Environmental Bankruptcy Law:

A Practice Guide

ALAN S. TENENBAUM and JEANNE T. COHN

AMERICAN BAR ASSOCIATION
Environment, Energy, and Resources Section

Cover design by Carolina Martinez/ABA Design

Printed in the United States of America.

27 26 25 24 23   5 4 3 2 1

ISBN 978-1-63905-286-8

A catalog record for this book is available from the Library of Congress.

Dedicated to my fellow stewards of the environment,
in our efforts to care for the earth, air, and water.

Jeanne T. Cohn

Dedicated with special gratitude to my understanding and supportive wife Mary Tenenbaum, son Kevin Tenenbaum and his fiancé Caroline Bass, close family friend Julie Pettis, and our pets Cooper, George, Kent, Tyler, and Pookie.

Alan S. Tenenbaum

Contents

Preface

JEANNE T. COHN

When I first began my practice in environmental bankruptcy work, I had already been a lawyer of many years, well-versed in Superfund matters. It was the early 2000s and I was brought onto an environmental bankruptcy case involving an environmental response trust. While I was experienced in Superfund law, brownfield redevelopment, and regulatory enforcement matters, I was new to bankruptcy law and had only a passing knowledge of environmental trusts. I searched for a practice primer to help guide me with the bankruptcy components of the work but it was tough to find one. I hope this Practice Guide serves as that primer for other lawyers who find themselves in similar circumstances.

In this book, Alan and I have made an effort to deconstruct key environmental bankruptcy concepts, describe how bankruptcy law overlaps with environmental law, and explain some of the policy implications underlying environmental bankruptcy law. We also describe the timing of an environmental bankruptcy case and each of the various steps in a case. In addition, we have covered more nuanced topics in several of the later chapters.

I hope that this Practice Guide will be of help to both environmental law practitioners and bankruptcy practitioners alike, and that it will be useful to starting lawyers as well as more seasoned lawyers practicing in the environmental bankruptcy arena. Last, this book may be of interest to others, including policy experts, students, and lay persons who want to better understand the law in this complicated area.

ALAN S. TENENBAUM

This Practice Guide tells the story of the conflict between environmental law and bankruptcy law. These complex bodies of law have dramatically different purposes and have often come into conflict over the last four decades. I hope that this book will help government and private environmental and bankruptcy attorneys navigate the difficult complexities at the intersection of environmental and bankruptcy law by providing in one place a fulsome summary of the law in this area.

The Practice Guide seeks throughout to provide insights and practice tips that can guide practioners and help them understand the logic of the Bankruptcy Code and court decisions harmonizing environmental and bankruptcy law. As set forth in Chapter 8 and discussed throughout the book, the process of harmonization seeks to reconcile the provisions of these weighty bodies of law. By doing so, courts have maximized the most beneficial provisions of each, resulting in a cleaner environment and protection of public health and safety while preserving viable bankrupt entities and jobs through corporate reorganization.

I have found environmental bankruptcy law to be a fascinating area of the law and it has been a source of great professional satisfaction to me in my work at the Department of Justice for the last thirty-four years. The federal, state, and private attorneys working in this field of the law are an exemplary group of dedicated individuals. My hope is that readers of this Practice Guide and practitioners in this area will agree. This book seeks to explain the differing perspectives of government attorneys and debtor's attorneys in this area. By fostering mutual understanding of where each side is coming from, settlements are more likely and, as a result, costly litigation can hopefully be avoided. If this book helps make that possible, I will view it as a great success.

Joint Acknowledgments

This book is the result of the efforts of many. We've tried to identify as many people as we could but our thanks go to all those who provided assistance. We appreciate the efforts of each person who helped, whether listed here or not.

First and foremost, we'd like to thank our professional colleagues who provided essential advice and comments throughout the course of reviewing and editing the book. Their insights were immeasurable. Special thanks go, in alphabetic order, to Kevin Barrett, Karen Cordry, Larry Kirsch, Mary Koks, and Margarita Padilla for their careful peer review and input. We'd also like to give credit to the former and present lawyers at Kirkland & Ellis LLP who assisted with drafting and editing portions of the book: Stefanie Gitler, Nacif Taousse, Alistair Fatheazam, Kimberly Pageau, and Miriam Peguero Medrano. Thanks also for the much appreciated assistance, in alphabetical order, of: Madison Beasley, Daniel Esrick, Donald Frankel, Kate Konschnik, Leslie Lara, Mary Lee Morrison, Margaret Newell, Erica Pencak, Allison Rafert, Savannah Wormley, and Caroline Zhang.

We would also like to thank the American Bar Association for helping to guide this book at each step along the way, and a special thanks to Grant Wilkinson, our ABA editor, who oversaw this effort, and helped with focusing the material, editing the book, offering insights, and keeping us on schedule, all through the years of the pandemic and after. His contributions were invaluable. Thanks to Margrethe Kearney and Randy Hill for their instrumental role in moving forward with the idea of this Practice Guide.

Supplemental Acknowledgments

JEANNE T. COHN

There are many people to acknowledge for their hard work in bringing this Practice Guide to fruition. Most are identified in our joint acknowledgment, but a few reflect more personal connections.

For me, it has been a long trajectory, from my earliest days handling environmental bankruptcy work at Kirkland & Ellis, where Walt Lohmann and the late Mark Grummer gave me my start, to the groundbreaking *Tronox* bankruptcy case, where, as debtors' environmental counsel I spearheaded the enormous multistate environmental settlement among the federal government, numerous states, several municipal entities, and the Navajo Nation, to my current role at DOJ, where I represent the government in tackling these difficult cases.

Aside from thanking my former colleagues where I first began my practice in environmental bankruptcy law, I thank my DOJ colleagues, including Jeff Sands and Tom Mariani. I would also especially like to thank my co-author and colleague, Alan Tenenbaum, for his focus, thoughtfulness, and deep knowledge of the subject as we have worked together over the years and in the process of organizing, selecting, and writing the material in this Practice Guide.

I'd also like to thank two of my college professors: Nancy Gish who first taught me expository writing at the University of Pennsylvania, and the late Paul Korshin, also in the English Department at Penn, who was a source of encouragement over the years. I'd also like to thank Pamela Toutant, who leads a local writing group that helped me further refine my writing skills and stressed the importance of writing from your own perspective.

Thanks also to several of my professors at the University of Chicago Law School, including the late Wally Blum and his well-regarded and challenging corporate restructuring class; Cass Sunstein, who taught administrative law when I was a law student which covered the early environmental law cases; and Doug Baird, for his course in secured transactions which proved invaluable both in my practice and in understanding certain of the bankruptcy law concepts. And thanks also go to my students at the University of Chicago Law School, where I have been teaching a seminar on the interface between environmental and bankruptcy law, for their incisive and thoughtful questions and input.

Finally, a big thank you to my family, my now adult children, for their encouragement and support: Hannah, Adrian, and Eileen Connor, and my husband, devoted friend and supporter, Mark Wolfe.

ALAN S. TENENBAUM

Thanks and gratitude to all of our peer reviewers and Grant Wilkinson (who are included in our joint acknowledgment) whose insights were of enormous value to this book. Thanks also to the numerous federal and state attorneys across the country I have had the pleasure of working with on environmental bankruptcy matters over my career. While many of these attorneys did not work directly on this Practice Guide, my interactions with them are what helped me learn and apply the legal concepts set forth in this book, and I therefore acknowledge and appreciate them all, including Andrea Madigan, Bob Roberts, and John Wheeler and many others at EPA, as well as DOJ attorneys, who are too numerous to mention. Thanks and acknowledgment to Cindy Brooks, Elliott Laws, Roberto Puga, Jay Steinberg, and Dan Silver for their work as environmental response trustees in managing site cleanups and helping protect public health and safety under environmental bankruptcy settlements that were the fruition of many of the concepts set forth in this book.

Thanks and acknowledgment to my supervisors for their guidance and direction over the years in my work in the environmental bankruptcy field that made this book possible: Tom Mariani, Ben Fisherow, Bruce Gelber, Jeff Wood, John Cruden, Joel Gross, David Buente, and Scott Fulton.

I would especially like to thank my co-author and colleague, Jeanne Cohn, for sharing her valuable expertise from working as debtors' counsel on some of the nation's key environmental bankruptcy cases, her hard work and her keen writing and editing skills that help to make these complex topics accessible to a broader audience. Finally, special thanks to my wife Mary, son Kevin and his fiancé Caroline Bass, and close family friend Julie Pettis for all their support and encouragement while I was working on this book.

About the Authors

Alan S. Tenenbaum is the National Bankruptcy Coordinator with the U.S. Department of Justice's Environmental Enforcement Section in the Environment and Natural Resources Division. Alan has worked at DOJ since 1988 and supervises or participates in many of the Department's environmental bankruptcy cases for federal client agencies. Alan has helped coordinate federal and state agency participation in numerous bankruptcy cases, including *Asarco*, *General Motors*, *Tronox*, *FirstEnergy*, *Philadelphia Energy*, *Peabody*, *Exide*, *Alpha*, *Fruit of the Loom*, and *Eagle-Picher*.

In 2022, Alan was named as a Presidential Rank Award Distinguished Senior Professional Winner. In 2010, Alan was a recipient of the Attorney General's Distinguished Service Award. Alan is a frequent speaker on many of the environmental bankruptcy law topics covered in this Practice Guide. Alan has also presented many training sessions to federal and state attorneys on environmental bankruptcy law topics.

Alan earned a BA in mathematics from Cornell University in 1978. He graduated from Harvard Law School in 1981 where he was an executive editor on the *Harvard Law Review*. He clerked for Judge Jon Newman on the Second Circuit Court of Appeals from 1981 to 1982. Alan is originally from North Bellmore, New York. In his spare time, Alan plays tournament bridge and is an Emerald Life Master.

Jeanne T. Cohn is a Trial Attorney and Bankruptcy Coordinator in the Environmental Enforcement Section at the U.S. Department of Justice. Before joining DOJ, she was a partner in the law firm of Kirkland and Ellis LLP where she served as primary environmental counsel for numerous debtors and others. In that role, she worked on some of the largest bankruptcies in the country including *Tronox, Energy Future Holdings, Philadelphia Refinery, Hovensa, GenOn Energy Holdings*, and *Sherwin Alumina.* As debtors' environmental counsel for *Tronox*, she led the global environmental settlement negotiations that resulted in the establishment of five separate environmental response trusts covering several thousand properties.

Jeanne's legal work has resulted in commendations from publications including the *Legal 500 US* and *Law360.* Jeanne has been recognized in Best Lawyers, Washington DC. Prior to her move to Washington DC, she had practiced law in Portland, Maine, and New York City. While in Maine, she served as general counsel to the Maine Low-Level Radioactive Waste Authority. Jeanne was also instrumental in negotiating an innovative liability transfer settlement for a Maine State Superfund site, the first of its kind in the nation.

Jeanne currently teaches a seminar at the University of Chicago Law School covering environmental bankruptcy law and has been a guest lecturer at other law schools. She is a graduate of the University of Chicago Law School where she was a Hinton Moot Court Semi-Finalist. She graduated with a BA from the University of Pennsylvania, cum laude, with a major in history and minor in English, where she also studied honors theoretical calculus and sciences.

Jeanne has spoken extensively at environmental law conferences. She has co-written two manuals on environmental law in Maine and was a contributing author to the ABA Book: *Implementing Institutional Controls at Brownfields and Other Contaminated Sites.* Jeanne also authored *Environmental Settlements in Bankruptcy: Practice Pointers for the Business Lawyer* for an ABA periodical.

While in private practice, Jeanne also had an active pro bono caseload, ranging from negotiating amendments to the Violence Against Women Act to handling child immigration and anti-trafficking cases. She appeared in both the national and international press for her pro bono work. On a personal note, Jeanne was a Girl Scout troop leader for many years and is an avid hiker and camper.

Disclaimer and Note

All views expressed in this book are solely those of the two authors and not necessarily those of the United States or the Department of Justice or any other governmental agency or law firm. Any errors or omissions in this Practice Guide are the sole responsibility of the authors.

CHAPTER 1

Introduction

Environmental law and bankruptcy law are two complex bodies of law that were created for starkly different purposes and that directly conflict with each other in key respects. Environmental law seeks to protect public health and safety by holding liable parties responsible, potentially forever, for addressing environmental harms they have caused.[1] In contrast, bankruptcy law seeks to provide debtors with a "fresh start" free and clear of their past problems.[2] One commentator long ago perceptively christened this conflict as a "Clash of the Titans."[3] How then are courts and lawyers to reconcile and harmonize these two bodies of law with such profoundly contrary goals? This question has vexed courts and attorneys on numerous occasions for more than 30 years.[4]

1. The Comprehensive Environmental Response, Compensation and Liability Act (CERCLA), 42 U.S.C. §§ 9601–9675, and Resource Conservation and Recovery Act (RCRA), 42 U.S.C. §§ 6901–6992, are two key environmental statutes encountered in bankruptcy cases. *See Burlington N. & Santa Fe Ry. Co. v. United States*, 556 U.S. 599, 602 (2009) (CERCLA was designed to ensure that "the costs of cleanup efforts were borne by those responsible for the contamination"); *Meghrig v. KFC Western, Inc.*, 516 U.S. 479, 483 (1996) (a primary purpose of RCRA is to "ensure the proper treatment, storage, and disposal" of generated waste to minimize threats to human health and the environment); *City of Chi. v. Env't Def. Fund*, 511 U.S. 328, 331 (1994) (RCRA provides for "cradle to grave" regulation of hazardous wastes).

2. *Schwab v. Reilly*, 560 U.S. 770, 791 (2010); *Grogan v. Garner*, 498 U.S. 279, 286–87 (1991).

3. Jill Thompson Losch, *Bankruptcy v. Environmental Obligation: Clash of the Titans*, 52 LA. L. REV. 137 (1991).

4. *See, e.g., In re Chicago, Milwaukee, St. Paul & Pacific R. Co.*, 3 F.3d 200, 201 (7th Cir. 1993) ("We attempt again to reconcile the conflicting goals of environmental

This Practice Guide tells the story of this conflict and provides a guide to how the courts have dealt with environmental bankruptcy issues since the 1980s. Its primary focus is to help environmental lawyers—both private practitioners, including counsel for debtors and creditors, and government attorneys—understand environmental bankruptcy law and provide a summary of the law in one place. We, therefore, assume familiarity with environmental laws and do not discuss them except for some general background in this chapter and then occasionally when details are relevant to particular environmental bankruptcy cases discussed in this Practice Guide.[5]

We begin the Practice Guide by providing a more fulsome discussion of general bankruptcy law: a brief history of bankruptcy law and its general purposes and key concepts (Chapter 2), the different chapters of the Bankruptcy Code (Chapter 3), the timeline of a typical bankruptcy case (Chapter 4), key statutory provisions (Chapter 5), obtaining information in bankruptcy cases (Chapter 6), and filing proofs of claim and administrative expense applications (Chapter 7)—all of which assume no prior bankruptcy law knowledge. We next tackle how the courts have generally resolved the conflicts posed by environmental law and bankruptcy law by attempting to harmonize federal statutes and deciding when federal law preempts state law. Next, we cover in Chapter 8 two important concepts in the law: (1) the distinction

---

cleanup and a 'fresh start' for bankruptcy debtors. . . . The tension between these fundamental aspects of our national policy is profound."); *In re Jensen*, 995 F.2d 925, 927–28 (9th Cir. 1993) ("The intersection of environmental cleanup laws and federal bankruptcy statutes is somewhat messy."); *In re Combustion Equip. Assocs., Inc.*, 838 F.2d 35, 37 (2d Cir. 1988) ("The conflict begins at a basic level, since the goal of CERCLA—cleaning up toxic waste sites promptly and holding liable those responsible for the pollution—is at odds with the premise of bankruptcy, which is to allow debtors a fresh start by freeing them from liability."). *See* Sarah Schenck, *Buoying Environmental Burden in Bankruptcy Floodwaters*, 45 Urban Law. 449, 449 (2013); Anne Lawton & Lynda Oswald, *Scary Stories and the Limited Liability Polluter in Chapter 11*, 65 Wash. & Lee L. Rev. 451, 459-60 (2008); Ingrid Hillinger & Michael Hillinger, *Environmental Affairs in Bankruptcy*, 12 Am. Bankr. Inst. L. Rev. 331, 333–34 (2004).

5. For more detailed discussions, *see* Arlene Elgart Mirsky, Richard J. Conway & Geralyn G. Humphrey, *The Interface between Bankruptcy and Environmental Laws*, 46 Bus. Law. 623, 627–34 (1991); Pamela Elkow & Thomas Sansone, *Treatment of Environmental Liabilities in Bankruptcy*, ch. 7, *in* Environmental Aspects of Real Estate Transactions 193–95 (American Bar Association, 2020).

between the treatment of compliance obligations versus the treatment of monetary liabilities under environmental bankruptcy law, and (2) the differences in treatment based on whether an environmental bankruptcy issue involves "property of the estate." The Practice Guide then examines the case law that addresses:

1. the obligation to comply with nonbankruptcy law in managing and operating "property of the estate" (Chapter 9),
2. the scope of the police or regulatory exception to the automatic stay (Chapter 10),
3. equitable remedies such as cleanup orders and bankruptcy law (Chapter 11),
4. the priority of environmental claims and compliance obligations compared to other claims and liabilities (Chapter 12),
5. when environmental claims arise and become dischargeable in bankruptcy (Chapter 13),
6. options for dealing with contaminated property owned by the bankruptcy estate (Chapter 14),
7. free and clear sales of contaminated property under bankruptcy law (Chapter 15),
8. plan confirmation objections based on feasibility, provisions forbidden by law, and the permissible scope of discharge of environmental liabilities (Chapter 16),
9. estimation and adjudication of environmental claims in bankruptcy (Chapter 17),
10. abandonment of contaminated property in bankruptcy (Chapter 18), and
11. insurance coverage when addressing environmental liabilities in a bankruptcy proceeding (Chapter 19).

We conclude with discussions of jurisdictional and standing issues in environmental bankruptcy cases including withdrawal of the reference (Chapter 20) and environmental settlements (Chapter 21).

ENVIRONMENTAL LAW

Congress enacted modern environmental laws in response to nationwide concern over environmental tragedies such as the 1969 Santa Barbara oil spill, the Love Canal hazardous waste dump site, the Cuyahoga River fire, the Exxon Valdez oil spill, and the chronic smog surrounding much of New York and Los Angeles in the mid-twentieth century.[6] Many federal environmental laws that appear in environmental bankruptcy cases were enacted in the 1960s through 1990s, including the Comprehensive Environmental Response, Compensation, and Liability Act (CERCLA),[7] the Resource Conservation and Recovery Act (RCRA),[8] the Clean Air Act (CAA),[9] the Clean Water Act (CWA),[10] the Oil Pollution Act (OPA),[11] the Surface Mining Control and Reclamation Act (SMCRA),[12] and the Toxic Substances Control Act (TSCA).[13] The U.S. Environmental Protection Agency (EPA) was created in 1970 with responsibility for maintaining and enforcing numerous environmental laws.[14]

Several of the federal statutes, including RCRA, CAA, CWA, and SMCRA, involve forms of cooperative federalism whereby both federal and state governmental authorities have certain enforcement authority.[15] Many states also have parallel or supplemental environmental statutes of their own.[16] The two federal statutes that most frequently appear in environmental bankruptcy cases are CERCLA and RCRA.

CERCLA, which created the "Superfund," authorizes EPA to require potentially responsible parties (PRPs) to clean up sites

---

6. Frank P. Grad, Treatise on Environmental Law § 1.01 (1985); Donald W. Stever & Eliza A. Dolin, Environmental Law and Practice § 1.01 (1993); Thomas M. Hoban & Richard O. Brooks, Green Justice: The Environment and the Courts 4 (2d ed. 1996); Erin Blakemore, *The Shocking River Fire That Fueled the Creation of the EPA* (updated Dec. 1, 2020), https://www.history.com/news/epa-earth-day-cleveland-cuyahoga-river-fire-clean-water-act; EPA, *Clean Air Requirements and History, Clean Air Act Overview* (updated Aug. 12, 2021), https://www.epa.gov/clean-air-act-overview/clean-air-act-requirements-and-history.

7. 42 U.S.C. §§ 9601–9675.

8. *Id.* §§ 6901–6992.

9. *Id.* §§ 7401–7671.

10. 33 U.S.C. §§ 1251–1388.

11. *Id.* §§ 2701–2762.

12. 30 U.S.C. §§ 1201–1328.

13. 15 U.S.C. §§ 2601–2697.

14. U.S. Env't Prot. Agency, The Origins of EPA, https://www.epa.gov/history/origins-epa.

15. Philip J. Weiser, *Towards a Constitutional Architecture for Cooperative Federalism*, 79 N.C. L. Rev. 663, 671 (2001).

16. Richard L. Revesz, *Federalism and Environmental Regulation: A Public Choice Analysis*, 115 Harv. L. Rev. 553, 578–624 (2001).

contaminated with hazardous substances and holds them liable for clean-up costs and natural resource damages.[17] PRPs fall within one of four categories, including current and former owners and operators of sites contaminated with hazardous substances, transporters of hazardous substances, as well as those that arrange for the disposal of hazardous substances.[18] CERCLA seeks to ensure that those who created a contamination problem are held accountable, bear the burden of their actions, and are deterred from creating additional pollution problems.[19]

RCRA imposes strict controls on entities that manage solid waste and hazardous waste.[20] Owners and operators of hazardous waste treatment, storage, or disposal facilities must obtain either a permit or "interim status" in order to operate legally.[21] The United States and those states with delegated RCRA authority can order the owner or operator of a permitted or interim status facility to comply with applicable RCRA regulations, conduct closure, implement corrective action, or take other response measures as necessary to protect human health and the environment.[22] Where EPA determines that the past or present handling, storage, treatment, transportation, or disposal of any solid waste or hazardous waste may present an imminent and substantial endangerment to health or the environment, it can issue an order or seek injunctive relief to address the threat.[23]

BANKRUPTCY LAW

The U.S. Constitution gives Congress the power to establish "uniform Laws on the subject of Bankruptcies throughout the United

17. 42 U.S.C. §§ 9604, 9006, 9607, 9622; *see B.F. Goodrich Co. v. Murtha*, 958 F.2d 1192, 1197–99 (2d Cir. 1992).

18. 42 U.S.C. § 9607(a)(1)–(4).

19. *Burlington N.*, 556 U.S. at 602; *Metro. Water Reclamation Dist. of Greater Chi. v. N. Am. Galvanizing & Coatings, Inc.*, 473 F.3d 824, 836 (7th Cir. 2007); *Tippins Inc. v. USX Corp.*, 37 F.3d 87, 95 (3d Cir. 1994); *United States v. Nicolet, Inc.*, 857 F.2d 202, 210 (3d Cir. 1988).

20. *See* 42 U.S.C. §§ 6921–6925; 40 C.F.R. subch. I.

21. 42 U.S.C. § 6925.

22. *Id.* §§ 6924(u), (v), 6925(c)(3), 6928.

23. *Id.* § 6973.

States."[24] Congress passed the first federal bankruptcy law in 1800, the Bankruptcy Act of 1800, which has had several successors.[25] Most recently, Congress enacted the Bankruptcy Reform Act of 1978, which codified the current Bankruptcy Code.[26] As further described in Chapter 2, the general purpose of bankruptcy law is to rehabilitate viable debtors by providing them with a fresh start and one forum for efficiently dealing with competing stakeholders.[27] Chapters 2 through 7 of this Practice Guide will provide a more detailed background of bankruptcy law as the building blocks to help environmental practitioners understand how the courts have grappled with the convergence of these competing bodies of law.

---

24. U.S. Const. art. 1, § 8, cl. 4.

25. *See* Emily Slagle, *Troubled Waters: What the Gulf Oil Spill Reveals about the Consequences of Bankruptcy*, 13 Vt. J. Env't L. 361, 365–67 (2011); C. Tabb, *The History of the Bankruptcy Laws in the United States*, 3 Am. Bankr. Inst. L. Rev. 5 (1995); J. Czarnetzky, *Time, Uncertainty, and the Law of Corporate Reorganizations*, 67 Fordham L. Rev. 2939, 2966–70 (1999).

26. 11 U.S.C. §§ 101–1532.

27. *Schwab v. Reilly*, 560 U.S. 770, 791 (2010); *Grogan v. Garner*, 498 U.S. 279, 286–87 (1991).

CHAPTER 2

History, Purposes, and Key Concepts of Bankruptcy Law

BRIEF HISTORY OF BANKRUPTCY LAW

A principal purpose of bankruptcy law is to grant a "fresh start" to the "honest but unfortunate debtor."[1] In addition, bankruptcy law seeks to balance the rehabilitative need of debtors with the rights of creditors and the orderly and fair payment of claims.[2] The Constitution of the United States gives Congress the power "[t]o establish . . . . uniform laws on the subject of Bankruptcies throughout the United States."[3] In the first one hundred years after the ratification of the Constitution, Congress exercised its bankruptcy powers cautiously, enacting short-term federal laws such as the Bankruptcy Act of 1800, the Bankruptcy Act of 1841, and

---

1. *Marrama v. Citizens Bank*, 549 U.S. 365 (2007) (quoting *Grogan v. Garner*, 498 U.S. 279 (1991)).

2. *See* ABI Commission to Study the Reform of Chapter 11, *2012–2014 Final Report and Recommendations, Background on the Commission and the Study Project*, pt. III, at 8–9, https://abiworld.app.box.com/s/pwtg5hi7ln3ty3kelnnt [hereinafter Chapter 11 Commission Final Report]; Pamela Elkow & Thomas Sansone, *Treatment of Environmental Liabilities in Bankruptcy*, *in* Environmental Aspects of Real Estate Transactions, ch. 7, at 192–93, 195–96 (ABA 2020); *In re Venoco LLC*, 998 F.3d 94 (3d Cir. 2021) (equitable distribution of debtor's property among creditors is a critical bankruptcy function).

3. U.S. Const. art. I, § 8, cl. 4.

the Bankruptcy Act of 1867.[4] Each of these laws was enacted in response to an economic crisis, and when the crisis subsided each of these laws was repealed after only a few years.[5] Of note, voluntary bankruptcy was not permitted under American bankruptcy law until the Bankruptcy Act of 1841, which was repealed just two years later.[6] Until that point, bankruptcy was viewed as solely a creditor's remedy. It was not until the Bankruptcy Act of 1898 that Congress introduced procedures for corporate reorganization and a system to adjudicate bankruptcy claims.[7]

Modern American bankruptcy law originates from the Bankruptcy Reform Act of 1978, which was enacted as title 11 of the United States Code (Bankruptcy Code)[8] and replaced the Bankruptcy Act of 1898.[9] The Bankruptcy Code is divided into nine chapters, six of which provide for various types of bankruptcy relief for particular types of debtors. Chapters 1, 3, and 5 of the Bankruptcy Code contain provisions designed to apply generally in all bankruptcy cases. These provisions are applicable in any case under any chapter of the Bankruptcy Code.[10] Section 101 of the Code, in Chapter 1, includes definitions of key terms, including for "claim," "debt," "person," and "governmental unit." Chapter 7 of the Bankruptcy Code contains provisions governing liquidation cases. Chapter 9 of the Bankruptcy Code concerns itself with the debts of municipalities (i.e., cities and counties, but not states or

---

4. Daniel A. Austin, *Bankruptcy and the Myth of "Uniform Laws,"* 42 Seton Hall L. Rev. 1081, 1084 (2012).

5. *Id.*

6. *Id.*

7. *Id.* at 1084–85. For additional historical background, *see* Chapter 11 Commission Final Report, *supra* note 2, at 8–10; *Central Virginia Community College v. Katz*, 546 U.S. 356 (2006); Karen Gebbia, *The Keepers of the Code: Evolution of the Bankruptcy Community*, 91 Am. Bankr. L.J. 183 (2017).

8. 11 U.S.C. §§ 101–1532.

9. Austin, *supra* note 4, at 1085 (citing Pub. L. No. 95-598, 92 Stat. 2549) (codified as amended at 11 U.S.C. §§ 101–1532 (2006)). For a brief history of the development of modern bankruptcy law, *see* Emily Slagle, *Troubled Waters: What the Gulf Oil Spill Reveals about the Consequences of Bankruptcy*, 13 Vt. J. Env't L. 361, 365–67 (2011); Charles Jordan Tabb, *The History of the Bankruptcy Laws in the United States*, 3 Am. Bankr. Inst. L. Rev. 5 (1995); *Time, Uncertainty, and the Law of Corporate Reorganizations*, 67 Fordham L. Rev. 2939, 2966–70 (1999).

10. 1 Collier on Bankruptcy ¶ 1.01[2][a] (16th ed. 2019).

the United States).[11] Chapter 11 of the Bankruptcy Code governs reorganization cases while Chapter 13 of the Bankruptcy Code provides for repayment plans by certain individual debtors.[12] In 1986, Congress enacted Chapter 12 of the Bankruptcy Code to govern the restructuring of debts of farmers or fishermen.[13] And, finally, in 2005, Congress added Chapter 15 of the Bankruptcy Code to address international, cross-border insolvency cases.[14]

The procedural aspects of proceedings under the Bankruptcy Code are governed by the Federal Rules of Bankruptcy Procedure (Fed. R. Bankr. P.), which provide rules for filing motions, claims, and adversary proceedings,[15] and rules governing hearings and various deadlines.[16]

GOALS AND OBJECTIVES OF BANKRUPTCY LAW

"[A] chief purpose of the bankruptcy laws is to secure a prompt and effectual administration and settlement of the estate of all bankrupts within a limited period."[17] Other commentators have stated that "[t]he essence of contemporary bankruptcy practice is the adjustment of the debtor-creditor relationship. For consumer bankruptcy, the purpose of bankruptcy is a 'fresh start,' which means that the debtor's unsecured debts and obligations are

11. U.S. Courts, *Chapter 9—Bankruptcy Basics*, https://www.uscourts.gov/services-forms/bankruptcy/bankruptcy-basics/chapter-9-bankruptcy-basics.

12. *Id. Chapter 13,* https:// www.uscourts.gov/services-forms/bankruptcy/bankruptcy-basics/chapter-13-bankruptcy-basics.

13. *Id. Chapter 12,* https:// www.uscourts.gov/services-forms/bankruptcy/bankruptcy-basics/chapter-13-bankruptcy-basics.

14. *Id. Chapter 15,* https:// www.uscourts.gov/services-forms/bankruptcy/bankruptcy-basics/chapter-13-bankruptcy-basics.

15. An "adversary proceeding" is a matter that must be initiated by a complaint as set forth in Bankruptcy Rule 7001 and includes proceedings to recover money, determine liens or interest in property, determine dischargeability, and seek injunctive or declaratory relief.

16. *See* Fed. R. Civ. P. 81(a)(2); Fed. R. Bankr. P. 1001. Each judicial district also has its own local bankruptcy rules that can be found on its bankruptcy court website. Some judges also have their own general or case-specific rules and procedures that should be consulted.

17. *Katchen v. Landy*, 382 U.S. 323, 328 (1966) (quotation omitted).

completely or partially discharged."[18] For a corporate bankruptcy, there is a similar goal of providing the debtor entity with a "fresh start," although in some cases, the corporate entity is past saving, in which case, the bankruptcy is used to create an orderly liquidation process. In either case, the Bankruptcy Code's intent is to "provide a procedure by which certain insolvent debtors can reorder their affairs, make peace with their creditors, and enjoy 'a new opportunity in life with a clear field for future effort, unhampered by the pressure and discouragement of preexisting debt.'"[19]

A central purpose of a Chapter 11 business reorganization, an essentially American invention, is to prevent a viable debtor "from going into liquidation, with an attendant loss of jobs and possible misuse of economic resources."[20] A reorganization plan should "enable the debtor to restructure its pre-bankruptcy debts, pay its creditors, and return to active operation as a viable enterprise, free from judicial control and scrutiny."[21] Bankruptcy is also an orderly collective process for the benefit of creditors whereby the status quo is preserved and a race to the courthouse prevented. The debtor's assets (or their value) are divided up for the benefit of creditors while taking into account the debtor's need for assets so that it can be feasibly rehabilitated.[22]

GOOD FAITH REQUIREMENT

Bankruptcy is designed to deal with honest, but unfortunate debtors who find themselves in precarious financial circumstances which are often caused by factors beyond their control. It seeks to make lemonade out of lemons by fashioning a solution that may be painful for debtors and creditors alike but makes the best out of a

18. Austin, *supra* note 4, at 1086.

19. *Grogan v. Garner*, 498 U.S. 279, 286 (1991) (quoting *Local Loan Co. v. Hunt*, 292 U.S. 234, 244 (1934)).

20. *NLRB v. Bildisco & Bildisco*, 465 U.S. 513, 528 (1984).

21. *In re Great Am. Pyramid Joint Venture*, 144 B.R. 780, 788 (Bankr. W.D. Tenn. 1992). The "two recognized policies underlying" Chapter 11 are "preserving going concerns" and "maximizing property available to satisfy creditors." *Bank of Am. Nat'l Tr. & Sav. Assoc. v. 203 N. LaSalle St. P'ship*, 526 U.S. 434, 453 (1999).

22. *See In re Frontier Ins. Grp., Inc.*, 585 B.R. 685, 693 (Bankr. S.D.N.Y. 2018); Elkow & Sansone, *supra* note 2, at ch. 7, 192–93, 195–96.

bad situation. Bankruptcy is not intended to be a litigation tactic. A Chapter 11 petition that is not filed in good faith but rather to gain tactical advantages in litigation or to evade a regulatory scheme can be dismissed for cause or converted to Chapter 7 liquidation. Alternatively, the bankruptcy court may determine that retaining the case in Chapter 11, but appointing a Chapter 11 trustee or examiner, is in the best interest of creditors.[23] Companies that are not in financial distress are not intended to be allowed to file for bankruptcy in order to gain an advantage from Bankruptcy Code provisions.[24] Even lawsuits for large amounts may not be appropriate grounds for bankruptcy if a judgment that will cause financial or operational ruin is not imminent.[25] Recently, some large well-financed companies facing mass tort claims have used divisional merger statutes to try to separate themselves from such liabilities by creating a separate entity which assumes the liabilities, files for bankruptcy, and then seeks a nondebtor release for the other part of the company. These cases are at risk of being dismissed as bad faith bankruptcies on the ground that they seek tactical litigation advantage or present inadequate evidence of financial distress.[26] Some older bankruptcy cases with serious environmen-

---

23. 11 U.S.C. § 1112(b); *see In re 15375 Mem'l Corp.*, 589 F.3d 605 (3d Cir. 2009); *In re Cedar Shore Resort, Inc.*, 235 F.3d 375 (8th Cir. 2000); *In re C-TC 9th Ave. P'ship*, 113 F.3d 1304 (2d Cir. 1997); *In re Nat'l Rifle Ass'n of Am.*, 628 B.R. 262 (Bankr. N.D. Tex. 2021); *In re Forest Hill Funeral Home & Mem'l Park-East, LLC*, 364 B.R. 808, 822 (Bankr. E.D. Okla. 2007); *In re First Plus Fin. Enter., Inc.*, 99 B.R. 751 (Bankr. W.D. Tex. 1989). *See generally* 7 Collier on Bankruptcy ¶ 1112.07 (16th ed. 2019).

24. *In re Integrated Telecom Express, Inc.*, 384 F.3d 108 (3d Cir. 2004).

25. *See In re SGL Carbon Corp.*, 200 F.3d 154 (3d Cir. 1999). However, entry of large judgments causing serious financial or managerial difficulties threatening long-term viability can be grounds for a good faith filing even in the absence of proof of insolvency. *Id.* at 164; *In re Marsch*, 36 F.3d 825 (9th Cir. 1994); *In re Cohoes Indus. Terminal Inc.*, 931 F.2d 222 (2d Cir. 1991); *In re Little Creek Dev. Co.*, 779 F.2d 1068 (5th Cir. 1986). *See also In re Texaco, Inc.*, 84 B.R. 893 (Bankr. S.D.N.Y. 1988), which dealt with the bankruptcy filed by Texaco to protect its ability to appeal and/or settle a judgment in excess of $8 billion, which substantially exceeded the world's entire bonding capacity at the time. While Texaco could have paid the entire amount, at least in theory, the automatic stay imposed by the filing allowed it to negotiate a settlement of "only" $3 billion and to pay all of its other creditors in full.

26. *In re LTL Mgmt., LLC*, 58 F.4th 738 (3d Cir. 2023) (funding agreement precluded finding of true financial distress). Potential grounds for objecting to nondebtor releases in such cases are discussed in Chapter 16 (Plan Objections) infra. The divisional merger statutes preserve causes of action for fraudulent conveyance

tal issues were dismissed where there was a pending state court environmental proceeding and the bankruptcy court determined that a bankruptcy case might undermine the protection of public health and safety.[27]

FRESH START AND DISCHARGE

A debtor, in most bankruptcy cases, is ultimately able to receive a "fresh start" at the end of the bankruptcy proceeding through what is known as the "discharge injunction."[28] Section 524 of the Bankruptcy Code describes the effect of discharge, which voids judgments against a debtor for debts and operates as an injunction against acts to collect on pre-petition debt.[29] The discharge injunction was enacted to prevent creditors from harassing discharged debtors by prohibiting those creditors from using state courts to collect on discharged debts.[30] The discharge injunction is intended to be broad, and "unambiguously voids past and future *in personam* judgments on discharged debts at any time obtained."[31] However, the discharge injunction only applies to a debtor's personal liability on a debt, and does not eliminate underlying secured debt or *in rem* liability.[32] As discussed in Chapter 19 (Insurance) of this Practice Guide, a discharge also does not provide an insurer a

---

if the newly created entity has inadequate assets to deal with its liabilities. However, a fraudulent conveyance action common to all creditors would be brought by the bankruptcy estate and thus must be addressed as part of the bankruptcy case.

27. *See, e.g., In re Com. Oil Serv., Inc.*, 58 B.R. 311 (Bankr. N.D. Ohio 1986), *aff'd*, 88 B.R. 126 (N.D. Ohio 1987); *In re Mattiace Indus., Inc.*, 76 B.R. 44 (Bankr. E.D.N.Y. 1987); *In re Charles George Land Reclamation Tr.*, 30 B.R. 918 (Bankr. D. Mass. 1983). Dismissal may not be in the interest of federal or state environmental agencies if it will create a race to the courthouse between authorities and other parties in interest or if the agencies would benefit from a stay of commercial creditors' attempt to seize valuable assets.

28. 1 Collier on Bankruptcy ¶ 1.02[1] (16th ed. 2019). Discharge is not available in corporate liquidations under Chapter 7 or Chapter 11. 11 U.S.C. §§ 727(a), 1141(d)(3).

29. 11 U.S.C. § 524(a); *Taggart v. Lorenzen*, 139 S. Ct. 1795, 1801 (2019); *Cent. Va. Cmty. Coll. v. Katz*, 546 U.S. 356, 364 (2006).

30. *See Houghton v. Foremost Fin. Servs. Corp.*, 724 F.2d 112, 116 (10th Cir. 1983).

31. *In re Gray*, 573 B.R. 868, 876 (10th Cir. 2017) (quotation omitted).

32. Teresa M. Schreffler & The Honorable Janice Miller Karlin, *Walking the Balance Beam of the Bankruptcy Code's Discharge Injunction*, 87 J. Kan. Bar Ass'n 38, 40 (2018).

release of its liability to creditors for a debtor's debts under an insurance policy.

The discharge injunction only applies to debts that are eligible for discharge, which varies based on whether the debtor is an individual or corporate debtor and on the chapter of the bankruptcy case. The injunction does not apply to corporate liquidations under Chapter 7 or to corporate cases under Chapter 11 involving the liquidation of all or substantially all of the debtor's estate.[33] Section 523 of the Bankruptcy Code currently lists 19 nondischargeable debts in *individual* debtor cases, including debts for money obtained by false pretenses;[34] debts obtained by fraud while acting in a "fiduciary capacity, embezzlement, or larceny";[35] unlisted and unscheduled debts;[36] domestic support obligations;[37] debts for willful and malicious injury by the debtor to another entity or to the property of another entity;[38] and debts to the government for a fine, penalty, or forfeiture that is not compensation for loss;[39] among others. In contrast, Section 1141 of the Bankruptcy Code sets forth a narrower list of nondischargeable debts in Chapter 11 cases involving *corporate* debtors that includes only certain of the fraud exceptions. Additionally, general due process rules may also result in an exception to discharge if the company fails to notify its known creditors.[40] While creditors are not required to file a complaint to determine nondischargeability (with a few exceptions),[41] a debtor or creditor may file an adversary proceeding complaint to determine whether a debt is excepted from discharge under

33. 11 U.S.C. §§ 727(a), 1141(d)(3).

34. *Id.* § 523(a)(2)(A).

35. *Id.* § 523(a)(4).

36. *Id.* § 523(a)(3) (unless the creditors had notice or actual knowledge of the case).

37. *Id.* § 523(a)(5).

38. *Id.* § 523(a)(6).

39. *Id.* § 523(a)(7); *see Whitehouse v. LaRouche*, 277 F.3d 568 (1st Cir. 2002). *See also Kelly v. Robinson*, 479 U.S. 36 (1986) (criminal restitution obligations of individual debtors are not discharged).

40. 11 U.S.C. § 1141(d)(6). Section 1141(d)(6) and the due process-based exception to discharge are discussed in Chapter 13 (Discharge) *infra*.

41. Complaints alleging nondischargeability under 11 U.S.C. § 523(a)(2), (4), (6) must be filed within 60 days of the first date set for the meeting of creditors under 11 U.S.C. § 341(a). There is no deadline for complaints to determine other dischargeability issues. Fed. R. Bankr. P. 4007.

Section 523 of the Bankruptcy Code.[42] A determination of nondischargeability may also be made in the nonbankruptcy forum for most debts excepted from discharge.[43] Chapter 13 (Discharge) of this Practice Guide provides for a more detailed discussion of several discharge issues that have come up in environmental bankruptcy cases.

If a creditor takes actions to collect on a discharged debt, the discharge may be enforced through a contempt proceeding upon the debtor's reopening of the bankruptcy case.[44] The bankruptcy court that issues the discharge injunction order has the power alone to enforce compliance with and punish contempt of that order, although dischargeability may be determined as a defense in an action brought in a nonbankruptcy court.[45] The Supreme Court recently held that the "objective fair ground of doubt" standard that traditionally governs civil contempt proceedings also governs contempt under the Bankruptcy Code's statutory injunctions.[46] Under that standard, a bankruptcy court may hold a creditor in civil contempt for violating a discharge injunction "where there is not a 'fair ground of doubt' as to whether the creditor's conduct might be lawful under the discharge order."[47] The Supreme Court rejected both a solely subjective good faith standard and a strict liability standard that would make subjective intent wholly irrelevant.[48]

---

42. Fed. R. Bankr. P. 4007(a), (b).

43. *Whitehouse v. LaRouche*, 277 F.3d at 578–79. However, debts for money obtained by false pretenses (§ 523(a)(2)(A)), debts obtained by fraud (§ 523(a)(4)), and debts for willful and malicious injury (§ 523(a)(6)) require a determination of nondischargeability by the bankruptcy court by filing a timely adversary proceeding complaint against the debtor. *See* 11 U.S.C. § 523(c)(1).

44. 1 Collier on Bankruptcy ¶ 1.02[1] (16th ed. 2019); *Taggart v. Lorenzen*, 139 S. Ct. 1795, 1801 (2019).

45. *In re McLean*, 794 F.3d 1313, 1318–19 (11th Cir. 2015) ("It is settled that 'the court that issued the injunctive order alone possesses the power to enforce compliance with and punish contempt of that order,' and this 'power to sanction contempt is jurisdictional.'") (quoting *Alderwoods Grp., Inc. v. Garcia*, 682 F.3d 958, 970 (11th Cir. 2012)). *See* Chapter 20 (Jurisdiction) *infra*; *In re Apex Oil Co.*, 406 F.3d 538, 542 (8th Cir. 2005); *Eden v. Robert A. Chapski, Ltd.*, 405 F.3d 582, 586 (7th Cir. 2005); *Whitehouse v. LaRouche*, 277 F.3d at 578–79; *Erspan v. Badgett*, 647 F.2d 550, 556 (5th Cir. 1981); *Signature Combs, Inc. v. United States*, 253 F. Supp. 2d 1028 (W.D. Tenn. 2003).

46. *Taggart*, 139 S. Ct. at 1804.

47. *Id.*

48. *Id.* at 1802–03.

Courts have stated that "[c]ertain actions [by creditors] are facially impermissible and are plainly prohibited by Section 524(a)(2), including dunning letters, collection calls, and collection actions. . . . [S]ome actions that are 'facially permissible' can nevertheless violate the discharge injunction if the effect of the actions is to coerce payment of discharged debts."[49] With respect to damages, bankruptcy courts may "award actual damages, attorney fees, and punitive damages as sanctions for willful violations of the discharge injunction."[50]

AUTOMATIC STAY AND BREATHING ROOM

Upon the commencement of a bankruptcy proceeding, Section 362 of the Bankruptcy Code provides debtors with the protection of another statutory injunction referred to as the "automatic stay." Unless one of the enumerated exceptions applies,[51] the automatic stay prohibits creditors (and other entities) from taking any action outside of the bankruptcy court to collect on pre-petition claims or judgments against the debtor or obtain possession or exercise control over property of the bankruptcy estate.[52] The automatic stay is "one of the fundamental protections that the Bankruptcy Code affords to debtors,"[53] and provides a debtor breathing room from creditors by halting all collection efforts, harassment, and foreclosure actions to permit a debtor to move forward with repayment or reorganization.[54] It maintains the status quo, prevents dismemberment of the estate, and permits an orderly distribution of the debtor's assets.[55] The automatic stay remains in effect until a case is dismissed, a discharge order is entered, or the court grants relief with respect to a particular creditor pursuant to Section 362(d)–(f)

49. *In re Montano*, 488 B.R. 695, 708 (Bankr. D.N.M. 2013).
50. *In re Peyrano*, 2017 WL 2731299, at *6 (B.A.P. 10th Cir. June 26, 2017).
51. 11 U.S.C. § 362(b).
52. *Id.* § 362.
53. *In re Jamo*, 283 F.3d 392, 398 (1st Cir. 2002).
54. *Constitution Bank v. Tubbs*, 68 F.3d 685, 691 (3d Cir. 1995); *see In re Guzman*, 513 B.R. 202 (Bankr. D. P.R. 2014).
55. *In re Denby-Peterson*, 941 F.3d 115, 122–23, 126 (3d Cir. 2019).

of the Bankruptcy Code.[56] The purpose of the automatic stay is to protect debtors and property of the estate from creditors during the pendency of their bankruptcy proceeding.[57] Actions taken in violation of the automatic stay may be void or voidable depending on the jurisdiction.[58]

The scope of the automatic stay is broad, and a creditor who violates the automatic stay may be found in contempt for doing so.[59] Threats to take action against a debtor or a debtor's property constitute violations of the automatic stay. In some cases, debtors may contend that merely sending bills on account of a pre-petition debt violates the automatic stay if they appear to be coercive or harassing.[60] However, the automatic stay does not preclude informational notices about a debtor's liability so long as there is no coercion or harassment amounting to an act to collect.[61] A creditor can also seek relief from the automatic stay under Section 362 of the Bankruptcy Code by showing sufficient cause to lift or modify the stay,[62] or by showing that the debtor lacks an equity

---

56. *In re Jamo*, 283 F.3d at 398; *see also* 11 U.S.C. § 362.

57. *In re Zotow*, 432 B.R. 252 (B.A.P. 9th Cir. 2010).

58. 3 Collier on Bankruptcy ¶ 362.12[1] (16th ed. 2019).

59. *See In re Windstream Holdings, Inc.*, 627 B.R. 32 (Bankr. S.D.N.Y. 2021). Additionally, in *Taggart*, the Supreme Court left open whether the objective "fair ground of doubt" standard for discharge violations applies to findings of contempt for automatic stay violations, noting that the statute providing for the stay also had language (using the word "willful") that needed to be considered. 139 S. Ct. at 1803–04. However, the Supreme Court's description of what it called the "old soil" applicable to the "potent weapon" of civil contempt, 139 S. Ct. at 1801, makes the "fair ground of doubt" standard a likely starting point of analysis.

60. *See In re Siegal*, 591 B.R. 609, 623–24 (Bankr. D. Md. 2018) (citing *In re Robinson*, 2011 WL 832857, at *2 (Bankr. E.D. Va. Mar. 3, 2011).

61. *LTV Corp. v. Gulf States Steel, Inc.*, 969 F.2d 1050, 1059 (D.C. Cir. 1992).

62. Courts consider many factors to determine whether there is cause to lift the automatic stay. *See In re Sonnax Indus., Inc.*, 907 F.2d 1280, 1286 (2d Cir. 1990) (Factors used to determine whether litigation should continue in another forum are "(1) whether relief would result in a partial or complete resolution of the issues; (2) lack of any connection with or interference with the bankruptcy case; (3) whether the other proceeding involves the debtor as a fiduciary; (4) whether a specialized tribunal with the necessary expertise has been established to hear the cause of action; (5) whether the debtor's insurer has assumed full responsibility for defending it; (6) whether the action primarily involves third parties; (7) whether litigation in another forum would prejudice the interests of other creditors; (8) whether the judgment claim arising from the other action is subject to equitable subordination; (9) whether movant's success in the other proceeding would result in a judicial lien avoidable by the debtor; (10) the interests of judicial economy and

interest in the property in question and that such property is not necessary to that debtor's reorganization.[63]

Section 362(b) of the Code currently lists 29 exceptions to the automatic stay. The most important exception for environmental bankruptcy cases is the police or regulatory exception, which permits governmental agencies to continue without interruption to exercise their police and regulatory powers against debtors and their properties. This exception is set forth in Section 362(b)(4), which allows "the commencement or continuation of an action or proceeding by a governmental unit . . . to enforce such governmental unit's . . . police and regulatory power, including the enforcement of any judgment other than a money judgment, obtained in an action or proceeding by such governmental unit to enforce such governmental unit's . . . police or regulatory power."[64]

COLLECTION OF ASSETS AND FAIR AND ORDERLY DISTRIBUTION

A major function of the bankruptcy process is to distribute property from the debtor to creditors so that creditors can apply such payments to the debtor's debts.[65] The Bankruptcy Code determines which assets of a debtor's estate are to be distributed and to whom, as well as the priority scheme that applies to such distributions.[66] Section 541 of the Bankruptcy Code defines "property of the estate" and what is excluded from "property of the estate."[67] Broadly speaking, "property of the estate" is any property in which a debtor has an interest as of the petition date.[68]

---

the expeditious and economical resolution of litigation; (11) whether the parties are ready for trial in the other proceeding; and (12) impact of the stay on the parties and the balance of harms.").

63. 11 U.S.C. § 362(d).

64. *Id.* § 362(b)(4). *See generally* Chapter 10 (Police or Regulatory Exception) *infra*.

65. 1 Collier on Bankruptcy ¶ 1.03 (16th ed. 2019).

66. *Id.*

67. 11 U.S.C. § 541.

68. 1 Collier on Bankruptcy ¶ 1.03[1] (16th ed. 2019); *see* further discussion of Section 541 and property of the estate in Chapter 5 (Key Provisions) *infra*.

A debtor satisfies allowed claims using property of the estate.[69] A "claim" under the Bankruptcy Code is defined as a "right to payment, whether or not such right is reduced to judgment, liquidated, unliquidated, fixed, contingent, matured, unmatured, disputed, undisputed, legal, equitable, secured, or unsecured," or a "right to an equitable remedy for breach of performance if such breach gives rise to a right to payment."[70] A creditor may have a secured debt if it has a lien or a "charge against or interest in property to secure payment of a debt or performance of an obligation."[71] Generally, claims may be secured in three ways: by a perfected security agreement, a judicial lien, or a statutory lien.[72]

BAR DATES AND FILING CLAIMS

Section 501 of the Bankruptcy Code and Bankruptcy Rules 3002 and 3003 govern filing proofs of claim.[73] A creditor asserts its pre-petition claims against the debtor by filing a proof of claim.[74] Once a bankruptcy petition is filed, the bankruptcy court will set a deadline by which proofs of claim must be filed. This deadline is referred to as the claims "bar date." In Chapter 7 and Chapter 13 cases, most creditors must file a proof of claim no later than 70 days after the petition date, while governmental units are allowed 180 days after the date of the order for relief, which is typically the date the bankruptcy petition is filed.[75] In Chapter 11 cases, the bar date is set through a motion; however, governmental units are allowed by statute at least 180 days after the date of the order for relief.[76] The bar date is necessary to allow the administration of a case to move forward without delay, and to allow a debtor to

69. 1 Collier on Bankruptcy ¶ 1.03[2] (16th ed. 2019).
70. 11 U.S.C. § 101(5).
71. *Id.* § 101(37).
72. 1 Collier on Bankruptcy ¶ 1.03[2][a] (16th ed. 2019).
73. 11 U.S.C. § 501; Fed. R. Bankr. P. 3002.
74. *See* Chapter 7 (Proofs of Claim) *infra* for further discussion about the filing of proofs of claim.
75. Fed. R. Bankr. P. 3002(c); 11 U.S.C. § 502(b)(9).
76. Fed. R. Bankr. P. 3003; 11 U.S.C. § 502(b)(9).

definitively ascertain the number, amount, and substance of claims asserted against the estate.[77]

Under Section 502(a) of the Bankruptcy Code, "[a] claim or interest, proof of which is filed under Section 501 of this title, is deemed allowed, unless a party in interest . . . objects."[78] Section 502(b) of the Bankruptcy Code sets forth limited grounds for disallowance of a claim.[79]

If an objection is made to a proof of claim, the bankruptcy court will adjudicate the validity and amount of the claim.[80] The bankruptcy court will apply state or federal nonbankruptcy law except under the very limited circumstances that Section 502(b) of the Code provides otherwise.[81] If the bankruptcy court disallows the claim, then the holder of the claim is not permitted to share in a distribution of assets.[82]

GENERAL DESCRIPTION OF BANKRUPTCY PRIORITIES

The scheme of priorities provided for by the Bankruptcy Code reflects another fundamental principle of bankruptcy administration—that similarly situated claims should be treated similarly.[83]

---

77. 14 Collier on Bankruptcy ¶ 5.03 (16th ed. 2019) (citing Bankr. Form 5.03-1).

78. 11 U.S.C. § 502(a).

79. Claims that are not allowable include, but are not limited to, claims that are not otherwise enforceable outside of bankruptcy as well as claims for "for a tax assessed against property of the estate if such claim exceeds the value of the interest of the estate in such property," claims "for services of an insider or attorney of the debtor, [if] such claim exceeds the reasonable value of such services," claims resulting "from a reduction, due to late payment, in the amount of an otherwise applicable credit available to the debtor in connection with an employment tax on wages, salaries, or commissions earned from the debtor," and untimely filed claims, among others. *See* 11 U.S.C. § 502(b).

80. 4 Collier on Bankruptcy ¶ 502.03[1][a] (16th ed. 2019); *see* Chapter 17 (Claim Objections) *infra* for a discussion of objections to proofs of claim.

81. *See* Chapter 17 (Claim Objections) *infra*; *Travelers Cas. & Sur. Co. of Am. v. Pac. Gas & Elec. Co.*, 549 U.S. 443, 449 (2007).

82. 4 Collier on Bankruptcy ¶ 502.03[1][c] (16th ed. 2019).

83. A "cardinal principle[] underlying bankruptcy law is equality of treatment of similarly situated creditors." 7 Collier on Bankruptcy ¶ 1122.03 (16th ed. 2019). *See, e.g., Begier v. Internal Revenue Serv.*, 496 U.S. 53, 58 (1990); *In re W.R. Grace & Co.*, 729 F.3d 332, 342–46 (3d Cir. 2013); *In re UAL Corp.*, 468 F.3d 456, 461 (7th Cir. 2006); *In re Dow Corning Corp.*, 280 F.3d 648, 660 (6th Cir. 2002).

Priority is given to secured debt since secured claims have superior rights over unsecured claims outside of bankruptcy.[84] In addition, under the absolute priority rule, an objecting class of senior creditors (i.e., creditors holding claims with higher priority) must be paid in full before more junior creditors (i.e., creditors holding claims with lower priority) are paid anything.[85]

Bankruptcy law makes a distinction between claims arising from pre-petition activities and those arising from post-petition activities. Those arising post-petition that represent "actual, necessary costs and expenses of preserving the estate" are referred to as "administrative expense claims."[86] Costs normally incident to the operation of a business during the bankruptcy proceeding are entitled to administrative expense priority.[87] These everyday liabilities are often referred to as "ordinary course" expenses and can be paid in the regular course during the case. Other administrative expense claims (those not in the ordinary course) are generally entitled to be paid in full upon confirmation of a Chapter 11 plan, unless a creditor has agreed to a different treatment.

Pre-petition claims are claims arising before the petition is filed. Those pre-petition claims that are not secured are typically treated as general unsecured claims and generally not paid in full. Where the debtor's assets are not sufficient to cover all of its debts, the lower priority claims are paid in what one commentator referred

---

84. Elkow & Sansone, *supra* note 2, at ch. 7, 192–93.

85. *See* 11 U.S.C. § 1129(b)(2); *Czyzewski v. Jevic Holding Corp.*, 137 S. Ct. 973, 983–84 (2017); *Norwest Bank Worthington v. Ahlers*, 485 U.S. 197 (1988); *Zachary v. Cal. Bank & Tr.*, 811 F.3d 1191, 1194 (9th Cir. 2016); *In re Pac. Lumber Co.*, 584 F.3d 229, 244 (5th Cir. 2009). As outside of bankruptcy, priority among secured creditors in the same collateral is ordinarily set by the time of perfection of security interest. *See, e.g., In re First River Energy, L.L.C.*, 986 F.3d 914, 923 (5th Cir. 2021); *Diesel Props S.r.l. v. Greystone Bus. Credit II LLC*, 631 F.3d 42, 55 (2d Cir. 2011); *In re Barton Indus., Inc.*, 104 F.3d 1241, 1247 (10th Cir. 1997). However, superliens can prime prior perfected liens in certain circumstances under nonbankruptcy law. *See In re 229 Main St. Ltd. P'ship*, 262 F.3d 1, 4 (1st Cir. 2001). In addition, 11 U.S.C. § 364 permits bankruptcy courts to provide lenders providing for financing for the bankruptcy case with a first priority lien if they are unable to obtain financing without such a lien and existing lienholders are adequately protected.

86. 11 U.S.C. § 503(b)(1)(A).

87. *See, e.g., Reading Co. v. Brown*, 391 U.S. 471 (1968); *Ellis v. Westinghouse Elec. Co., LLC*, 11 F.4th 221 (3d Cir. 2021).

to as "tiny bankruptcy dollars,"[88] which are typically well under 100 cents on the dollar. For example, there may only be enough to pay general unsecured claims 40 cents on the dollar, which would mean that if $10,000 was the amount of the debt, $4,000 would be the payment. Thus, whether or not a particular claim is afforded general unsecured status versus administrative priority status is critical as to the ultimate recovery by the creditor. Chapter 12 (Priorities) of this Practice Guide discusses the application of priorities to environmental matters.

88. Jay Westbrook, *A Functional Analysis of Executory Contracts*, 74 MINN. L. REV. 227, 252–53 (1989).

CHAPTER 3

Distinguishing Chapter 11 and Chapter 7 and Other Chapters

OVERVIEW

The two key chapters in the Bankruptcy Code governing corporate bankruptcies are Chapter 7 and Chapter 11. This chapter of the Practice Guide distinguishes between Chapter 7 and Chapter 11 and concludes by briefly describing the remaining chapters of the Bankruptcy Code that provide bankruptcy relief to debtors.

Chapter 7 specifically provides for the liquidation of a business, with the goal of disposing of the assets to generate as much value as possible for distribution to creditors. Chapter 11, on the other hand, is the traditional vehicle for the reorganization of a business. It entails, among other things, the securing of debtor-in-possession (DIP) financing or the use of cash collateral during the bankruptcy proceeding (see discussion later in this chapter), the determination of available assets and liabilities, and an eventual agreement on the resolution of debts. The ultimate goal in a Chapter 11 proceeding is to enable the debtor to emerge from bankruptcy as a going concern business, though sometimes a Chapter 11 case will result in a liquidation as discussed later.

Another key distinction between the two chapters is that Chapter 11 allows a debtor to act as a "debtor-in-possession," with the authority to run its own affairs during the bankruptcy.[1] Chapter 7, on the other hand, takes this power away from the debtor, providing instead for a court-appointed trustee to control the estate until the case ends.[2]

Proceedings under both Chapter 7 and Chapter 11 of the Bankruptcy Code are subject to oversight by the U.S. Trustee Program, sometimes referred to as the U.S. Trustee.[3] The U.S. Trustee Program is a component of the U.S. Department of Justice that plays an important role in both Chapter 7 and Chapter 11 cases. For Chapter 7 cases, the U.S. Trustee maintains a panel of private trustees (from which it will appoint one trustee in each case) and supervises those trustees and reviews their reports at the conclusion of the cases. In Chapter 11 cases, the U.S. Trustee acts as a party in interest who serves as a "watchdog" over the debtor's actions (or those of a private trustee if there is one) and who may file objections to any aspect of the case it believes does not comply with the Bankruptcy Code or the Federal Rules of Bankruptcy Procedure (Bankruptcy Rules).[4]

In recent years, corporate debtors have increasingly utilized Chapter 11 for liquidation after a sale of substantially all of their assets under Section 363(f) of the Bankruptcy Code.[5] These liqui-

---

1. *See* U.S. Courts, *Chapter 11—Bankruptcy Basics*, https://www.uscourts.gov/services-forms/bankruptcy/bankruptcy-basics/chapter-11-bankruptcy-basics [hereinafter Chapter 11 Bankruptcy Basics]; 7 Collier on Bankruptcy ¶ 1100.06 (16th ed. 2019).

2. *See* 11 U.S.C. §§ 701–704; U.S. Courts, *Chapter 7—Bankruptcy Basics*, https://www.uscourts.gov/services-forms/bankruptcy/bankruptcy-basics/chapter-7-bankruptcy-basics [hereinafter Chapter 7 Bankruptcy Basics]; 6 Collier on Bankruptcy 700.01, at 1122–26 (16th ed. 2019). Once a trustee has been appointed, governmental authorities should include the trustee in discussions or negotiations regarding the debtor or property of the estate.

3. In the bankruptcy courts in Alabama and North Carolina, the Bankruptcy Administrator performs functions similar to those performed by the U.S. Trustees in other districts. The bankruptcy administrator program is administered by the Administrative Office of the U.S. Courts, while the U.S. Trustee program is administered by the U.S. Department of Justice.

4. *See generally In re Columbia Gas Sys., Inc.*, 33 F.3d 294 (3d Cir. 1994).

5. *See* Ashley Suarez, *An Analysis of § 363 Sales: Justified Deviations or Just Deviations*, 22 U. Pa. J. Bus. L. 988, 990–92 (2020); Jacob A. Kling, *Rethinking 363 Sales*, 17 Stan. J.L. Bus. & Fin. 258, 260 (2012); Bryant P. Lee, *Imagining Future Uses of 11 U.S.C.*

dating debtors have relied on Chapter 11 rather than Chapter 7 in order to remain in control of the liquidation process, continue to operate the business between the filing and the Section 363 sale, and save the cost of a trustee. Secured creditors may also prefer that the process remain in Chapter 11 with a debtor-in-possession and that the process is guided by professional asset managers approved by the secured creditors. The secured creditors may provide financing to the debtor for the costs of staying in Chapter 11 and may also bid the amount of their debt (or portion thereof) as a basis for purchasing the assets being sold (referred to as credit bidding).[6]

CHAPTER 7

In a Chapter 7 bankruptcy proceeding, an independent private trustee selected by the U.S. Trustee controls the debtor's estate during the bankruptcy case. The trustee marshals and protects the assets in the estate; sells or liquidates property of the estate; and evaluates and settles or objects to claims against the estate.[7] The trustee stands in the shoes of the debtor and its estate and is generally bound by the same rights and obligations subject to the provisions of the Bankruptcy Code.[8] Unlike Chapter 11, where

---

§ 363 to Accomplish Chapter 7 Liquidation Goals in Chapter 11 Reorganizations, 2009 COLUM. BUS. L. REV. 520, 523–24, 544–63 (2009); Douglas G. Baird & Robert K. Rasmussen, *The End of Bankruptcy*, 55 STAN. L. REV. 751 (2002).

6. *See* 11 U.S.C. § 363(k); Chapter 15 (Section 363 Sales) *infra.*

7. 11 U.S.C. § 704 (duties of the trustee); *Chapter 7 Bankruptcy Basics*, *supra* note 2.

8. *Cook v. Tullis,* 85 U.S. 332, 341 (1873) (trustee is subject to same legal and equitable rights and obligations as bankrupt); *Hays & Co. v. Merrill Lynch, Pierce, Fenner & Smith, Inc.*, 885 F.2d 1149, 1154 (3d Cir. 1989) (trustee is bound by arbitration clause of securities broker's customer agreements with debtor); *Paul v. Monts*, 906 F.2d 1468 (10th Cir. 1990) (trustee is bound by debtor's authorized actions); *In re Gebco Inv. Corp.*, 641 F.2d 143, 146 (3d Cir. 1981) (trustee "stands in the shoes" of the debtor); *Jenson v. Cont'l Fin. Corp.*, 591 F.2d 477, 482 (8th Cir. 1979) (trustees are bound by their debtor's nonexecutory contracts); *In re Magnus Harmonica Corp.*, 262 F.2d 515, 517 (3d Cir. 1959) (trustee in bankruptcy "takes over the bankrupt's situation as he finds it"); *In re S. Rachles, Inc.*, 131 B.R. 782, 785 (Bankr. D.N.J. 1991) ("Upon conversion and appointment, a trustee steps into the shoes of the debtor-in-possession with respect to all rights, responsibilities and liabilities."); *In re Light*, 23 B.R. 482, 484 (Bankr. E.D. Mich. 1982) (debtor's pre-petition arson precludes recovery by the trustee under a fire insurance policy). *See also In re Abbott,*

the business can automatically continue to operate, the Chapter 7 trustee is expected to operate the business, if at all, for only a limited period of time and may do so only with court authorization and upon a determination that operation is in the best interest of the estate and consistent with an orderly liquidation.[9] At the end of the case, unless the business has been sold as a going concern as part of the liquidation process, it will cease operations and be shut down.[10]

Trustee's Final Report

The Chapter 7 trustee must prepare a final report as soon as the estate's assets have been liquidated, all money has been distributed to creditors, and the bar date for filing creditor claims has passed. The report summarizes all actions that the trustee took in administering the case. It must include details such as the specific disposition of each asset of the estate and all financial transactions entered into by the trustee. The report is also the trustee's opportunity to request compensation and expense reimbursements. Finally, the report must lay out the proposed distributions to all creditors that have filed timely claims in accordance with the priorities in Section 726(a) of the Bankruptcy Code.[11] The U.S. Trustee reviews the trustee's report to assess whether the case has been administered in accordance with the provisions of the Bankruptcy Code. Once the U.S. Trustee's review is completed, assuming no objections, the trustee files the final report with the bankruptcy court. Professional compensation applications (e.g., for the attorneys and financial professionals who were authorized by the bankruptcy court to work on the case) should also be filed with or prior to the trustee's report. All creditors are given notice of the report's filing and opportunity to object. After all funds have been distributed to the creditors pursuant to the trustee's report and all

---

23 B.R. 484, 487 (Bankr. W.D. Okla. 1982) (debtor-in-possession bound by debtor's obligation to insure mortgage collateral).

9. 11 U.S.C. § 721.

10. *See, e.g., In re Triangle Transp., Inc.*, 419 B.R. 603 (Bankr. D.N.J. 2009).

11. U.S. Dep't of Just., *Handbook for Chapter 7 Trustees*, https://www.justice.gov/ust/private-trustee-handbooks-reference-materials/chapter-7-handbooks-reference-materials.

checks have cleared, the trustee submits a second report, known as the trustee's final account, to the U.S. Trustee, which is also filed with the bankruptcy court. If the final account is approved, the bankruptcy court officially closes the Chapter 7 case and discharges the trustee.[12]

CONVERSION

Generally, corporate bankruptcy proceedings are conducted under either Chapter 7 or Chapter 11. However, a Chapter 11 case (whether a reorganization or a liquidation) can be converted to a Chapter 7 liquidation. Under the Bankruptcy Code, the debtor has a right to convert its case unless the debtor is not a debtor-in-possession (i.e., a trustee has been appointed) or the bankruptcy case was commenced involuntarily. Alternatively, a "party in interest"[13] in a Chapter 11 case, such as a creditor, may file a motion to have the case converted "for cause."[14] The factors that establish cause for conversion are listed in Section 1112(b)(4) of the Bankruptcy Code. They include, among other things, gross mismanagement of the estate, unauthorized use of cash collateral to the detriment of creditors, or failure to comply with a bankruptcy court order.[15]

A key factor that the bankruptcy court considers when ruling on a motion to convert a case to Chapter 7 is the likelihood of the business's rehabilitation if it stays in Chapter 11.[16] This determination is fact-specific but includes questions such as the business's income and ability to generate future income. To decide whether the estate will suffer continuing loss by remaining in Chapter 11, the bankruptcy court looks at the business's cash flow and the potential depreciation of its assets. Another factor that bankruptcy courts consider is whether the debtor filed the Chapter 11 petition

---

12. *Id.*

13. *See* 11 U.S.C. § 1109 (providing a nonexclusive list of parties in interest); Chapter 20 (Jurisdiction) *infra*.

14. 11 U.S.C. § 1112.

15. *Id.* § 1112(b)(4).

16. John B. Newman, *Conversion of a Bankruptcy from Chapter 11 to Chapter 7*, Newman, Simpson & Cohen LLP, https://nscattorneys.com/conversion-of-a-bankruptcy-from-chapter-11-to-chapter-7-2/.

in bad faith. In such an instance, the bankruptcy court will seek to determine if the Chapter 11 case was filed for legitimate reasons.[17] Finally, the bankruptcy court, instead of converting a Chapter 11 case to Chapter 7, can appoint a Chapter 11 trustee if it determines that such an appointment is in the best interest of creditors and the estate.[18]

Conversion from Chapter 11 to Chapter 7 does not result in the commencement of an entirely new bankruptcy case. For instance, all claims that creditors filed during the Chapter 11 case are carried over to the Chapter 7 case.[19] The debtor-in-possession in the Chapter 11 case is also required to turn over "all records and property of the estate" under its control to a Chapter 7 trustee.[20]

Conversion from Chapter 7 to Chapter 11 (or to Chapter 13 in individual cases) is also permitted in the discretion of the bankruptcy court as long as eligibility requirements are met and the case has not been previously converted to Chapter 7 from another chapter, such as a conversion under Section 1112 of the Code.[21] Such conversions are rare and will not be granted where prejudicial to creditors or where confirmation of a plan would be futile.[22]

CHAPTER 11

In a Chapter 11 case, the debtor continues to run its business usually under its existing management while preparing for its emergence from bankruptcy. During the bankruptcy proceeding, the entity running the business is often referred to as the debtor-in-possession.[23]

---

17. *Id.* Petitions filed in bad faith may be dismissed. *See* Chapter 2 (History and Purposes) *supra.*

18. 11 U.S.C. § 1112(b)(1).

19. Fed. R. Bankr. P. 1019.

20. *Id.*

21. 11 U.S.C. § 706.

22. *See Marrama v. Citizens Bank of Mass.*, 549 U.S. 365, 375 (2007); *In re First Conn. Consulting Grp., Inc.*, 579 B.R. 673 (Bankr. D. Conn. 2018); *In re Decker*, 535 B.R. 828 (Bankr. D. Alaska 2015) (granting conversion where individual debtor was expected to have disposable future income).

23. Chapter 11 Bankruptcy Basics, *supra* note 1. Many large corporate bankruptcies involve multiple debtors each of which has its own docket number. The bankruptcy court typically administratively consolidates the related cases under a lead docket number into which all filings are made.

Frequently, in order to fund its operations during the bankruptcy proceeding, the debtor-in-possession, as a Chapter 11 debtor who remains in control of its business after the bankruptcy filing, obtains financing commonly referred to as DIP financing. Ultimately, the debtor (or, less often, another party in interest) proposes a plan of reorganization, according to which creditors are divided into separate classes, priorities of payment among the classes are outlined, and provisions for distributing the available assets are made.[24] When the bankruptcy court confirms a plan of reorganization, all debts that arose before confirmation are discharged, unless otherwise provided in the plan or the Bankruptcy Code.[25] While the discharge is a tremendous benefit for debtors, it does come with heightened scrutiny and various safeguards to ensure adequate notice and overall fairness. In recent years, the debtor-in-possession has frequently employed a professional manager, commonly referred to as a chief restructuring officer, to manage the Chapter 11 process and the business and affairs of the debtor.

Chapter 11 is available to individual as well as corporate debtors. Bankruptcy legislation enacted in 2005 tightened requirements with respect to individual debtors so as to make clear that their post-filing income is property of the estate, which makes Chapter 11 less attractive to individuals.[26]

DIP Financing

Post-petition financing is usually necessary to enable the debtor to conduct its operations while in bankruptcy. This financing, known as debtor-in-possession (or DIP) financing, is one of the most important components of a bankruptcy and is governed by Section 364 of the Bankruptcy Code.[27]

---

24. *See Czyzewski v. Jevic Holding Corp.*, 137 S. Ct. 973, 978–79 (2017).

25. 11 U.S.C. § 1141; *Chapter 11 Bankruptcy Basics*, *supra* note 1, at *Discharge*. Confirmation of a plan does not result in a discharge if the plan provides for the liquidation of all or substantially all of the property of the estate. 11 U.S.C. § 1141(d)(3). For discussions of exceptions to discharge, *see* Chapter 2 (History and Purposes) *supra*, Chapter 13 (Discharge) *infra*.

26. 11 U.S.C. § 1115; *see Zachary v. Cal. Bank & Tr.*, 811 F.3d 1191 (9th Cir. 2016); *Ice House Am., LLC v. Cardin*, 751 F.3d 734 (6th Cir. 2014); *In re Lively*, 717 F.3d 406 (5th Cir. 2013); *In re Maharaj*, 681 F.3d 558 (4th Cir. 2012).

27. *See, e.g.*, *In re hhgregg, Inc.*, 949 F.3d 1039 (7th Cir. 2020); *In re Calore Express*

Section 364(a) of the Code allows a debtor to obtain unsecured credit extensions or loans in the ordinary course of business, and grants the new debt "administrative expense" status, giving it higher priority for being paid from estate assets than pre-petition unsecured claims. There is a deliberate policy reason for giving post-petition debt a higher priority than pre-petition debt. If a debtor's business is continuing while in bankruptcy, there is a presumption that its assets are worth more as a going concern than in liquidation. Therefore, unsecured claims—even those subordinate to the new debt—should, in theory, benefit from a loan that allows the business to avoid liquidation and continue to generate income to pay claims. Section 364(b) allows for new unsecured debt to be incurred outside the ordinary course of business, but only after notice and a hearing. For post-petition secured debt, Section 364(c) applies and requires court approval. New debt issued under Section 364(c) is given priority over unsecured claims, but not over pre-petition secured claims.

Finally, Section 364(d) exists as a last resort. This subsection not only authorizes new secured debt but also grants it a priority equal to or higher than pre-petition secured debt. Since this is a deviation from the default priority rules, however, the loan must meet two requirements to qualify for it. First, the debtor must show that it could not obtain funding under Section 364(a)–(c), that is, credit that would have a more junior priority status is not otherwise available.[28] This is often true, since most lenders are reluctant to finance a bankrupt company without collateral and an advantageous priority position. Second, the debtor must provide existing creditors with adequate protection, as defined in Section 361 of the Bankruptcy Code, which is intended to protect existing secured creditors from diminution in the value of their collateral.[29]

Lending to a company in bankruptcy is a risky endeavor and, therefore, only certain lenders have the knowledge, sophistication, and risk appetite to do so. Often, lenders who provide DIP

Co., 288 F.3d 22 (1st Cir. 2002); *In re Babcock & Wilcox Co.*, 250 F.3d 955 (5th Cir. 2001); 3 Collier on Bankruptcy ¶ 364 (16th ed. 2019); *see* Chapter 5 (Key Provisions (post-petition financing)) *infra*.

28. 3 Collier on Bankruptcy ¶ 364.05 (16th ed. 2019).

29. *Id.*

financing, frequently referred to as DIP lenders, are pre-petition secured creditors who seek to use their position as existing creditors to negotiate favorable terms with the debtor-in-possession for post-petition financing or protection of their pre-petition secured debt. Regardless of the identity of the lenders providing financing, DIP financing pursuant to a DIP loan offers DIP lenders an opportunity to wield influence over the debtor and estate. Most companies in bankruptcy have an urgent need for liquidity in order to survive, even if they only need to survive long enough to sell off their assets.[30] Potential lenders are taking significant risks but also may recognize the debtors' vulnerability and sometimes use their leverage to negotiate more aggressive terms than they normally could outside bankruptcy. These terms often include higher interest rates or liens that place them ahead of all other pre-petition and post-petition secured creditors.[31]

For pre-petition lenders, agreeing to provide DIP financing is not only good from the standpoint of negotiating favorable terms or seeking to influence the reorganized company but can also be better for the lenders than a nonconsensual "cash collateral order."[32] The lender's cash collateral is the portion of the debtor's cash that is encumbered by the lender's pre-petition liens. The debtor's ability to use this encumbered cash to fund operations during the bankruptcy proceeding is naturally more restricted than unencumbered cash would be. Bankruptcy court orders authorizing DIP financing often also authorize the use of the lender's cash collateral. If a debtor is unable to obtain DIP financing, however, a bankruptcy court can authorize the debtor to use a lender's cash collateral *without* the lender's consent as long as adequate protection is provided.[33]

---

30. *In re hhgregg*, 949 F.3d at 1042.

31. *See generally* Adam Levitin, *Purdue's Poison Pill: The Breakdown of Chapter 11's Checks and Balances*, 100 Tex. L. Rev. 100, 116 (2022).

32. Richard M. Kohn, Alan P. Solow & Douglas P. Taber, *Pure Debtor-in-Possession Financing*, The Secured Lender, https://www.goldbergkohn.com/media/publication/51_kohn_DebtorinPossession.pdf.

33. *Id.*; Stephen A. Stripp, *Balancing the Interests in Orders Authorizing the Use of Cash Collateral in Chapter 11*, 21 Seton Hall L. Rev. 562, 565–66 (1991); *In re James Wilson Assocs.*, 965 F.2d 160, 171 (7th Cir. 1992); *In re Proalert LLC*, 314 B.R. 436, 442 (9th Cir. B.A.P. 2004).

DIP financing and/or authority to use cash collateral are often sought in first day motions on an interim basis with a final hearing to follow.[34] The language in the proposed bankruptcy court approval orders for financing should be carefully reviewed because such orders can have significant impacts, and objections should be made to improper terms.[35]

The Plan of Reorganization

While the DIP loan (or court-approved use of cash collateral) keeps the debtor's business on its feet during bankruptcy, the debtor (or, less often, creditors) must come up with a proposal to show to the creditors and the court describing what will become of the business after bankruptcy and what creditors will receive. The proposal is the plan of reorganization (or in some cases a liquidation plan), which is the culmination of all the negotiations that happen both before and after the commencement of the bankruptcy proceeding. While any party in interest can ultimately propose a plan, the debtor has the exclusive right to do so in the first 120 days of the case, and, subject to court approval for cause shown, up to as much as 18 months from the commencement of the case. If the debtor proposes a plan in that time period, it is given another 60 days of exclusive authority (referred to as "exclusivity") in which to solicit votes on the plan without having to compete with other plans.[36] Most plans of reorganization are proposed by debtors, but if the exclusivity period expires, any party in interest may propose a plan.[37] Where more than one party in interest wants to propose a plan, competitive bidding may result, which benefits creditors.[38] The Bankruptcy Code has numerous requirements in Sections 1123–1129 regarding the contents of the plan and the notice and solicitation procedures related to the plan. In order to be confirmed by the bankruptcy court, the plan must meet all of them.

34. *See* Chapter 4 (Timeline) *infra*.

35. For a discussion of issues creditors or governmental agencies need to look for in DIP financing and use of cash collateral motions, *see* Chapter 5 (Key Provisions (post-petition financing)) *infra*.

36. 11 U.S.C. § 1121.

37. *Id.*

38. *See, e.g., In re Asarco LLC*, 420 B.R. 314 (S.D. Tex. 2009) (full payment plus interest plan confirmed).

Requirements for Confirmation of the Plan of Reorganization under Chapter 11

Classification of Claims

A plan of reorganization must divide the claims of creditors and shareholders into classes and propose a particular treatment for each class.[39] Claims or interests[40] that are dissimilar cannot be in the same class.[41] This means, for instance, that a general unsecured claim cannot be in the same class as a secured claim or an equity interest (e.g., ownership of stock in a company such as by a parent company or shareholder(s)). It also generally means that each secured claim must be in a class by itself. This is because secured claims are not only for different amounts but can be secured by different collateral or different liens, and may have different priorities relative to other secured claims. While the general rule is that claims that are substantially similar or have the same legal entitlements belong together, the Bankruptcy Code does permit separate classification of similar claims for a legitimate reason as long as the reason for separate classification is not to gerrymander the vote of an impaired class of creditors. As discussed in more detail later, creditors' votes are used to determine whether or not a class of creditors accepts the plan. Gerrymandering the classes though, solely to create a class that will provide a supporting vote, is not permitted.[42]

A class is considered unimpaired if it will be paid in full under the plan, but impaired if it receives anything less. Unimpaired creditors do not have a right to vote on the plan; they are deemed to accept it, since they are being treated no worse than if the bankruptcy was not occurring.[43] Impaired classes do get to vote and

---

39. 11 U.S.C. § 1123.

40. Although not defined in the Code, "interests" refer to the equity interests of shareholders of the debtor.

41. 11 U.S.C. § 1122.

42. *See In re Boston Post Road Ltd. P'ship*, 21 F.3d 477, 482–83 (2d Cir. 1994); *In re Greystone III Joint Venture*, 995 F.2d 1274, 1279 (5th Cir. 1991); *In re Jersey City Med. Ctr.*, 817 F.2d 1055, 1061 (3d Cir. 1987); *In re Novinda*, 585 B.R. 145, 155–56 (10th Cir. B.A.P. 2018); *In re W.R. Grace & Co.*, 475 B.R. 34, 109–10 (D.N.J. 2012).

43. Unimpaired creditors should carefully scrutinize the plan to determine if they are in fact unprejudiced, because some debtors may have an incorrect view of what it means to be unimpaired. Plans should be scrutinized to see if they

are invited to study the plan. To help their decision-making, the Bankruptcy Code requires the issuance of what is referred to as a disclosure statement, which must be approved by the bankruptcy court.

Disclosure Statement

A disclosure statement is a document intended to give all parties in interest "adequate information" regarding the debtor's proposed plan so that all parties can make an informed decision prior to their vote.[44] This requirement stems out of a concern for the preservation of due process and the provision of adequate notice and opportunity to object and be heard.

The Bankruptcy Code defines "adequate information" as information that is reasonably sufficient, given the circumstances of the case, to allow an investor typical of holders of claims or interests in that case to make an informed judgment on the proposed plan.[45] Disclosure statements can vary in length, but typically provide background information concerning the debtor's business and the reason for the filing of the petition, a detailed summary of the proposed plan, and information regarding actions that the parties in interest will have to take to protect their rights for the remainder of the bankruptcy process.

Another important component of the disclosure statement is the "liquidation analysis," which is a financial analysis typically conducted by financial advisors retained by the debtor (or other plan proponent). The liquidation analysis is a projection of creditors' and shareholders' recoveries in a hypothetical liquidation of the company under Chapter 7 (as opposed to the reorganization

---

adversely affect rights against the debtor or nondebtors. A plan may not impair claims but seek to affect adversely other rights. Some plans do not impair rights against the debtor but provide for a nonconsensual (or consensual) third-party release of claims or rights against nondebtors. Nondebtor releases are often vigorously contested. *See* Chapter 16 (Plan Objections) *infra*.

44. Chapter 11 Bankruptcy Basics, *supra* note 1. An exception to the requirement of a separate disclosure statement may occur if the debtor is a small business and the court determines that the plan itself contains adequate information, and, in that case, a separate disclosure statement is not required. 11 U.S.C. § 1125(f) (enacted as part of a new "small business" Subchapter V of Chapter 11 in 2019).

45. 11 U.S.C. § 1125(a); *In re Cardinal Congregate I*, 121 B.R. 760, 765 (Bankr. S.D. Ohio 1990).

that is being proposed). This is an important analysis because, as discussed later, the plan must propose recoveries that are at least as large as those that would occur in a Chapter 7 liquidation.[46] While there are numerous pieces of information that a disclosure statement must include, plan proponents sometimes initially submit an incomplete disclosure statement in the interest of time, and seek to file supplemental materials later as they become available.[47]

Once again, the concept of adequate notice is a crucial consideration. In addition to the disclosure statement, under the Code all parties in interest must receive at least 28 days' notice of the objection deadline and the disclosure statement hearing. During the objection period, any party in interest, such as a lender, a vendor, a governmental agency, or the U.S. Trustee, can file objections to the disclosure statement. Objections can pertain to many different aspects of the disclosure statement, such as adequacy of the descriptions of the treatment of the classes or the proposed plan's implementation. Objectors may want, and in some cases are required, to propose language that would cure their informational-type objections. Parties in interest should also review and consider objecting to any related motions such as those relating to voting procedures or procedures to opt out of nondebtor releases.[48]

Objections to disclosure statements may contend that a plan is patently unconfirmable and that it would be a waste of time and money to proceed further on what is obviously an invalid and therefore unconfirmable plan.[49] While the vast majority of such objections to the disclosure statement are deferred for consideration until plan confirmation, where they are treated as objections

---

46. 11 U.S.C. § 1129(a)(7)(A)(ii); Gary L. Kaplan, *What to Know About Drafting Ch. 11 Disclosure Statements*, Law360, https://www.friedfrank.com.

47. *Id.* The court, however, may delay approval of the disclosure statement and delay progress on the plan process if the information or changes are important enough to warrant a fair opportunity to object to the new information.

48. Nondebtor releases are discussed in detail in Chapter 16 (Plan Objections) *infra.*

49. *See, e.g.*, *In re Am. Cap. Equip., LLC*, 688 F.3d 145, 154 (3d Cir. 2012); *In re FirstEnergy Solutions Corp.*, 606 B.R. 720, 731–32 (Bankr. N.D. Ohio 2019); *In re K Lunde*, LLC, 513 B.R. 587, 598 (Bankr. D. Colo. 2014); *In re Mahoney Hawkes, LLP*, 289 B.R. 285, 294 (Bankr. E.D. Mass. 2002); *In re Cardinal Congregate I*, 121 B.R. 760, 763–64 (Bankr. S.D. Ohio 1990).

to confirmation, they are occasionally granted.[50] Further, even though disclosure statement objections on the ground that a plan is unconfirmable are generally denied at the disclosure statement stage, they can serve an important educational function for the bankruptcy court with respect to whether the plan should ultimately be confirmed.

Once the objection deadline for the disclosure statement passes, the plan proponents prepare responses to each objection. The responses are often accompanied by an amended plan and amended disclosure statement. These responses are filed, and then the objecting parties come to the disclosure statement hearing ready to defend their objections, unless they want to withdraw their objections.[51] In larger cases, the process often results in the filing of multiple amended plans and disclosure statements both before and after the disclosure statement hearing.

After the bankruptcy court approves the debtor's disclosure statement, the debtor (or other plan proponent) must mail to the U.S. Trustee and all creditors and shareholders the proposed plan, the approved disclosure statement, a notice of time within which to file an acceptance or rejection of the plan, and any other information the bankruptcy court requires or approves.[52]

Voting on the Plan

Equipped with sufficient information, those parties whose interests are impaired may now vote on the plan and, where applicable, opt out of or opt in to any proposed nondebtor releases.[53] A class that is entitled to vote on a plan is considered to have accepted it if more than 50 percent of its *voting* members, holding collectively two-thirds or more of the amount of the *voting* members' claims, vote to accept the plan. For instance, in order to meet both requirements—(1) if there are 100 creditors in a class and only ten cast ballots, six votes constitute a majority in number and (2) if that class's claims total $1 million and only claims

50. *See* cases cited in previous footnote.
51. Kaplan, *supra* note 46.
52. Fed. R. Bankr. P. 3017(d).
53. *See* Chapter 16 (Plan Objections) *infra* for a discussion of nondebtor releases in plans.

aggregating $100,000 actually vote on the plan—the two-thirds in amount requirement would be satisfied with votes of claims aggregating at least $66,667.[54] Confirmation of the plan requires acceptance from at least one impaired class of claimholders.[55]

Section 1129 Requirements

Section 1129 of the Bankruptcy Code contains additional requirements for plan confirmation, a few of which bear explanation. A plan must specifically provide for payment of certain types of expenses, such as any unpaid administrative expenses, which are the costs of conducting a bankruptcy case (such as bankruptcy professionals' fees) and the costs of operating a business during the bankruptcy case. These must be paid in full and in cash on the plan's effective date.[56] While this is typically feasible, if it presents challenges, holders of administrative claims may sometimes agree to reduce or delay the payment owed to them to allow the plan to proceed.[57] The Bankruptcy Code also requires plans to set aside cash for payment of pre-petition taxes and obligations to employees such as employee benefits.[58]

Requirements that may be relevant to environmental bankruptcy cases include whether the plan is consistent with other Bankruptcy Code provisions,[59] the plan is proposed in good faith and not by any means forbidden by law,[60] administrative expenses are being paid in full,[61] similar claims are receiving similar treatment,[62] and the plan is "feasible," a requirement described in more

---

54. 11 U.S.C. § 1126.
55. *Id.* § 1129(a)(10).
56. *Id.* § 1129(a)(9)(A).
57. *See* J. Lathrop & Ryan Messina, *The Rising Trend in Administrative Claimants Programs Leading To "Agreement" to a Lesser Treatment in Major Retail Cases*, 30-6 Bankr. L. & Prac. (Dec. 2021).
58. 11 U.S.C. § 1129(a)(9)(B).
59. *Id.* § 1129(a)(1).
60. *Id.* § 1129(a)(3).
61. *Id.* § 1129(a)(9).
62. *Id.* § 1129(a)(1); "One of the cardinal principles underlying bankruptcy law is equality of treatment of similarly situated creditors." 7 Collier on Bankruptcy ¶ 1122.03, at 1122–26 (16th ed. 2019); *see* Ralph Brubaker, *Bankruptcy Injunctions and Complex Litigation: A Critical Reappraisal*, 1997 Univ. Ill. L. Rev. 959, 981–86 (1997); *Begier v. Internal Revenue Serv.*, 496 U.S. 53, 58 (1990); *In re W.R. Grace & Co.*, 729 F.3d 332, 342–46 (3d Cir. 2013); *In re W.R. Grace & Co.*, 729 F.3d 311, 327–28

detail later.[63] Under the absolute priority rule, an objecting class of creditors must be paid in full before more junior creditors are paid anything.[64]

Cramdown

If at least one impaired class of creditors has voted to approve the plan, it is possible for the plan proponent to have the plan confirmed even though one or more classes of impaired creditors has voted to reject the plan. This is known as a cramdown. In order to "cram down" a plan, a plan may not discriminate unfairly against any dissenting classes and must treat such classes in a fair and equitable manner within the meaning of the Bankruptcy Code.[65]

Confirmation

Assuming the plan gets the minimum requisite creditor support, a bankruptcy court must still consider any legal objections to the plan by creditors or interested parties and enter a confirmation order for it to take effect. The most common potential objections to confirmation in environmental bankruptcy cases are discussed in Chapter 16 (Plan Objections) of this Practice Guide. The proposed confirmation order should be carefully reviewed as it often contains important provisions, and the confirmation order usually

---

(3d Cir. 2013); *In re UAL Corp.*, 468 F.3d 456, 461 (7th Cir. 2006); *In re Dow Corning Corp.*, 280 F.3d 648, 660 (6th Cir. 2002).

63. 11 U.S.C. § 1129(a)(11). Section 1123(a)(5) of the Code likewise requires that a plan provides adequate means for its implementation. 11 U.S.C. § 1123(a)(5). *See* Chapter 16 (Plan Objections) *infra*.

64. *See* 11 U.S.C. § 1129(b)(2); *Czyzewski v. Jevic Holding Corp.*, 137 S. Ct. 973, 983–84 (2017); *Norwest Bank Worthington v. Ahlers*, 485 U.S. 197 (1988); *Zachary v. Cal. Bank & Tr.*, 811 F.3d 1191, 1194 (9th Cir. 2016); *In re Pac. Lumber Co.*, 584 F.3d 229, 244 (5th Cir. 2009). In *Jevic*, the Supreme Court rejected the possibility of plans or structured dismissals providing for final distributions that bypassed classes of creditors by way of "gifts" from a superior class as contrary to the Code. 137 S. Ct. at 985–86. The Supreme Court left open limited departures from the absolute priority rule early in the case (such as payment of critical trade vendors or wages) where there is a clear reorganization purpose that would even make disfavored creditors better off. *Id.*

65. 11 U.S.C. § 1129(b); *In re Sunnyslope Hous. Ltd. P'ship*, 859 F.3d 637, 646 (9th Cir. 2017); *In re Tribune Co.*, 972 F.3d 228, 237–39 (3d Cir. 2020); *In re D & F Constr. Inc.*, 865 F.2d 673, 675 (5th Cir. 1989).

governs in terms of precedence in the event of a conflict between the order and the plan.

Before entering such an order, the court must assess the plan's feasibility (i.e., the likelihood that the business can continue post-bankruptcy without needing to liquidate or reorganize again).[66] For instance, a plan that leaves a debtor with too much outstanding debt is unlikely to be confirmed because of the risk that the debtor will need to refile for bankruptcy. In evaluating feasibility, the bankruptcy court can use information such as the adequacy of capital structure, earning power of the business, economic conditions, and management ability.[67]

In addition to the feasibility test, bankruptcy courts apply the "best interests of the creditors" test. A plan must give each class of creditors a recovery equal to or better than what they would have received in a hypothetical liquidation under Chapter 7 of the Bankruptcy Code.[68] This is where the liquidation analysis, discussed earlier in the chapter, becomes relevant. This is used as a baseline against which to judge the proposed plan's treatment of all classes, and generally confirms that the reorganization of a debtor as a going concern (or orderly liquidation under a plan) generates more value than a Chapter 7 liquidation of the debtor's business and assets.[69] In some cases, creditors who are unsatisfied with their expected payments under a proposed plan will object and seek to demonstrate that the debtor's liquidation analysis undervalues the payments that would likely be made in a liquidation.

After a plan is confirmed through the bankruptcy court's entry of the confirmation order, the debtor must meet the plan's conditions before becoming effective. On the effective date, the property of the estate is vested in the reorganized debtor free and clear of claims and interests of creditors.[70] Confirmation of the plan generally discharges a reorganizing debtor that is not liquidating from

---

66. 11 U.S.C. § 1129(a)(11); *see* Chapter 16 (Plan Objections) *infra.*

67. *In re U.S. Truck Co.*, 800 F.2d 581, 589 (6th Cir. 1986).

68. 11 U.S.C. § 1129(a)(7)(A)(ii).

69. A plan may provide for payments over time or present risks or delays for recoveries to creditors. The plan must provide creditors at least as much value as they would receive immediately in a liquidation.

70. 11 U.S.C. § 1141(b), (c).

debts arising before the date of confirmation except as otherwise provided in the plan or confirmation order.[71] In the case of a liquidating plan, a corporate debtor does not receive a discharge, and a liquidating trustee or plan administrator may handle the remaining assets in accordance with the liquidation plan, or, in some situations, the case is dismissed as part of a structured settlement.[72] The bankruptcy court may retain jurisdiction to hear disputes related to the plan, but its jurisdiction over some issues (such as whether a discharge precludes the filing of a future action against the reorganized debtor) is concurrent with other courts or tribunals having jurisdiction.[73] Once the plan has been fully administered, the bankruptcy case is closed, but can be reopened for cause.[74]

INVOLUNTARY BANKRUPTCY CASES

While most bankruptcy cases are voluntarily filed, Section 303 of the Bankruptcy Code allows an involuntary petition to be filed under Chapter 7 or Chapter 11 by three creditors with claims that are not contingent as to liability and that total over a required amount.[75] If the debtor contests the involuntary petition, the bankruptcy court will decide whether the debtor is generally paying its debts as they become due or whether the debts are subject to bona fide dispute.[76] Governmental agencies with unpaid claims may join in such filings but should be aware of the risk of an award of attorney's fees and costs in the event of a finding of bad faith.[77]

---

71. *Id.* § 1141(d)(1); Chapter 11 Bankruptcy Basics, *supra* note 1, at *Discharge*; *see* Chapter 13 (Discharge) *infra*.

72. 11 U.S.C. § 1112(b); *Czyzewski v. Jevic Holding Corp.*, 137 S. Ct. 973, 983–84 (2017) (discussing structured settlements); *see generally* John Anderson & Peter Wright, *Liquidating Plans of Reorganization*, 56 Am. Bankr. L.J. 29 (1982).

73. *See* Chapter 20 (Jurisdiction) *infra*.

74. *See* 11 U.S.C. § 350.

75. 11 U.S.C. § 303. One such creditor can file if there are fewer than 12 such creditors. *Id.* § 303(b)(2).

76. *Id.* § 303(h)(1).

77. *Id.* § 303(i). In accordance with 11 U.S.C. § 106 (waiver of sovereign immunity), governmental units may not be ordered to pay punitive damages. In *Blixseth v. Mont. Dep't of Revenue (In re Blixseth)*, Adv. Pro. No. 21-1274 (Bankr. D. Nev.), three states filed an involuntary case which was dismissed, and the debtor sued for significant fees and costs.

APPOINTMENT OF A TRUSTEE OR EXAMINER

While a private trustee is always appointed in a Chapter 7 case, a trustee can also be appointed in a Chapter 11 case under Section 1104 of the Bankruptcy Code to take over the affairs of the debtor for cause, such as fraud, dishonesty, incompetence, or gross mismanagement before or after filing of the case.[78] Section 1104(c) of the Bankruptcy Code alternatively allows for the appointment of an examiner to conduct an investigation of a debtor including allegations of fraud or misconduct.[79]

SUBCHAPTER V OF CHAPTER 11

Subchapter V of Chapter 11, a recent addition to the Bankruptcy Code enacted in 2019, provides a streamlined path to reorganization for small businesses that meet certain debt maximums.[80] Instead of a disclosure statement, the debtor's plan must include a brief history of its business operations, a liquidation analysis, and projections with respect to the ability to make payments under the proposed plan.[81] Subchapter V plans must dedicate certain income to supervision of or control by a trustee to aid in execution of the plan.[82] Key differences between Subchapter V cases and regular Chapter 11 cases include: (1) the absolute priority rule for payment of creditors does not apply, (2) a creditors' committee is not

78. 11 U.S.C. § 1104(a); *In re G-I Holdings, Inc.*, 385 F.3d 313 (3d Cir. 2004); *In re Marvel Ent. Grp., Inc.*, 140 F.3d 463 (1st Cir. 1998); *In re Sharon Steel Corp.*, 871 F.2d 1217 (3d Cir. 1989). The duties of a Chapter 11 trustee are set forth in 11 U.S.C. § 1106.

79. 11 U.S.C. § 1104(c). There is a split in authority as to whether appointment of an examiner is mandatory under Section 1104(c)(2) if requested where fixed unsecured debts exceed $5 million. *Compare In re Revco D.S., Inc.*, 898 F.2d 498 (6th Cir. 1990), *with In re Residential Capital, LLC*, 474 B.R. 112 (Bankr. S.D.N.Y. 2012).

80. 11 U.S.C. §§ 101(51)(D), 1181–1195; Chapter 11 Bankruptcy Basics, *supra* note 1. Congress has changed the maximum amount of debt permitted for a small business filing from time to time.

81. *See In re Pearl Res. LLC*, 622 B.R. 236 (S.D. Tex. 2020).

82. Paul W. Bonapfel, *A Guide to the Small Business Reorganization Act of 2019*, 93 Am. Bankr. L.J. 571, 586–87, 608–11, 616–18 (2019).

required, (3) the appointment of a trustee is for limited purposes,[83] (4) the debtor has the exclusive right to file a plan, (5) a provision exists for potential cramdown of a fair and reasonable plan even if all classes vote against it, (6) payment of administrative expenses can be made over time, and (7) there are no required U.S. Trustee quarterly fees.[84]

THE OTHER CHAPTERS: CHAPTERS 9, 12, 13, AND 15

Chapter 9 is available for municipalities, which are defined to include political subdivisions, public agencies, and instrumentalities but not the state itself.[85] Chapter 9 has its own version of a plan confirmation process and special provisions preserving state and municipal governmental power and relating to municipal special revenue bonds.[86]

Chapter 12 is available for family farmers and fishermen and Chapter 13 for individuals meeting debt limitations.[87] Both Chapter 12 and Chapter 13 involve payment plans for allowed claims and include a trustee.[88] The discharge for Chapter 13 debtors is

83. Unlike trustees in Chapter 7 or 11 cases, the Subchapter V trustee does not wholly displace the debtor and is, in fact, directed to facilitate the development of a consensual plan. 11 U.S.C. § 1183(b).

84. ABI, *Reflecting on More Than a Year of Subchapter V*, 40-8 Am. Bankr. Inst. J. 8 (Aug. 2021).

85. 11 U.S.C. §§ 101(40), 901–946. *See, e.g.*, *Puerto Rico v. Franklin Cal. Tax-Free Tr.*, 579 U.S. 115 (2016); *In re City of Detroit*, 504 B.R. 97 (Bankr. E.D. Mich. 2013); *In re Jefferson Cnty.*, 474 B.R. 228 (Bankr. N.D. Ala. 2012); *In re Las Vegas Monorail Co.*, 429 B.R. 770 (Bankr. D. Nev. 2010).

86. *See* Andrew B. Dawson, *Beyond the Great Divide: Federalism Concerns in Municipal Bankruptcy*, 11 Harv. L. & Pol'y Rev. 31 (2017); Clayton P. Gillette & David A. Skeel, *Governance Reform and the Judicial Role in Municipal Bankruptcy*, 125 Yale L.J. 1150 (2016); Michael J. Deitch, *Time for an Update: A New Framework for Evaluating Chapter 9 Bankruptcies*, 83 Fordham L. Rev. 2705 (2015); *see* U.S. Courts, *Chapter 9—Bankruptcy Basics*, https://www.uscourts.gov/services-forms/bankruptcy/bankruptcy-basics/chapter-9-bankruptcy-basics.

87. 11 U.S.C. §§ 101(18), (19); 109; 1201–1232; 1301–1330.

88. *See* U.S. Courts, *Chapter 13—Bankruptcy Basics*, https://www.uscourts.gov/services-forms/bankruptcy/bankruptcy-basics/chapter-13-bankruptcy-basics; U.S. Courts, *Chapter 12—Bankruptcy Basics*, https://www.uscourts.gov/services-forms/bankruptcy/bankruptcy-basics/chapter-12-bankruptcy-basics; *In re Hardzog*, 901 F.2d 858 (10th Cir. 1990) (explaining Chapter 12); *In re Blendheim*, 803 F.3d 477 (9th Cir. 2015) (explaining Chapter 13).

broader than under Chapter 7 or Chapter 11 for individual debtors, as certain claims such as penalty claims can be discharged if they are provided for in the payment plan, although criminal restitution and fines still cannot be discharged.[89] Further, a discharge in Chapter 13 is obtained only if the debtor completes the payments required under the plan, which can take three to five years.

Chapter 15 deals with cross-border debtors that have filed for bankruptcy in other countries and have assets in the United States.[90] A Chapter 15 case commences when a foreign representative petitions for recognition of the foreign proceeding.[91] Chapter 15 provides for bankruptcy courts' aid of and comity to foreign proceedings.[92] However, bankruptcy courts may refuse to take actions "manifestly contrary to the public policy of the United States."[93] And while Chapter 15 authorizes the bankruptcy courts to assist the foreign representative, they may do so "only if the interests of the creditors and other interested entities, including the debtor, are sufficiently protected."[94] State and federal governmental agencies may invoke these limitations to guard against any actions of foreign bankruptcy courts impacting contaminated property of the United States that are inconsistent with domestic law.[95]

---

89. *Compare* 11 U.S.C. § 1328(a)(2) *with* 11 U.S.C. § 523. *See* 11 U.S.C. § 1328(a)(3) (criminal restitution and fines not dischargeable).

90. 11 U.S.C. §§ 1501–1532; U.S. Courts, *Chapter 15—Bankruptcy Basics*, https://www.uscourts.gov/services-forms/bankruptcy/bankruptcy-basics/chapter-15-bankruptcy-basics; Melanie Cyganowski, *Chapter 15 Bankruptcy: A Concise Overview*, Distressed Asset Central (May 19, 2021), https://www.dailydac.com/what-is-chapter-15-bankruptcy/.

91. 11 U.S.C. § 1504.

92. *Id.* §§ 1504, 1509(b)(3), 1525(a).

93. *Id.* § 1506; *In re Vitro S.A.B. de CV*, 701 F.3d 1031 (5th Cir. 2012).

94. 11 U.S.C. § 1522(a); *Jaffe v. Samsung Elecs. Co., Ltd.*, 737 F.3d 14 (4th Cir. 2013).

95. For example, courts will not recognize or enforce nonconsensual third party releases of nondebtors by foreign courts without an adequate record of procedural fairness and due process. *See Vitro*, 701 F.3d 1031 (5th Cir. 2012); *In re PT Bakrie Telecom Tbk*, 601 B.R. 707 (Bankr. S.D.N.Y. 2021).

CHAPTER 4

Timeline of a Bankruptcy Case under Chapter 11

Timelines for bankruptcy cases under Chapter 11 vary depending upon the nature of the case. The three major types of corporate Chapter 11 cases are: (1) a traditional bankruptcy case, in which the debtor enters Chapter 11 without an agreed-upon path to emergence; (2) a prearranged case, in which the debtor has negotiated the terms of a plan of reorganization with certain creditors prior to filing the case; and (3) a prepackaged case, in which the debtor has already solicited and obtained votes on a plan of reorganization prior to filing its Chapter 11 petition.[1] The type of case will determine how long the proceedings may last and the various steps to resolution. While a traditional Chapter 11 case will take place over an extended period of time, cases with prearranged plans are generally completed within four to six months from the petition date, and prepackaged cases generally can be completed within 45 to 60 days from the date of filing, and sometimes within an even shorter period of time.[2] Prearranged or prepackaged cases

---

1. *See* 11 U.S.C. § 1125(g); *United Artists Theatre Co. v. Walton*, 315 F.3d 217 (3d Cir. 2003); *In re Genco Shipping & Trading Ltd.*, 509 B.R. 455, 461–62 (Bankr. S.D.N.Y. 2014).

2. Prepackaged cases have even been completed within a 24-hour period. *See* Soma Biswas, *Judge Approves FullBeauty's Record 24-Hour Bankruptcy Case*, Wall St. J. (Feb. 4, 2019), https://www.wsj.com/articles/fullbeauty-attempts-record-24-hour-bankruptcy-case-11549310368.

typically involve a consensual restructuring of major debts such as secured bond debt. Such cases provide for full payment of debts other than the restructured debts so that due process concerns do not arise on account of the limited time provided to such other creditors to review the plan closely prior to confirmation. Acceleration of the time frames specified by the Bankruptcy Code requires a truly consensual plan of reorganization.[3] On occasion, prepackaged or prearranged bankruptcies are delayed and become like traditional bankruptcy cases and extend over a longer period than anticipated.

PRE-BANKRUPTCY WORK BY PROSPECTIVE DEBTORS

The period before the bankruptcy petition is filed is one of the most important parts of the Chapter 11 process for prospective debtors. Careful planning for the filing is crucial, requiring input from a number of personnel at the company in order to develop and implement a highly tailored strategy. A debtor, with the help of its counsel, must conduct necessary due diligence, prepare a number of schedules, consider which entities should file for bankruptcy and in what venue, and determine how it will finance its business operations while in Chapter 11. Less commonly, a debtor may not have time to plan a filing and instead it ends up in what is known as a "free fall" bankruptcy, which is risky because it can lead to liquidation or substantially less value for creditors.

For a bankruptcy case involving environmental issues, it is important for the debtor to identify its environmental liabilities before filing. Counsel for the debtor typically works with the debtor's technical and in-house legal team to undertake extensive due diligence including the review of environmental documents, such as environmental site assessments, remedial investigation reports, monitoring reports, operational audits, regulatory orders,

3. The plan and confirmation order need to be clear that they do not impair or prejudice other creditors or governmental units. The U.S. Trustee's office or other governmental regulators may request language that confirms this or will otherwise have strong grounds to object to departures from Code requirements.

compliance history, notices of violation and environmental litigation. Counsel may also need to meet with debtor personnel to review and identify environmental issues, including contamination issues at or from current and former operations (including operations of predecessor entities) and third-party off-site disposal locations, nature of hazardous material used and generated, historical violations and how each was addressed, and compliance concerns, including voluntary compliance audits and current status of environmental permits.[4]

Discretion is critical in the prefiling period.[5] Faced with an imminent bankruptcy filing, employees may leave the company, vendors may stop providing shipments, creditors may curtail business or pursue legal remedies, and competitors may go after the debtor's business.[6] As a result, a debtor preparing for bankruptcy often will only share its plans with a limited group of management personnel, employees, counsel, and occasionally creditors, and will also take steps to ensure that all insolvency-related discussions remain confidential.[7] Debtors in heavily regulated industries who need to work with governmental agencies during the bankruptcy may decide to provide such agencies with limited advance notice to facilitate cooperation.[8]

FILING THE PETITION

After careful preparation, each debtor begins the official bankruptcy case by filing its bankruptcy petition and paying the filing

---

4. *See also* Chapter 14 (Debtor-Owned Contaminated Property) *infra* (discussing identification of debtor sites with environmental liabilities).

5. John D. Ayer, Michael Bernstein & Jonathan Friedland, *The Life Cycle of a Chapter 11 Debtor through the Debtor's Eyes: Part I*, 22 Am. Bankr. Inst. J. 2 (Sept. 2003), https://www.kirkland.com/-/media/publications/article/2003/09/chapter-11-101–the-life-cycle-of-a-chapter-11-deb/friedland–life-cycle-of-a-chapter-11-debtor.pdf [hereinafter *Life Cycle Part I*].

6. *Id.*

7. *Id.*

8. Some statutes require debtors to notify regulators of a bankruptcy filing. *See, e.g.*, for the Nuclear Regulatory Commission: 10 C.F.R. §§ 30.34(h), 40.41(f), 70.32(a)(9), 72.44(b)(6). It is important for debtors with significant environmental compliance obligations and facing liquidity issues to keep regulators informed about their situation. As noted later, Question 12 of the bankruptcy petition inquires whether the debtor has any property requiring immediate attention.

fee.[9] The filing of the bankruptcy petition commences every bankruptcy case and constitutes the "order for relief" in a voluntary case.[10] In the petition, each debtor lists its name, its social security number or tax ID number, and the location of its principal assets; announces its plan or its intention to file a plan; and requests relief under Chapter 11.[11] Further, in a voluntary Chapter 11 case, the debtor must file, along with its petition, a complete list of creditors (including federal, state, and local government creditors), co-debtors, and parties to executory contracts and unexpired leases,[12] as well as a list of noninsider creditors holding the 20 largest unsecured claims.[13] The typical Chapter 11 debtor may also choose to file a number of "first-day motions" (discussed later in this chapter) at the time the debtor files the bankruptcy petition to facilitate the operation of the business and the administration of the bankruptcy case.

For an environmental bankruptcy case, Question 12 on the petition (Question 14 for individual debtors) will be of particular relevance. This is the question often referred to as the "environmental question." The question requires that the debtor disclose "any real property or personal property that needs immediate attention" from the perspective of potential imminent and identifiable hazards or property "that needs to be physically secured or protected from the weather."[14] Debtors often take the position that the "imminent and identifiable" standard is a very high threshold and, as a result, determine that most of their properties do not meet the standard for inclusion in the response to Question

9. 11 U.S.C. § 301.

10. However, in an involuntary case, the court must enter an actual order for relief. 11 U.S.C. §§ 301–303.

11. *See, e.g.*, U.S. Courts, Official Bankruptcy Form B 201 Voluntary Petition for Non-Individuals Filing for Bankruptcy, https://www.uscourts.gov/sites/default/files/form_b_201.pdf.

12. Fed. R. Bankr. P. 1007(a). *See also* 4 Collier on Bankruptcy ¶ 521.03[1] (16th ed. 2019). In an involuntary case, the debtor must file the list within 14 days after the order for relief. *Id.* Debtors may amend such lists as a matter of right any time before the case is closed, so long as they pay additional fees and provide notice to those affected. Fed R. Bankr. P. 1009(a).

13. Fed. R. Bankr. P. 1007(d). Debtors often seek extensions of time to meet some of these filing requirements.

14. https://www.uscourts.gov/sites/default/files/form_b_201.pdf; https://www.uscourts.gov/sites/default/files/form_b_101.pdf.

12. However, this position poses some risks for debtors, because if something deleterious occurs on a debtor's property during the pendency of the bankruptcy, then the bankruptcy court and governmental agencies may question the debtor's failure to disclose, which could undermine the debtor's position with the court. The authors are not aware of any cases to date that have addressed the scope of Question 12 or the legal consequences of failure to disclose.

As soon as the bankruptcy petition is filed, the debtor becomes a "debtor-in-possession"[15] and its property becomes property of the bankruptcy estate.[16] The petition filing also activates the automatic stay, an important protection for the Chapter 11 debtor and its creditors, but one that is limited by some exceptions, including the police and regulatory exception.[17]

FIRST-DAY HEARING

The first-day hearing takes place on either the day that the debtor files the petition or the next available business day following the filing. The hearing is the debtor's first and best opportunity to lay out a narrative explaining why it filed for Chapter 11 protection, describing its business, and, most importantly, if credible, setting forth the debtor's view of the path to exiting the bankruptcy process.[18]

During the first-day hearing, the court may also consider a number of first-day motions. First-day motions are generally filed on the same day as the bankruptcy petition itself and range from purely procedural to substantive requests.[19] Typical administrative

---

15. 11 U.S.C. §§ 1101(1), 1107(a) (debtor-in-possession has rights, powers, duties, and functions of a trustee); ABI Commission to Study the Reform of Chapter 11, *2012–2014 Final Report and Recommendations, Commencing the Case*, pt. IV, at 21–22, https://commission.abi.org.

16. 11 U.S.C. § 541. *See* Chapter 5 (Key Provisions (property of the estate)) *infra*.

17. 11 U.S.C. § 362(a), (b)(4). *See* Chapter 2 (History and Purposes) *supra*, Chapter 10 (Police or Regulatory Exception) *infra*.

18. Often this narrative will echo the information set forth in a "first-day declaration," signed by a member of the debtor company's upper management and submitted concurrently with the bankruptcy petition.

19. John W. Weiss, *Timeline of a Chapter 11 Case*, *in* Creditors' Rights in Chapter 11 Cases (2013 ed.), 2013 WL 936385, at *1–2.

first-day motions include joint administration motions that would allow the cases of related entities to be administered using a single docket and calendar, and case management motions. Typical operational first-day motions include cash collateral use authorization and DIP financing motions,[20] which help the debtor fund operations throughout the bankruptcy case, and motions authorizing the debtor to pay taxes, utilities, insurance premiums, and/or employee wages and benefits. Whereas a debtor generally is barred from using or incurring obligations on property of the estate during the first 21 days after filing,[21] these motions can provide interim relief which, if granted, helps "minimize the disruption" of the bankruptcy process.[22] Substantive motions, such as for cash collateral use authorization and DIP financing, are generally only approved on an interim basis at a first-day hearing since many interested parties may not be able to attend or have an adequate opportunity for review on short notice.[23]

While most first-day motions should not impact environmental creditors, careful attention should be paid to the first-day motions and the language in the debtor's proposed orders, including DIP financing and cash collateral motions,[24] motions relating to environmental bonding,[25] and motions relating to the bankruptcy

20. Section 364 of the Bankruptcy Code, 11 U.S.C. § 364, provides for DIP financing and is discussed briefly in Chapter 3 (Code Chapters) *supra*, Chapter 5 (Key Provisions (post-petition financing)) *infra*.

21. Fed. R. Bankr. P. 6003(b).

22. *Life Cycle Part I*, *supra* note 5, at 1.

23. *See, e.g.*, Fed. R. Bankr. P. 4001(b)(2), (c)(2). For a discussion of issues to look for in DIP financing and use of cash collateral motions, *see* Chapter 5 (Key Provisions (post-petition financing)) *infra*.

24. For a discussion of issues to look for in DIP financing and use of cash collateral motions, *see* Chapter 5 (Key Provisions (post-petition financing)) *infra*. Orders should be reviewed carefully to ensure that they do not provide the debtor any discretion to modify compliance obligations or change the applicable rules and standards of environmental law. Reputable bankruptcy attorneys would not seek such relief in a first-day order (if ever) and bankruptcy judges would not grant such relief if the language is brought to their attention as it is beyond their authority. *See* Chapter 9 (Operating Estate Property) *infra*.

25. This type of motion often seeks authority for the debtor to continue paying premiums on bonding and is thus in the interest of beneficiaries of the bonding. If the motion attachments omit relevant bonds or provide discretion in compliance with legal requirements, which is contrary to 28 U.S.C. § 959(b), *see* Chapter 9 (Operating Estate Property) *infra*, correction may be sought.

automatic stay.[26] First-day motions are typically accompanied by a first-day declaration that provides useful information about the debtors and the plans for the case.

SCHEDULES AND THE STATEMENT OF FINANCIAL AFFAIRS

Within 14 days of the petition filing, a Chapter 11 debtor must file a schedule of assets and liabilities, a schedule of current income and expenditures, a schedule of executory contracts and unexpired leases, and a statement of financial affairs (SOFA).[27] A corporate Chapter 11 debtor must also file a list of equity security holders within the 14-day period,[28] and in a voluntary Chapter 11 reorganization, the debtor must also file a list containing the name, address, and claim of noninsider creditors holding the 20 largest unsecured claims.[29] In a complex Chapter 11 case, the compilation of this information can be a labor-intensive task, so debtors may file a request for additional time to file the schedules and SOFAs as part of the first-day motions.[30] Such motions generally request a 30-day extension to file schedules and statements, with the right to extend the time further if necessary. While requests for extensions are usually granted within reason, they can be objected to by a party that needs the information sooner in order to participate in matters pending in the bankruptcy case.

With respect to the schedules and the SOFAs, debtors must disclose a host of historical and current information about each filing entity. Together, the documents provide a snapshot of a debtor's debts and operations at the time of filing, including what it

26. Although less common nowadays, some debtors have sought a court order implementing the bankruptcy automatic stay. It is important to review the proposed orders carefully to ensure that they incorporate the Bankruptcy Code's exceptions to the automatic stay (i.e., the police or regulatory exception) and to ensure that they do not otherwise seek to modify or expand the stay.

27. 11 U.S.C. § 521(a)(1)(B); Fed. R. Bankr. P. 1007(b)–(c).

28. Fed. R. Bankr. P. 1007(a)(3).

29. *Id.* 1007(d).

30. *See id.* 1007(c) and 9006(b) (providing that the bankruptcy court may extend the schedules and SOFAs filing deadline "for cause"). The debtor also has the right to amend the schedules at any time before the case is closed, provided that it pays additional fees and provides notice to those affected. *Id.* 1009(a).

owes and to whom. The schedules also help to identify creditors and usher in the claims administration process.

Part 12 of the SOFA for a corporate debtor (Part 10 for an individual debtor) requests detailed information about environmental matters.[31] This information includes identifying the debtor's known environmental liabilities for which notice has been given, proceedings under environmental law in which the debtor has been a party, and any notifications to governmental authorities regarding releases of hazardous materials.[32] Given that the responses are not limited to a specific time period, preparation of the responses in Part 12 can be time-consuming for a debtor. In addition, other sections of the SOFA may touch on environmental matters, such as Question 7 of Part 3, which asks the debtor to identify legal actions, proceedings, or investigations by regulatory agencies in the last year. The information in the schedules and SOFA is a good first source of information for regulators.

THE 341 MEETING AND CREDITORS' COMMITTEE

The U.S. Trustee must call a meeting of creditors "[w]ithin a reasonable time" after the filing of the petition.[33] (The meeting requirement may, however, be waived for prepackaged bankruptcies.)[34] In a Chapter 11 bankruptcy, this "341 meeting" must be held from 21 to 40 days after the order for relief.[35] Notice of the meeting must be given to all creditors, the debtor, and the bankruptcy trustee (if one is appointed).[36] The U.S. Trustee or an Assistant U.S. Trustee presides over this meeting. The debtor must appear and submit to examination under oath by the creditors or their agents, the U.S. Trustee, or any trustee or examiner.[37] The meeting is an

31. This information is in addition to the information discussed above that is required by Question 12 on the petition for relief.

32. *See* Official Bankruptcy Form B207 (nonindividuals); Official Bankruptcy Form B107 (individuals).

33. 11 U.S.C. § 341(a).

34. *Id.* § 341(e).

35. Fed. R. Bankr. P. 2003(a).

36. *Id.* 2002(a)(1).

37. 11 U.S.C. §§ 341(d), 343.

opportunity for creditors to obtain information, but creditors do not need to attend the meeting in order to assert their claims.[38] The U.S. Trustee may also convene a meeting of equity security holders, though he or she is not required to do so.[39]

In a Chapter 11 case, the U.S. Trustee is also required to appoint a committee of unsecured creditors "as soon as practicable after the order for relief."[40] The U.S. Trustee also has the authority to appoint additional official creditors' committees or equity security committees.[41] Ordinarily, the committees consist of the persons holding the seven largest claims who are willing to serve.[42] Official committees may seek compensation from the bankruptcy estate for their work on the bankruptcy case. Creditors may also band together in unofficial, ad hoc committees to advance their particular interests.[43] In a number of cases, state and local governmental creditors have acted collectively, on an ad hoc basis, often with the assistance of the National Association of

---

38. "In most consumer bankruptcy cases, few creditors attend the meeting because the expenditure of time and money necessary is rarely justified by significant benefits derived from attending. . . . In some business cases, creditors may have reason to attend the meeting. The section 341 meeting represents a unique opportunity for a creditor, particularly one with a significant claim, to conduct a wide-ranging examination that may help determine whether a debtor has a realistic prospect for reorganization and what a reorganized debtor might look like." 3 Collier on Bankruptcy ¶ 341.02[5][a] (16th ed. 2019). During the COVID pandemic, meetings of creditors have been conducted virtually.

39. 11 U.S.C. § 341(b).

40. *Id.* § 1102(a)(1).

41. *Id.* § 1102(a)(2).

42. *Id.* § 1102(b)(1)–(2). The statute's use of the term "ordinarily" allows the U.S Trustee some leeway in who may be appointed. The term "person," though, is defined in 11 U.S.C. § 101(41) to exclude most governmental agencies other than pension regulators. *See In re Mansfield Tire & Rubber Co.*, 39 B.R. 974 (N.D. Ohio 1983); *In re VTN, Inc.*, 65 B.R. 278 (Bankr. S.D. Fla. 1986). Governmental agencies have historically served as ex officio members of committees, such as in the *LTV* and *Uniroyal* cases, which can benefit both the committees and agencies in their work on the case. More recently, committees have been less receptive to this.

43. *See* 3 Collier on Bankruptcy ¶ 1102.06 (16th ed. 2019) ("While section 1102 provides for the creation of official committees of creditors and of equity security holders, nothing in section 1102 prohibits creditors or equity security holders from forming additional committees."). In a Chapter 11 case, the ad hoc committees are generally required to file a "verified statement" laying out "pertinent facts and circumstances" concerning the formation of the committee and its membership. Fed. R. Bankr. P. 2019(b)–(c).

Attorneys General (NAAG).[44] In bankruptcy cases involving numerous environmental liabilities, the Department of Justice, Environment and Natural Resources Division, has coordinated with states on conference calls and in the filing of joint briefs. Interested governmental agencies and creditors may wish to file a notice of appearance and request for service of papers during the first few weeks of the bankruptcy case so that they can stay informed about developments in the case.[45]

THE BAR DATE AND FILING PROOFS OF CLAIM

The debtor's schedules are the first step in the claims administration process.[46] If a debtor schedules a creditor's claim in an amount and priority that the creditor agrees with, it need not do more unless the claim is scheduled as disputed, contingent, or unliquidated (though creditor's counsel may advise that the creditor file a claim all the same).[47] Any creditor whose claim is not

44. Unlike creditors' committee members, state governmental creditors are unable to obtain reimbursement of their expenses under Section 503(b)(4). However, they may seek reimbursement of attorney's fees and expenses if they make a "substantial contribution" to resolving the case. 11 U.S.C. § 503(b)(3)(D), (4). NAAG's bankruptcy counsel obtained such an award for helping 31 states and the debtor resolve cleanup cost issues for the debtor's 1,100 stores and gas stations in the Circle K Corp. bankruptcy in the 1990s. The $30 million settlement in this case was the successful result of a three-way negotiation among NAAG (for the states), the debtor, and landlord/owner/operators who could access the funds to pay their costs as they did the work. *See* David Hird, *Settlement Allows Circle K to Resolve Environmental & Financial Problems*, Env't Compliance & Litig. Strategy 4 (Apr. 1994).

45. *See* 11 U.S.C. § 342 (notice); Fed. R. Bankr. P. 2002 (notice), 1010(b) (appearance). The bankruptcy court's local rules should be consulted for any special requirements for appearances or requests for service of papers. Some bankruptcy court local rules require that out-of-state parties have local counsel and that out-of-state attorneys file pro hac vice motions if they wish to appear. At least one key bankruptcy court allows state agency attorneys to appear by filing a certification. *See, e.g.*, Del. Local Bankr. Ct. Rule 9010-1(e)(i). While federal attorneys may always appear in bankruptcy court pursuant to 28 U.S.C. § 516, they should consider also filing any certifications or notices required by local rules to accommodate such preference of the courts.

46. John D. Ayer, Michael Bernstein & Jonathan Friedland, *The Life Cycle of a Chapter 11 Debtor through the Debtor's Eyes: Part II*, 22 Am. Bankr. Inst. J. (Oct. 2003), https://www.kirkland.com/siteFiles/kirkexp/publications/2455/Document1/Friedland%20-%20Life%20Cycle%20of%20a%20Chapter%2011%20Debtor%202.pdf [hereinafter *Life Cycle Part II*].

47. Fed. R. Bankr. P. 3003(b). *See also, e.g., Life Cycle Part II*, *supra* note 46.

on the appropriate schedule is listed as disputed, contingent, or unliquidated, or is listed in an amount or priority that the creditor does not agree with, however, must file a proof of claim before the "bar date."[48] Even if a claim is correctly listed when schedules are first filed, filing a proof of claim avoids the risk that the creditor will miss a subsequent amendment of the schedule that changes the listed amount of the claim and, consequently, miss the opportunity to file a proof of claim if the creditor disagrees with the change. Such changes can be easy to miss because they may be buried in long lists without particularized or prominent notice to the creditor. If a creditor's claim is scheduled as disputed or unliquidated, it must file a proof of claim if it wishes to protect its ability to recover on a claim.

The bar date is the court-ordered deadline for submission of proofs of claim, affording the debtor the ability to determine its liability on a claim with finality. The bar date in Chapter 11 cases is set by court order upon motion of the debtor, typically within the first few months of a case.[49] In any event, nongovernmental creditors must receive at least 21 days' notice of the bar date.[50] If a claim is not filed by the bar date, it will normally be disallowed as untimely.[51] By statute, governmental units are entitled to at least 180 days after the petition date to file proofs of claim (the government bar date) and this period may not be shortened.[52]

---

48. Fed. R. Bankr. P. 3003(c)(2)–(3).

49. Weiss, *supra* note 19, at *3.

50. The bar date may be extended for a particular creditor on the basis of insufficient notice. Fed. R. Bankr. P. 3002(c)(6).

51. There are, however, several exceptions to the bar date. Among them: the date only applies to governmental units if it is set more than 180 days after the order for relief. The court may in its discretion extend the filing deadline for infants or incompetent persons. Fed. R. Bankr. P. 3002(c)(2). The bar date is also extended for certain claims arising from the bankruptcy process itself: unsecured claims arising from the result of judgments by the estate or claims arising from the debtor's rejection of an executory contract or unexpired lease. Fed. R. Bankr. P. 3002(c)(2)–(3). In Chapter 11, the bar date may also be extended on the basis of insufficient notice or excusable neglect. Fed. R. Bankr. P. 3002(c)(6); *Pioneer Inv. Servs. v. Brunswick Assocs.*, 507 U.S. 380 (1993); *In re CJ Holding Co.*, 27 F.4th 1105 (5th Cir. 2022); *In re Zilog, Inc.*, 450 F.3d 996, 1007 (9th Cir. 2006); *Jones v. Chemetron Corp.*, 212 F.3d 199 (3d Cir. 2000).

52. *See* Fed. R. Bankr. P. 3002(c)(1); 11 U.S.C. § 502(a)(9); *In re Metrocall, Inc.*, No. 02-11579 (Bankr. D. Del. June 6, 2002); *In re George Transfer, Inc.*, 212 B.R. 475 (Bankr. D. Md. 1997); *Hill v. McDermott, Inc.*, 827 F.2d 1040, 1043 (5th Cir. 1987) (court may grant relief where an order "obviously conflicts with a clear statutory mandate.").

After claims are asserted through the schedules and the creditors' filed proofs of claim, the debtor and potentially other parties in interest may raise objections to such claims, either on a claim-by-claim basis or on an omnibus basis.[53] Common objections include duplicative claims, untimeliness, invalidity under nonbankruptcy law, or assertion of claims of the wrong priority.[54] Debtors may also seek the estimation of an unliquidated or contingent claim, if waiting until the claim is fixed or liquidated would unduly delay the administration of the bankruptcy case.[55]

PLAN, DISCLOSURE STATEMENT, SOLICITATION PERIOD, AND CONFIRMATION HEARING

A key purpose of the Chapter 11 case is to confirm and consummate a Chapter 11 plan, but the process of achieving that confirmation varies, depending on whether the plan is traditional, prearranged, or prepackaged, and whether it is a reorganization or a liquidation after a sale of substantially all of the debtor's assets.

Traditional, prearranged, and prepackaged cases share several fundamental elements: the disclosure statement, an informational document used to satisfy the Bankruptcy Code's disclosure requirements;[56] solicitation, the process of soliciting, receiving, and tabulating votes by voting parties to accept or reject the proposed plan from parties who are entitled to vote; and the plan supplement, composed of documents that support the plan and which is considered part of the plan.

Where the categories of cases—traditional, prearranged, and prepackaged—differ is in their timing. In the traditional case, the plan is negotiated after the Chapter 11 filing. Generally, a debtor in a traditional case will try to take advantage of the exclusivity period, during the first 120 days of a case, in which the debtor is

53. 11 U.S.C. § 502; Fed. R. Bankr. P. 3007. As discussed in Chapter 17 (Claim Objections) *infra*, some courts limit the ability of interested parties to file objections where the trustee or debtor-in-possession is handling objections.

54. Fed. R. Bankr. P. 3007(d); *Life Cycle Part II*, *supra* note 46.

55. *See* 11 U.S.C. § 502(c); Chapter 17 (Claim Objections) *infra*.

56. *See* 11 U.S.C. § 1125(a)(1); Chapter 3 (Code Chapters) *supra*.

the only party who may file a plan.[57] The bankruptcy court may extend debtor's exclusivity period upon notice and hearing, but only up to 18 months after the commencement of the case.[58] The prearranged case differs from the traditional case in that the prearranged plan is negotiated before the Chapter 11 filing, with the debtor filing a disclosure statement and plan at the same time that it files the bankruptcy petition. The prepackaged case differs further in that the plan is fully negotiated and drafted and solicitation has occurred prior to filing, and the disclosure statement and confirmation hearing occur shortly thereafter.[59]

During the exclusivity period, the debtor determines, after consultation with other interested parties, how to formulate a proposed plan. Options include: (1) a standalone reorganization, (2) the liquidation of its business, (3) a Section 363 sale of some or all assets, or (4) any combination thereof. If there are significant environmental liabilities, debtors may consider utilizing a liability transfer or assumption arrangement or environmental response trust to address environmental issues.[60] In recent years, Section 363 sales of assets have become increasingly common, sometimes under the pressure of secured creditors who may want to purchase the assets or equity or secure the proceeds from a sale.[61] If the debtor wishes to pursue a sale, it may determine to pursue the sale separate from, and usually prior to, confirmation of a plan, or it may incorporate the sales process into the plan process or provide for it to be carried out post-confirmation.[62]

In certain complex cases, the debtor will seek approval of a solicitation and confirmation timeline in a motion for a "scheduling" order. Otherwise, the deadlines to vote on and object to the plan, the confirmation hearing date, and related record dates are set in connection with approval of the disclosure statement. Parties in interest must receive at least 28 days' notice of the disclosure

---

57. 11 U.S.C. § 1121.

58. *Id.* § 1121(d)(1)–(d)(2)(A).

59. *See id.* § 1126(b); Fed. R. Bankr. P. 3018(b); 9 Collier on Bankruptcy ¶ 3018.02 (16th ed. 2019).

60. *See* Chapter 14 (Debtor-Owned Contaminated Property) *infra.*

61. *See* Chapter 16 (Plan Objections) *infra.*

62. *See id.*

statement objection deadline and hearing date.[63] If the disclosure statement is approved by the court, the solicitation period will usually begin five to seven days later, after solicitation packages have been customized and printed. However, in the prepackaged case, the solicitation period takes place before the disclosure statement hearing, in accordance with special rules for pre-petition and "straddle" (i.e., both pre-petition and post-petition) votes.[64]

During the solicitation period, the debtor obtains votes from interested parties to approve or reject the proposed plan. This right to solicit votes is exclusive to the debtor for the first 180 days after petition date, with the solicitation exclusivity period extendable up to a hard cap of 20 months after commencement of a case.[65] Interested parties whose claims are "not impaired" (that is, parties whose claims will be satisfied in full, according to the Code's provisions) are deemed to have accepted the plan. Conversely, parties whose claims are wiped out (that is, parties who receive nothing under the plan) are deemed to have rejected the plan.[66] The remaining parties in interest are entitled to vote on the plan and the plan supplement,[67] with ballots to be received within a time period set by the bankruptcy court.[68]

The bankruptcy court sets the particular dates and time period for plan voting and for the confirmation hearing according to the needs of the case.[69] Creditors must ordinarily be notified at least 28 days before the deadline for objections to the plan and

---

63. Fed. R. Bankr. P. 2002(b), 3017(a).

64. 11 U.S.C. § 1126(b); Fed. R. Bankr. P. 3018(b); 9 Collier on Bankruptcy ¶ 3018.01[2] (16th ed. 2019).

65. 11 U.S.C. § 1121(d).

66. *Id.* § 1126(f)–(g).

67. The plan supplement is a filing made by the debtor, and includes organizational documents for the reorganized company, a schedule of retained causes of action, schedules of contracts and leases to be assumed and to be rejected, exit financing documents, and other documents and disclosures. Usually, the plan supplement must be submitted at least seven days before the voting deadline. *See, e.g.*, Del. L. Bankr. R. 3016-2.

68. 11 U.S.C. § 1126(a).

69. Fed. R. Bankr. P. 3017(c); 9 Collier on Bankruptcy ¶ 3018.01[3] (16th ed. 2019).

the confirmation hearing.[70] Usually, though, the court allows more than 28 days for the solicitation period, especially in large cases.[71]

Votes are tabulated on a class-by-class basis, with each class deemed to have accepted a plan if it is accepted by a majority of voting creditors of that class as long as such creditors also hold at least two-thirds of the monetary amount of the claims of the voting creditors of that class.[72] If all classes permitted to vote on the plan accept it, the plan proponent will ask the court to confirm the plan; if every voting class rejects the plan, the plan is dead.[73] If some classes vote to accept and some to reject, the plan proponent may pursue a "cramdown."[74]

Along with voting to accept or reject the plan, interested parties (including creditors, equity security holders, indenture trustees, debtors, committees, and regulatory agencies) may file an objection to the plan.[75] The bankruptcy court may set a deadline by which objections must be filed, which is often the same as the voting deadline but which is sometimes extended to permit negotiations. In many cases, the ballot for voting may have an option to opt in or out of a third-party release of certain nondebtors.[76] The permissibility of such releases is controversial and varies from circuit to circuit.[77] The rules for effectuating an opt-out from or an opt-in to the third-party nondebtor release can vary from case to case and should be carefully reviewed.

---

70. Fed. R. Bankr. P. 2002(b)(2). The 28-day period may be shortened for cause in accordance with Fed. R. Bankr. P. 9006.

71. 9 Collier on Bankruptcy ¶ 3018.01[3] n.17 (16th ed. 2019).

72. 11 U.S.C. § 1126(c). If the debtor and creditor do not agree on the amount of the claim, the court may estimate it for purposes of voting. *See* Chapter 17 (Claim Objections) *infra.*

73. 11 U.S.C. § 1129(a)(10).

74. *See id.* § 1129(b)(1); Chapter 3 (Code Chapters) *supra.*

75. 11 U.S.C. § 1109(a)–(b); Fed. R. Bankr. P. 3020.

76. Nondebtor releases are discussed in detail in Chapter 16 (Plan Objections) *infra.*

77. *See id.*

CONFIRMATION HEARING

After voting and the passage of the objection deadline, the bankruptcy court holds the "confirmation hearing."[78] At this hearing, the bankruptcy court reviews voting results, considers objections to the plan, and determines whether the plan complies with the relevant statutory requirements set forth in the Bankruptcy Code, including the "best interests test," feasibility, good faith, not forbidden by law requirements, and other requirements set forth in Section 1129(a) of the Code.[79] The confirmation hearing may be an evidentiary hearing with witnesses on factual issues. If the bankruptcy court finds that the plan meets the requirements, it issues a confirmation order with findings of fact and conclusions of law. The confirmation order is a critical document and usually takes precedence over provisions in a plan (which may have been the subject of objections). In contested cases, bankruptcy courts often require that the confirmation order be filed in advance so that parties in interest can review it and raise any objections.[80]

Debtors view confirmation "as the end goal of a filing."[81] With confirmation comes the vesting of all of the property of the estate in the reorganized debtor (unless sold) free and clear of claims and interests of creditors.[82]

EMERGENCE OR LIQUIDATION

If the plan is confirmed, the debtor "exits" Chapter 11 on the "effective date," which is usually at least 14 days after confirmation during which the bankruptcy court's confirmation order is stayed

78. 11 U.S.C. § 1128.

79. *See id.* § 1129(a); Fed. R. Bankr. P. 3020(e); Chapter 16 (Plan Objections) *infra*.

80. However, the time permitted for such a review may be just a day or two or less. In the event that a confirmation order has important substantive errors or addresses matters that were not presented to the court, parties in interest have 14 days to file a request for amendment under Federal Rule of Bankruptcy Procedure 9023, which incorporates Federal Rule of Civil Procedure 59. Federal Rule of Bankruptcy Procedure 9024 also incorporates Federal Rule of Civil Procedure 60's provisions for relief from a judgment or order, but subject to the limitations of 11 U.S.C. § 1144 on revocation of an order of confirmation.

81. *Life Cycle Part II*, *supra* note 46.

82. 11 U.S.C. § 1141(b)–(d); *see* Chapter 3 (Code Chapters) *supra*, Chapter 13 (Discharge) *infra*.

to permit an appeal.[83] It is, however, common for the debtor to seek and obtain a waiver of the stay. Without a stay, if a plan becomes effective and is consummated, the debtor may contend that an appeal is equitably moot.[84]

During the period between confirmation and emergence, the debtor finalizes all necessary documentation, such as organizational documents and exit financing agreements, and obtains necessary regulatory approvals to effectuate the transactions contemplated by the plan.[85] It is on the effective date of emergence that environmental or other monetary claims may be discharged in accordance with the plan, and, if applicable, an environmental response trust may be established or an environmental liability transaction may be consummated.

Post-emergence, the debtor's Chapter 11 case continues, sometimes for years, for the purpose of resolving certain bankruptcy-related matters (e.g., disputed claims and related distributions), usually out of the limelight. Moreover, the debtor remains bound to carry out the terms of the plan.[86] To that end, the bankruptcy court is authorized to direct the debtor or other parties to effect transfers of property and to perform any other acts necessary to consummate the plan.[87] In the case of a liquidation, many plans utilize a liquidation trust to administer the debtor's remaining assets.

When the estate has been "fully administered," that is, the plan has been substantially consummated, the bankruptcy court enters a final decree.[88] Notwithstanding the entry of the final decree, the case may not be entirely finished. In some situations, distributions under the plan might still be required to be administered, and the

---

83. Fed. R. Bankr. P. 3002(e). Appeals must be brought within 14 days of entry of the confirmation order, Fed. R. Bankr. P. 8002, and are governed by Part VIII of the Federal Rules of Bankruptcy Procedure (Rules 8001–8026).

84. *See* Chapter 16 (Plan Objections) *infra*.

85. Modifications to a plan after confirmation can only be made after notice and hearing. 11 U.S.C. § 1127(b). In some limited situations, the effective date of a plan has been substantially delayed, which can be objected to if prejudicial. *See In re Potomac Iron Works Inc.*, 217 B.R. 170 (Bankr. D. Md. 1997); Leslie Masterson, *The Effective Date of a Chapter 11 Plan: Delay and Danger*, 29 Am. Bankr. Inst. J. 24 (2010); John Ayer, *Confirmation Is Not the End of the Case*, 24 Am. Bankr. Inst. J. 32 (2005).

86. 11 U.S.C. § 1142(a).

87. *Id.* § 1142(b).

88. *Id.* § 350(a); Fed. R. Bankr. P. 3022.

bankruptcy court's retained jurisdiction provided for in the plan or confirmation order may be invoked to enforce or interpret the bankruptcy court's own orders.[89] However, the final decree represents the substantial consummation of the plan and, with it, the closing of the Chapter 11 case.[90]

89. Notes of Advisory Committee on Rules—1991 Amendment, FED. R. BANKR. P. 3022 (Aug. 1, 1991).

90. *Id.*; 11 U.S.C. § 350(a); FED. R. BANKR. P. 3022. Once a case is closed, it can only be reopened by the filing of a motion demonstrating cause. 11 U.S.C. § 350(b); *In re Apex Oil Co.*, 406 F.3d 538 (8th Cir. 2005); *In re Shondel*, 950 F.2d 1301 (7th Cir. 1991).

CHAPTER 5

Thumbnail Sketch of Bankruptcy Rules and Key Statutory Provisions

THE BANKRUPTCY RULES

Bankruptcy proceedings are governed by the Federal Rules of Bankruptcy Procedure, which incorporate many but not all of the Federal Rules of Civil Procedure.[1] The Federal Rules of Bankruptcy Procedure contain procedural rules on commencing a case (Part I), case administration (Part II), assertion of claims and distributions to creditors (Part III), the debtor's duties and benefits (Part IV), bankruptcy courts and clerks' offices (Part V), collection and liquidation of the estate (Part VI), adversary proceeding complaints (Part VII), bankruptcy appeals (Part VIII),[2] and general provisions

1. *See* Fed. R. Civ. P. 81(a)(2); Fed. R. Bankr. P. 1001.

2. Bankruptcy appeals are governed by 28 U.S.C. § 158. Initial appeals in the First, Sixth, Eighth, Ninth, and Tenth Circuits are to Bankruptcy Appellate Panels consisting of three bankruptcy judges unless any party provides notice of an election to proceed in district court. In other circuits, initial appeals are to the district court. Special provisions permit a limited number of appeals that meet specific requirements to proceed directly to the circuit courts. 28 U.S.C. § 152(d)(2)(A). *See also* Chapter 20 (Jurisdiction) *infra*.

(such as for contested matters that are not adversary proceedings) (Part IX).[3]

Bankruptcy Rule 7001 sets forth those matters that must be initiated by a complaint as an adversary proceeding and includes proceedings to recover money, determine liens or interest in property, determine dischargeability, or obtain injunctive or declaratory relief. All other relief must be requested by motion and is considered a "contested matter" governed by Bankruptcy Rule 9014. Part VII and Bankruptcy Rule 9014 specify which rules of the Federal Rules of Civil Procedure apply to bankruptcy proceedings and which of the Federal Rules of Civil Procedure have been modified to address the requirements unique to bankruptcy proceedings.

JURISDICTION, REFERENCE, AND CORE PROCEEDINGS: 28 U.S.C. §§ 157, 1334

28 U.S.C. § 1334 provides the U.S. district courts with bankruptcy jurisdiction. The statute provides for exclusive jurisdiction over the case and property of the estate, but nonexclusive jurisdiction over proceedings arising under the Bankruptcy Code or arising in or related to bankruptcy cases.[4] 28 U.S.C. §§ 151 and 157(a) designate bankruptcy courts as units of district courts and authorize the district courts to "refer" bankruptcy cases and proceedings to bankruptcy judges. 28 U.S.C. § 157(b)(1) provides that bankruptcy judges can hear and determine cases under title 11 of the United States Code and certain "core proceedings." 28 U.S.C. § 157(c)(1) and Article III of the Constitution require that, for certain matters requiring an Article III judge, the bankruptcy courts can only submit proposed findings of fact and conclusions of law to a district court judge who will review the matter de novo.[5] Greater detail and background on all of these provisions can be found in Chapter 20 (Jurisdiction) of this Practice Guide.

3. Each judicial district also has its own local bankruptcy rules that can be found on its bankruptcy court website. Some judges also have their own general or case specific rules and procedures that should be consulted.

4. 28 U.S.C. § 1334(a), (b), (d).

5. *Stern v. Marshall*, 564 U.S. 462, 503 (2011); *Executive Benefits Ins. Agency v. Arkison*, 573 U.S. 25, 38 (2014).

WITHDRAWAL OF THE REFERENCE: 28 U.S.C. § 157(D)

Although bankruptcy courts hear most matters that are automatically referred to them by local rules from district courts, 28 U.S.C. § 157(d) provides that the district court "shall, on timely motion of a party" withdraw the reference of a proceeding if the court determines that resolution of the proceeding requires consideration of both bankruptcy law and "laws of the United States regulating organizations or activities affecting interstate commerce." That section also provides for permissive withdrawal of the reference "for cause shown." Greater detail on this provision can be found in Chapter 20 (Jurisdiction). As noted therein, withdrawal of the reference is most likely to occur in environmental bankruptcy cases where: (1) the court will be required to interpret or apply unsettled nonbankruptcy law such as on an objection to a proof of claim, or (2) the matter arises from the intersection of or requires resolution of conflict between environmental law and bankruptcy law.

PROPERTY OF THE ESTATE; TURNOVER: 11 U.S.C. §§ 541, 542

Section 541 of the Bankruptcy Code provides that the commencement of a bankruptcy case creates an estate consisting of all legal or equitable interests of the debtor wherever located and by whomever held, which is referred to as "property of the estate."[6] Property may include real or personal property, cash, causes of action, contracts, leases, licenses, and permits.[7] Many provisions of the Bankruptcy Code revolve around property of the estate.[8]

6. *See United States v. Whiting Pools*, 462 U.S. 198, 204–05 (1983).

7. Where a license or permit is a revocable privilege that can never be assigned, it has been found not to be property of the estate. *See Phila. Ent. & Dev. Partners LP v. Dep't of Revenue,* 860 Fed. Appx. 25 (3d Cir. 2021), *affirming* 623 B.R. 114 (E.D. Pa. 2020) *and* 611 B.R. 51 (Bankr. E.D. Pa. 2019). But where a governmental license or permit can be assigned, it may have value and be property of the estate even if governmental approval for the assignment is required since assignment may be a quicker and less expensive process than applying for an entirely new permit or license.

8. *See, e.g.*, 11 U.S.C. § 542 (turnover of property of the estate, *see City of Chi. v. Fulton*, 141 S. Ct. 585 (2021)); 11 U.S.C. § 362 (a)(3) (acts to obtain possession or property of the estate stayed); 11 U.S.C. § 363 (sales of property of the estate); 11

Insurance policies are property of the estate because the estate holds legal title to them, but whether or not the equitable interest in the proceeds constitutes property of the estate varies depending on the facts and types of policy involved.[9] Letters of credit and surety bonds are specifically designed so they are not property of the estate in order that the beneficiaries (including the government) may rely on them without delay on account of the bankruptcy case.[10] Trust funds or dedicated escrow funds held by debtors are property of the estate insofar as they hold legal title, but the equitable interest held by nondebtor beneficiaries in the trust or escrow funds is not property of the estate.[11] Similarly,

---

U.S.C. § 1141 (vesting of property of the estate in reorganized debtor). Section 522 of the Code permits the individual debtor to list as exempt certain limited property that will then not become part of the estate so that the debtor can be rehabilitated and obtain a fresh start. 11 U.S.C. § 522. Creditors can object before the specified deadline. *See* Fed. R. Bankr. P. 4003(b).

9. *See In re OGA Charters, LLC*, 901 F.3d 599, 602–03 (5th Cir. 2018). For further discussion of governmental interests under debtors' insurance policies, *see* Chapter 19 (Insurance) *infra*.

10. *See In re Builders Transp., Inc.*, 471 F.3d 1178, 1186 (11th Cir. 2006) (letter of credit); *Kaiser Grp. Int'l*, 399 F.3d 558, 566 (3d Cir. 2005) (letter of credit); *In re Graham Square, Inc.*, 126 F.3d 823, 827 (6th Cir. 1997) (letter of credit); *In re Mansfield Tire & Rubber Co.*, 660 F.2d 1108, 1113 (6th Cir. 1981) (surety bonds); *In re Lockard*, 884 F.2d 1171, 1177 (9th Cir. 1989) (surety bonds); *In re Kmart Corp.*, 297 B.R. 525, 529 (N.D. Ill. 2003) (letters of credit); *In re McLean Trucking Co.*, 74 B.R. 820, 827–28 (Bankr. W.D.N.C. 1987) (surety bonds). If related documents such as a settlement agreement provide a debtor with rights, such rights may be property of the estate. For example, the estate might have a separate collateral agreement, a residual interest in unused proceeds, or might have certain rights of approval. If bond proceeds are being used to reimburse a monetary claim against a debtor, the debtor might contend that collecting bond proceeds violates the automatic stay. *See In re War Eagle Constr. Co.*, 283 B.R. 193 (S.D. W. Va. 2002). The government would contend that the liability being pursued was against the bonding company, not the debtor. The question would not arise if the government was using bond money to perform police or regulatory action since such actions can in any event be pursued even to enforce judgments under the police or regulatory exception to the automatic stay. *See* Chapter 10 (Police or Regulatory Exception) *infra*. The law as to when various instruments constitute property of the estate can vary from circuit to circuit.

11. *See* 11 U.S.C. § 541(d); *In re NTA, LLC*, 380 F.3d 523, 531 (1st Cir. 2004); *Gulf Petroleum, S.A. v. Collazo*, 316 F.2d 257, 261 (1st Cir. 1963); *In re Jazzland, Inc.*, 322 B.R. 610, 616–17 (E.D. La. 2005); *In re ANR Advance Transp. Co.*, 247 B.R. 771 (Bankr. E.D. Wis. 2000) (escrow was not property of the estate because grantor had only limited right to review invoices for reasonableness and could not veto or otherwise control funds); *In re O.P.M. Leasing Servs., Inc.*, 46 B.R. 661, 667 (Bankr. S.D.N.Y. 1985). It is helpful for parties intending to create trust interests (or dedicated escrow funds) to use express language to create and define a trust interest and state that the interest is irrevocable. *See In re Web2b Payment Sols., Inc.*, 815 F.3d 400, 405 (8th Cir. 2016); *O.P.M. Leasing*, 46 B.R. at 667–68.

parties may contend that where a debtor holds funds in constructive or resultant trust for another party, such funds are not property of the estate as the Bankruptcy Code does not authorize a debtor to distribute another's property to its own creditors.[12] Government grant funds held by a debtor are not property of the estate where a governmental agency maintains supervision over how funds are spent.[13]

BANKRUPTCY AUTOMATIC STAY AND POLICE OR REGULATORY EXCEPTION: 11 U.S.C. § 362(A), (B)(4)

The bankruptcy automatic stay provides a debtor with some breathing space to try to reorder its affairs and obtain a fresh start through the bankruptcy process and to preserve the status quo for an orderly resolution.[14] For example, Section 362(a)(1) stays the commencement of judicial proceedings that were or could have been commenced before the petition was filed; Section 362(a)(2) stays the enforcement of judgments obtained before the petition was filed; Section 362(a)(3) stays acts to obtain possession of or control of property of the estate; Section 362(a)(4) and (5) stay acts to create, perfect, or enforce liens; and Section 362(a)(6) stays acts to collect, assess, or recover claims that arose before the petition was filed. Section 362(b) currently lists 29 exceptions to the automatic stay. As explained more fully in Chapter 10 (Police or Regulatory Exception) of this Practice Guide, the police and regulatory exception to the automatic stay in Section 362(b)(4) provides

12. *See Perlman v. Reliance Ins. Co.*, 371 U.S. 132, 135–36 (1962); *In re Montreal, Maine & At. Ry. Ltd.*, 888 F.3d 1, 9–10 (1st Cir. 2018); *In re Miss. Valley Livestock, Inc.*, 745 F.3d 299, 305–07 (7th Cir. 2014); *In re Computrex, Inc.*, 403 F.3d 807, 811 (6th Cir. 2005); *In re Foster*, 275 F.3d 924, 926 (10th Cir. 2001); Andrew Kull, *Restitution in Bankruptcy: Reclamation and Constructive Trust*, 72 Am. Bankr. L.J. 265 (1988). Some courts are reluctant to impose constructive trusts in bankruptcy if they have not been found by a court pre-bankruptcy. *See In re Web2b Payment*, 815 F.3d at 408; *In re Newpower*, 233 F.3d 922, 931–33 (6th Cir. 2000).

13. *In re LAN Tamers, Inc.*, 329 F.3d 204 (1st Cir. 2003); *Westmoreland Human Opportunities, Inc. v. Walsh*, 246 F.3d 233 (3d Cir. 2001); *In re Joliet-Will Cnty. Cmty. Action Agency*, 847 F.2d 430 (7th Cir. 1988); *In re Nev. Fire Safe Council*, 2017 WL 6553395, at *6 (9th Cir. B.A.P. Dec. 21, 2017).

14. *See* Chapter 2 (History and Purposes) *supra* for additional discussion.

that the automatic stay does not apply to police or regulatory actions, although enforcement of money judgments resulting from such actions is stayed. A creditor can seek relief from the automatic stay under Section 362(d) by showing sufficient cause to lift or modify the stay.

TRUSTEES' AND DEBTOR-IN-POSSESSION'S DUTY TO MANAGE AND OPERATE PROPERTY OF THE ESTATE IN COMPLIANCE WITH NONBANKRUPTCY LAW: 28 U.S.C. § 959(B)

28 U.S.C. § 959(b) requires trustees and debtors-in-possession to "manage and operate" the property in their possession "according to the requirements of the valid laws of the State in which such property is situated."[15] Section 959(b) reflects Congress's intent that bankruptcy courts not become a safe haven or refuge for wrongdoers.[16] The courts are split on the question of the applicability of 28 U.S.C. § 959(b) to Chapter 7 trustees or liquidating debtors who are not actively operating a business.[17] Application of Section 959(b) to environmental compliance is discussed in Chapter 9 (Operating Estate Property) of this Practice Guide.

15. 11 U.S.C. § 1101(1) defines "debtor in possession" to mean a debtor in Chapter 11 except when a trustee has been appointed. 11 U.S.C. § 1107(a) provides that debtors-in-possession have most rights and duties of trustees.

16. *In re Steenes*, 918 F.3d 554, 558 (7th Cir. 2019); *In re Nortel Networks, Inc.*, 669 F.3d 128, 137 (3d Cir. 2011); *S.E.C. v. Brennan*, 230 F.3d 65, 71 (2d Cir. 2000); *In re Commonwealth Cos., Inc.*, 913 F.2d 518, 527 (8th Cir. 1990); *United States v. Nicolet, Inc.*, 857 F.2d 202, 207–08 (3d Cir. 1988); *City of New York v. Exxon Corp.*, 932 F.2d 1020, 1024 (2d Cir. 1991); *In re Commerce Oil Co.*, 847 F.2d 291, 297 (6th Cir. 1988); *Commodity Futures Trading Comm'n*, 700 F.2d 1279, 1283 (9th Cir. 1983).

17. *See* Chapter 9 (Operating Estate Property) *infra*.

PROOFS OF CLAIM; APPLICATIONS FOR ADMINISTRATIVE EXPENSE: 11 U.S.C. §§ 502, 503, 507

11 U.S.C. § 502 and Bankruptcy Rule 3001 cover the requirements for filing proofs of claim and applications for administrative expense.[18] The proof of claim is the form that is filed by creditors so that creditors with pre-petition claims can share in the estate's assets in accordance with the Bankruptcy Code's priority scheme. While compliance or regulatory obligations are not "claims" under Section 101(5) of the Bankruptcy Code and therefore are not dischargeable, governmental agencies sometimes file "protective" proofs of claim, which state the government's position that a proof of claim need not be filed, but covers these obligations in the alternative in the event a bankruptcy court disagrees with the government's position that the obligation in question is not a claim.[19] The administrative expense application is the mechanism for creditors to seek recovery for liabilities accruing during the administration of the bankruptcy case. Administrative expense claims, which include claims for post-petition response costs with respect to property of the estate and post-petition penalties, have a higher priority for payment than unsecured, pre-petition claims.[20] Proofs of claim and administrative expense applications are discussed in Chapter 7 (Proofs of Claim) of this Practice Guide.

CLAIMS: 11 U.S.C. § 101(5)

Section 101(5) of the Bankruptcy Code defines a claim to include a "right to payment" and an "equitable remedy for breach of performance if [the] breach gives rise to a right to payment."[21] As noted repeatedly throughout this Practice Guide, whether a liability is a "claim" under this definition, as opposed to a compliance obligation, is an important issue under environmental bankruptcy law.

18. *See* Chapter 7 (Proofs of Claim) *infra*.
19. *See* Chapter 11 (Compliance Obligations) *infra*.
20. *See* Chapter 12 (Priorities) *infra*.
21. 11 U.S.C. § 101(5).

This issue is discussed in greater detail in Chapter 11 (Compliance Obligations) of this Practice Guide.

DISCHARGE: 11 U.S.C. §§ 524, 727, 1141(D)

Discharge is the mechanism for the honest debtor to obtain the fresh start envisioned by the Bankruptcy Code.[22] The scope of discharge depends on the bankruptcy petition chapter and whether the debtor is an individual or corporate entity. Section 523(a) has various exceptions to discharge for individual debtors,[23] but only certain fraud exceptions apply to corporate debtors.[24] Liquidating corporations in Chapter 7 or Chapter 11 are not entitled to a discharge since they are ceasing operations and do not need a fresh start.[25] In Chapter 11, the Bankruptcy Code discharges "debts" that "arose" by the date of confirmation.[26] In evaluating whether a liability will be discharged, one must determine whether the liability: (1) is found to have arisen by the time of the filing of the bankruptcy petition (or confirmation of a Chapter 11 plan), (2) whether it falls under the Bankruptcy Code's definition of "claim," and (3) whether it is excepted from discharge.[27]

PREFERENCE ACTIONS: 11 U.S.C. § 547

One of the features of the Bankruptcy Code is the equivalent treatment of similarly situated creditors.[28] Accordingly, the Bankruptcy

---

22. *See* Chapter 2 (History and Purposes) *supra*; U.S. Courts, *Discharge in Bankruptcy—Bankruptcy Basics*, https://www.uscourts.gov/services-forms/bankruptcy/bankruptcy-basics/discharge-bankruptcy-bankruptcy-basics.

23. Section 1141(d)(2) (applying Section 523) and Section 1141(d)(5) also govern the discharge for individual debtors in Chapter 11.

24. *See* 11 U.S.C. §§ 523(a), 1141(d)(6)(A) (applying fraud exception to discharge under subsections 523(a)(2)(A), (B) to corporate debtors under Chapter 11); *see* Chapter 2 (History and Purposes) *supra*, Chapter 13 (Discharge) *infra*.

25. *See* 11 U.S.C. §§ 727(a)(1), 1141(d)(3).

26. *See id.* § 1141(d)(1). Debts are defined as a "liability on a claim." 11 U.S.C. § 101(12).

27. *See* Chapters 11 (Compliance Obligations), 13 (Discharge) *infra*.

28. "One of the cardinal principles underlying bankruptcy law is equality of treatment of similarly situated creditors." 7 COLLIER ON BANKRUPTCY ¶ 1122.03, at

Code provides for the avoidance and return to the estate of payments to creditors that were made just before filing for bankruptcy on account of preexisting claims unless they fall within certain specified exceptions.[29] Otherwise, such payments would result in such creditors being preferred over other unpaid creditors. Section 547 of the Bankruptcy Code thus provides for the recovery of such preferential payments made within 90 days of the petition (or one year for insiders).[30] Defenses are provided for, inter alia, ordinary course of business payments and the provision of new value.[31] Permit renewal and similar environmental fees and charges have been found to be ordinary course of business payments not subject to avoidance.[32] However, certain criminal restitution payments have been found to be preferential payments subject to avoidance.[33]

FRAUDULENT CONVEYANCE ACTIONS: 11 U.S.C. §§ 544, 548, 550(A)

The Bankruptcy Code also provides that the trustee or debtor-in-possession may recover pre-petition fraudulent transfers.[34] The

1122–26 (16th ed. 2019). *See, e.g., In re W.R. Grace & Co.*, 729 F.3d 332, 342–46 (3d Cir. 2013); *In re UAL Corp.*, 468 F.3d 456, 461 (7th Cir. 2006); *In re Dow Corning Corp.*, 280 F.3d 648, 660 (6th Cir. 2002).

29. *See Begier v. Internal Revenue Serv.*, 496 U.S. 53, 58 (1990). State entities are potentially subject to preference actions notwithstanding sovereign immunity. *Cent. Va. Cmty. Coll. v. Katz*, 546 U.S. 356 (2006). Unauthorized post-petition payments may be avoided under 11 U.S.C. § 549.

30. *See, e.g., In re Wagenknecht*, 971 F.3d 1209, 1212 (10th Cir. 2020); *In re BFW Liquidation LLC*, 899 F.3d 1178, 1188 (11th Cir. 2018); *In re C.W. Mining Co.*, 798 F.3d 983, 987 (10th Cir. 2015).

31. *See, e.g.*, 11 U.S.C. § 547(c)(2), (4).

32. *See, e.g., In re New Page Corp.*, 555 B.R. 444 (Bankr. D. Del. 2016).

33. *See, e.g., In re Silverman*, 616 F.3d 1001 (9th Cir. 2001) (restitution payments made pursuant to state court prosecution for insurance fraud subject preference action even though restitution obligation was not discharged under Section 523(a)(7). In *In re Grooms*, 572 B.R. 559 (Bankr. W.D. Pa. 2017), the court acknowledged that pre-petition criminal restitution payments were exempted from being recovered as preference payments by the Mandatory Victims Restitution Act, 18 U.S.C. § 3613, but found a preference where a payment was made prior to entry of the charging instrument and the judgment mandating restitution.

34. When the trustee or debtor-in-possession refuses to bring an action for recovery of a fraudulent transfer, a court may authorize a creditors' committee or creditor to bring such action derivatively on behalf of the estate. *See, e.g., In re*

Bankruptcy Code provides its own fraudulent transfer provision[35] but also allows the estate to utilize state fraudulent transfer statutes to return property to the estate.[36] State fraudulent transfer provisions frequently have longer statutes of limitations than the two-year statute of limitations provided in Section 548 of the Bankruptcy Code.[37] However, there is a separate two-year statute of limitations from the filing of the petition governing when the estate must bring avoidance actions, which include fraudulent conveyance actions.[38] Fraudulent transfer statutes are divided into two categories: actual fraudulent transfers and constructive fraudulent transfers.[39] Actual fraudulent transfer cases involve transactions made with an intent to hinder, delay, or defraud creditors.[40] Constructive fraudulent transfer cases involve transactions for less than equivalent value at a time of insolvency or that cause insolvency, regardless of the debtor's actual intent in making the transfer (including potentially even involuntary transfer such as a foreclosure or seizure of property).[41] Fraudulent conveyance actions have resulted in significant recoveries for estates in environmental bankruptcies such as: Tronox ($5.5 billion),[42] Asarco

---

Trailer Source, Inc., 555 F.3d 231 (6th Cir. 2009); *Official Comm. of Unsecured Creditors of Cybergenics v. Chinery*, 330 F.3d 548 (3d Cir. 2003) (en banc).

35. 11 U.S.C. § 548.

36. *Id.* § 544(b).

37. *See, e.g., In re Tronox, Inc.*, 429 B.R. 73 (Bankr. S.D.N.Y. 2010). Additionally, multiple transactions in a fraudulent transfer scheme can be collapsed into the late stages of the scheme for purposes of statute of limitations analysis. *In re Tronox, Inc.*, 503 B.R. 239, 269 (Bankr. S.D.N.Y. 2013); *In re Maxus Energy Corp.*, 641 B.R. 467 (Bankr. D. Del. 2022).

38. *See* 11 U.S.C. § 546(a). This limitation period also applies to the recovery of preferential transfers under Section 547.

39. *See Suvicmon Dev., Inc. v. Morrison*, 991 F.3d 1213 (11th Cir. 2021).

40. Actual fraudulent conveyance is different from actual fraud and involves consideration of factors known as badges of fraud. *See, e.g., In re Ritz*, 832 F.3d 560 (5th Cir. 2016). Proof of misrepresentation is not required. *Husky Int'l Elecs., Inc. v. Ritz*, 578 U.S. 356, 361–62 (2016).

41. *See, e.g., In re Chicago Mgmt. Consulting Grp. Inc.*, 929 F.3d 803 (7th Cir. 2019); *In re Fruehauf Trailer Corp.*, 444 F.3d 203 (3d Cir. 2006).

42. *In re Tronox Inc.*, 503 B.R. 239 (Bankr. S.D.N.Y. 2013); *In re Tronox, Inc.*, 2014 WL 5819821 (Bankr. S.D.N.Y. July 22, 2014), *aff'd*, 549 B.R. 21 (S.D.N.Y. 2016), *aff'd*, 855 F.3d 84, 100, 106 (2d Cir. 2017).

($1.79 billion),[43] and Magnesium Corp. ($213 million).[44] In large cases, fraudulent conveyance actions can be pursued even after plan confirmation for the benefit of creditors.[45] The amount that can be recovered in a fraudulent conveyance proceeding is not capped by the amount of unpaid claims against the estate, so long as the recovery is "for the benefit of the estate," which has been interpreted broadly.[46] Section 550 of the Bankruptcy Code governs whether fraudulent transfers can be recovered from subsequent transferees to whom the Code extends certain limited defenses. Section 546(e) of the Bankruptcy Code creates a safe harbor for certain constructive fraudulent transfers involving financial institutions or securities agencies, which some transferees have sought to expand beyond what was intended and use as a loophole.[47]

SALE OF ASSETS: 11 U.S.C. § 363

Section 363 of the Bankruptcy Code permits a debtor to sell its property free and clear of liens and interests. In recent times, many large debtors have utilized Section 363 to sell substantially all of

---

43. *In re Asarco LLC*, 441 B.R. 813 (S.D. Tex. 2010); *Asarco LLC v. Americas Mining Corp.*, 404 B.R. 150 (S.D. Tex. 2009); *Asarco LLC v. Americas Mining Corp.*, 396 B.R. 278 (S.D. Tex. 2008).

44. *In re Magnesium Corp. of Am.*, 2017 WL 946729, 682 Fed. Appx. 24 (2d Cir. 2017), *aff'g Buchwald v. Renco Grp.*, No. 13-cv-7958 (S.D.N.Y. Aug. 19, 2015).

45. As noted in Chapter 16 (Plan Objections) *infra*, a plan may provide for a distribution of proceeds from fraudulent conveyance actions and creditors may object to the resolution of fraudulent conveyance actions proposed in a plan. Where a creditor has a special or unique claim not common to general creditors, the creditor's and estate's rights are more complex. The Federal Debt Collection Procedures Act provides the United States with certain rights with respect to fraudulent transfers made to hinder collection of federal debts. 28 U.S.C. § 3304. If a debtor or transferee has potential liability under this Act, the status of such liability during and after the bankruptcy case should be evaluated. An example of such a fraudulent transfer situation occurred in the *Tronox* case, which is discussed in Chapter 21 (Settlements) *infra*. *See also* Chapter 16 (Plan Objections) n.47.

46. *See In re Acequia, Inc.*, 34 F.3d 800, 811 (9th Cir. 1994); *In re Tronox Inc.*, 464 B.R. 606, 614–15 (Bankr. S.D.N.Y. 2012). For example, the estate may be benefited on account of creditors taking a risk on the outcome of fraudulent conveyance proceedings.

47. 11 U.S.C. § 546(e). *See Merit Mgmt. Grp., LP v. FTI Consulting, Inc.*, 138 S. Ct. 883 (2017) (requiring examination of overarching transfer rather than component transactions); *In re Tribune Co. Fraudulent Conveyance Litig.*, 946 F.3d 66 (2d Cir. 2019).

their assets and then liquidate through a plan of liquidation.[48] This trend has become so marked that, at least for some kinds of cases, property sales followed by liquidations have become more common than traditional reorganization under the Bankruptcy Code. In some instances, sales are forced by secured creditors seeking to recover on loans and/or utilize credit bidding to acquire the debtor's business and operations.[49] As discussed in greater detail in Chapter 15 (Section 363 Sales) of this Practice Guide, Section 363 sales do not relieve the purchaser of environmental liability that a future owner of contaminated property is subject to as an owner or operator under nonbankruptcy law, regardless of whether the contamination originated before such entity or individual became the owner of the property.

ABANDONMENT: 11 U.S.C. § 554

Section 554 of the Bankruptcy Code allows trustees and debtors-in-possession to abandon property of inconsequential value and benefit to the estate. The Supreme Court has held that bankruptcy courts do "not have the power to authorize an abandonment without formulating conditions that will adequately protect the public's health and safety."[50] Property may not be abandoned "in contravention of a state statute or regulation that is reasonably designed to protect the public health or safety from identified hazards," but "the abandonment power is not to be fettered by laws or regulations not reasonably calculated to protect the public or health or safety from imminent and identifiable harm."[51] Abandonment and its implications for environmental bankruptcies are discussed in greater detail in Chapter 18 (Abandonment) of this Practice Guide.

48. *See* Ashley Suarez, *An Analysis of § 363 Sales: Justified Deviations or Just Deviations*, 22 U. Pa. J. Bus. L. 988, 990–92 (2020); Jacob A. Kling, *Rethinking 363 Sales*, 17 Stan. J.L. Bus. & Fin. 258, 260 (2012); Bryant P. Lee, *Imagining Future Uses of 11 U.S.C. § 363 to Accomplish Chapter 7 Liquidation Goals in Chapter 11 Reorganizations*, 2009 Colum. Bus. L. Rev. 520, 523–24, 544–63 (2009); Douglas G. Baird & Robert K. Rasmussen, *The End of Bankruptcy*, 55 Stan. L. Rev. 751 (2002).

49. *See* Chapter 15 (Section 363 Sales) *infra*.

50. *Midlantic Nat'l Bank v. N.J. Dep't of Env't Prot.*, 474 U.S. 494, 507 (1986).

51. *Id.* at 506–07 & n.9.

EXECUTORY CONTRACTS: 11 U.S.C. § 365

Section 365(a) permits trustees and debtors-in-possession to assume or reject executory contracts or leases.[52] Governmental oil, gas, and coal leases can be considered executory contracts, but permits, licenses, and administrative or court orders are not considered executory contracts because they have the force of law separate and apart from contract law.[53] Careful review is therefore warranted of any schedules of executory contracts that may be assumed or rejected to determine if any permits, licenses, administrative or court orders have been mistakenly included. Under Section 365(d)(1), Chapter 7 trustees have 60 days to assume or reject an executory contract or lease, or it is deemed rejected if the bankruptcy court has not extended the deadline. Until a decision is made, a debtor must continue to perform if the nondebtor party is continuing its performance.[54]

In order to assume an executory contract or lease, the debtor (or purchaser if there is a sale of assets) must pay amounts to cure monetary defaults and provide adequate assurance of future performance under the contract or lease.[55] Assumption of a contract or lease must be done based on the complete "burdens and

---

52. An executory contract is a contract where both parties have unperformed obligations, the breach of which excuses the performance of the other party. *See, e.g., In re Weinstein Co. Holdings LLC*, 997 F.3d 511 (3d Cir. 2021); *In re Interstate Bakeries Corp.*, 690 F.3d 1069, 1073 (8th Cir. 2012); *In re Exide Techs.*, 607 F.3d 957, 962 (3d Cir. 2010); *In re Robert L. Helms Constr. & Dev. Co.*, 139 F.3d 702, 705 (9th Cir. 1998); *In re Murexco Petroleum, Inc.*, 15 F.3d 60, 63 (5th Cir. 1994). *See also Mission Prod. Holdings, Inc. v. Tempnology, LLC*, 139 S. Ct. 1652, 1662 (2019).

53. *See United States v. ITT Cont'l Banking Co.*, 420 U.S. 223, 236 (1975); *Saline River Props., LLC v. Johnson Controls, Inc.*, 2011 WL 4916681 (E.D. Mich. 2011); *United States v. Am. Nat'l Can Co.*, 126 F. Supp. 2d 521, 531 (N.D. Ill. 2000); *FDIC v. Frates*, 44 F. Supp. 2d 1176, 1201 (N.D. Okla. 1999). Judicial orders, including consent orders and judgments, are not executory contracts. *See Roxse Homes, Inc. v. Roxse Homes Ltd. P'ship*, 83 B.R. 185, 187 (D. Mass. 1988), *aff'd*, 860 F.2d 1072 (1st Cir. 1988); *In re Baver*, 2021 WL 5815643 (Bankr. S.D. Ohio Nov. 2, 2021); *In re Smith*, 269 B.R. 629, 632–33 (Bankr. E.D. Tex. 2001); *In re Bassett*, 74 B.R. 361, 362 (Bankr. D. Colo. 1987); *In re Brick House Props. LLC*, 633 B.R. 410, 417–19 (Bankr. D. Utah June 11, 2021).

54. *Nat'l Labor Relations Bd. v. Bildisco & Bildisco*, 465 U.S. 513 (1984). If the debtor defaults, the nondebtor can move to lift the automatic stay to seek termination of the contract. *See In re W. Elecs. Inc.*, 852 F.2d 79 (3d Cir. 1988).

55. 11 U.S.C. § 365(b)(1)(A). Cure amounts must be paid in full if the contract is to be assumed and are not reduced on account of the bankruptcy.

benefits" under the contract as a whole; a debtor may not pick and choose provisions to assume.[56] If a contract is assumed, it must therefore be assumed in its entirety. Once a debtor assumes a contract or lease, Section 365(f)(2) authorizes the assignment of such contracts if adequate protection of future performance is provided. However, the Bankruptcy Code does not permit assignment without consent where applicable law excuses a counterparty from accepting performance from a party other than the debtor.[57]

Rejection of a contract or lease constitutes a breach thereof (not a rescission of the contract) that is deemed to relate back to the petition date.[58] The consequences of a breach are the same in bankruptcy as outside of bankruptcy. The estate does not need to continue performance, but continuing rights of the counterparty are not revoked.[59] Monetary claims for the breach are considered

---

56. *See In re Nat'l Gypsum Co.*, 208 F.3d 498, 506 (5th Cir. 2000); *Bennu Oil & Gas, LLC v. Bluewater Indus., L.P.*, 517 B.R. 756, 759–60 (Bankr. S.D. Tex. 2014).

57. 11 U.S.C. §§ 365(c)(1)(A) (precluding assignment where applicable law excuses counterparty from accepting performance from another entity), 11 U.S.C. § 365(f)(2) (permitting assignment except as provided in subsections (b) and (c)). The circuit courts have adopted various interpretations of the interplay between the various provisions of Section 365, which should be consulted in any case presenting such issues. *See, e.g., In re Mirant Corp.*, 440 F.3d 238 (5th Cir. 2006); *In re Sunterra Corp.*, 361 F.3d 257 (4th Cir. 2004); *In re Catapult Ent., Inc.*, 165 F.3d 747 (9th Cir. 1999); *In re W. Elecs., Inc.*, 852 F.2d 79 (3d Cir. 1988); *Institut Pasteur v. Cambridge Biotech Corp.*, 104 F.3d 489 (1st Cir. 1997). Under some of these cases, parties may have potential grounds for objection to a debtor's assumption of an executory contract if applicable law does not permit assignment. Many governmental executory contracts and leases (such as for coal or oil and gas) require governmental approval of any assignment. *See, e.g.*, 41 U.S.C. § 6305; 43 U.S.C. § 1337(e); 30 U.S.C. § 187; 30 C.F.R. §§ 556.62, 556.72; 43 C.F.R. §§ 3453.3-1, 3453.3-2.

58. 11 U.S.C. § 365(g); *Mission Prod. Holdings, Inc. v. Tempnology, LLC*, 139 S. Ct. 1652, 1662 (2019).

59. *Id.*; Michael T. Andrew, *Executory Contracts in Bankruptcy*, 59 U. Colo. L. Rev. 845 (1988). Whether specific performance can be obtained from the debtor in connection with a rejected contract is a difficult question on which parties disagree. *See, e.g., In re Nine Point Energy Holdings, Inc.*, 633 B.R. 124, 135–36 (Bankr. D. Del. 2021); *In re Extraction Oil & Gas*, 622 B.R. 608, 623–24 (Bankr. D. Del. 2020); *In re Hughes*, 166 B.R. 103, 105 (Bankr. S.D. Ohio 1994); *In re Noco, Inc.*, 76 B.R. 839, 844 (Bankr. N.D. Fla. 1987). Likewise, whether a debtor must comply with a restrictive covenant running with the land relating to a rejected contract is a controversial question. *See Extraction Oil & Gas*, 622 B.R. at 620–24; *In re Southland Royalty Co.*, 623 B.R. 64, 97–99 (Bankr. D. Del. 2020); *In re Chesapeake Energy Corp.*, 622 B.R. 274, 281–82 (Bankr. S.D. Tex. 2020); *In re Alta Mesa Res., Inc.*, 613 B.R. 90 (Bankr. S.D. Tex. 2019); *In re Badlands Energy, Inc.*, 608 B.R. 854, 874 (Bankr. D. Colo. 2019); *In re Sabine Oil & Gas Corp.*, 550 B.R. 59 (Bankr. S.D.N.Y. 2016).

general unsecured claims except that the acceptance of continued post-petition performance can sometimes be entitled to administrative expense priority.[60]

ANTI-DISCRIMINATION: 11 U.S.C. § 525

Section 525 prohibits discrimination by the government based upon: (1) the filing of a bankruptcy case, (2) the nonpayment of a debt that is discharged or dischargeable in a bankruptcy case, or (3) insolvency whether the insolvency occurs before or during the bankruptcy case. The government may not deny, revoke, suspend, or refuse to renew a license, permit, charter, or other similar grant for these reasons. In *F.C.C. v. NextWave Personal Communications Inc.*,[61] the Supreme Court held that Section 525 prevented the F.C.C. from cancelling a broadband license due to the failure of the debtor to make payments for the purchase of the license. *NextWave*, however, does not preclude denials, revocations, or suspensions based on police or regulatory requirements that are different from the nonpayment of debt and are not based on previous insolvency. Governments may deny or revoke licenses and permits for other valid reasons that apply to debtors and nondebtors alike. Chapter 13 (Discharge) of this Practice Guide discusses anti-discrimination in greater detail.

POST-PETITION FINANCING: 11 U.S.C. § 364

Section 364 allows debtors operating a business to obtain post-petition financing through the grant of a superpriority lien and administrative expense status where unsecured credit is not available (which will almost always be the case).[62] Existing liens are

60. *See, e.g., Mission Prod.*, 139 S. Ct. at 1662; *In re Whistler Energy II, L.LC.*, 931 F.3d 432, 443 (5th Cir. 2019); *In re Sharon Steel Corp.*, 161 B.R. 934, 937 (W.D. Pa. 1994).

61. 537 U.S. 293 (2003).

62. *See, e.g., In re hhgregg, Inc.* 949 F.3d 1039 (7th Cir. 2020); *In re Calore Express Co.*, 288 F.3d 22 (1st Cir. 2002); *In re Babcock & Wilcox Co.*, 250 F.3d 955 (5th Cir. 2001). *See* Chapter 3 (Code Chapters) *supra*.

entitled to adequate protection.[63] Post-petition financing and liens are often granted on an interim basis early in the case with little advance notice, but are subject to final approval no sooner than 14 days after service of the motion for financing.[64] Governmental agencies or creditors that may have significant rights at issue in a bankruptcy case should carefully review motions and proposed orders for post-petition financing as they sometimes contain prejudicial provisions that could have large impacts.[65] Issues to look for include: (1) restrictions on expenditures and other budget requirements that need lender approval, thereby potentially limiting a debtor's ability to comply with nonbankruptcy law during the bankruptcy case;[66] (2) whether the lender improperly seeks to prioritize its rights over governmental security interests, governmental rights to financial assurance or setoff, or the debtor fails to provide adequate protection of such interests; (3) whether the lender seeks to limit its potential liability as an operator under nonbankruptcy law or seeks factual findings that it will not be an operator;[67] (4) whether the lender seeks pre-approval of a right to credit bid on any sale of assets in the bankruptcy case;[68] or (5) whether the proposed order seeks to dictate terms of a sub rosa plan.[69] Attention should be paid to terms that limit or restrict challenges to the security interests of secured creditors.

---

63. 11 U.S.C. § 364(d)(1)(B).

64. *See* Fed. R. Bankr. P. 4001(c)(2).

65. *See generally* Adam Levitin, *Purdue's Poison Pill: The Breakdown of Chapter 11's Checks and Balances*, 100 Tex. L. Rev. 100, 112–16 (2022).

66. This would be contrary to 28 U.S.C. § 959(b). *See* Chapter 9 (Operating Estate Property) *infra*.

67. Lenders are not normally liable under CERCLA so long as they do not assert control over the debtors' environmental decision-making or management. *See, e.g.*, 42 U.S.C. § 9601(20)(F); *United States v. Fleet Factors Corp.*, 901 F.2d 1550 (11th Cir. 1990); Note, *Cleaning Up the Debris After Fleet Factors: Lender Liability and CERCLA's Security Interest Exemption*, 104 Harv. L. Rev. 1249 (1991). Seeking a ruling on lender liability in advance of an enforcement action violates prohibitions on pre-enforcement review. *See* 42 U.S.C. § 9613(h); *re Combustion Equip. Assocs., Inc.*, 838 F.2d 35 (2d Cir. 1988); *Lone Pine Steering Comm. v. United States*, 777 F.2d 882, 887–88 (3d Cir. 1985).

68. Under 11 U.S.C. § 363(k), credit bids may be objected to "for cause." *See* Chapter 15 (Section 363 Sales) *infra*.

69. *See In re Latam Airlines Grp. S.A.*, 620 B.R. 722 (Bankr. S.D.N.Y. 2020).

SETOFF: 11 U.S.C. § 553

Section 553 of the Bankruptcy Code provides that the right to offset (a synonym for setoff) mutual debts between a creditor and debtor is not affected by the Bankruptcy Code. This provision can have significant impact, as it allows a creditor to receive the full value of its claim (as a reduction in what the creditor must otherwise pay the debtor for the setoff liability in real (not "tiny bankruptcy")[70] dollars) even if other creditors are receiving pennies on the dollar or nothing.[71] A key requirement is that the offsetting debts be mutual.[72] Mutuality requires that both debts be either pre-petition or post-petition and involve the same debtor entity.[73] The United States is considered unitary for purposes of setoff.[74] Therefore, an environmental claim can be set off against a mutual receivable owed to a debtor by another federal agency such as a tax refund, amounts due under a government contract, or contribution liability of a federal agency under environmental law. While a creditor seeking a setoff can freeze or hold onto a payment owed to a debtor pending a ruling, it must obtain an order from the bankruptcy court lifting the automatic stay before it can effectuate the setoff.[75] If a creditor plans on releasing funds to a debtor that it believes may be applied as a setoff, it should consider protecting its setoff rights by entering into an adequate protection stipulation or agreement approved by the bankruptcy court in order to avoid any contention that the government's setoff rights were not

---

70. *See* Chapter 2 (History and Purposes) *supra* (citing Jay Westbrook, *A Functional Analysis of Executory Contracts*, 74 MINN. L. REV. 227, 252–53 (1989)).

71. *See, e.g.*, *In re Orexigen Theraputics, Inc.*, 990 F.3d 748 (3d Cir. 2021).

72. *See, e.g.*, *id.*; *In re Meyer Medical Physicians Grp., Ltd.*, 385 F.3d 1039 (7th Cir. 2004); *In re Larbar Corp.*, 177 F.3d 439 (6th Cir. 1990).

73. *See In re United Sciences of Am., Inc.*, 893 F.2d 720 (5th Cir. 1990); *In re SemCrude, L.P.*, 399 B.R. 388 (Bankr. D. Del. 2009). With respect to environmental liabilities, the mutuality issue can raise difficult questions regarding when environmental claims arise in connection with whether they are considered pre-petition or post-petition. *See, e.g.*, *In re MetCo Mining & Minerals, Inc.*, 171 B.R. 210 (Bankr. W.D. Pa. 1994); Chapter 13 (Discharge) *infra*.

74. *See United States v. Maxwell*, 157 F.3d 1099, 1102–03 (7th Cir. 1998); *In re Hal, Inc.*, 122 F.3d 851 (9th Cir. 1997); *In re Chateaugay*, 94 F.3d 772 (2d Cir. 1996); *In re Turner*, 84 F.3d 1294 (10th Cir 1996) (en banc).

75. *See Citizens Bank of Maryland v. Strumpf*, 516 U.S. 16, 18 (1995); *Maxwell*, 157 F.3d at 1102–03.

preserved.[76] Although seemingly contrary to the literal language of Section 553, which provides that bankruptcy does not "affect" setoff rights, the Third Circuit appears to require a creditor to identify its setoff claims by the time of plan confirmation in some circumstances.[77] Therefore, it is important to review the terms of a plan and confirmation order to ensure that the right of setoff is identified and preserved.[78] Other courts have been more definitive that a bankruptcy discharge does not impair a right of setoff meeting mutuality requirements.[79]

SOVEREIGN IMMUNITY

Section 106(a) of the Bankruptcy Code provides for a broad abrogation of sovereign immunity as to governmental units for actions under most Bankruptcy Code provisions, subject to the limitations of the 11th Amendment for states. The 11th Amendment precludes bankruptcy court in personam jurisdiction against a state, but may permit certain actions furthering in rem jurisdiction relating to the debtor's estate.[80] The applicability of the 11th Amendment to bankruptcy and other matters involving states has been controversial and subject to close Supreme Court rulings and, therefore, may be the subject of further litigation in the future.[81]

---

76. *See Strumpf*, 516 U.S. at 20; *In re Lifestyle Furnishings, LLC*, 418 B.R. 382, 387 (Bankr. D. Idaho 2009); *In re Gehrke*, 158 B.R. 465, 468 (Bankr. N.D. Iowa 1993).

77. *See In re Continental Airlines*, 134 F.3d 536, 542 (3d Cir. 1998).

78. *See* Karen Cordry, *Setoff, Plan Provisions and Espinosa*, 29 Am. Bankr. Inst. J. 12 (Dec./Jan. 2011).

79. *See In re Luongo*, 259 F.3d 323, 333 (5th Cir. 2001); *In re De Laurentiis Ent. Grp., Inc.*, 963 F.2d 1269, 1276 (9th Cir. 1992) (right of offset survived confirmation of a Chapter 11 plan); *In re Davidovich*, 901 F.2d 1533, 1539 (10th Cir. 1990) (discharge no bar to exercise of right to offset, even where creditor did not file a claim).

80. *See Cent. Va. Cmty. Coll. v. Katz*, 546 U.S. 356 (2006); *Tenn. Student Assistance Corp. v. Hood*, 541 U.S. 440 (2004); *In re Venoco LLC*, 998 F.3d 94 (3d Cir. 2021); *In re Sherwin Alumina Co.*, 952 F.3d 229, 234 (5th Cir. 2020).

81. Many states believe that *Katz* misapprehends the historical record as to state immunity in bankruptcy. For more detailed discussions of 11th Amendment issues relating to bankruptcy, *see* Karen Cordry, *Central Va. Cmty. College v. Katz: How Is It Faring Fifteen Years On?*, 30–33 J. Bankr. L. & Prac. NL Art. 2 (June 2021); Karen Cordry, *Hood, How Not to Decide a Case—And the Ramifications of What Was Decided*, 3 DePaul Bus. & Com. L.J. 187 (2005); Karen Cordry, *Of State Sovereign Immunity and Prospective Remedies: The Bankruptcy Discharge as Statutory Ex Parte Young Relief: A Response*, 77 Am. Bankr. L.J. 23 (2003); Karen Cordry, *Seminole Seven*

Section 106(a) provides that any order, process, or judgment must be consistent with nonbankruptcy law applicable to the governmental unit.[82] Therefore, a debtor may not seek a pre-enforcement determination of liability under environmental law where such law would not otherwise allow for such a determination.[83] The filing of a proof of claim waives sovereign immunity but only as to claims arising from the same transaction or occurrence underlying the claims asserted in the proof of claim.[84]

Years On, 2003 NORTON ANNUAL SURVEY OF BANKR. LAW 383 (2003); Karen Cordry, *Eleventh Amendment Immunity: Everything Old Is New Again*, 1999 NORTON ANNUAL SURVEY OF BANKR. LAW 8 (1999).

82. 11 U.S.C. § 106(a)(4).

83. *See, e.g.*, 42 U.S.C. § 9613(h); *Reardon v. United States*, 947 F.2d 1509 (1st Cir. 1991) (CERCLA); *Voluntary Purchasing Grps., Inc. v. Reilly*, 889 F.2d 1380 (5th Cir. 1989) (CERCLA); *Amoco Oil Co. v. United States Env't Prot. Agency*, 959 F. Supp. 1318 (D. Colo. 1997) (RCRA).

84. 11 U.S.C. § 106(b); *Shieldalloy Metallurgical Corp. v. N.J. Dep't of Env't Prot.*, 743 F. Supp. 2d 429, 437–38 (D.N.J. 2010).

CHAPTER 6

Obtaining Information in Bankruptcy Cases

There are a number of ways creditors and other interested parties obtain information about debtors during a bankruptcy proceeding. One way to monitor a bankruptcy case and obtain a wealth of information is directly from the internet. Most corporate debtors of any significant size use a private service company, sometimes referred to as a claims service, that maintains an internet site that allows creditors and other interested parties to obtain key background information as well as review the docket and filings as often as they wish without having to go through a court website such as PACER.[1] Another quick early way to obtain information about a case is to look at the debtor's "first-day declaration" of its corporate officer, which will provide key information about the debtor and its bankruptcy plans.[2] Other sources of information on the internet may include SEC or other regulatory filings of

1. As of this writing, key service companies with such websites include (in alphabetical order): BMC Group; Donlin Recano; Epic; Kroll Restructuring Administration (formerly Prime Clerk); Kutzman Carson Consultants LLC (KCCLLC); and Stretto. Some service companies offer an option for interested parties to sign up for direct email updates of docket entries.

2. The first-day declaration is generally filed along with a number of "first-day motions" at the same time that the debtor files the bankruptcy petition or shortly thereafter, as discussed in Chapter 4 (Timeline) of this Practice Guide.

a debtor. In addition, some environmental agencies have websites with information about enforcement actions against a debtor.

Much information is also required to be provided by the debtor in the early stages of a case, as set forth in the Bankruptcy Code. The discussion that follows describes the kinds of information to be provided and the timing for providing it.

Debtors have a set of disclosure duties, outlined in Section 521 of the Bankruptcy Code, with which they must comply at the outset of their bankruptcy proceedings. These reporting duties are intended to promote transparency, shape and inform plan negotiations, and give notice to parties in interest by providing them with adequate information concerning, among other things, the debtor's assets and liabilities, and corporate governance. To fulfill its disclosure duties, a debtor must file a list of creditors (sometimes referred to as a creditor matrix), schedules of assets and liabilities, and a statement of financial affairs (SOFA) at the beginning of its bankruptcy case. For voluntary debtors, these statements and schedules are to be filed with the petition or within 14 days thereafter unless an extension is obtained.[3] In voluntary Chapter 11 cases, the debtor must also file a list of the 20 largest unsecured claims.[4] The bankruptcy petition, also referred to as a petition for relief, and SOFAs have specific questions relating to environmental liabilities, which are discussed later. Operating debtors must also file monthly operating reports with financial information.[5]

This comprehensive set of guidelines for providing information is intended to ensure that the case progresses in an orderly and transparent fashion. The petition, schedules, and SOFAs operate together to accurately capture a broad view of the debtor's

3. Fed. R. Bankr. P. 1007(c); 11 U.S.C. §§521(a)(1)(B)(i), 1106(a)(2). *See* 4 Collier on Bankruptcy ¶ 521.03[1] (16th ed. 2019); Chapter 4 (Timeline) *supra.* Debtors often seek extensions of the deadlines, which are usually granted. The bankruptcy court will grant an extension only for cause shown and on notice to the U.S. Trustee as well as to any trustee, elected committee, or other party as required by the court. Fed. R. Bankr. P. 1007(a)(5); 4 Collier on Bankruptcy ¶ 521.03[1] (16th ed. 2019). In some jurisdictions, including the Southern District of New York and the District of Delaware, an automatic extension (called a bridge) is allowed when a timely motion to extend is filed until the motion is resolved by the court. Bankr. S.D.N.Y. R. 9006-2; Bankr. D. Del. R. 9006-2.

4. Fed. R. Bankr. P. 1007(d).

5. *See id.* 2015.3.

financial affairs at the time the bankruptcy case is filed and allow parties in interest to assess the debtor's financial situation and plan their participation in the bankruptcy case accordingly. Creditors also have the opportunity to ask questions to obtain information at the Section 341 meeting of creditors conducted early in the case.[6] Finally, parties in interest have the ability to request additional information pursuant to Bankruptcy Rule 2004, which is a discovery rule unique to bankruptcy, and gives interested parties the ability to obtain more detailed information about the debtor's finances and obligations.

THE PETITION, SCHEDULES, AND SOFA

The bankruptcy petition itself may contain useful information.[7] For example, Question 2 of the petition requires the debtor to reveal all corporate names it has used in the past eight years. Question 9 asks about prior bankruptcies. Question 10 asks about pending or related bankruptcies including names of affiliates. Question 12 in nonindividual cases and Question 14 in individual cases ask specifically whether the debtor owns or has possession of real or personal property that needs immediate attention and, if so, requires the identification of hazards that may pose a threat of an imminent and identifiable hazard to public health and safety. The wording of Question 12 is based on terms used by the Supreme Court in the *Midlantic* case, but the meaning of the terms is subject to significant debate and disagreement among the lower courts.[8] Although the authors are not aware of any case law to date, a debtor's failure to identify property presenting risk that then harms public health and safety after the petition is filed could pose problems for a debtor for filing an inaccurate petition.

---

6. The U.S. Trustees' office is required to set the time for and "convene and preside at" such meetings under Section 341 of the Bankruptcy Code. *See* Chapter 4 (Timeline) *supra*.

7. Official Bankruptcy Forms B101 (individuals) and B201 (non-individuals): https://www.uscourts.gov/sites/default/files/form_b_201.pdf; https://www.uscourts.gov/sites/default/files/form_b_101.pdf

8. *See* Chapter 18 (Abandonment) *infra*.

Schedules and SOFAs also provide interested parties insight into the debtor's financial affairs at the beginning of a Chapter 11 case. A corporate debtor is required to complete schedules that identify the debtor's real and personal property, its creditors (both secured and unsecured), its executory contracts and leases, and its co-debtors.[9] The schedule of creditors must include all known creditors. A "creditor" is defined under Bankruptcy Code Section 101(5) as any entity that has a claim against the debtor, with a "claim" encompassing all rights to payment and certain equitable remedies that have given rise to a right to payment.[10] In the environmental context, creditors may include federal, state, and local regulatory authorities; third-party property owners; co-liable "potentially responsible parties" with contribution claims; off-site disposal facility owners; environmental contractors; bonding companies; and predecessors-in-interest. Any of these may have claims against the debtor for environmental matters. Chapter 11 debtors are also required to file a list of the holders of the 20 largest unsecured claims holders, for the purpose of selecting an unsecured creditors' committee under Bankruptcy Code Section 1102.[11] Schedules allow creditors to understand the debtor's financial health as well as the breadth of the debtor's contracts and claims. Sometimes the debtor's listing of the creditor will provide useful information concerning the debtor's understanding of its liability to the creditor.[12]

---

9. *See* Fed. R. Bankr. P. 1007. Official Bankruptcy Form B206A/B, Official Bankruptcy Form B206D, Official Bankruptcy Form B206E/F (Schedules of Assets and Liabilities); Official Bankruptcy Form B206G (Schedule of Executory Contracts and Unexpired Leases).

10. 11 U.S.C. § 101(5). *See* 2 Collier on Bankruptcy ¶ 101.05[1] (16th ed. 2019); Chapter 11 (Compliance Obligations) *infra*.

11. *See* 4 Collier on Bankruptcy ¶ 521.03[4] (16th ed. 2019).

12. Some debtors try to provide little if any information about the liability other than the name and address of the creditor and a designation of the liability as disputed and unliquidated. In theory, a motion could be filed to require a debtor to provide more useful information, but the debtor may resist as there is not much case law on the subject of debtor's duties to provide more specific information. Seeking discovery under Rule 2004 (as discussed later) will often be a quicker and more reliable route to obtaining further information. Many debtors will voluntarily provide governments with information about locations and details of potential liabilities in lieu of a Rule 2004 examination.

While schedules capture the debtor's financial state at the time of the filing, SOFAs are designed and intended to show a broader view of the debtor's finances in that they illustrate the debtor's operating history, past transactions, and financial history. SOFAs include questions on revenue, payments made to creditors, property transfers, lawsuits, the debtor's business, environmental information, and other financial information.[13] Schedules and SOFAs must substantially comply with the official bankruptcy forms created by the Judicial Conference of the United States (Official Forms), and therefore must contain all the information set out in the Official Forms. However, this substantial compliance does not necessitate completion of the schedules or portions of the SOFA that are inapplicable to the debtor's particular situation. Rather, while Bankruptcy Rule 1007(b) necessitates the use of Official Forms, Rule 9009 allows appropriate modifications as applicable to the debtor's financial structure, including combination of forms and rearrangement of contents for greater economy.

In prepackaged bankruptcy cases under Bankruptcy Code Section 1125(g), in which the debtor presents a plan that it has pre-negotiated with its main creditors for approval,[14] most of the information generally set forth in the schedules and SOFAs has already been revealed to the creditors in the course of negotiating the prepackaged case. In addition, Bankruptcy Code Section 1126(b)(2) provides that pre-petition acceptances or rejections may be used post-petition to seek confirmation of the prepackaged plan provided that disclosure of "adequate information" was given. As a result, bankruptcy courts recognize that requiring the debtor in such cases to go through the process of creating and filing schedules and SOFAs would be wastefully duplicative, and often grant motions waiving the filing requirement. Since governmental

13. Official Bankruptcy Form B207 (non-individuals); Official Bankruptcy Form B107 (individuals). The SOFA also provides information concerning the governance of a debtor, including directors and officers of the debtor.

14. *See United Artists Theatre Co. v. Walton*, 315 F.3d 217, 224 n.5 (3d Cir. 2003); 16 Collier on Bankruptcy ¶ 21.14[1] (16th ed. 2019) (describing how Section 1125(g) "enables a debtor to file a prepackaged plan of reorganization that has been solicited and accepted or rejected by holders of claims or interests entitled to vote on the plan before a disclosure statement has been approved by the Bankruptcy Court").

units would generally not be part of any prepackaged activities, debtors may need to agree to language that passes through all liabilities to governmental units as if the case had never been filed (i.e., liabilities to the government are unchanged) and otherwise preserves the governmental unit's rights. Otherwise, governmental units may object to the waiver of the Code's disclosure requirements and expedited approval of the prepackaged plan so that they are not prejudiced.

With respect to environmental information, Part 12 of a corporate debtor SOFA and Part 10 of an individual debtor SOFA list questions that specifically ask a debtor to disclose information about certain of its environmental liabilities. Parts 12 and 10 respectively request information on: (1) any notices that governmental authorities have provided to the debtor indicating that the debtor is potentially liable under environmental law, (2) any proceedings under environmental law in which the debtor has been a party, and (3) any notifications that the debtor has provided to governmental authorities concerning releases of hazardous materials.[15] These questions are open-ended as to time (and include the debtor's predecessors) and are not restricted as to just unresolved liabilities or proceedings. Therefore, a debtor in operation for many years could potentially be required to provide a large amount of information. In addition, there are other parts of the SOFA where information pertinent to environmental matters may be responsive. These include Question 7 of Part 3 which requests a list of legal actions, proceedings, investigations, and other legal actions.[16] It is worthwhile to review the SOFA broadly for information about environmental issues concerning the debtor. Other general information, such as locations of real property and transfers in the last two years not in the ordinary course of business, may also be of interest in helping to assess the bankruptcy case.

15. *See* Official Bankruptcy Form B207 (non-individuals); Official Bankruptcy Form B107 (individuals).

16. As discussed in Chapter 5 (Key Provisions (executory contracts)) *supra*, the debtor's schedule of executory contracts should not include licenses, permits, orders, and consent judgments because they have the force of law independent of any contractual arrangement. If they are included though, parties in interest should note that their treatment may be an issue in the case and should check the plan and any filings related to executory contracts.

DISCOVERY IN BANKRUPTCY (BANKRUPTCY RULE 2004)

While the schedules and SOFAs provide a baseline amount of information regarding the company, Bankruptcy Rule 2004 allows any "party in interest" to further "examine" the debtor.[17] As the basic discovery device used in bankruptcy cases,[18] parties in interest can use Bankruptcy Rule 2004 examinations for a variety of purposes, including assessing the debtor's financial condition, identifying claims against the estate, more closely analyzing the debtor's past transactions (often to determine whether to bring preference or fraudulent conveyance actions), and identifying the bankruptcy estate's assets and location. Bankruptcy Rule 2004 examinations are commenced generally by filing a Rule 2004 motion with the bankruptcy court seeking an order authorizing the requesting party to proceed with the examination, which can include a request for production of documents.[19]

Unlike examinations governed by the Federal Rules of Civil Procedure, permissible inquiries under Bankruptcy Rule 2004 have a much broader scope than the narrowly tailored discovery for civil cases.[20] Indeed, these inquiries have sometimes been seen as amounting to a "fishing expedition."[21] Bankruptcy Rule 2004 provides that permissible examinations include examination regarding acts, conduct, or property of the estate; the liabilities and financial conditions of the debtor; and any matter that might affect the discharge of the debtor's estate.[22] In Chapter 11 cases, permissible Bankruptcy Rule 2004 examinations also cover the operation of any business of the debtor and the desirability of its continuance, the

17. Fed. R. Bankr. P. 2004; 11 U.S.C. § 1109 (defining "party in interest").

18. *See In re French*, 145 B.R. 991, 992 (Bankr. D.S.D. 1992).

19. The applicable local rules for the bankruptcy court should be consulted as they may have special requirements such as trying to work out an agreement with the debtor for discovery in advance of filing a motion. Other local rules may not require the filing of a motion before proceeding with a Rule 2004 examination or document request.

20. *In re Enron Corp.*, 281 B.R. 836, 840 (Bankr. S.D.N.Y. 2002); *In re Drexel Burnham Lambert Grp., Inc.*, 123 B.R. 702, 711 (Bankr. S.D.N.Y. 1991); *In re GHR Energy Corp.*, 33 B.R. 451, 453 (Bankr. D. Mass. 1983).

21. *In re Blinder, Robinson & Co., Inc.*, 127 B.R. 267, 274 (D. Colo. 1991); *In re Wilcher*, 56 B.R. 428, 433 (Bankr. N.D. Ill. 1985).

22. Fed. R. Bankr. P. 2004(b).

source of any money or property the debtor plans to acquire to consummate the plan as well as the consideration given or offered for it, and any other matter relevant to the case or to the formulation of a plan.[23] While the scope of allowable discovery under Bankruptcy Rule 2004 is broad, it is not unlimited and requires a showing of legitimate need or cause and is dependent on the discretion of the bankruptcy court.[24] Courts have limited Bankruptcy Rule 2004 examinations where a previous settlement agreement limited the scope of the discovery,[25] where the examination was initiated to abuse or harass,[26] and/or where the examination was intended for matters outside the administration of the bankruptcy estate.[27] Bankruptcy Rule 2004 only applies pre-litigation; once an adversary proceeding or other litigation has begun, further discovery takes place pursuant to the discovery rules in the other litigation or the rules for bankruptcy adversary proceedings in Part VII of the Bankruptcy Rules rather than under Bankruptcy Rule 2004.[28] Courts also are hesitant to allow Bankruptcy Rule 2004 to be used when it appears that it is being leveraged in an attempt to bypass the restrictions placed on discovery in other proceedings.[29]

---

23. *Id. See also Bennett Funding Grp., Inc.*, 203 B.R. 24, 28 (Bankr. N.D.N.Y. 1996) (recognizing that generally Rule 2004 examinations are appropriate tools for revealing the nature and extent of the bankruptcy estate); *In re Strecker*, 251 B.R. 878, 882 (Bankr. D. Colo. 2000) (holding that Rule 2004 examinations may also be used for "discovering assets, examining transactions, and determining whether wrongdoing has occurred").

24. *See In re Sunedison Inc.*, 572 B.R. 482, 491 (Bankr. S.D.N.Y. 2017); *In re Millennium Lab Holdings II, LLC*, 562 B.R. 614, 626 (Bankr. D. Del. 2016); *Drexel Burnham Lambert Grp.*, 123 B.R. at 712.

25. *See, e.g., In re Gawker Media LLC*, 2017 WL 2804870, at *7 (Bankr. S.D.N.Y. June 28, 2017).

26. *In re Mittco, Inc.*, 44 B.R. 35, 36 (Bankr. E.D. Wis. 1984)

27. *Millennium Lab Holdings*, 562 B.R. at 627–28; *In re J & R Trucking, Inc.*, 431 B.R. 818, 821–22 (Bankr. N.D. Ind. 2010).

28. *See, e.g., Sunedison Inc.*, 572 B.R. at 490 (pending proceeding rule); *In re Washington Mutual, Inc.*, 408 B.R. 45, 50 (Bankr. D. Del. 2009) (pending proceeding rule); *In re Enron Corp.*, 281 B.R. 836, 840 (Bankr. S.D.N.Y. 2002); *In re Blinder, Robinson & Co.*, 127 B.R. 267, 274 (D. Colo. 1991); *In re Kipp*, 86 B.R. 490, 491 (Bankr. W.D. Tex. 1988) (stating that discovery devices in Rules 7026–7037 of Fed. R. Bankr. P. apply after adversary proceeding has been initiated).

29. *See In re Snyder*, 52 F.3d 1067 (5th Cir. 1995); *In re Cont'l Forge Co.*, 73 B.R. 1005, 1007 (Bankr. W.D. Pa. 1987); *In re GHR Energy Corp.*, 35 B.R. 534, 536–38 (Bankr. D. Mass. 1983); *In re GHR Energy Corp.*, 33 B.R. 451, 455 (Bankr. D. Mass. 1983); *In re Inv. Bankers, Inc.*, 30 B.R. 883, 888–89 (Bankr. D. Colo.1983).

Section 1109 of the Bankruptcy Code identifies a "party in interest" as including the debtor, the trustee, a creditors' committee, an equity security holders' committee, a creditor, and an indenture trustee, but this list of entities is not exclusive.[30] Courts have extended the right to commence Bankruptcy Rule 2004 examinations to these parties. In addition, courts have extended the right to commence Bankruptcy Rule 2004 examinations to U.S. Trustees and any trustee or examiner appointed by the bankruptcy court.[31] The breadth of the discovery tool is intended to allow both an assessment of the nature and extent of the estate as well as discovery of the assets of the debtor that may have been concealed (intentionally or unintentionally).[32]

OBTAINING INFORMATION FROM KEY PLAYERS IN THE BANKRUPTCY CASE

In addition to the aforementioned resources and mechanisms for obtaining information, creditors or parties in interest should also consider more informal ways to obtain information. Bankruptcy works best as a collaborative settlement-like process.[33] As such, other parties in the case are often willing to provide useful information that can save time and expense. Counsel for the creditors' committee is a good candidate to start with in this regard, given that the creditors' committee has fiduciary duties to all unsecured creditors and may be aligned in some respects with environmental unsecured creditors in terms of overall creditor recovery in the bankruptcy case.[34] Governmental parties should check to see if the Department of Justice or other states (or the National Association

---

30. 11 U.S.C. § 1109; *In re Thorpe Insulation Co.*, 677 F.3d 869 (9th Cir. 2012); *In re Global Indus. Techs., Inc.*, 645 F.3d 201 3d Cir. 2011); *In re James Wilson Assocs.*, 965 F.2d 160 (7th Cir. 1992).

31. *In re Davis*, 452 B.R. 610, 615–17 (Bankr. E.D. Mich. 2011) (U.S. Trustees); *In re FiberMark, Inc.*, 339 B.R. 321, 324 (Bankr. D. Vt. 2006) (examiner).

32. *See, e.g., In re Cinderella Clothing Indus., Inc.*, 93 B.R. 373, 377–78 (Bankr. E.D. Pa. 1988); *In re Wilcher*, 56 B.R. 428, 433–34 (Bankr. N.D. Ill.1985); *In re GHR Energy Corp.*, 35 B.R. 534, 536–37 (Bankr. D. Mass. 1983).

33. *See* Chapter 16 (Plan Objections) *infra*.

34. *See Westmoreland Human Opportunities, Inc. v. Walsh*, 246 F.3d 233, 256 (3d Cir. 2001).

of Attorneys General (NAAG)) are involved in the case and have useful information.[35] If so, it is common for interested governmental parties to coordinate and share information. The Assistant U.S. Trustee assigned to a case might also have useful information, and governmental parties may coordinate with him or her from time to time, especially if there may be potential evidence of fraudulent conduct. Where there are other private co-liable parties with a debtor, counsel for such parties might also be a good contact for coordination. Finally, sometimes counsel for the debtor (who has fiduciary duties to creditors)[36] is willing to cooperate and share information because that advances the debtor's goal of reaching agreement on a consensual plan of reorganization.

35. Bankruptcy court filings or service lists may disclose the names of attorneys involved for such parties.

36. *See Wolf v. Weinstein*, 372 U.S. 633, 649 (1963).

CHAPTER 7

Proofs of Claim and Applications for Administrative Expense

Bankruptcy cases are collective proceedings involving multiple parties in interest where the assets of a debtor are divided up for the benefit of creditors. Chapter 11 reorganizations also take into account: (1) whether the debtor can be rehabilitated and provided a fresh start, and (2) the means for accomplishing the debtor's feasible reorganization.[1] In many cases, creditors and parties in interest can benefit from value provided through reorganization of the debtor and continued business activities. However, where reorganization is not feasible, bankruptcy becomes a collective liquidation process.[2]

PROOFS OF CLAIM

The Bankruptcy Code provides for the filing of proofs of claim for the purpose of distributions to creditors in either the reorganization or liquidation context.[3] A proof of claim is the form used by a creditor to indicate that the creditor claims the debtor owes it

1. *See In re Frontier Ins. Grp., Inc.*, 585 B.R. 685, 693 (Bankr. S.D.N.Y. 2018).
2. *See* Chapters 2 (History and Purposes), 3 (Code Chapters) *supra*.
3. *See* 11 U.S.C. § 501; Fed. R. Bankr. P. 3001, 3002.

money and, if known, the amount owed. A creditor may file more than one proof of claim. Proofs of claim are deemed "allowed" unless and until a proof of claim is the subject of objection.[4] Contingent or unliquidated proofs of claim, which are claims that a creditor believes it may have if certain conditions are met or occur, can be estimated if necessary to avoid unduly delaying the administration of the bankruptcy case.[5] For further information on objections and requests for estimation of claims, see Chapter 17 (Claim Objections). For further information on the priority of claims under the Bankruptcy Code, see Chapter 12 (Priorities).

The Bankruptcy Code defines "claim" broadly at Section 101(5) to include a right to payment as well as a right to an equitable remedy for breach of performance where the breach gives rise to a right to payment, whether or not such rights are contingent or unliquidated.[6] As discussed in Chapter 11 (Compliance Obligations) of this Practice Guide, certain equitable remedies such as injunctions, orders, and other compliance obligations are not within the definition of a claim if breach of the equitable remedy does not give rise to the government seeking a right of payment (i.e., spending funds and seeking reimbursement in lieu of enforcement of the equitable remedy).

Given the disagreement and uncertainty about what constitutes a "claim," which is discussed in Chapter 11 (Compliance Obligations), governmental agencies often file protective proofs of claim for environmental cleanup and compliance obligations, which note the government's position that a proof of claim is not required, but that the filing is being made protectively should the bankruptcy court disagree with the government's position.[7] The

4. 11 U.S.C. § 501(e).

5. *Id.* § 502(c). Requests for estimation of environmental proofs of claims for unliquidated future cleanup costs have been made in several cases which are discussed in Chapter 17 (Claim Objections) *infra*.

6. *Midland Funding, LLC*, 137 S. Ct. 1407, 1412 (2017); *Johnson v. Home State Bank*, 501 U.S. 78, 85 (1991); *Penn. Dep't of Public Welfare v. Davenport*, 495 U.S. 552, 558 (1990).

7. If the government has a monetary claim such as for penalties or past response costs, it can file a proof of claim protectively in part with respect to the compliance obligations. State agencies should consider the issue of waiver of sovereign immunity under the 11th Amendment in connection with the wording of any protective proof of claim. *See* Chapter 11 (Compliance Obligations) *infra*, Chapter 5 (Key

government's protective proof of claim would state that the filing is not an election of remedies and reserves the government's right to seek affirmative compliance from the debtor. Protective proofs of claim are frequently filed by governmental agencies out of an abundance of caution that a court may take a position contrary to the governmental agency with respect to environmental cleanup and compliance obligations. Protective proofs of claim also alert interested parties and the bankruptcy court to the fact that environmental cleanup and compliance obligations may need to be addressed in the case.[8] To date, the authors are not aware of any rulings by courts that preclude the filing of protective proofs of claim or grant challenges by debtors or other parties to such filings.[9]

Bankruptcy courts set bar dates for filing nongovernmental proofs of claim in Chapter 11 cases.[10] Governments, however, are provided by statute at least 180 days from the filing of the bankruptcy petition (in voluntary cases) to file proofs of claim, or such later time provided under the Bankruptcy Rules, 11 U.S.C. § 502(b)(9).[11] This requirement may not be shortened by a bankruptcy court.[12] In Chapter 11 cases, bar date orders generally provide the government the later of 180 days or the deadline set for nongovernmental creditors to file.[13] For Bankruptcy Code Chapters

---

Provisions (sovereign immunity)) *supra*. The filing of a proof of claim waives sovereign immunity but only as to claims arising from the same transaction or occurrence. 11 U.S.C. § 106(b); *Shieldalloy Metallurgical Corp. v. N.J. Dep't of Env't Prot.*, 743 F. Supp. 2d 429, 437–38 (D.N.J. 2010).

8. *See* Chapter 12 (Priorities) *infra* (discussing where compliance obligations fit into bankruptcy priorities), Chapter 16 *infra* (discussing objections to plans of reorganization that do not provide for environmental compliance).

9. *See* Chapter 11 (Compliance Obligations) *infra* for samples of language for protective proofs of claim. Courts have ruled on the legal issues presented by protective proofs of claim in only a limited number of cases which are discussed in Chapter 11 (Compliance Obligations).

10. Fed. R. Bankr. P. 3003(c)(3).

11. *See also id.* 3002(c)(1) (applicable to filing proofs of claim in Chapter 7, 12, and 13 cases).

12. *In re George Transfer, Inc.*, 212 B.R. 475, 479 (Bankr. D. Md. 1997); *In re Metrocall, Inc.*, No. 02-11579 (Bankr. D. Del. June 6, 2002) ("the court lacks authority to shorten" the 180-day period and a bar date order so providing "cannot be valid").

13. Local rules should also be consulted as some local rules automatically provide the government 180 days from the filing of the bankruptcy petition (in voluntary cases) without making clear that a later date may apply if the court sets a later

7, 12, and 13, the deadline for nongovernmental creditors is 70 days from the filing of the petition for relief (90 days in involuntary cases), but the deadline for governmental creditors is 180 days from the filing of the petition.[14]

If a creditor does not file a proof of claim by the bar date, the creditor may lose out on having its claim allowed in the bankruptcy case. In Chapter 9 or 11 cases, late proofs of claim can be allowed as if timely filed based on a showing of excusable neglect.[15] In Chapter 7, 12, and 13 cases, late proofs of claims are permitted as timely only for the narrow specific reasons set forth in Bankruptcy Rule 3002(c)(6).[16] Historically, extensions of the bar date after it has passed have been difficult to obtain in Chapter 7, 12, and 13 cases, somewhat unbelievably even where the creditor was not provided any notice of the bar date.[17] The mixed case law on this subject results from very literal applications of Bankruptcy Rules 3002(c) and 9006(b)(3).[18] Fortunately, Bankruptcy Rule 3002(c)(6) was

---

deadline for claims by other creditors. A local rule should not be read to override Bankruptcy Rule 3003(c)(3), which permits the court to set the bar date in Chapter 11 cases. Section 502(b)(9) of the Code expressly provides the government the ability to file at later dates if so provided for in the Bankruptcy Rules. Governmental parties may wish to seek clear language in the court's bar date order as to the governmental deadline to avoid the possibility of disputes or prejudice in districts with such local rules.

14. Fed. R. Bankr. P. 3002(c).

15. *See id.* 9006(b)(1); *Pioneer Inv. Sers. Co. v. Brunswick Assocs. Ltd. P'ship*, 507 U.S. 380 (1993); *DPWN Holdings (USA), Inc.*, 246 F. Supp. 3d 680, 692 (E.D.N.Y. 2017). *See also* Fed. R. Bankr. P. 9006(b)(3). However, Fed. R. Bankr. P. 3002(c)(1) permits governmental units to seek extensions of a bar date before it expires. And Fed. R. Bankr. P. 3002(c)(6) has been interpreted by some courts to permit late claims by creditors who lacked notice of a bar date because the debtor knew of the potential claim but failed to list the creditor on its list of creditors resulting in the creditor not receiving notice. *See In re Vanderpol*, 606 B.R. 425 (Bankr. D. Colo. 2019); *In re Mazik*, 592 B.R. 812 (Bankr. E.D. Pa. 2018).

16. *Pioneer*, 507 U.S. at 390 n.4. The narrow reasons listed in the rule relate only a debtor's failure to timely file the list of creditors or where notice is mailed to a foreign address.

17. *See* David Cisar & Christopher Koehnke, *Revised Rule 3002: Is Lack of Notice Grounds for a Late-Filed Claim?*, 39-2 Am. Bankr. Inst. J. 15 (Feb. 2020). However, Section 726(a)(2)(C) of the Bankruptcy Code permits the payment of tardily filed claims in Chapter 7 cases as if they were timely filed where there was lack of notice or actual knowledge in time to file and a proof of claim is filed in time to permit payment. 11 U.S.C. § 726(a)(2)(C).

18. *See* Cisar & Koehnke, *supra* note 17, at 15. Bankruptcy Rule 9006(b)(3) on enlargements of time expressly carves out extensions on grounds beyond those specified in certain other rules including Bankruptcy Rule 3002(c)(6), which governs

amended effective December 2022 to expressly permit bankruptcy courts to allow an extension of time to file proofs of claim in Chapter 7, 12, and 13 cases where there was insufficient notice.[19] Finally, in the rare full payment case, where creditors are paid fully, tardy proofs of claim can receive distributions after other proofs of claim are paid in full.[20]

The Bankruptcy Rules have a standard form for a proof of claim that is often required to be used.[21] Governments (and sometimes other claimants) often use the form as a cover sheet and attach a more detailed supplemental statement of the basis of the proof of claim as an attachment.[22] The attachment typically provides factual background and describes the legal basis for the proof of claim, including a recitation of how the key elements of liability under the statute giving rise to the claim are met.

For bankruptcy cases involving the submission of proofs of claims for response costs, the attachment typically provides a calculation of past response costs through an identified recent date and an estimate or range of estimate of future response costs. While unliquidated proofs of claim for future response costs are permitted,[23] that is, claims for an unknown and unstated amount, it

---

certain extensions to the filing of proofs of claim in Chapters 7, 12, and 13. Chapter 11 proof of claims are governed by Bankruptcy Rule 3003, which provides for court enlargements of time after expiration. Rule 3003, though, is not referred to in Rule 9006(b)(3). In *In re Vanderpol*, 606 B.R. 425 (Bankr. D. Colo. 2019), the court found that narrowly construing Rule 3002(c)(6) to a failure to file a list of creditors would render that section a nullity and would be contrary to principles of due process.

19. *See* https://www.govinfo.gov/content/pkg/CDOC-117hdoc108/pdf/CDOC-117hdoc108.pdf.

20. *See, e.g.*, 11 U.S.C. § 726(a)(4).

21. Fed. R. Bank. P. Form 410. This form can be found on bankruptcy court websites and the website of the U.S. Courts at uscourts.gov/forms/bankruptcy-forms.

22. Fed. R. Bank. P. Form 9009 limits alterations to required forms, but permits variations provided for by other rules. According to the website for the United States Courts' list of "Permitted Changes to Official Bankruptcy Forms," alterations are permitted to Form 410 as long as the proof of claim "conform[s] substantially to the appropriate Official Form." US Courts.gov, Services & Forms, Permitted Changes (citing to Fed. R. Bankr. P. 3001(a)). Governments (and sometimes private parties) will often specify "see attached" on their proof of claim cover sheets in response to questions that are covered in more detail in their attachments.

23. *See, e.g.*, 11 U.S.C. § 101(5) ("claim" includes unliquidated claims); 11 U.S.C. § 502(c) (providing for estimation of unliquidated claims); *Ellis v. Westinghouse Elec. Co.*, 11 F.4th 221, 237–38 (3d Cir. 2021) (creditor may file protective claim to put debtor on notice without amount); *In re FirstEnergy Sols. Corp.*, 606 B.R. 720, 743

is best practice to provide an estimated amount or estimated range of amounts where possible and a reservation of the right to supplement the proofs of claim. Such estimates put the other parties in interest on notice of the potential magnitude of the proof of claim and may help minimize any risks in neglecting to update the proof of claim over time. Likewise, it is best practice for proofs of claim to note where other viable parties may be jointly and severally liable with the debtor for the claim (such as under CERCLA)[24] in order to provide the court and other parties in interest appropriate context for the liability. Proofs of claim for penalties or fines may state or estimate the penalty sought by the government, if known, or cite to the statutory maximum for penalties, if the amount sought has not yet been determined. If the government expects to seek liquidation of the amount of a penalty or the amount of past response costs in another forum with jurisdiction to determine the amount, the proof of claim should so note.[25] The proof of claim should also note if funds in the estate, such as escrow or trust accounts, are earmarked for environmental liabilities or if the government or private party is the beneficiary of financial assurance such as bonds, letters of credit, or insurance. The proof of claim should state the legal position that the equitable interest in such funds or proceeds is not property of the estate and/or provides a secured interest.[26]

In most large corporate bankruptcy cases, proofs of claim can be filed electronically with the debtor's claims service.[27] Proofs of claim can be signed and filed by non-attorneys. They should be signed by someone with knowledge of the facts or access to people

(Bankr. N.D. Ohio. 2019).

24. *See, e.g.*, *In re Nat'l Gypsum Co.*, 139 B.R. 397, 414–15 (N.D. Tex. 1992); Chapter 17 (Claim Objections) *infra*.

25. Actions to liquidate the amount of a judgment for penalties fall under the police or regulatory exceptions to the automatic stay (but judgments may not be enforced outside of the proof of claim process). *See* 11 U.S.C. § 362(b)(4); Chapter 10 (Police or Regulatory Exception) *infra*.

26. The rights of the party filing the proof of claim will depend on the nature of its interest and may be disputed by the debtor. *See* Chapter 5 (Key Provisions (property of the estate)) *supra*.

27. In many cases, proofs of claim can be filed with the bankruptcy court through PACER. However, where a bar date order requires filing with a claims service, filing the proofs of claim through PACER may be technically defective. Proofs of claims of creditors can usually be viewed on the websites of claims services and sometimes through PACER.

with knowledge of the facts so that they can certify under penalty of perjury that the proof of claim is correct to the best of their knowledge.[28]

Creditors should review the debtor's proposed bar date orders carefully, as they sometimes seek to create requirements beyond those required by the Bankruptcy Code or the Bankruptcy Rules and, in those instances, creditors may want to object to such provisions. For example, the debtor may include language that would seem to bar late claims for excusable neglect or create documentary or affidavit requirements not provided for in the Bankruptcy Rules.[29] In large administratively consolidated cases, creditors are typically required to file separate proofs of claim in the case of each particular debtor that the creditor believes liable unless the bankruptcy court has approved the filing of consolidated proofs of claim.

Where a creditor fails to file an official proof of claim, it is possible that its pleading will be treated as a valid informal proof of claim. An informal proof of claim requires a bankruptcy court filing evidencing an intent to assert a claim and seek recovery from the estate.[30]

EPA has issued nonbinding guidance on the factors it considers when evaluating whether it will file a proof of claim or

---

28. Fed. R. Bank. P. Form 410. Signatures by non-attorneys avoids the risk of discovery against the signatory attorney as to the basis for filing under penalty of perjury. If an attorney signs, he or she may want to limit their signature to legal contentions only.

29. Bankruptcy Rule 3001 has various requirements for documentary attachments to proofs of claim for certain types of secured claims. These requirements do not apply to general unsecured proofs of claim. Documentary production requirements for unsecured proofs of claim are governed by the discovery rules that apply to contested matters under Bankruptcy Rule 9014(c).

30. *See In re Nowak*, 586 F.3d 450, 455 (6th Cir. 2009); *In re American Classic Voyages Co.*, 405 F.3d 127, 130–32 (3d Cir. 2005); *In re Nikoloutsos*, 199 F.3d 233, 236 (5th Cir. 2000); *In re Reliance Equities Inc.*, 966 F.2d 1338, 1345 (10th Cir. 1992); *In re Charter Co.*, 876 F.2d 861, 863–64 (11th Cir. 1989); *In re Pizza of Hawaii, Inc.*, 761 F.2d 1374, 1381 (9th Cir. 1985); *Wilkens v. Simon Bros., Inc.*, 731 F.2d 462, 464–65 (7th Cir. 1984). As discussed in these cases, the concept of informal proofs of claim is equitable in nature. As such, the facts underlying a request to recognize an informal proof of claim might also be used to justify a late claim on the basis of excusable neglect. If a creditor has made the debtor and other parties aware of its claim in a court filing, the creditor's actions might be found to be more understandable and less prejudicial to the estate.

otherwise participate in bankruptcy cases.[31] These factors include the likelihood of recovery in the bankruptcy case; the impact on agency resources; fairness to parties co-liable with a debtor; the culpability of the debtor; strength of evidence against the debtor; the deterrence value of taking action; and the interests of justice and equity.[32]

If the government (or another creditor) does not file a proof of claim, the debtor or trustee may file a proof of claim on its behalf (sometimes called a surrogate proof of claim) within 30 days of the bar date.[33] Likewise, if the government (or another creditor) does not file a proof of claim, a creditor liable with the debtor on the claim may file a proof of such claim within 30 days of the bar date.[34] The government (or other creditor) should closely monitor adjudication of surrogate proofs of claim filed on its behalf to avoid prejudice and handle any recoveries consistent with its policies and requirements.[35]

Amendments to proofs of claim are liberally granted to update dollar amounts (such as for cleanup costs), to cure defects, or describe a claim with greater particularity.[36] Additional theories of recovery have also been permitted where they are based on

31. *Guidance on EPA Participation in Bankruptcy Cases* (Sept. 30, 1997), found at epa.gov.

32. *Id.* at 2-6.

33. *See* 11 U.S.C. § 501(c); Fed. R. Bankr. P. 3004; *In re Hemingway Transp., Inc.*, 993 F.2d 915, 928 (1st Cir. 1993).

34. *See* 11 U.S.C. § 501(b); Fed. R. Bankr. P. 3005(a); *Hemingway Transp.*, 993 F.2d at 928. Such a filing enables the co-liable party to reduce its liability to the extent claims are paid given that contingent claims for contribution are disallowable under Section 502(e) of the Code.

35. Where appropriate, the government or other creditor may wish to consider intervening or participating as an interested party to protect its interests in connection with any proceedings on an objection to the surrogate proof of claim. *See* Fed. R. Bankr. P. 2018(a); 11 U.S.C. § 1109; *In re Bicoastal Corp.*, 122 B.R. 771, 773–74 (Bankr. M.D. Fla. 1990).

36. *See In re Enron Corp.*, 419 F.3d 115, 133 (2d Cir. 2005); *In re Ben Franklin Hotel Assocs.*, 186 F.3d 301, 309 (3d Cir. 1999); *Hemingway Transp.*, 954 F.2d at 10; *In re Roberts Farms Inc.*, 980 F.2d 1248, 1251–52 (9th Cir. 1992); *In re Unioil, Inc.*, 962 F.2d 988, 992–93 (10th Cir. 1992); *In re SemCrude, L.P.*, 443 B.R. 472, 477–78 (Bankr. D. Del. 2011); *In re Lee Way Holding Co.*, 178 B.R. 976, 979 (Bankr. S.D. Ohio 1995). Bankruptcy Rule 9014 may apply Federal Rule of Civil Procedure 15 and Bankruptcy Rule 7015 by analogy to proof of claim amendments. *See In re Stavriotis*, 977 F.2d 1202, 1204 (7th Cir. 1992).

the same transactions originally alleged.[37] However, brand new claims, asserted in the guise of amending an existing claim, have been rejected as prejudicial to the debtor.[38] Under some plans of reorganization, it can be more difficult to amend a proof of claim post-confirmation, such as where amendment might render the plan infeasible or alter the distribution to other creditors provided for in the plan.[39] Where post-confirmation claims litigation is contemplated though, such prejudice is unlikely.[40]

APPLICATIONS FOR ADMINISTRATIVE EXPENSE

Applications for administrative expense are requests for reimbursement for the costs and expense of preserving the bankruptcy estate.[41] In the environmental context, administrative expenses may include cleanup or response costs incurred post-petition with respect to property of the bankruptcy estate and penalties for the debtor's post-petition violations of environmental laws. These are discussed in greater detail in Chapter 12 (Priorities) of the Practice Guide and are examples of environmental claims that may be entitled to administrative expense priority. Section 503(b) provides that administrative expenses are to be allowed after notice and hearing. Unlike proofs of claim, the Bankruptcy Rules do not have provisions governing applications for administrative expense claims. Each

---

37. *See, e.g., Hemingway Transp.*, 954 F.2d at 10; *In re Int'l Horizons, Inc.*, 751 F.2d 1213, 1216 (11th Cir. 1985); *In re Black, Davis & Shue Agency, Inc.*, 460 B.R. 407, 417 (Bankr. M.D. Pa. 2011).

38. *See, e.g., In re Unroe*, 937 F.2d 346, 350 (7th Cir. 1991); *In re Exide Techns.*, 601 B.R. 271, 292–94 (Bankr. D. Del. 2019), *aff'd*, 613 B.R. 79 (D. Del. 2020).

39. *See In re Winn-Dixie Stores, Inc.*, 639 F.3d 1053, 1056–57 (11th Cir. 2011); *Holstein v. Brill*, 987 F.2d 1268 (7th Cir. 1993). These situations can arise under res judicata principles where a plan makes specific provision of the amount of cash or stock to be paid for a claim allowed under the plan. *See* Chapter 16 (Plan Objections) *infra* (discussing res judicata effect of plans). In contrast, plans that contemplate post-confirmation claim adjudication and are elastic enough to accommodate updated (but not new) claims should be governed by a more flexible standard for amendment.

40. *See, e.g., In re Appalachian Fuels, LLC*, 521 B.R. 779, 803 (Bankr. E.D. Ky. 2014); *In re Waterscape Resort LLC*, 520 B.R. 424, 434–35 (Bankr. S.D.N.Y. 2014).

41. *See* 11 U.S.C. §§ 503(b), 507(a)(2), 726(a)(1), 1129(a)(9); *Hartford Underwriters Ins. Co. v. Union Planters Bank*, 530 U.S. 1, 4–5 (2000).

bankruptcy court may therefore establish its own rules, procedures, and deadlines for filing administrative expense claims. In Chapter 11 cases, the plan of reorganization and confirmation order typically contain the relevant requirements and deadlines. Where a debtor needs to know the magnitude of administrative expense claims before confirmation, in order to be able to assess feasibility of a plan, an administrative expense bar date order may be established by the bankruptcy court. However, because administrative expenses continue to be incurred throughout the case, such a bar date order needs to cover claims through a specified date so as to provide the claimant a reasonable amount of time to file its claim and permit the future filing of claims that have not yet arisen. On rare occasions, a bankruptcy court will therefore have multiple bar date orders over time for filing administrative expense claims. Many bankruptcy courts require that administrative expense claims be filed by motion and may require the filing of a memorandum of law in support of the motion that describes the legal basis for the filing. Other courts have replicated proof of claim procedures by requiring the filing of an administrative expense claim form with a claims service. Some plans or confirmation orders provide that administrative expense applications do not need to be filed for ordinary course of business expenses during the bankruptcy case, which may include environmental-related expenses such as application fees, registration fees, permit fees, report fees, and routine payments of costs under a consent decree. These payments are then made in the ordinary course.

Where a creditor may have a claim for response costs with respect to property of the estate or for penalties for violations of environmental law during the bankruptcy case, it is important to pay close attention to the applicable deadline in the case for filing an administrative expense claim. As noted earlier, while not typical, such deadlines can occur periodically during the bankruptcy case. Deadlines in confirmed plans can apply not just to administrative expenses pre-confirmation but also to penalties or response costs incurred after the confirmation hearing but before the effective date of the plan.[42] If the debtor failed to provide notice of the

42. *See, e.g.*, *Ellis v. Westinghouse Elec. Co., LLC*, 11 F.4th 221 (3d Cir. 2021) (barring claim arising during eight-month delay between confirmation and effective

deadline to a known creditor and such creditor did not have actual knowledge of the bar date, the creditor's claim will not be discharged.[43] If a deadline is missed, creditors may want to consider seeking authority to file a late administrative expense application. Depending on the facts and circumstances, a debtor might not be prejudiced by a late administrative expense application such as where the debtor was aware of the liability and the plan provided for administrative expenses to be paid by the reorganized debtor as part of ongoing operations.[44]

---

date). If a plan or other order does not provide for notice of a bar date for administrative expense claims, they are not discharged. *Id.* at 235.

43. *See* Chapter 13 (Discharge) *infra*; *Ellis v. Westinghouse*, 11 F.4th at 236.

44. *See* note 15 *supra* (discussing authority for filing late proofs of claim).

CHAPTER 8

Harmonization of Bankruptcy Law and Environmental Law

How have courts harmonized and reconciled bankruptcy law and environmental law, that is, the "Clash of the Titans" representing such vastly different and conflicting goals and purposes?[1] The approach taken by courts has been similar to how courts have addressed conflicts between other bodies of law. When two bodies of federal law conflict, courts use traditional tools of statutory interpretation to determine whether Congress expressed an intent as to how the statutory schemes should interact.[2] If the environmental laws at issue are state laws as opposed to federal laws, then the legal analysis becomes one of whether federal bankruptcy law preempts state environmental law under the Supremacy Clause of the Constitution.[3] In either situation (conflicting federal statutes or preemption of state statutes), the touchstone of analysis is determining the intent of Congress through express language or statutory structure and purpose as to the interaction between environmental law and bankruptcy law.[4] In addition, courts have

1. *See* Chapter 1 (Introduction) *supra*, at note 4 (citing Jill Thompson Losch, *Bankruptcy v. Environmental Obligation: Clash of the Titans*, 52 La. L Rev. 137 (1991).

2. *POM Wonderful v. Coca-Cola Co.*, 573 U.S. 102, 112 (2014).

3. U.S. Const. art. VI, cl. 2. Several federal environmental laws themselves expressly preserve separate state environmental laws. 42 U.S.C. §§ 6929 (RCRA), 9614(a) (CERCLA), 9652(d) (CERCLA).

4. *Medtronic, Inc. v. Lohr*, 518 U.S. 470, 485–86 (1996); *United States v. Ron Pair*

emphasized that federal law is presumed not to preempt laws grounded in state police power unless Congress has clearly and manifestly so provided.[5]

In the absence of statutory language from which congressional intent can be determined, federal laws that conflict with each other must be harmonized and reconciled, if at all possible, so as to achieve the goals and purposes of each to the maximum extent possible.[6] Clues as to Congress's intent concerning how the laws should be harmonized and reconciled should be looked for in each body of law. The goal is not to prefer one statute over the other, but to maximize achievement of the provisions and purposes of each as reflected in the text and structure of the statute.[7] Only as a last resort, where two federal statutes are irreconcilable, either: (1) the more specific statute may be found to control over a

---

Enterprises, Inc., 489 U.S. 235, 242–46 (1989); *see* Caleb Nelson, *Preemption*, 86 Va. L. Rev. 225 (2000); Stephen A. Gardbaum, *The Nature of Preemption*, 79 Cornell L. Rev. 767 (1994).

5. *Wyeth v. Levine*, 555 U.S. 555, 565 & n.3 (2009); *Medtronic*, 518 U.S. at 485; *Midlantic Nat'l Bank v. N.J. Dep't of Env't Prot.*, 474 U.S. 494 (1986); *Rice v. Santa Fe Elevator Corp.*, 331 U.S. 218, 230 (1947); *Atay v. County of Maui*, 842 F.3d 688, 699 (9th Cir. 2016); *Saravia v. 1736 18th St., N.W. Ltd. P'ship*, 844 F.2d 823 (D.C. Cir. 1988); *Penn Terra Ltd. v. Dep't of Env't Res.*, 733 F.2d 267, 273 (3d Cir. 1984); *In re Chi. Rapid Transit Co.*, 129 F.2d 1, 5 (7th Cir. 1942); *see* Robert W. Miller, *A Comprehensive Framework for Conflict Preemption in Federal Insolvency Proceedings*, 123 W. Va. L. Rev. 423 (2020); Josef Athanas & Peter Knight, *Resolving Conflicts between the Bankruptcy Code and Other Federal and State Laws*, 11 J. Bankr. L & Prac. 237, 253–54 (2002).

6. *Morton v. Mancari*, 417 U.S. 535, 551 (1974) ("The courts are not at liberty to pick and choose among congressional enactments, and when two statutes are capable of co-existence, it is the duty of the courts . . . to regard each as effective."); *see Epic Systems Corp. v. Lewis*, 138 S. Ct. 1612, 1624 (2018); *POM Wonderful v. Coca-Cola Co.*, 573 U.S. at 112–21; *J.E.M. Ag. Supply, Inc. v. Pioneer H-Bred Int'l, Inc.*, 534 U.S. 124, 143–44 (2001).

7. *See Chi., Milwaukee, St. Paul & Pacific R.R. Co.*, 3 F.3d 200, 201 (7th Cir. 1993) ("if possible, these two conflicting objectives should be reconciled"); *In re Jensen*, 995 F.2d 925, 927 (9th Cir. 1993) (recognizing the obligation of the courts to reconcile the conflicting objectives of environmental law and bankruptcy law); *In re Nat'l Gypsum Co.*, 139 B.R. 397, 404 (N.D. Tex. 1992) (The pivotal question is not whether a given environmental statute or the Bankruptcy Code is "accorded primacy over the other, but rather what interaction between the two statutes serves most faithfully the policy objective embodied in the two separate enactments of Congress.").

general one, or (2) a later statute may be found to impliedly repeal the former.[8]

Applying these principles, bankruptcy courts have, on a number of occasions, harmonized and reconciled bankruptcy and environmental law (whether federal or state) through the application of particular provisions of the Bankruptcy Code (or other law such as the Judicial Code (28 U.S.C.)) that expressly provide for or presume compliance with nonbankruptcy or police or regulatory law.[9] For example, Section 959(b) of Title 28 provides that trustees and debtors-in-possession must manage and operate their property in accordance with nonbankruptcy law.[10] Likewise, the Bankruptcy Code's automatic stay has an express police or regulatory exception that permits governmental units to bring actions to enforce their police or regulatory power, including enforcement of judgments for injunctive relief.[11] And the Bankruptcy Code's definition of "claim" excludes certain "equitable remedies," which may include injunctive actions such as undertaking cleanups or mitigation activities.[12] While the Bankruptcy Code favors reorganization where possible, "it does not permit anything and everything that might advance that goal."[13] Rather, Congress did not have a "single purpose" but "st[ruck] a 'balance' among multiple competing interests."[14] On the other hand, courts have preempted state laws

---

8. *Pliva, Inc. v. Mensing*, 564 U.S. 604, 622 (2011); *Nat'l Ass'n of Homebuilders v. Defenders of Wildlife*, 551 U.S. 644, 662–63 (2007); *Matsushita Elec. Indus. Co. v. Epstein*, 516 U.S. 367, 380 (1996); *Morton*, 417 U.S. at 550–52.

9. *Midlantic Nat'l Bank v. N.J. Dep't of Env't Prot.*, 474 U.S. 494, 502 (1986) ("Congress has expressly provided that the efforts of the trustee to marshal and distribute the assets of the estate must yield to governmental interest in public health and safety."); *In re Commerce Oil Co.*, 847 F.2d 291, 297 (6th Cir. 1988) ("plain meaning" of the Bankruptcy Code is that preservation of the debtor's estate is not of "greater priority" than enforcement of environmental protection laws).

10. *See* 28 U.S.C. § 959(b); Chapter 9 (Operating Estate Property) *infra*.

11. *See* 11 U.S.C. § 362(b)(4); Chapter 10 (Police or Regulatory Exception) *infra*.

12. *See* 11 U.S.C. § 101(5); Chapter 11 (Compliance Obligations) *infra*.

13. *Mission Prod. Holdings, Inc. v. Tempnology, LLC*, 139 S. Ct. 1652, 1665 (2019); *Ellis v. Westinghouse Elec. Co., LLC*, 11 F.4th 221, 230 (3d Cir. 2021) ("debtor's interest in a fresh start is not absolute, as the Bankruptcy Code tries to strike" a delicate balance between competing interests).

14. *Mission Prod. Holdings*, 139 S. Ct. at 1665. (quoting *Florida Dep't of Revenue v. Piccadilly Cafeterias, Inc.*, 554 U.S. 33, 51 (2008)); *see Bartenwerfer v. Buckley*, 143 S. Ct. 665, 675 (2023) ("the Code . . . balances multiple, often competing interests").

found to be plainly inconsistent with the Bankruptcy Code's provisions for discharge of monetary liabilities.[15]

In harmonizing and reconciling bankruptcy law and environmental law, two general recurring themes are worth noting up front.

DISTINCTION BETWEEN COMPLIANCE OBLIGATIONS AND MONETARY LIABILITIES

The first recurring theme is the distinction between compliance obligations and monetary liabilities, which is of fundamental importance. Based on the statutory language covered in the preceding discussion, environmental law has primacy when environmental compliance obligations are involved. Congress sought to protect and preserve compliance obligations so that no one, including debtors and trustees, would be above the law and public health and safety would be paramount.[16] Congress did not want bankruptcy courts to become a safe haven or refuge for wrongdoers, scofflaws, and lawbreakers.[17] On the other hand, bankruptcy law will be paramount when the treatment of monetary liabilities is at issue, such as the obligation to reimburse the government or a nondebtor private party for its costs of cleanup. Monetary liabilities and their treatment are squarely addressed by the statutory language of the Bankruptcy Code, which also reflects

15. *Perez v. Campbell*, 402 U.S. 637 (1971) (Bankruptcy Code preempts state statute whose purpose was to permit accident victims to recover debts from drivers without insurance).

16. "The Bankruptcy Code cannot reasonably be read to enlist the judiciary's aid in permitting debtors to violate the law." *In re Steenes*, 918 F.3d 554, 558 (7th Cir. 2019). *See* Daniel J. Bussel, *Doing Equity in Bankruptcy*, 34 Emory Bankr. Dev. J. 13, 46–47 (2017) ("The correct resolution in environmental clean-up cases requires a balancing of bankruptcy and nonbankruptcy policies in the light of the specific circumstances of the case, understanding that in cases where public health and safety is directly threatened by continuing noncompliance, nonbankruptcy policy may have the casting vote.").

17. *Steenes*, 918 F.3d at 557–58; *In re Nortel Networks, Inc.*, 669 F.3d 128, 137 (3d Cir. 2011); *S.E.C. v. Brennan*, 230 F.3d 65, 71 (2d Cir. 2000); *In re Commonwealth Cos., Inc.*, 913 F.2d 518, 527 (8th Cir. 1990); *United States v. Nicolet, Inc.*, 857 F.2d 202, 207–08 (3d Cir. 1988); *City of New York v. Exxon Corp.*, 932 F.2d 1020, 1024 (2d Cir. 1991); *CFTC v. Co Petro Mktg. Grp., Inc.*, 700 F.2d 1279, 1283 (9th Cir. 1983).

congressional intent.[18] This first recurring theme follows from the express provisions of the Bankruptcy Code and the United States Code manifesting congressional intent; it is analyzed throughout this Practice Guide.[19]

This distinction between health and safety obligations and financial or monetary liabilities was key to the result in *Midlantic Nat'l Bank v. New Jersey Dep't of Env't Prot.*, a seminal decision on harmonizing bankruptcy law and environmental law in the context of the proposed abandonment of contaminated property.[20] As recounted in a book and article by Professor Mann,[21] the decision in *Midlantic* was a very close call with the outcome in doubt until late in the Supreme Court's deliberations. Ultimately, the distinction between those obligations affecting public health and safety and those that were simply financial or monetary in nature was determinative to the Supreme Court's *Midlantic* opinion, which did not allow abandonment without conditions protecting public health and safety.[22]

Distinguishing between compliance obligations and monetary obligations is wise, because the reputation and beneficial work of the bankruptcy system could be undermined if the failure to require compliance resulted in a public health and safety disaster. Environmental harms could become associated in the public mind with a dysfunctional bankruptcy system. Moreover, bankruptcy courts often do not have the necessary expertise or time to second-guess compliance obligations. In contrast, issues about

18. *See, e.g.*, Chapter 2 (History and Purposes) *supra*; Chapters 7 (Proofs of Claim), 9 (Operating Estate Property) *infra*.

19. *See* 11 U.S.C. §§ 101(5), 362(b)(4); 28 U.S.C. § 959(b); Chapters 9 (Operating Estate Property), 10 (Police or Regulatory Exception), 11 (Compliance Obligations) *infra*. Some of the most difficult and interesting cases arise when governments and debtors disagree as to whether compliance obligations and/or monetary liabilities are at issue.

20. *Midlantic Nat'l Bank v. N.J. Dep't of Env't Prot.*, 474 U.S. 494 (1986), discussed more fully in Chapter 18 (Abandonment) *infra*.

21. Ronald J. Mann, *Balancing Bankruptcy and Environmental Law: Midlantic National Bank v. New Jersey Department of Environmental Protection*, 42 J. S. Ct. Hist. 101–17 (Mar. 2017); Ronald J. Mann, Bankruptcy and the Supreme Court 125–45 (2017).

22. *See* Mann, *supra* note 21, at 112–13. According to Professor Mann's summary, the Court voted at the original conference to permit abandonment but Justice Stevens had a change of heart because of his concern that abandonment could have public health consequences and was more than about who pays. He was also concerned about consistency with the Court's "normal preemption analysis." *Id.* at 113.

monetary liabilities, claims, debts, and judgments for money actually expended by environmental creditors are more straightforward and are covered by the generic provisions of the Bankruptcy Code that address all monetary liabilities, claims, debts, and judgments for money.[23] Although there are some exceptions,[24] Congress generally intended that such Bankruptcy Code provisions relating to monetary liabilities be applied to environmental creditors just as they would be to competing creditors. This is the bread and butter of bankruptcy courts and Congress wanted environmental creditors to participate in the bankruptcy process for monetary liabilities alongside other creditors and on generally similar terms.

PROPERTY OF THE BANKRUPTCY ESTATE

The second recurring theme in the cases harmonizing bankruptcy law and environmental law relates to differences in treatment based on whether or not an environmental issue involves property of the bankruptcy estate. When "property of the estate" is involved,[25] Section 959(b) of title 28 of the United States Code requires that it be managed and operated in accordance with nonbankruptcy law.[26] The Bankruptcy Code does not exempt debtors from all of the burdens and requirements "that generally applicable

23. *See, e.g.*, 11 U.S.C. §§ 101(5), 502; *Ohio v. Kovacs*, 469 U.S. 274, 283 (1985), where the Court held that, when the government had put the debtor into receivership, done the work itself, and solely sought repayment for its costs, it was clear that "the cleanup order had been converted into an obligation to pay money."

24. One partial exception is the police or regulatory exception to the automatic stay, which permits governments to proceed to judgment on monetary claims, but stays enforcement outside the bankruptcy process. 11 U.S.C. § 362(b)(4); Chapter 10 (Police or Regulatory Exception) *infra*. This partial exception derives from Congress's intent that bankruptcy courts not become a safe haven from law enforcement for defendants in police or regulatory cases seeking to avoid trials and entry of judgments meant to have a deterrent effect on wrongdoers. *See Nicolet*, 857 F.2d 202; *City of New York*, 932 F.2d 1020. However, in an attempt to harmonize regulatory and bankruptcy law purposes, Congress made the exception partial and stayed enforcement (i.e., collection) of the money judgment other than through the bankruptcy process. *See* Chapter 10 (Police or Regulatory Exception) *infra*.

25. Section 541 of the Bankruptcy Code defines property of the estate and is discussed further in Chapter 5 (Key Provisions (property of the estate)) *supra*.

26. *See* Chapter 9 (Operating Estate Property) *infra*.

law . . . imposes on property owners."[27] No one owning property "may maintain a nuisance . . . or refuse to remove the source of such conditions."[28] Property of the estate is administered and overseen by the debtor-in-possession or trustee and bankruptcy court as part of the bankruptcy case.[29] Indeed, even the debtor-in-possession or trustee may not want to see environmental damage or disaster result from violations of the law on their watch.[30]

However, whether property of the estate is involved is not always decisive to the outcome. As detailed in Chapter 11 (Compliance Obligations) of this Practice Guide, Section 101(5) of the Bankruptcy Code[31] carves out certain "equitable remedies" from its definition of "claim." Thus, even if an equitable environmental remedy such as a cleanup order does not relate to property of the estate, the environmental remedy may not be subject to aspects of bankruptcy law applicable to "claims," including discharge.[32] On the other hand, pre-petition response costs incurred by the government, including for cleaning up property of the estate, may be treated as general unsecured claims if the government does not have a security interest for its response costs given the language of the Bankruptcy Code governing monetary liabilities.[33]

Throughout this Practice Guide we will look at more specific examples of the harmonization of environmental law and bankruptcy law and how the courts, to date, have tried to resolve the "Clash of the Titans." By harmonizing these important bodies of law, courts have maximized the most beneficial provisions of each, resulting in a cleaner environment and protection of public health and safety while preserving viable economically distressed companies and jobs through corporate reorganization.

27. *Mission Products*, 139 S. Ct. 1652, 1665–66 (2019).

28. *Kovacs*, 469 U.S. at 285.

29. *See In re NP Mining Co.*, 963 F.2d 1449, 1458 (11th Cir. 1992) (noting as a significant factor that mining sites with violations were not property of the estate); *In re Globe Bldg. Materials, Inc.*, 345 B.R. 619, 640 (Bankr. N.D. Ind. 2006) (whether estate still owned storage tanks was determinative as to whether it could be ordered to abate hazards from seeping tanks).

30. Accordingly, many debtors and trustees will seek to cooperate with the government on environmental issues provided that the law provides a supporting basis.

31. 11 U.S.C. § 101(5).

32. *See* Chapter 11 (Compliance Obligations) *infra*.

33. *See* Chapter 12 (Priorities) *infra*.

CHAPTER 9

The Obligation to Comply with Nonbankruptcy Law in Managing and Operating Property of the Estate

This chapter examines Section 959(b) of Title 28 of the United States Code, 28 U.S.C. § 959(b), which actually is not part of the Bankruptcy Code (Title 11) itself, but whose statutory predecessors have been part of the United States Judicial Code (Title 28) since 1887.[1] This statutory provision is an important one for environmental bankruptcy cases and the interpretation of it has been critical in a number of cases, as it establishes that a filing for bankruptcy does not excuse compliance with the law. By its own wording, Section 959(b) entails two key concepts at the heart of environmental bankruptcy law as noted throughout this Practice Guide, the importance of: (1) the distinction between compliance obligations and monetary liabilities, and (2) determining whether an environmental issue pertains to property of the estate.[2]

---

1. *See* 28 U.S.C. §§ 124, 125 (1887); 28 U.S.C. §§ 124, 125 (1911); 28 U.S.C. § 959 (1948); *Diners Club, Inc. v. Bumb*, 421 F.2d 396 (9th Cir. 1970); *In re Jefferson Cnty.*, 484 B.R. 427, 457–59 (Bankr. N.D. Ala. 2012); Robert W. Miller, *A Comprehensive Framework for Conflict Preemption in Federal Insolvency Proceedings*, 123 W. Va. L. Rev. 423, 451 (2020).

2. *See* Chapter 8 (Harmonization) *supra*.

Importantly, Section 959(b) requires a trustee or debtor-in-possession to "manage and operate" the *property* in its possession "according to the requirements of the valid laws of the State in which such property is situated." Section 959(b) is a key indicator of Congress's intent that bankruptcy courts not become a safe haven or refuge for wrongdoers and scofflaws or provide debtors with immunity from compliance with police or regulatory statutes protecting public health and safety, including but not limited to environmental laws.[3] Courts have relied on this statute to hold that debtors and trustees must comply with environmental laws regulating their operations and property.[4] Thus, for example, a debtor operating in Chapter 11 must comply with environmental laws, including but not limited to the Resource Conservation and Recovery Act (RCRA), with respect to hazardous wastes it generates, and

3. *In re Steenes*, 918 F.3d 554, 558 (7th Cir. 2019); *In re Nortel Networks, Inc.*, 669 F.3d 128, 137 (3d Cir. 2011); *S.E.C. v. Brennan*, 230 F.3d 65, 71 (2d Cir. 2000); *In re Commonwealth Cos., Inc.*, 913 F.2d 518, 527 (8th Cir. 1990); *United States v. Nicolet, Inc.*, 857 F.2d 202, 207–08 (3d Cir. 1988); *City of New York v. Exxon Corp.*, 932 F.2d 1020, 1024 (2d Cir. 1991); *In re Commerce Oil Co.*, 847 F.2d 291, 297 (6th Cir. 1988); *Commodity Futures Trading Comm'n*, 700 F.2d 1279, 1283 (9th Cir. 1983); *Bickford v. Lodestar Energy, Inc.*, 310 B.R. 70, 76 (E.D. Ky. 2004); *United States v. ILCO, Inc.*, 48 B.R. 1016, 1023 (N.D. Ala. 1985). *See United States v. Wheeling-Pittsburgh Steel Co.*, 818 F.2d 1077, 1087 (3d Cir. 1987) (Defendant's "pending Chapter 11 status is not a basis on which the district court could have permissibly relied for its order relieving [defendant] of its obligation to comply with the relevant environmental statute, regulations and consent decree provisions.").

4. *In re H.L.S. Energy Co.*, 151 F.3d 434, 438 (5th Cir. 1998) (debtor must comply with Texas law requiring plugging wells that have not been productive for a year); *In re Wall Tube & Metal Prods. Co.*, 831 F.2d 118, 121–22 (6th Cir. 1987) (trustee had obligation to comply with Tennessee waste disposal statute which supported state's right to priority reimbursement of cleanup); *In re Jager*, 609 B.R. 156, 161 (Bankr. W.D. Pa. 2019) (upholding dismissal of case when debtors failed to remove manure piles from their property to comply with state water pollution laws); *In re Gollnitz*, 456 B.R. 733 (Bankr. W.D.N.Y. 2011) (Chapter 13 debtor must comply with New York's petroleum bulk storage laws at owned property); *Wilner Wood Prods. v. Maine*, 128 B.R. 1, 2–3 (D. Me. 1991) (debtor-in-possession must comply with air pollution laws and obtain permit if it wishes to continue to operate); *In re Am. Coastal Energy Inc.*, 399 B.R. 805, 810 (Bankr. S.D. Tex. 2009) (debtor was required to plug inactive wells); *In re Grace Coal Co.*, 155 B.R. 5, 6 (Bankr. E.D. Ky. 1993) (Kentucky could order Chapter 11 debtor to cease mining activities without a permit.); *In re Becker Indus. Corp.*, 57 B.R. 611, 624 (Bankr. S.D.N.Y. 1986) (Chapter 11 debtor must comply with laws regulating mine usage.); *In re Laurinburg Oil Co.*, 49 B.R. 652, 653–54 (Bankr. M.D.N.C. 1984) (state could require debtor to restore waste water lagoon to comply with state water pollution laws).

must maintain compliant financial assurance if the debtor wishes to continue its operations.[5]

Although Section 959(b) literally only refers to "laws of the State" where the property is situated, courts have interpreted Section 959(b) to apply to compliance obligations under federal laws as well.[6] These courts do not expressly address the statutory wording "valid laws of the State." However, federal laws are certainly valid and binding laws in all states and it would make no sense for a trustee or debtor-in-possession under federal bankruptcy law to have to comply with state laws but not federal laws applicable to its property.[7] If Congress meant for such an odd result, it would have expressly said so. This reasoning is consistent with the Supreme Court's analysis in *Midlantic National Bank v. New Jersey Department of Environmental Protection*, which specifically refers to "state and federal laws" in noting that if Congress wished to grant a

---

5. *In re Commonwealth Oil Refining Co.*, 805 F.2d 1175 (5th Cir. 1986) (RCRA and state law); *Safety-Kleen, Inc. (Pinewood) v. Wyche*, 274 F.3d 846 (4th Cir. 2001) (RCRA financial assurance).

6. *Mission Prod. Holdings, Inc. v. Tempnology, LLC*, 139 S. Ct. 1652, 1666 (2019) (trustee must manage estate "in accordance with applicable law" in a trademark case); *Safety-Kleen, Inc. (Pinewood) v. Wyche*, 274 F.3d at 864–66 (a Chapter 11 debtor could not avoid enforcement of RCRA, including financial assurance requirements during bankruptcy); *Commonwealth Oil*, 805 F.2d at 1185–86 (same); *see also Wheeling-Pittsburgh*, 818 F.2d at 1086 (a Chapter 11 debtor was obligated to comply with the Clean Air Act during bankruptcy); *Norris Square Civic Ass'n v. Saint Mary Hosp.*, 86 B.R. 393, 398 (E.D. Pa. 1988) ("28 U.S.C. § 959(b) requires a debtor to conform with applicable federal, state, and local law in conducting its business"); *In re Sewanee Land, Coal & Cattle, Inc.*, 34 B.R. 696, 697 (N.D. Ala. 1983) (the bankruptcy court's injunction of the Department of the Interior's closure of an unpermitted mining operation violated section 959(b)); *In re Am. Coastal Energy Inc.*, 399 B.R. at 810 ("Bankruptcy debtors are no different from any citizen in that they must comply with state and federal laws."); *In re Trans World Airlines, Inc.*, 275 B.R. 712, 722 (Bankr. D. Del. 2002) ("A debtor which continues to operate post-petition is obligated to do so in accordance with its other legal obligations. To fail to do so may subject the debtor to suit.").

7. Moreover, many environmental laws such as RCRA, the Clean Air Act, and the Clean Water Act are partially delegated to states as lead. State environmental regulations are the applicable law under these circumstances and EPA as well as states may enforce them. *See, e.g.*, 33 U.S.C. § 1319 (Clean Water Act); 42 U.S.C. §§ 6924(u), (v), 6925(c)(3), 6928 (RCRA); 42 U.S.C. § 9413 (Clean Air Act).

trustee "an extraordinary exemption from nonbankruptcy law" its intention would have been clearly expressed.[8]

The courts, though, are split on the question of whether Section 959(b) applies to Chapter 7 trustees or liquidating debtors who are not actively operating a business.[9] In *Midlantic*, the Supreme Court cited to, but did not explicitly rely on, Section 959(b) in holding that a Chapter 7 trustee could not abandon property in violation of environmental laws and that the Bankruptcy Code did not preempt state laws designed to protect public health or safety from identified hazards.[10] The Supreme Court's citation to Section 959(b) in *Midlantic*, a case involving a liquidating debtor, suggests that Section 959(b) applies to a liquidating debtor. In *Kovacs*,[11] which also was a Chapter 7 case (although of an individual debtor), the Supreme Court, without citing to Section 959(b), stated that it did not question "that anyone in possession of the [hazardous waste] site [including] the bankruptcy trustee must comply with the environmental laws of the State. . . . Plainly that person or firm may not maintain a nuisance, pollute the waters of the State or refuse to remove the source of such conditions."

Nevertheless, several courts have stated that Section 959(b) only applies to operating businesses, and not to liquidating businesses where the trustees or debtors-in-possession are only

---

8. *Midlantic Nat'l Bank v. N.J. Dep't of Env't Prot.*, 474 U.S. 494, 501 (1986). *See In re St. Lawrence Corp.*, 248 B.R. 734, 739 n.4 (D.N.J. 2000) (debtors may not violate federal laws by abandonment).

9. *Compare, e.g.*, *Wall Tube*; *HLS Energy*; *In re Stevens*, 68 B.R. 774, 781 (D. Me. 1997); *In re Coal Stripping, Inc.*, 222 B.R. 78 (Bankr. W.D. Pa. 1998), *with In re N.P. Mining*, 963 F.2d 1449, 1460–61 (11th Cir. 1992); *SEC v. Wealth Mgmt., LLC*, 628 F.3d 323, 334 (7th Cir. 2010); *In re Valley Steel Prods. Co.*, 157 B.R. 442, 447–49 (E.D. Mo. 1993); *In re Globe Bldg. Materials Inc.*, 345 B.R. 619, 637 (Bankr. N.D. Ind. 2006); *In re St. Lawrence Corp.*, 239 B.R. 720, 725 (Bankr. D.N.J. 1999). It should be noted that the statements in some of the cases finding that section 959 does not apply to liquidations are actually dicta because either: (1) property of the estate may not have been involved, or (2) the issue before the court was a bankruptcy priority issue relating to a claim rather than a direct question of whether a bankruptcy estate had to comply with nonbankruptcy law.

10. *Midlantic* was an abandonment case that is discussed further in Chapter 18 (Abandonment) *infra*.

11. *Ohio v. Kovacs*, 469 U.S. 274, 285 (1985). In *Kovacs*, the individual debtor no longer owned the property in question because his assets had been placed in receivership. *Kovacs* is discussed further in Chapter 11 (Compliance Obligations) *infra*.

maintaining the status quo until estate assets can be distributed to creditors.[12] Governments have disagreed with such rulings because they ignore that the express language of Section 959(b) provides that trustees and debtors-in-possession "shall manage *and* operate" their property in accordance with valid laws of the state. If Congress had meant for this provision only to apply to trustees or debtors-in-possession that "operate" a business, Congress would not have also used the word "manage" in addition to the word "operate."[13] Moreover, Section 959(a), a preceding subsection of the same statute, uses the more limited wording "acts or transactions in carrying on business connected with such property" when permitting suits against trustees outside of the appointing court. If Congress had wanted to limit compliance with nonbankruptcy law in Section 959(b) to operating businesses it could have used the more limited language it employed in Section 959(a).[14] Debtors might contend that Section 959(b) does not apply to the actual process of liquidating property, including those activities leading up to liquidation, since, they would argue, such liquidation-related activities are not within the meaning of "management."[15] However, the converse argument made by governmental agencies is that Section 959(b) requires that the bankruptcy estate manage its property in accordance with nonbankruptcy law pending actual liquidation.[16] In addition, governmental agencies would note that interpreting Section 959(b) as being inapplicable to the management of property in advance of liquidation would be at odds with the rules of

12. *See, e.g.*, *NP Mining* and certain other cases in note 9 *supra*.

13. As noted in Miller, *supra* note 1, at 451 (citing Merriam-Webster.com), the dictionary definition of manage is "to handle or direct with a degree of skill."

14. Indeed, even where Congress used clearer language in 28 U.S.C. § 960(a) ("conducting any business"), the Supreme Court still found that liquidating entities were required to pay state taxes because even this language was not clear enough to create an exemption from state law applicable to property. *Cal. State Bd. of Equalization v. Sierra Summit, Inc.*, 490 U.S. 844 (1989). *See* Miller, *supra* note 1, at 480–81.

15. However, *In re Highland Capital Mgtmt.*, L.P., 48 F.4th 419, 432–33 (5th Cir. 2022), the Fifth Circuit held that winding down a business after confirmation constituted engaging in business within the meaning of 11 U.S.C. § 1141(d)(3) (no discharge for liquidating debtor that does not engage in business after confirmation). If winding down a business for purposes of liquidation constitutes engaging in business, then it may be considered operation or management of the business as well.

16. For a thorough critique of those cases holding that section 959(b) does not apply to liquidations, *see* Miller, *supra* note 1, at 474–81.

harmonization of conflicting statutes set forth in Chapter 8 (Harmonization) of this Practice Guide because such an interpretation would ignore the express language of Section 959(b) (which evidences Congress' intent) as well as the established presumption of not disturbing laws protecting public health and safety absent clear language.[17]

In any event, although there are still areas of controversy, Section 959(b) is broadly applied and provides a strong guidepost to courts in harmonizing bankruptcy and environmental law.

17. *See* Chapter 8 (Harmonization) *supra*.

CHAPTER 10

The Police or Regulatory Exception to the Automatic Stay

GENERAL DISCUSSION

This chapter reviews the police or regulatory exception to the bankruptcy automatic stay, codified at 11 U.S.C. § 362(b)(4). The exception is a key statutory provision by which Congress expressed its intent to distinguish the treatment of compliance obligations (obligations to take action) and monetary claims (obligations to pay money) in bankruptcy.[1]

As explained in Chapter 2 of this Practice Guide, the bankruptcy automatic stay provides a debtor with breathing room to try to reorder its affairs and obtain a fresh start through the bankruptcy process while preserving the status quo for an orderly allocation of its assets. But there are important exceptions for police or regulatory actions.

The major components of the bankruptcy automatic stay are as follows: 11 U.S.C. § 362(a)(1) stays the commencement or continuation of judicial proceedings that were or could have been

1. *See* Chapters 8 (Harmonization), 9 (Operating Estate Property) *supra*.

commenced before the petition was filed; 11 U.S.C. § 362(a)(2) stays the enforcement of judgments obtained before the petition was filed; 11 U.S.C. § 362(a)(3) stays acts to obtain possession of or exercise control over property of the estate; 11 U.S.C. § 362(a)(4) and (5) stay acts to create, perfect, or enforce liens; and 11 U.S.C. § 362(a)(6) stays acts to collect, assess, or recover claims that arose before the petition was filed.[2]

Although the provisions cited here provide debtors with some breathing space, Congress did not intend for bankruptcy courts to become a refuge for wrongdoers and scofflaws or to provide immunity to debtors from complying with laws and regulations of general applicability, including environmental regulatory statutes protecting public health and safety by allowing the automatic stay to bar or delay environmental proceedings.[3] Congress thus harmonized these conflicting policy goals through the police or regulatory exception to the automatic stay, which enables federal and state environmental agencies to continue to enforce their police and regulatory powers through the pendency of the bankruptcy proceeding.[4]

The police or regulatory exception in Section 362(b)(4) provides that the automatic stay does not apply to the:

> commencement or continuation of an action or proceeding by a governmental unit . . . to enforce such governmental unit's . . . police and regulatory power, including the enforcement of a judgment other than a money judgment, obtained in an action or

---

2. *See* Chapter 2 (History and Purposes) *supra.* The automatic stay does not preclude informational notices about a debtor's environmental liability so long as there is no coercion or harassment amounting to an act to collect a debt. *LTV Corp. v. Gulf States Steel, Inc.*, 969 F.2d 1050, 1059 (D.C. Cir. 1992).

3. *In re Steenes*, 918 F.3d 554, 558 (7th Cir. 2019); *In re Nortel Networks, Inc.*, 669 F.3d 128, 137 (3d Cir. 2011); *S.E.C. v. Brennan*, 230 F.3d 65, 71 (2d Cir. 2000); *In re Commonwealth Cos., Inc.*, 913 F.2d 518, 527 (8th Cir. 1990); *City of New York v. Exxon Corp.*, 932 F.2d 1020, 1024 (2d Cir. 1991); *United States v. Nicolet, Inc.*, 857 F.2d 202, 207–08 (3d Cir. 1988); *In re Commerce Oil Co.*, 847 F.2d 291, 297 (6th Cir. 1988); *Commodity Futures Trading Comm'n v. Co Petro Mktg. Grp.*, 700 F.2d 1279, 1283 (9th Cir. 1983); *Bickford v. Lodestar Energy, Inc.*, 310 B.R. 70, 76 (E.D. Ky. 2004); *United States v. ILCO, Inc.*, 48 B.R. 1016, 1023 (N.D. Ala. 1985).

4. *See* Chapter 8 (Harmonization) *supra.* The exception was adopted in 1978 in response to bankruptcy courts' stretching the automatic stay so as to interfere with the enforcement of environmental laws. *Midlantic Nat'l Bank v. N.J. Dep't of Env't Prot.*, 474 U.S. 494, 504 (1986).

proceeding by the governmental unit to enforce such governmental unit's or organization's police or regulatory power.

By its terms, the exception applies only to 11 U.S.C. § 362(a)(1), (2), (3), and (6), and does not apply to the stay of actions to enforce a money judgment. The police or regulatory exception does not apply to Section 362(a)(4) and (5)'s stay of actions to create, perfect, or enforce liens.[5] Thus, the police or regulatory exception not only harmonizes environmental and bankruptcy law, it also is an important example of the distinction between enforcing compliance obligations and monetary claims.[6]

The first issue to consider when evaluating the applicability of the police or regulatory exception is to determine whether a particular governmental[7] action is police or regulatory. Most courts of

---

5. However, the Bankruptcy Code does permit the perfection of superliens under statutes providing priority over prior filed liens. *See* 11 U.S.C. §§ 362(b)(3), 546(b); *In re 229 Main St. Ltd. P'ship*, 262 F.3d 1 (1st Cir. 2001); *In re Perona Bros., Inc.*, 186 B.R. 833 (D.N.J. 1995); *In re Microfab, Inc.*, 105 B.R. 152 (Bankr. D. Mass. 1989).

6. It should be noted that Section 362(b)(4) was amended in 1998 to combine former subsections 362(b)(4) and 362(b)(5), and to clarify that it applies to Section 362(a)(3) and (6) as well as (a)(1) and (a)(2). The stay exception in Section 362(b)(4) initially only applied to Section 362(a)(1) and a separate exception in Section 362(b)(5) applied to Section 362(a)(2). *See* 105 Cong. Rec. H10950-01 (Nov. 13, 1997); *In re Allegheny Health Educ. & Rsch. Found.*, 252 B.R. 309 (W.D. Pa. 1999). Older case law thus sometimes refers to Section 363(b)(5) as well as (b)(4) even though (b)(5) was repealed and integrated into (b)(4) in 1998. Courts have held that given the lack of significant change to the language of the exception, prior case law is generally still applicable. *In re United States v. Alsol Corp.*, 2014 WL 46775, at *4 n.4 (D.N.J. 2014); *In re Fairchild*, 2009 WL 4546581, at *4 n.19 (Bankr. D. Del. 2009); *In re Burns*, 2008 WL 3246244, at *2 n.4 (Bankr. M.D. Pa. 2008); *Mohawk Greenfield Motel Corp.*, 239 B.R. 1, 5 n.6 (Bankr. D. Mass. 1999).

7. The Bankruptcy Code defines "governmental unit" as including, inter alia, the United States, States, and municipalities, agencies thereof, and any "other foreign or domestic government." 11 U.S.C. § 101(27). At least for purposes of determining whether Congress waived sovereign immunity of tribes, courts have disagreed as to whether or not tribes fall under "other domestic government." *Compare Meyers v. Oneida Tribe of Indians of Wisconsin*, 836 F.3d 818 (7th Cir. 2016) (not included), *and In re Greektown Holdings, LLC*, 917 F.3d 451 (6th Cir. 2019) (not included), *with In re Coughlin*, 33 F.4th 600 (1st Cir. 2022) (included), *and Krystal Energy Co. v. Navajo Nation*, 357 F.3d 1055 (9th Cir. 2004) (included). Courts have held that citizen groups seeking to enforce environmental laws on behalf of the government may not proceed under the police or regulatory exception, *United States v. Env't Waste Control, Inc.*, 131 B.R. 410 (N.D. Ind. 1991); *In re Chateaugay Corp.*, 118 B.R. 19 (Bankr. S.D.N.Y. 1990); *In re Revere Copper & Brass, Inc.*, 28 B.R. 584 (Bankr. S.D.N.Y.), *aff'd*, 32 B.R. 725 (S.D.N.Y. 1983). However, bankruptcy courts have nonetheless sometimes granted a request to lift the automatic stay so that a citizens group could

appeal have established specific tests to evaluate whether a governmental action is police or regulatory. Generally speaking, two tests have developed. The first is called the "pecuniary advantage" or "pecuniary interest" test; the second is called the "public purpose" or "public policy" test. Courts in each circuit have adopted slightly different versions of one or both of these tests.[8] Under the pecuniary advantage or interest test, courts consider whether the purpose of a governmental action is to advance the government's pecuniary interest, or instead to protect public health and safety and the general welfare.[9] Under the public purpose test, courts consider whether the government is seeking to effectuate public policy or merely adjudicate private rights.[10] Under either test, the government's primary purpose governs over any secondary interests or motivations.[11] Actions under environmental laws have generally been found to have public purposes to protect public health and safety and that any pecuniary interests, if any, to be at most secondary.[12] As the Third Circuit held in *Penn Terra*, when

---

proceed under the applicable test for lifting the stay. *See, e.g.*, *In re Edison Mission Energy*, 502 B.R. 830 (N.D. Ill. 2013).

8. *In re Kupperstein*, 994 F.3d 673 (1st Cir. 2021); *Parkview Adventist Med. Ctr. v. United States*, 842 F.3d 757 (1st Cir. 2016); *In re Spookyworld, Inc.*, 346 F.3d 1 (1st Cir. 2003); *In re Methyl Tertiary Butyl Ether Prods. Liab. Litig.*, 488 F.3d 112, 133 (2d Cir. 2007); *In re Nortel Networks, Inc.*, 669 F.3d 128, 139–40 (3d Cir. 2011); *Safety-Kleen, Inc.(Pinewood) v. Wyche*, 274 F.3d 846, 865 (4th Cir. 2001); *In re Halo Wireless, Inc.*, 684 F.3d 581 (5th Cir. 2012); *Chao v. Hosp. Staffing Servs., Inc.*, 270 F.3d 374 (6th Cir. 2001); *In re Commerce Oil Co.*, 847 F.2d 291, 295 (6th Cir. 1988); *In re Fulton*, 926 F.3d 916 (7th Cir. 2019); *In re Commonwealth Cos.*, 913 F.2d 518 (8th Cir. 1990); *Lockyer v. Mirant Corp.*, 398 F.3d 1098 (9th Cir. 2005); *Edelman v. United States Dep't of Labor*, 923 F.2d 782 (10th Cir. 1991); *Brock v. Rusco Indus., Inc.*, 842 F.2d 270 (11th Cir. 1988).

9. *See* cases cited note 8 *supra*.

10. *See* cases cited note 8 *supra*. The two tests are overlapping and in many courts, if either test is met, the action falls under the police or regulatory exception. *See, e.g.*, *Mirant*, 398 F.3d at 1108.

11. *Commerce Oil*, 847 F.2d at 296; *Bickford v. Lodestar*, 310 B.R. 70, 77–78 (E.D. Ky. 2004); *In re Yellow Cab Coop Ass'n*, 132 F.2d 591, 597 (10th Cir. 1997); *In re Universal Life Church, Inc.*, 128 F.3d 1294, 1298–99 (9th Cir. 1997).

12. *See Safety-Kleen*, 274 F.3d 846 (RCRA); *In re Hemingway Transp., Inc.*, 993 F.2d 915 (1st Cir. 1993) (CERCLA); *City of New York v. Exxon Corp.*, 932 F.2d. 1020 (2d Cir. 1991) (CERCLA); *Nicolet, Inc.*, 857 F.2d 202 (CERCLA); *Commerce Oil Co.*, 847 F.2d 291 (Tennessee Water Control Act); *United States v. Wheeling-Pittsburgh Steel Corp.*, 818 F.2d 1077 (3d Cir. 1987) (Clean Air Act); *In re Commonwealth Oil Ref. Co.*, 805 F.2d 1175 (5th Cir. 1986) (RCRA); *United States v. Jones & Laughlin Steel Corp.*, 804 F.2d 348 (6th Cir. 1986) (Clean Air Act); *United States v. Oil Transp. Co.*, 172

addressing an action for reclamation for environmental violations by a mining company, "[n]o more obvious exercise of the State's power to protect the health, safety, and welfare of the public can be imagined."[13] The legislative history for the police or regulatory exception specifically refers to environmental protection laws as falling under the police or regulatory exception.[14] The express language of the exception applies to all police or regulatory actions and is therefore not limited to situations threatening imminent and identifiable harm or urgent public necessity or actions involving property of the estate.[15] In determining the threshold issue of whether a matter is police or regulatory, a court should not scrutinize the validity or merits of the governmental action as part of its initial determination.[16]

It is well settled that the tribunal in which a matter is pending has concurrent jurisdiction with the bankruptcy court to determine applicability of the police or regulatory exception to the

---

B.R. 834 (E.D. La. 1994) (Oil Pollution Act); *In re Mateer*, 205 B.R. 915 (C.D. Ill. 1997) (Illinois Environmental Protection Act); *United States v. Mattiace Indus. Inc.*, 73 B.R. 816 (E.D.N.Y. 1987) (CERCLA); *United States v. Standard Metals Corp.*, 49 B.R. 623 (D. Colo. 1985) (Clean Water Act); *In re Gandy*, 327 B.R. 796 (Bankr. S.D. Tex. 2005) (Solid Waste Disposal Act and Clean Air Act); *In re Lenz Oil Service, Inc.*, 65 B.R. 292 (Bankr. N.D. Ill. 1986) (hazardous waste cleanup). However, (1) an action to collect recycling fees that were unconnected to violations and were reimbursements for services provided, *In re Iezzi*, 504 B.R. 777, 788 (Bankr. E.D. Pa. 2014), and (2) a state water district's action that was akin to a private suit for money, *In re Fairchild Corp.*, 2009 WL 4546581 (Bankr. D. Del. 2009), were found to be pecuniary actions outside of the police or regulatory exception.

13. *Penn Terra Ltd. v. Dep't of Env't Res.*, 733 F.2d 267, 272 (3d Cir. 1984) ("It is indisputable that the Commonwealth is normally empowered to regulate the environment, in its role as protector of the public health and welfare."). *See also Nicolet, Inc.*, 857 F.2d at 208–09 (citing *Midlantic*, 474 U.S. at 503–04, and *Wheeling-Pittsburgh*, 818 F.2d at 1086) (exception applies to enforcement of compliance with federal environmental laws).

14. "Thus, where a governmental unit is suing a debtor to prevent or stop violation of fraud, *environmental protection*, consumer protection, safety or similar police or regulatory laws, or attempting to fix damages for violation of such law, the action or proceeding is not stayed under the automatic stay." H.R. Rep. No. 95-595 at 343; S. Rep. No. 95-989 at 52 (italics added).

15. *See, e.g.*, *In re Commonwealth Companies, Inc.*, 913 F.2d 518, 522 (8th Cir. 1990); *In re Commonwealth Oil Ref.*, 805 F.2d at 1184; *Nicolet*, 857 F.2d at 209; *California ex rel. Brown v. Villalbos*, 453 B.R. 404, 411 (D. Nev. 2011); *Hagman v. New Jersey*, 151 B.R. 696, 699 (D.N.J. 1993).

16. *Bd. of Governors of the Fed. Reserve Sys. v. MCorp. Fin., Inc.*, 502 U.S. 32, 40 (1991); *In re Gandy*, 327 B.R. at 805–06; *In re Enron Corp.*, 314 B.R. 524, 535 (Bankr. S.D.N.Y. 2004).

automatic stay.[17] No ruling from the bankruptcy court is necessary because the exception, like the stay itself, is automatic, and a stay therefore does not need to be lifted since the stay never applied in the first place.[18] Although state courts and administrative tribunals also have jurisdiction to adjudicate whether the exception applies to matters before them, there is some risk that a debtor might later seek to collaterally attack an adverse ruling in bankruptcy court.[19] In such a dispute, the state government would emphasize principles of res judicata and contend that that the state court or administrative tribunal was only interpreting and applying the exception to the facts before it.[20] A debtor could contend that the state court or administrative tribunal was acting contrary to the automatic stay so that the ruling was void ab initio or should be voided.[21] In close cases, it may be prudent and provide comfort for the government to seek a declaratory ruling from the bankruptcy court regarding applicability of the police or regulatory exception to a particular action, but if it is determined that the stay applies, then only the bankruptcy court has authority to lift the stay.[22]

Once a court has determined that a matter is police or regulatory and thus fits within the exception to the automatic stay, then

17. *Lockyer v. Mirant Corp.*, 398 F.3d 1098, 1106 (9th Cir. 2005); *Chao v. Hosp. Staffing Servs., Inc.*, 270 F.3d 374, 384–85 (6th Cir. 2001); *Picco v. Global Marine Drilling Co.*, 900 F.2d 846, 850 (5th Cir. 1990); *Brock v. Morysville Body Works, Inc.*, 829 F.2d 383, 387 (3d Cir. 1987); *NLRB v. Edward Cooper Painting, Inc.*, 804 F.2d 934, 936 (6th Cir. 1996); *Hunt v. Bankers Trust Co.*, 799 F.2d 1060, 1069 (5th Cir. 1986); *In re Baldwin-United Corp.*, 765 F.2d 343, 347 (2d Cir. 1985).

18. *See Lockyer*, 398 F.3d at 1107; *Edward Cooper*, 804 F.2d at 939. If the matter is raised in both jurisdictions, the first-filed rule should govern which jurisdiction will decide the issue. *See City of New York v. Exxon Corp.*, 932 F.2d 1020, 1026 (2d Cir. 1991); *Baldwin-United Corp. Litig.*, 765 F.2d at 349.

19. *See Gandy*, 327 B.R. at 801; *In re Gruntz*, 202 F.3d 1074 (9th Cir. 2000). *But see Inn World Report, Inc. v. MB Financial Bank NA*, 2022 WL 17841529 (2d Cir. Dec. 20, 2022) (disagreeing with *Gruntz*).

20. *Picco*, 900 F.2d at 850. *See also Durfee v. Duke*, 375 U.S. 106 (1963) (where court had jurisdiction to determine its jurisdiction that decision was not subject to collateral attack); *In re Athens/Alpha Gas Corp.*, 715 F.3d 230 (8th Cir. 2013) (applying *Durfee* in bankruptcy); *Inn World Report*, 2022 WL 17841529 Karen Cordry, *The Ninth Circuit and Gruntz,* 2000 Norton Bankr. L. Advisor 1; Chapter 20 (Jurisdiction) *infra* (under Rooker-Feldman doctrine federal courts do not have appellate authority over decisions of state courts acting within their jurisdiction).

21. *ACandS, Inc. v. Travelers Cas. & Sur. Co.*, 435 F.3d 252, 261 (3d Cir. 2006); *In re Dunbar*, 245 F.3d 1058, 1063 (9th Cir. 2001) (relying on *Gruntz*, 202 F.3d at 1080–84).

22. *Gandy*, 327 B.R. at 801.

the scope of relief that can be obtained depends on whether the government is pursuing injunctive relief, cost recovery, penalties, or financial assurance.

INJUNCTIVE RELIEF

Police or regulatory actions for injunctive relief such as an action to require compliance with regulatory requirements or compelling site cleanup may proceed to judgment and the judgments can also be enforced because Section 362(b)(4) expressly allows for the "enforcement of a [police or regulatory] judgment other than a money judgment."[23] The Bankruptcy Code does not define "money judgment"; courts therefore look to the term's traditional or common definition or understanding.[24] Traditionally, money judgments are for a definite sum certain and they typically compensate a party for past wrongful acts as opposed to seeking protection against potential future harm.[25] The courts have held that, notwithstanding that compliance actions will often cost money, judgments

23. *Penn Terra Ltd. v. Dep't of Env't Res.*, 733 F.2d 267, 275 (3d Cir. 1984) (state mining laws); *In re Commonwealth Oil Ref. Co.*, 805 F.2d 1175 (5th Cir. 1986) (RCRA); *United States v. Jones & Laughlin Steel Corp.*, 804 F.2d 348 (6th Cir. 1986 (CWA and CAA); *United States v. Tronox Pigments (Savannah), Inc.*, 2009 WL 256459 (S.D. Ga. 2009) (CAA, CWA, RCRA, CERCLA); *New York v. Mirant N.Y., Inc.*, 300 B.R. 174 (S.D.N.Y. 2003) (CAA); *In re Madison Indus., Inc.*, 161 B.R. 363 (D.N.J. 1993) (RCRA); *United States v. ILCO, Inc.*, 48 B.R. 1016 (N.D. Ala. 1985) (RCRA); *Illinois v. Elec. Utils.*, 41 B.R. 874 (N.D. Ill. 1984) (TSCA); *In re Fernandez*, 2010 WL 731672 (Bankr. S.D. Fla. 2010) (state law); *In re Gandy*, 327 B.R. 796 (CAA and state Solid Waste Disposal Act); *United States v. Pharmacia Corp.*, No. 02-0749 (N.D. Ala. Sept. 9, 2004) (CERCLA); *In re Norwesco Dev. Corp.*, 68 B.R. 123 (Bankr. W.D. Pa. 1986) (state water laws); *In re Williston Oil Corp.*, 54 B.R. 10 (Bankr. D.N.J. 1984) (state law); *In re Laurinburg Oil Co.*, 49 B.R. 652 (Bankr. M.D.N.C. 1984) (state water laws). *See also United States v. HVI Cat Canyon, Inc.*, No. CV-11-5097 (C.D. Cal. Aug. 26, 2019) (CWA and OPA); *United States v. RG Steel Wheeling, LLC*, No. 12-00019 (N.D. W. Va. July 9, 2012) (CAA and RCRA).

24. *See, e.g., Penn Terra.*, 733 F.2d at 275; Adam M. Back, *Crossroads: The Collision of Bankruptcy's Automatic Stay and Environmental Law's Injunctive Relief*, 20 J. Nat. Res. & Env't L. 103, 110–13 (2005–06).

25. *In re Commonwealth Oil Ref.*, 805 F.2d at 1186; *Penn Terra*, 733 F.2d at 276–77; *United States v. Price*, 688 F.2d 204, 212 (3d Cir. 1982); *In re Security Gas & Oil, Inc.*, 70 B.R. 786, 790–91 (Bankr. N.D. Cal. 1987). *See also Cournoyer v. Town of Lincoln*, 790 F.2d 971, 976 (1st Cir. 1986). Courts have reached similar conclusions as to the meaning of the term "money judgment" under other statutory provisions. *See, e.g., Eaves v. County of Cape May*, 239 F.3d 527, 533 (3d Cir. 2001) (collecting cases).

requiring such actions are not traditional money judgments, and therefore enforcement of such judgments is not stayed.[26] Likewise, regulatory requirements can be enforced because they are not money judgments.[27]

It should be noted that notwithstanding the preceding discussion, debtors may contend that cleanup orders and judgments are money judgments if the government has the potential to convert or reduce them to money judgments.[28] Most governments would likely vigorously contest such contentions as contrary to the plain meaning of the statute. Nonetheless, where a debtor is expected to dispute whether an action for injunctive relief or compliance falls within the police or regulatory exception, it may be prudent for the government to seek a declaratory ruling regarding applicability of the police or regulatory exception from the forum in which the police or regulatory action is pending or in the bankruptcy court if time permits.[29]

---

26. *See, e.g., Commonwealth Oil Ref.*, 805 F.2d at 1183–84; *Penn Terra*, 733 F.2d at 274–78; *Security Gas & Oil*, 70 B.R. at 790–92; *Lenz Oil Service, Inc.*, 65 B.R. at 294; *ILCO*, 48 B.R. at 1023–24. As noted by these courts, the police or regulatory exception would otherwise "be narrowed into virtual nonexistence," *Penn Terra*, 733 F.2d at 277–78, as almost all regulatory requirements necessitate some expenditures in order to comply. However, one court has held that where the government actually sought in the alternative an award of damages equal to the cost of cleanup, the government was seeking to enforce a monetary claim which was stayed. *In re Goodwin*, 163 B.R. 825, 826 (Bankr. D. Idaho 1993). This court found the matter fully stayed because at that time the police or regulatory exception did not apply to attempts to collect claims which fell within 11 U.S.C. 362(a)(6)'s stay of collection of claims. *Id.* at 829. Congress clarified that the exception does apply to (a)(6) in 1998, *see* note 6 *supra*.

27. *See, e.g., In re Commonwealth Oil Ref.*, 805 F.2d 1175 (RCRA compliance); *Cournoyer v. Town of Lincoln*, 790 F.2d 971 (zoning requirements); *In re Albion Disposal, Inc.*, 203 B.R. 884 (Bankr. W.D.N.Y. 1996) (landfill regulations); *In re Scotia Dev., LLC*, 2007 WL 1192137 (Bankr. S.D. Tex. 2007) (clean water regulations for logging company); *In re Beker Industries Corp.*, 57 B.R. 611 (Bankr. S.D.NY. 1986) (mining regulations).

28. This is similar to the argument debtors make as to why they believe some cleanup orders are dischargeable bankruptcy claims. This argument is discussed in Chapter 11 (Compliance Obligations) *infra*.

29. By seeking such a ruling, the government keeps the focus on the protection of public health and safety and prevents debtors from obscuring or diverting attention from their violations by raising allegations of violation of the automatic stay by the government. However, there may not always be time to seek a court ruling where time is of the essence in order to protect public health and safety. Obtaining such a ruling is not necessary since the police or regulatory exception operates automatically. Seeking such a ruling may be useful for state agencies which intend

If an action exercising police or regulator power is not yet pending, consideration should also be given as to whether to file an action by adversary proceeding in bankruptcy court rather than in the forum that would otherwise have jurisdiction.[30] On the one hand, bankruptcy courts are often able to act faster than other forums. On the other hand, bankruptcy courts may be perceived as having less environmental expertise than the alternative forum or as being more concerned with the debtor and monetary creditors than with protection of public health and safety.[31] If the government chooses to proceed in bankruptcy court, the vast majority of courts have held that a filing in the bankruptcy court does not itself violate the automatic stay.[32] Questions may be raised as to whether the bankruptcy court has jurisdiction to hear such substantive matters, but arguably there is either "related to" jurisdiction or jurisdiction under federal environmental law given that bankruptcy courts are units of district courts.[33]

---

to proceed in state forums because it will alleviate the risk of a collateral attack on state proceedings. *See* notes 19–21 *supra.*

30. For examples of environmental actions filed in bankruptcy court as adversary proceedings, *see, e.g., W. Va. Dep't of Env't Prot. v. Revelation Energy, LLC,* Adv. Proc. No. 3:20-3002 (Bankr. S.D. W. Va. 2020) (Main Case—*In re Blackjewel, LLC,* No. 19-30289 (Bankr. S.D. W. Va.)); *In re Outboard Marine Corp.*, 2004 WL 1254128 (N.D. Ill. June 7, 2004); *In re Globe Bldg. Materials, Inc.*, 345 B.R. 619 (Bankr. N.D. Ind. 2006).

31. Additional cost may be a factor for some state agencies if the bankruptcy case is filed out of state. In addition to travel costs, some bankruptcy court local rules require the hiring of local counsel. State agencies may also wish to consider whether filing an adversary proceeding in bankruptcy may result in a waiver of sovereign immunity under the Eleventh Amendment relating to matters raised. *See* Chapter 5 (Key Provisions (sovereign immunity)) *supra.* Consideration should be given to the litigation risks presented as well. In *In re Venoco LLC,* 572 B.R. 105, 114–15 (Bankr. D. Del. 2017), the court denied a request for injunctive relief against a liquidating debtor because it believed that public health was not at risk, the site was not property of the estate, and the liability was a claim because money had been sought to be held as a reserve.

32. *See, e.g., In re Bird,* 229 B.R. 90, 95 (Bankr. S.D.N.Y. 1999). *But see In re Roman Catholic Church of Archdiocese of Santa Fe,* 627 B.R. 916 (Bankr. D.N.M. 2021) (noting but disagreeing with majority rule). Regardless of where filed, the complaint can seek a declaration that the action falls under the police or regulatory exception to the automatic stay.

33. *See* Chapter 20 (Jurisdiction) *infra.* If proceeding under "related to" jurisdiction, the bankruptcy court may need to make recommended findings and conclusions of law unless the parties consent to judgment by the bankruptcy court. *See id.* This could slow down the proceedings. Where a state proceeds under state law, if the bankruptcy court is unwilling to hear the matter, it may abstain in favor of a state court proceeding under 28 U.S.C. § 1334(c).

COST RECOVERY CLAIMS

Courts have permitted cost recovery actions under CERCLA to proceed to judgment outside of bankruptcy court (but not enforcement of the judgment) notwithstanding the automatic stay of Section 362(a) of the Bankruptcy Code.[34] Actions for the recovery of response costs under Section 107 of CERCLA are viewed by the courts as exercises of police or regulatory power under the exception of Section 362(b)(4). Courts have pointed out that such actions are an effective deterrent to potential polluters who realize that they will be held responsible to reimburse the government's costs of cleanup of contamination they have caused.[35] The legislative history for the police or regulatory exception specifically provides that it was meant to include "attempting to fix damages" for violations of environmental protection laws.[36] Thus, a cost recovery action can be pursued to judgment even after a bankruptcy petition has been filed, but the judgment can then only be enforced through the process for monetary claims in the bankruptcy proceeding.[37]

---

34. *City of New York v. Exxon Corp.*, 932 F.2d 1020 (2d Cir. 1991) (CERCLA); *United States v. Nicolet, Inc.*, 857 F.2d 202 (3d Cir. 1988) (CERCLA); *see, e.g., In re Mystic Tank Lines Corp.*, 544 F.3d 524, 527 (3d Cir. 2008); *In re Hemingway Transp., Inc.*, 993 F.2d 915, 924 n.8 (1st Cir. 1993); *Commerce Oil*, 847 F.2d at 296; *In re Commonwealth Oil Ref. Co.*, 805 F.2d 1175, 1186 n.12 (5th Cir. 1986); *United States v. Fed. Res. Corp.*, 525 B.R. 759, 766–67 (D. Idaho 2015); *United States v. Alsol Corp.*, 2014 WL 46775 (D.N.J. 2014); *In re Mateer*, 205 B.R. 915 (C.D. Ill. 1997); *United States v. Oil Transp. Co.*, 172 B.R. 834 (E.D. La. 1994); *In re Madison Indus., Inc.*, 161 B.R. 363 (D.N.J. 1993); *United States v. Acme Solvents Reclaiming, Inc.*, 154 B.R. 72, 74 (N.D. Ill. 1993); *United States v. Mattiace Indus., Inc.*, 73 B.R. 816, 818–19 (E.D.N.Y. 1987); *In re New York Trap Rock Corp.*, 153 B.R. 642, 645 (Bankr. S.D.N.Y. 1993); *In re Lenz Oil Serv., Inc.*, 65 B.R. 292 (Bankr. N.D. Ill. 1986).

35. *See Exxon Corp.*, 932 F.2d at 1024; *Nicolet*, 857 F.2d at 210.

36. "Thus, where a governmental unit is suing a debtor to prevent or stop violation of fraud, *environmental protection*, consumer protection, safety or similar police or regulatory laws, or attempting to *fix damages for violation of such law*, the action or proceeding is not stayed under the automatic stay." H.R. Rep. No. 95-595 at 343; S. Rep. No. 95-989 at 52 (italics added).

37. For nonenvironmental cases discussing how the police or regulatory exception applies to cases for monetary relief, *see, e.g., In re Halo Wireless, Inc.*, 684 F.3d 581, 587 (5th Cir. 2012); *S.E.C. v. Brennan*, 230 F.3d 65, 71 (2d Cir. 2000); *In re First Alliance Mortgage Co.*, 263 B.R. 99 (B.A.P. 2001).

ACTIONS FOR CIVIL PENALTIES

Courts have similarly permitted actions for civil penalties for violation of environmental laws or regulations to proceed to judgment pursuant to the police or regulatory exception of Section 362(b)(4).[38] Civil penalties are a critical police and regulatory tool that create an important deterrent effect.[39] They create both a specific deterrent effect on the party involved and a general deterrent effect on other regulated parties who can see the potential consequences to them if they do not attend to compliance issues.[40] Companies facing financial difficulties should not be able to avoid consequences if they violate the law. While the government can pursue an action to determine the amount of a civil penalty under the police or regulatory exception, once a judgment is obtained, the judgment can only be enforced through the claims process for monetary claims in the bankruptcy proceeding, since Section 362(b)(4) only allows enforcement of police and regulatory judgments that are not money judgments.

ACTIONS FOR FINANCIAL ASSURANCE

Courts have found that actions requiring a debtor to establish financial assurance for regulatory compliance also fall within the

---

38. *Commerce Oil*, 847 F.2d at 296; *United States v. Jones & Laughlin Steel Corp.*, 804 F.2d 348, 350–51 (6th Cir. 1986); *Penn Terra Ltd. v. Dep't of Env't Res.*, 733 F.2d 267, 274 n.7 (3d Cir. 1984); *United States v. Tronox Pigments (Savannah), Inc.*, 2009 WL 256459 (S.D. Ga. 2009); *United States v. LTV Steel Co.*, 269 B.R. 576 (W.D. Pa. 2001); *Mateer*, 205 B.R. 915; *United States v. Sugarhouse Realty, Inc.*, 162 B.R. 113, 115 (E.D. PA. 1993); *Mattiace*, 73 B.R. 816 (E.D.N.Y. 1987); *United States v. Standard Metals Corp.*, 49 B.R. 623 (D. Colo. 1985); *Ill. v. Elec. Utils.*, 41 B.R. 874 (N.D. Ill. 1984); *United States v. Energy Int'l, Inc.*, 19 B.R. 1020 (S.D. Ohio 1981); *In re Williston Oil Corp.*, 54 B.R. 10 (Bankr. D.N.J. 1984); *In re Neman*, 5 E.A.D. 450 (EPA Env't. App. Bd. 1994). *See also In re W.R. Grace & Co.*, 412 B.R. 657, 662–64 (D. Del. 2009).

39. *W.R. Grace & Co.*, 412 B.R. at 663–64; *LTV Steel*, 269 B.R. at 583.

40. *See, e.g.*, *W.R. Grace*, 412 B.R. at 663–64; *In re Emerald Casino, Inc.*, 2003 WL 23147946 (N.D. Ill. 2003); *Standard Metals Corp.*, 49 B.R. at 625. In a nonenvironmental case, one court stated that given the importance of deterrent effect on future violations, it would be contrary to separation of powers principles for a court to refuse to consider an action brought by an executive branch agency that falls under the police or regulatory exception based on the likelihood of actual recovery of a penalty on account of bankruptcy. *United States v. Rupari Food Servs., Inc.*, 254 F. Supp. 3d 1367, 1375–76 (Ct. Int. Trade 2017) (penalties for customs disclosure regulation violations).

police or regulatory exception.[41] Although, in some sense, financial assurance sounds more monetary (or "financial") than other kinds of regulatory obligations, courts have found actions regarding financial assurance requirements to fall under the police or regulatory exception because of their strong connection to protection of public health and safety through deterrence of environmental misconduct or sloppy operations.[42] Maintaining required financial assurance generally applicable to a debtors' business also conforms to the requirements of 28 U.S.C. § 959(b) that debtors manage and operate their property in accordance with nonbankruptcy law.[43] Since requirements for financial assurance are regulatory requirements as opposed to traditional money judgments, they may be fully enforced under the police or regulatory exception to the automatic stay.[44]

A related but different question is whether an action for the use of financial assurance previously provided falls within the police or regulatory exception. Some forms of financial assurance, such as letters of credit and surety or performance bonds, are specifically designed to be bankruptcy-free (i.e., easily accessible without need to involve the bankruptcy court) and not to be property of the estate under what is known as the "doctrine of independence."[45]

---

41. *See, e.g.*, *Safety-Kleen, Inc. (Pinewood) v. Wyche*, 274 F3d 846 (4th Cir. 2001) (hazardous waste facilities); *Bickford v. Lodestar*, 310 B.R. 70 (E.D. Ky. 2004) (mining); *In re Molycorp., Inc.*, No. 15-11357 (Bankr. D. Del. Oct. 22, 2015) (Docket No. 718, at 49–51) (idled mine in care and maintenance mode).

42. *Safety-Kleen*, 274 F.3d at 865–66; *Bickford*, 310 B.R. at 77–78. *See* Chapter 5 (Key Provisions (property of the estate)) *supra*.

43. *See* Chapter 9 (Operating Estate Property) *supra*; *Gillis v. Cal.*, 293 U.S. 62, 63–67 (1934) (court-appointed receiver must obtain surety bonds required by state law to guarantee payment of gas taxes); *Duffey v. Dollison, 734 F.2d 265, 273 (6th Cir. 1984)* (debtors must comply with financial responsibility requirements for automobile licenses under Ohio law); *Safety-Kleen*, 274 F.3d at 864–66 (hazardous waste landfill operator in bankruptcy must comply with South Carolina's bond requirement for financial assurance for closure and post-closure); *Cumberland Farms, Inc. v. Fla. Dep't of Env't Prot., 116 F.3d 16, 20–21 (1st Cir. 1997)* (debtor liable for civil penalties based on noncompliance with financial assurance requirements during bankruptcy).

44. *See* discussion of *Injunctive Relief supra*.

45. *See, e.g.*, *In re Mansfield Tire & Rubber Co.*, 660 F.2d 1108, 1113 (6th Cir. 1981) (bond); *Lockard*, 884 F.2d 1171, 1177–79 (9th Cir. 1989) (bond); *In re McLean Trucking*, 74 B.R. 820, 826–28 (Bankr. W.D.N.C. 1987) (bond); *In re Builders Transp.*, 471 F.3d 1178, 1186 (11th Cir. 2006) (letter of credit); *In re Kaiser Grp. Int'l*, 399 F.3d 558,

While ancillary litigation or disputes may arise as to the proceeds from these instruments, it would defeat a central purpose of these instruments if the collection of proceeds from bonding companies or banks were stayed by a bankruptcy filing. Technically, such actions are not against the debtor or estate property and thus not within the scope of the automatic stay in the first place.[46] However, there may be situations where a debtor has a limited interest in financial assurance, which makes the financial assurance partially property of the estate, such as where the estate has legal title but not an equitable interest in certain types of insurance, trust funds, escrow accounts, or cash deposits. In such situations, governments may still contend that actions to secure cleanup or injunctive relief through the financial assurance mechanism fall under the police or regulatory exception or that the stay should be lifted in recognition of the government's equitable interest.[47] However, given the limited number of decisions in this area, if the particular facts raise any doubts, governmental agencies may decide to obtain an advance declaratory ruling that such an action falls within the police or regulatory exception or that, in the alternative, the automatic stay be lifted. Bankruptcy courts may lift the automatic stay for cause and are likely (or arguably required) to do so when the debtor's estate does not have an equitable interest (as opposed to mere legal title) in the financial assurance.[48]

---

566 (3d Cir. 2005) (letter of credit); *In re Graham Square*, 126 F.3d 823, 827 (6th Cir. 1997) (letter of credit).

46. The design and wording of bonds can vary. These distinctions are important. For example, where a bond has similarities to a trust or escrow account, a cash deposit, or insurance in which the debtor retains a legal or equitable interest, courts have sometimes found a particular performance bond technically to be property of the estate and relief from stay must be sought before the government can execute on the instrument. *See In re War Eagle Constr. Co.*, 243 B.R. 193, 195 (S.D. W. Va. 2002) (performance bond consisting of certificates of deposit with a bank); *In re Sec. Gas & Oil, Inc.*, 70 B.R. 786, 791 (Bankr. N.D. Cal. 1987) (undescribed performance bond found to be property of the estate based upon citation to insurance proceeds cases). Where a separate bonding company's assets are on the line, the bond is generally not property of the estate. *Lockard*, 884 F.2d at 1178.

47. *See War Eagle*, 283 B.R. at 199–200 (stay would need to be lifted to use financial assurance proceeds to pay a money judgment).

48. *See In re Fin. Oversight & Mgmt. Bd. for Puerto Rico*, 939 F.3d 340, 348 (1st Cir. 2019).

ADMINISTRATIVE PROCEEDINGS

The principles just described also apply to administrative proceedings brought by governmental units for penalties, cost recovery, financial assurance, and injunctive relief in the same manner as they do to judicial proceedings by governmental units. Specifically, a bankruptcy court should not evaluate the merits or legitimacy of the administrative action in determining the applicability of the exception. Instead, the court should determine solely whether the administrative action is a police or regulatory action. For example, in *Board of Governors v. MCorp Financial*,[49] the Supreme Court held that administrative actions by the Federal Reserve Board for violations of the Federal Reserve Act could continue under the police or regulatory exception. The Supreme Court rejected the contention that the bankruptcy court should scrutinize the legitimacy (merits) of the administrative action to decide if it should be allowed to go forward under the police or regulatory exception because scrutinizing numerous administrative or enforcement actions would be inconsistent with the limited authority of bankruptcy courts.[50]

CRIMINAL ACTIONS[51]

Several federal and state environmental statutes include provisions for criminal prosecutions.[52] The interplay of criminal law and bankruptcy law is a particularly complex area of law. Thus, it is important to carefully evaluate the impact a bankruptcy filing by an individual or corporate defendant may have on a federal or state criminal action against them. A number of Bankruptcy Code

49. 502 U.S. 32 (1991).

50. *Id.* at 40. The Court also found that the agency's action to determine whether the debtor had violated various regulations was not an action to control the debtor's assets. *Id.* at 40–41. It should be noted that this discussion pre-dates the 1998 clarification of the police or regulatory exception to make clear that it applies to acts to control property of the estate. *See* note 6 *supra*.

51. Special thanks to Margarita Padilla, former Supervising Deputy Attorney General, Environment Section, California Department of Justice, for her contributions to this section.

52. For a list of federal environmental statutes with criminal provisions, *see* https://www.justice.gov/enrd/federal-environmental-crimes-statute, Department of Justice, Environment and Natural Resources Division, Environmental Crimes Section, Federal Environmental Crimes, By Statute.

provisions may come into play depending on the type of debtor (individual or corporate) and the type of bankruptcy (i.e., Chapter 7, 11, or other Code chapter). For federal criminal proceedings, the Criminal Code supersedes the Bankruptcy Code as it specifically states that its provisions are "[n]otwithstanding any other Federal law."[53] With respect to state criminal actions, the Supreme Court has stated its "deep conviction that federal bankruptcy courts should not invalidate the results of state criminal proceedings."[54]

11 U.S.C. § 362(b)(1) contains a separate exception to the automatic stay for the "commencement or continuation of criminal actions or proceedings against the debtor."[55] Courts have recognized that the language of Section 362(b)(1) "unambiguously signals Congress's intent to exempt all parts of the process aimed at punishing a defendant for criminal conduct from any interruption by the Bankruptcy Code's automatic stay."[56] The majority view is that criminal proceedings may proceed notwithstanding the filing

---

53. The relevant enforcement provisions of the federal Criminal Code at 18 U.S.C. § 3613 include that: (1) the United States may enforce judgments imposing criminal fines against all property of the person fined, 18 U.S.C. § 3613(a); (2) federal criminal fines are not dischargeable in bankruptcy, 18 U.S.C. § 3613(e); and (3) the United States may enforce federal restitution orders which are also not dischargeable in bankruptcy, 18 U.S.C. § 3613(f). Courts have agreed that the Criminal Code makes clear that bankruptcy law should not interfere with the enforcement of a fine or restitution order imposed pursuant to a federal criminal judgment. *See In re Robinson*, 764 F.3d 554 (6th Cir. 2014); *United States v. Hyde*, 49 F.3d 103 (1st Cir. 2007); *In re Partida*, 862 F.3d. 909 (9th Cir. 2019).

54. *Kelly v. Robinson*, 479 U.S. 36, 47 (1986).

55. Some courts have given significant import to the language "against the debtor" and ruled in individual debtor cases that Section 362(b)(1) does not allow collection against the debtor's estate. *See, e.g., In re Robinson*, 764 F.3d 554, 559–60 (6th Cir. 2014) (although court found recovery of federal criminal restitution could not proceed under 362(b)(1) against estate assets, it could proceed under Section 3613 of the Criminal Code because its language clearly meant Congress intended for it to supersede the Bankruptcy Code). Section 541 of the Bankruptcy Code defines "property of the estate" and the scope of what is encompassed in property of the estate depends on the type of bankruptcy. *See* Chapters 2 (History and Purposes), 5 (Key Provisions (property of the estate)), 8 (Harmonization) *supra* regarding discussion of property of the estate under the Bankruptcy Code.

56. *United States v. Colasuonno*, 697 F.3d 164, 174 (2d Cir. 2012). The Bankruptcy Code's legislative history underscores that bankruptcy is not a haven for criminal offenders and that criminal actions and proceedings may proceed notwithstanding a bankruptcy filing. House Report No. 95-595, 95th Cong. 1st Sess. 342 (1977); Senate Report No. 95-989, 95th Cong. 2nd Sess. 51 (1978), *U.S. Code Cong.& Admin, News* 1978, at 5787, 5837, 5963, 6298.

of a bankruptcy petition, including collection efforts and probation revocation proceedings for failure to pay criminal restitution.[57] However, some courts have found that fines and restitution fall within the Bankruptcy Code's definition of claim and that an action for collection of a fine or restitution would be a civil action.[58]

As discussed further in Chapter 13 (Discharge), criminal liability is nondischargeable in bankruptcy in many situations.[59] Therefore once a bankruptcy case is over and the automatic stay no longer applies,[60] collection of nondischarged criminal liability may continue.[61]

---

57. *In re Gruntz*, 202 F.3d 1074, 1087 (9th Cir. 2000) (en banc); *Colasuonno*, 697 F.3d at 174 (Section 362(b)(1) allows federal probation revocation to proceed against debtor); *United States v. Caddell*, 830 F.2d 36, 39 (5th Cir. 1987) (same); *United States v. Coluccio*, 19 F.3d 1115, 1117 n.2 (6th Cir. 1994) (collection of criminal fine); *In re Hucke*, 992 F.2d 950 (9th Cir. 1993) (Section 362(b)(1) allows state criminal probation revocation to proceed against debtor), *overruled on other grounds* in *In re Gruntz*, 202 F.3d at 1085–87; *In re Rollins*, 140 F.3d 1043 (11th Cir. 1998), *aff'g*, 243 B.R. 540 (N.D. Ga. 1997) (state court criminal revocation proceeding allowed under 362(b)(1)); *United States v. Troxler Hosiery Co.*, 796 F.2d 723 (4th Cir. 1986), *aff'g*, 41 B.R. 457 (M.D.N.C. 1984) (collection of criminal fine); *United States v. Palm Beach Cruises*, 204 B.R. 634 (S.D. Fla. 1996) (financial conditions of criminal sentence for environmental violations not stayed).

58. A discussion of some contrary case law is summarized in *In re Bibbs*, 282 B.R. 876 (Bankr. E.D. Ark. 2002, and *In re Sori*, 513 B.R. 728 (Bankr. N.D. Ill. 2014). Notably, though, many of the cases finding that collection or probation revocation to be stayed were prior to amendment of the federal Criminal Code in 1996 by the Mandatory Victim Restitution Act, Pub. L. No. 104-132, 110 Stat. 1239 (1996) (codified at 11 U.S.C. § 3613) (as to federal criminal actions) and/or are based on *Pennsylvania Dep't of Pub. Welfare v. Davenport*, 495 U.S. 552, 560–61 (1990), where the Supreme Court stated in dicta that collection of criminal restitution orders was stayed in Chapter 13 cases (in the course of holding them dischargeable). Because Congress legislatively overruled *Davenport* in 1990 through the passage of the Criminal Victims Protection Act of 1990, Pub. L. No. 101-581, § 3, 104 Stat. 2865 (codified at 11 U.S.C. §1328 (a)(3)), the continued validity of such cases is in doubt. *See, e.g.*, *Bryan v. Rainwater*, 254 B.R. 273, 277 (N.D. Ala. 2000).

59. *See, e.g.*, 11 U.S.C. §§ 523(a)(13); 523(a)(7); 1328(a)(3); 18 U.S.C. § 3613(f) (restitution for federal crimes); *In re Partida*, 862 F.3d 909 (9th Cir. 2017); *In re Robinson*, 764 F.3d 554 (6th Cir. 2014); *United States v. Hyde*, 497 F.3d 103 (1st Cir. 2007); *In re Thompson*, 418 F.3d 362 (3d Cir. 2005).

60. The duration of the automatic stay depends on the particular facts of each proceeding but often is at the time discharges are granted or denied. 11 U.S.C. §§ 362(c)(2)(C); 362(c)(1), (2).

61. For a discussion of how a bankruptcy case could be contended to impact payments made on criminal matters before the case was filed, *see* Chapter 5 (Key Provisions (preferences)) *supra*.

SECTION 105 STAYS

Even where the police or regulatory exception to the automatic stay applies, several courts have raised the possibility of a bankruptcy court using its general equitable authority under Section 105 to enjoin police or regulatory actions that threaten the integrity of a bankruptcy case. These cases cite to the legislative history of Section 105, which identifies the possibility of a discretionary stay as opposed to Section 362's automatic stay.[62] These cases require the application of traditional factors for injunctive relief such as evaluating the likelihood of success, harm, and the public interest.[63] It should be noted though that to the authors' knowledge, with one exception in a case for penalties where a proof of claim was not filed,[64] no court has enjoined an environmental action under Section 105. Moreover, notwithstanding the legislative history, the recent trend has been to significantly limit bankruptcy courts' use of Section 105 equitable authority.[65] Many of the cases referring to discretionary stays under Section 105 are several decades old or rely on old case law. The more recent cases

---

62. *In re Commerce Oil Co.*, 847 F.2d 291, 297 (6th Cir. 1988); *In re Commonwealth Oil Ref. Co.*, 805 F.2d 1175, 1188 (5th Cir. 1986) (not deciding issue); *Penn Terra Ltd. v. Dep't of Env't Res.*, 733 F.2d 267, 273–74 (3d Cir. 1984); *In re Sec. Gas & Oil, Inc.*, 70 B.R. 786, 792–97 (Bankr. N.D. Cal. 1987); S. Rep. No. 95-989 at 51, 1978 U.S. Code Cong. & Ad. News at 5787, 5837; H. Rep. No. 95-595 at 342, 1978 U.S. Code Cong. & Ad. News at 5963, 6298.

63. *See, e.g., Commonwealth Oil Ref. Co.*, 805 F.2d at 1189 (debtors would need to show likelihood of success on underlying environmental actions).

64. *In re W.R. Grace & Co.*, 412 B.R. 657 (D. Del. 2009).

65. *Law v. Siegel*, 571 U.S. 415, 421 (2014); *Raleigh v. Ill. Dep't of Revenue*, 530 U.S. 15 (2000); *United States v. Reorganized CF&I Fabricators of Utah, Inc.*, 518 U.S. 213 (1996); *United States v. Noland*, 517 U.S. 535 (1996); *Norwest Bank Worthington v. Ahlers*, 485 U.S. 197, 206 (1988); *In re Reyes-Colon*, 922 F.3d 13 (1st Cir. 2019); *In re Archdiocese of Saint Paul & Minneapolis*, 888 F.3d 944 (8th Cir. 2018); *Willms v. Sanderson*, 723 F.3d 1094, 1103 (9th Cir. 2013); *In re Scrivner*, 535 F.3d 1258, 1263–65 (10th Cir. 2008); *In re Metromedia Fiber Network, Inc.*, 416 F.3d 136, 142 (2d Cir, 2005); *In re Joubert*, 411 F.3d 452, 455 (3d Cir. 2005); *In re Combustion Eng'g, Inc.*, 391 F.3d 190, 236 (3d Cir. 2004); *In re Holyoke Nursing Home, Inc.*, 372 F.3d 1, 5 (1st Cir. 2004); *In re Dairy Mart Convenience Stores, Inc.*, 351 F.3d 86 (2d Cir. 2003); *In re Highland Superstores, Inc.*, 154 F.3d 573 (6th Cir. 1998); *In re Sadkin*, 36 F.3d 473 (5th Cir. 1994); *In re Fesco Plastics Corp.*, 996 F.2d 152 (7th Cir. 1993); *In re Saybrook Mfg. Co.*, 963 F.2d 1490, 1495 (11th Cir. 1992); *In re Wolverine Radio Co.*, 930 F.2d 1132, 1140 (6th Cir. 1991); *United States v. Sutton*, 786 F.2d 1305, 1308 (5th Cir. 1986); *In re Purdue Pharma, L.P.*, 635 B.R. 26, 99–100 (S.D.N.Y. 2021); Douglas G. Baird, Elements of Bankruptcy 6 (6th ed. 2014); 2 Collier on Bankruptcy ¶ 105.01[1] (16th ed. 2019).

limit Section 105's use (as its language says) to support other provisions of the Bankruptcy Code and not in a manner that undermines other Bankruptcy Code provisions.[66] Governments can be expected to strenuously oppose the use of Section 105 to enjoin civil or criminal environmental actions that Sections 362(b)(1) and 362(b)(4) of the Bankruptcy Code and/or Section 959(b) of Title 28 permit to proceed.[67] To do otherwise would be to allow bankruptcy to become the safe haven for wrongdoers that Congress has forbidden.[68]

DISMISSAL OF BANKRUPTCY CASES DESIGNED TO EVADE REGULATORY SCHEMES

Bankruptcy petitions that are designed to evade police or regulatory statutes or litigation may also be dismissed for cause or converted to Chapter 7 unless the bankruptcy court determines that appointment of a Chapter 11 trustee or examiner is in the best

---

66. Section 105 does not authorize bankruptcy courts to create substantive rights that are otherwise unavailable under applicable law, or constitute a roving commission to do equity. *United States v. Sutton*, 786 F.2d 1305, 1308 (5th Cir. 1986); *see also* cases cited in note 65 *supra*.

67. An injunction against a criminal action would be contrary to the criminal exception to the automatic stay under Section 362(b)(1), and that the presumption that bankruptcy should not interfere with state criminal actions, *Kelly v. Robinson*, 479 U.S. 36, 47 (1986). Enjoining a state criminal proceeding would also need to overcome the requirements of *Younger v. Harris*, 401 U.S. 37 (1971), and the Anti-Injunction Act, 28 U.S.C. § 2283. *See In re Fussell*, 928 F.2d 712, 715–16 (5th Cir. 1991); *Barnette v. Evans*, 673 F.2d 1250, 1251–52 (11th Cir. 1982); *In re Davis*, 691 F.2d 176, 177–79 (3d Cir. 1982). Enjoining a federal criminal proceeding would also be contrary to 18 U.S.C. § 3613.

68. *See, e.g.*, *Wilbur Wood Prods. v. Maine*, 128 B.R. 1 (D. Me. 1991) (Section 105 may not be used to circumvent 28 U.S.C. § 959(b)'s requirement that debtors-in-possession comply with applicable environmental laws.); *In re Env't Waste Control, Inc.*, 125 B.R. 546 (N.D. Ind. 1991) (refusing to issue Section 105 injunction against government requiring compliance with environmental laws); David A. Brenningmeyer, *The Limited Power of Federal Bankruptcy Courts To Stay Enforcement of State Environmental Regulations*, 44 ME. L. REV. 485, 508–14 (1992).

interest of creditors.[69] The requirement of good faith for the filing of a bankruptcy petition and the dismissal of bad faith filings is further discussed in Chapter 2 (History and Purposes) of this Practice Guide.

69. 11 U.S.C. § 1112(b); *see In re 15375 Mem'l Corp.*, 589 F.3d 605 (3d Cir. 2009); *In re Cedar Shore Resort, Inc.*, 235 F.3d 375 (8th Cir. 2000); *In re Nat'l Rifle Ass'n of Am.*, 628 B.R. 262 (Bankr. N.D. Tex. 2021); *In re Forest Hill Funeral Home & Mem'l Park-East, LLC*, 364 B.R. 808, 822 (Bankr. E.D. Okla. 2007); *In re First Plus Fin. Enter., Inc.*, 99 B.R. 751 (Bankr. W.D. Tex. 1989).

CHAPTER 11

Compliance Obligations, Equitable Remedies, and Bankruptcy Discharge

This chapter considers issues relating to equitable remedies, the bankruptcy discharge, and post-bankruptcy compliance. It analyzes whether equitable remedies, including compliance obligations and cleanup orders, are dischargeable "claims" in bankruptcy, that is, whether these obligations no longer continue post-bankruptcy, after the debtor has emerged from bankruptcy.[1] Given the uncertainty in this area of the law, this chapter concludes with a discussion of protective proofs of claims for compliance obligations as well as considerations for moving forward with actions seeking to require compliance during a bankruptcy case.[2]

1. Since liquidating corporate debtors do not receive any discharge, 11 U.S.C. §§ 727(a)(1), 1141(d)(3), the issue of whether a liability is a dischargeable "claim" as analyzed in this chapter should not arise in the case of liquidating corporate debtors. The corporation will no longer exist when the bankruptcy is over. Issues about compliance during liquidation bankruptcy cases are discussed in Chapter 9 (Operating Estate Property) *supra* and Chapter 10 (Police or Regulatory Exception) *supra*.

2. While this chapter is focusing on discharge and post-bankruptcy compliance, such issues often come up during the bankruptcy case in connection with language in proposed plans and confirmation orders. Such language and potential objections thereto are discussed in Chapter 16 (Plan Objections) *infra*.

Before reaching these issues, it is important to note that evaluating a debtor's compliance with environmental law post-bankruptcy should be analyzed under different legal provisions than a debtor's compliance during the bankruptcy case. As previously discussed in Chapters 9 and 10, whether a debtor has to comply with environmental law during the bankruptcy case raises issues relating to: (1) the police or regulatory exception to the automatic stay, and (2) the duty to comply with laws with respect to property of the estate.[3]

DEFINITION OF "CLAIM"

The starting point for analyzing issues relating to the bankruptcy discharge and post-bankruptcy compliance is the Bankruptcy Code's definition of "claim." Section 101(5) of the Bankruptcy Code defines "claim" as a:

> (A) right to payment, whether or not such right is reduced to judgment, liquidated, unliquidated, fixed, contingent, matured, unmatured, disputed, legal, equitable, secured, or unsecured; or
>
> (B) *right to an equitable remedy for breach of performance if such breach gives rise to a right to payment*, whether or not such right to an equitable remedy is reduced to judgment, fixed, contingent, matured, unmatured, disputed, undisputed, secured, or unsecured.[4]

The distinction between compliance obligations and monetary claims reflected in this statutory language is a key concept in harmonizing environmental law and bankruptcy law and is seen throughout this chapter.

Whether a liability is a "claim" is critical to determining how bankruptcy may impact a debtor's post-bankruptcy obligations

---

3. Although the issues of compliance during and after the bankruptcy case are distinct, courts are not always clear in their analyses and sometimes cite to cases involving both situations. As noted in this chapter and Chapter 9 (Operating Estate Property) *supra* and Chapter 10 (Police or Regulatory Exception) *supra*, in both situations (during and after the bankruptcy case), the importance of environmental compliance has often been found to be paramount. Nonetheless, the legal analysis applicable to each is different.

4. 11 U.S.C. § 101(5) (italics added).

with respect to the liability because only "claims" are dischargeable under the Code. Section 1141(d)(1) of the Code provides that "the confirmation of a plan . . . discharges the debtor from any debt that arose before the date of such confirmation." The term "debt" is defined as "liability on a claim."[5] Therefore, if a compliance obligation does not fall within the definition of "claim," it is not dischargeable through bankruptcy.[6] In addition, many of the Code's provisions such as those governing classification, treatment, and voting under plans of reorganization only apply to "claims."[7]

Courts have long struggled with Congress's language to determine when equitable remedies (such as injunctions, orders, and other compliance obligations) fall within the definition of "claim."[8] The Supreme Court identified, but did not decide, the issue in one of the earliest environmental bankruptcy law cases, *Ohio v. Kovacs*.[9] In *Kovacs*, Ohio issued a cleanup order to Kovacs but instead of Ohio prosecuting Kovacs under environmental law or bringing contempt enforcement proceedings, the Supreme Court held that Ohio had converted the cleanup obligation to a monetary claim that was dischargeable in bankruptcy by securing the appointment of a receiver and divesting Kovacs of his authority over the site and use of his assets.[10] As such, and critical to the Court's analysis and ruling, Ohio had, in fact, conceded that it was only seeking the payment of money from the bankruptcy estate.[11] The Supreme Court carefully emphasized that it was not deciding

5. *Id.* § 101(12).

6. In addition, liquidating debtor corporations do not receive any discharge. 11 U.S.C. §§ 727(a)(1), 1141(d)(3). However, the corporation will no longer exist when the bankruptcy is over.

7. *See, e.g.*, 11 U.S.C. §§ 1122, 1124, 1126, 1129(a)(7)–(10). The government, as a "party in interest," may still object to how plans deal with compliance obligations that are not "claims." *See id.* § 1109(b) (providing for a right to be heard by a party in interest).

8. *See, e.g.*, *In re Chateaugay Corp.*, 944 F.2d 997, 1006–09 (2d Cir. 1991); Shan A. Haider, Ji Hun Kim & Nicholas M. McGrath, *After Apex, Debtors Must Clean Up After Themselves*, 29 Am. Bankr. Inst. J. 49 (2011); Jill Losch, *Bankruptcy v. Environmental Obligations: Clash of the Titans*, 52 La. Law. Rev. 137, 172–73 (1991).

9. 469 U.S. 274, 278–79 (1985).

10. *Id.* at 282–83. "As the case comes to us . . . Kovacs has been dispossessed and the State seeks to enforce his cleanup obligation by a money judgment." *Id.* at 285.

11. *Id.* at 283.

what the legal consequences would have been had a receiver not been appointed.[12] Significantly, the Supreme Court stated that anyone in possession of a site "must comply with the environmental laws" and may not "maintain a nuisance" or "refuse to remove the source of such conditions."[13] This statement suggests that compliance obligations are not dischargeable in bankruptcy.

The language of Section 101(5) of the Code literally provides that an equitable remedy for breach of performance is a "claim" if "such breach gives rise to a right to payment." Disagreements often arise regarding whether or not a particular breach "gives rise to a right to payment." Governments have contended that if they are seeking an equitable remedy such as an injunction requiring compliance or the cleanup of a contaminated site, and are not asking for the payment of money to the government, breach of performance of the equitable remedy has not given "rise to a right to payment" because the government has not spent money implementing the equitable remedy and is not seeking payment. Governments note that a polluter does not have the right to pay the government money in lieu of complying with an order to, for instance, clean up hazardous waste that is endangering public health and safety.[14]

Debtors, on the other hand, have focused on the portion of the statutory language that refers to a "right to payment" and contend that if the government has an alternative statutory remedy available that is monetary, such as cleaning up a site itself and suing to recover cleanup costs, then that alternative remedy makes the government's right to obtain injunctive relief a "claim," even if the government has not actually invoked that right or sought any payment from the debtor. Debtors contend that the government should not have the ability to decide whether an injunctive

12. *Id.* at 284. Courts analyzing *Kovacs* have noted that the ruling was based on the fact that Ohio had elected to convert its equitable remedy into a monetary liability. *See, e.g., In re Ben Franklin Hotel Assocs.*, 186 F.3d 301, 304 (3d Cir. 1999); *In re Udell*, 18 F.3d 403, 406 (7th Cir. 1994); *Chateaugay Corp.*, 944 F.2d at 1009; *In re Commonwealth Oil Ref. Co.*, 805 F.2d 1175, 1187 n.14 (5th Cir. 1986); *Cournoyer v. Town of Lincoln*, 790 F.2d 971, 975 (1st Cir. 1986).

13. *Kovacs*, 469 U.S. at 285.

14. *See Chateaugay*, 944 F.2d at 1008.

obligation is dischargeable simply by electing not to pursue a monetary remedy.

Governments may take the position that the theoretical alternative right to payment argument goes too far in its scope, as the government could frequently be contended to have the ability to seek money, as happened in *Kovacs* through the appointment of a receiver. The theoretical alternative right to payment argument therefore would risk making most equitable remedies dischargeable and that is contrary to the language of Section 101(5), which provides that only some equitable remedies are dischargeable, that is, when they have given rise to the government seeking a right to payment.

Additionally, debtors also often argue that if they must spend money to comply with an obligation, the obligation is effectively a monetary one (i.e., a right to payment). However, this argument has been rejected by most courts because it would make the limiting language of Section 101(5) meaningless, given that taking almost any action costs money and using that as a dividing line would mean that all equitable remedies would be "claims." Furthermore, where injunctive relief is implemented, money is not actually being paid to the government but to third parties.[15] Debtors have further emphasized the generally broad nature of the definition of "claim," but governments have responded that the language is clear that certain equitable remedies are not included in the definition (i.e.,

15. *Compare United States v. Apex Oil Co.*, 579 F.3d 734, 737–38 (7th Cir. 2009) (costs of compliance incurred by a debtor are not equivalent to a right to payment; Code created only a limited right to discharge of equitable remedies); *In re Torwico Electronics, Inc.*, 8 F.3d 146, 150 (3d Cir. 1993) (state is not seeking payment of money to state); *Penn Terra, Ltd. v. Dep't of Env't Res.*, 733 F.2d 267, 278–79 (3d Cir. 1984) (injunction which does not cost some money may be effective nullity); *United States v. Hubler*, 117 B.R. 160, 164 (W.D. Pa. 1990), *aff'd without opinion*, 928 F.2d 1131 (3d Cir. 1991), *with United States v. Whizco*, 841 F.2d 147, 150 (6th Cir. 1988) (finding a reclamation liability a claim to the extent it would require a vice president/sole shareholder to spend money to comply as opposed to performing the reclamation himself). As noted, most courts have rejected *Whizco*. Moreover, *Whizco* was an individual debtor case. If it was contended that *Whizco* should be applied to corporate debtors, governments might contend that a corporation can always perform the cleanup itself as set forth in *Whizco* since the acts of its employees and agents are normally attributed to it. *Meyer v. Holley*, 537 U.S. 280, 285–86 (2003); *Belmont v. MB Investment Partners, Inc.*, 708 F.3d 470, 494–95 (3d Cir. 2013).

where breach of performance has not given rise to the government seeking a right to payment.).[16]

Ultimately, the outcome of this disagreement may depend on how the courts interpret the phrase "gives rise" in the definition of "claim." Does the breach have to "give rise" to the government actually pursuing a right to payment or can it merely "give rise" to a theoretical right to payment that is never sought (because the government has not spent funds or sought funds to implement the equitable remedy itself) and still be considered to fall within the definition of "claim"?

APPLICATION TO STATUTES

Most courts have had little trouble concluding that equitable remedies under statutes that do not provide the government a right to monetary recovery are not dischargeable claims.[17] These courts have held that the focus of analysis should be on the statute that the government actually proceeded under and not on whether the government could have pursued a monetary claim under other statutes with different remedial schemes.[18]

---

16. As noted by the Supreme Court in *Kovacs*, earlier versions of the proposed statutory definition of "claim" would have included equitable remedies even if they did not rise to a right to payment. The enacted version was a compromise. 469 U.S. at 278, 280 & n.6 (citing H.R. 8200, 95th Cong. 1st Sess. 309–10 (1977).

17. *See, e.g., Apex*, 579 F.3d 734 (RCRA); *In re Mark IV Indus., Inc.*, 438 B.R. 460 (Bankr. S.D.N.Y. 2010), *aff'd*, 459 B.R. 173 (S.D.N.Y. 2011) (New Mexico Water Quality Act); *AM Int'l, Inc.*, 106 F.3d 1342 (7th Cir. 1997) (RCRA citizen's suit); *In re Outboard Marine Corp.*, 2004 WL 1254128 (N.D. Ill. 2004) (RCRA); *New York v. Mirant New York, Inc.*, 300 B.R. 174, 181 (S.D.N.Y. 2003) (Clean Air Act); *Davenport v. Neely*, 7 F. Supp. 2d 1219, 1231 (D. Ala. 1998) (RCRA citizen's suit); *In re Indus. Salvage, Inc.*, 196 B.R. 784 (S.D. Ill. 1996) (Illinois Environmental Protection Act); *United States v. Hubler*, 117 B.R. 160 (W.D. Pa. 1990) (Surface Mining Control and Reclamation Act), *aff'd without opinion*, 928 F.2d 1131 (3d Cir. 1991); *In re Taylor*, 572 B.R. 592 (Bankr. E.D.N.C. 2017) (RCRA and Clean Water Act). The reasoning of the one contrary decision, *Whizco*, 841 F.2d 147, has been criticized by these cases. In any event, *Whizco* can often be distinguished even in the Sixth Circuit on the ground that its self-described "narrow" ruling may be limited to a situation where the government seeks performance from an individual officer/shareholder debtor without the ability to perform. Moreover, *Whizco* agreed that the individual's liability to perform with his own equipment was not dischargeable. *Id.* at 151.

18. *See, e.g., Apex*, 579 F.3d at 736; *Torwico*, 8 F.3d at 151 n.6; *Mark IV*, 438 B.R. at 470, 459 B.R. at 185–86. *See also In re Kaiser Aluminum Corp.*, 2010 WL 2690322, 386 Fed. Appx. 201 (3d Cir. 2010) (remanding for a decision on whether each

With respect to statutes such as CERCLA, which provides the government the option to spend its own money and seek reimbursement, the results have been mixed. A number of courts have held that where the government is seeking cleanup of ongoing pollution and prevention of additional harm, the equitable remedy is not a claim, either because: (1) the government should not be required to accept money in lieu of stopping continued pollution,[19] or (2) the government should not have to accept the less beneficial remedy of money over cleanup.[20] For the government, carrying out a cleanup through government contracts, even if funding is provided, is less beneficial from the perspective of justice, fairness, and resources than a cleanup undertaken by a responsible party. For instance, having a private party prevent ongoing harm from its pollution by conducting a cleanup under governmental oversight is much less burdensome on limited governmental resources than a cleanup conducted by the government, even if funding were to be provided.

---

environmental cause of action asserted was a dischargeable claim). *But see In re Peabody Energy Corp.*, 958 F.3d 717, 724–25 (8th Cir. 2020).

19. This test could raise factual issues such as whether buried drums or contaminated soil present risks of continued pollution based on the particular facts of a case including the condition of drums or leachability of soils.

20. *Torwico*, 8 F.3d at 151 (order was not a dischargeable claim because State sought cleanup rather than money and the release of hazardous wastes was "threatened and ongoing," and was "an attempt to prevent additional damage"); *Chateaugay*, 944 FR.2d at 1008 ("[EPA] has no authority to accept a payment from a responsible party as an alternative to continued pollution. Thus, a cleanup order that accomplishes the dual objectives of removing accumulated wastes and stopping or ameliorating ongoing pollution emanating from such wastes is not a dischargeable claim."); *Mark IV*, 438 B.R. at 468, 459 B.R. at 188; *Thebes v. Pennsylvania*, 2012 WL 1802044 (M.D. Pa. 2012) (cleanup order was not a claim because government sought compliance with order to ameliorate ongoing pollution even though statute also permitted state to perform and seek cost recovery), *aff'g* 2011 WL 5005310 (Bankr. M.D. Pa. 2011); *Shieldalloy Metallurgical Corp.v. New Jersey Dep't of Env't Prot.*, 743 F. Supp. 2d 429, 442–43 (D.N.J. 2010) (future decommissioning obligation of reorganized debtor was not a claim where state was not seeking money for this obligation even though it had other monetary claims for response costs); *In re Buchanan*, 2019 WL 1982939, 1983955 (Bankr. D. Ariz. Apr. 30, 2019) (orders to remove improperly stored materials were not dischargeable claims even though claim for response costs was dischargeable); *In re Damm*, 2001 WL 34065016 (Bankr. N.D. Ill. 2001). *See also Gouveia v. Tazbir*, 37 F.3d 295 (7th Cir. 1994) (debtor cannot set aside restrictive land covenant through bankruptcy because even though landowner would have an action for damages, breaching landowner has no option to force other landowner to accept money damages in lieu of equitable relief).

Several courts, however, have ruled the other way, including several in cases where private parties were seeking cleanup.[21]

The key factor underlying all of these decisions is how courts interpret the language "gives rise to a right to payment." Courts that focus on whether the government is *actually* seeking the payment of money, as opposed to whether it *could* have spent money and then sought payment, tend to find that the government's equitable remedy is not a dischargeable claim.

For example, in *Apex*, the Seventh Circuit stressed that the government "is not seeking the payment of money and the injunction that it has obtained does not entitle it to payment,"[22] and referred to a "near consensus" and "general understanding" that discharge is limited to cases where an equitable remedy "gives rise to a right to payment because the equitable decree cannot be executed. . . ."[23] Although *Apex* involved a RCRA injunctive order rather than CERCLA, the manner in which the court addressed the issue of whether an equitable remedy is a "claim" could be contended to support the argument that CERCLA cleanup orders are not ordinarily dischargeable unless the government has actually converted the order into a request for payment of money to the government so that the equitable decree could no longer be executed. The *Apex* court's focus on whether an equitable remedy gives rise to a right to payment may apply even in situations where there is no threat of ongoing pollution, as required by *Chateaugay*, *Torwico*, and *Mark IV* under statutes with cost recovery options (like CERCLA). However, the extent to which the reasoning of *Apex* applies to statutes with cost recovery options will be contested as *Apex* involved RCRA, which does not have a cost recovery option. If courts find the statutory definition of "claim" unclear, then rules

21. *Peabody Energy Corp.*, 958 F.3d at 724–25; *In re G-1 Holdings, Inc.*, 514 B.R. 720 (Bankr. D.N.J. 2014), *aff'd* 654 Fed. Appx. 571 (3d Cir. 2016) (non-precedential); *Route 21 Assocs. of Belleville, Inc. v. MHC, Inc.*, 486 B.R. 75 (S.D.N.Y. 2012), *aff'd*, 542 Fed. Appx. 41 (2d Cir. 2013) (non-precedential summary order); *Gable v. Borges Constr., Inc.*, 792 F. Supp. 2d 117 (D. Mass. 2011); *In re Kaiser Aluminum Corp.*, 399 B.R. 596 (D. Del. 2009); *In re IT Grp., Inc.*, 339 B.R. 338 (D. Del. 2006); *In re Betancourt*, 2021 WL 438858 (Bankr. D.P.R. Feb. 8, 2021); *In re Flintkote Co.*, 533 B.R. 887 (Bankr. D. Del. 2015); *In re Goodwin*, 163 B.R. 825 (Bankr. D. Idaho 1993).

22. 579 F.3d at 737.

23. *Id.* at 738.

of harmonization of federal statutes to maximize the purposes of each could be contended to support a finding of ongoing pollution in order for a compliance obligation to be a nondischargeable equitable remedy, which would be a compromise position that arguably harmonizes bankruptcy law and environmental law.[24]

The question of when equitable remedies are "claims" also comes up in nonenvironmental cases when a party has an alternative right of payment that it has not invoked. For example, *In re Davis*[25] is a Fifth Circuit case involving a state court fraud judgment in a dispute among stockholders. The state court judgment provided for remedies of a resulting trust, partition, deed reformation, appointment of a receiver, and dissolution of a partnership. Davis filed for bankruptcy and contended that these remedies were dischargeable debts because if he failed to perform, he could be held liable for an award of money damages. The Fifth Circuit disagreed, noting that creditors are not required to select a "suboptimal remedy of money damages,"[26] and finding that payment of money was a suboptimal remedy to the prevention of future wrongs. The Fifth Circuit cited to an environmental case, *In re Chateaugay Corp.*, in support of its conclusion.[27]

Courts deciding other nonenvironmental cases have applied the following test: a cause of action is a claim, and therefore dischargeable, if the party had an adequate remedy at law for a breach.[28] This test is similar to that used in the environmental cases just described, which found that it is an inadequate or suboptimal remedy for the government to take money from a polluter instead of the polluter itself promptly stopping the ongoing environmental harm from the polluter's contamination. Payment of money that then has to be used to finance government cleanup contracts is burdensome to the government, given its limited resources and the number of activities it can pursue at one time.

24. *See* Chapter 8 (Harmonization) *supra*.

25. 3 F.3d 113 (5th Cir. 1993).

26. *Id.* at 116.

27. 944 F.2d 997, 1008 (2d Cir. 1991).

28. *Rederford v. U.S. Airways, Inc.*, 589 F.3d 30, 35–37 (1st Cir. 2009); *Kennedy v. Medicap Pharmacies, Inc.*, 267 F.3d 493, 495–98 (6th Cir. 2001); *In re Ben Franklin Hotel Assocs.*, 186 F.3d 301, 304–07 (3d Cir. 1999); *In re Cont'l Airlines*, 125 F.3d 120, 131–36 (3d Cir. 1997); *In re Udell*, 18 F.3d 403, 405–10 (7th Cir. 1994).

The test is also consistent with *Davis*, where payment of money was found to be an inadequate remedy for fraud in a partnership.[29]

Given the result described previously in *Kovacs* whereby the government was found to have converted its right to an equitable remedy to a dischargeable monetary bankruptcy claim (right to payment), governmental agencies should exercise great care not to cause such a conversion or waiver of their rights by their actions in a bankruptcy proceeding. In their communications with debtors, governmental agencies should make clear that they are seeking performance and not payment of money to the government.[30]

It certainly is possible for the government to seek cleanup work for some aspects of a site and seek monetary claims for reimbursement for other aspects.[31] However, the government will need to be clear and careful in this regard, as the courts will not permit the government to disguise monetary claims as nondischargeable equitable remedies.[32] Even in settlement negotiations, there is a risk that seeking money could undermine the government's position since settlement negotiations are not always found to be confidential for all purposes. Therefore, the government may wish to seek only performance through settlement and leave it to debtors to advocate for any monetary settlement. If a monetary settlement is nonetheless proposed or reached as a compromise, protective wording could be placed into the settlement to protect the gov-

29. In *In re United States Pipe & Foundry Co.*, 32 F.3d 1324 (11th Cir. 2022), the Eleventh Circuit held that an obligation to maintain a health retirement plan was a claim because breach of the obligation gave rise to a requirement for the payment of premiums. The Eleventh Circuit expressly limited its reasoning to the Coal Act and distinguished environmental laws. *Id.* at 1331.

30. In *In re Venoco LLC*, 572 B.R. 105, 116 (Bankr. D. Del. 2017), the court found that a request for a reserve for plugging and abandonment supported that the liability was a monetary claim.

31. A good example would be oversight costs. The government's claim for the cost of overseeing a remedy being performed by a debtor would be a monetary claim while the performance of the cleanup would be an equitable remedy that would not fall within the Bankruptcy Code's definition of claim. Another example would be where the government is approaching different operable units of a site in a different manner, that is, electing to perform cleanup at some operable units and seeking reimbursement and requiring potentially responsible parties to implement the cleanup at other operable units.

32. *See Torwico*, 8 F.3d 146, 151 (3d Cir. 1993) (this is not a "repackaging [of] a forfeited claim for damages") (quoting *In re CMC Heartland Partners*, 966 F.2d 1143, 1147 (7th Cir. 1992)).

ernment's position regarding this issue in the event that the settlement is not approved.

Regardless of whether a liability is found to fall within the Bankruptcy Code's definition of a "claim," environmental liability may spring anew where a reorganized debtor or other entity owns contaminated property post-bankruptcy. The leading case on this is *CMC Heartland Partners*,[33] where the Seventh Circuit found that even though the government may have had dischargeable CERCLA claims at the time of a bankruptcy, CERCLA liability runs with the land and does not disappear at confirmation. A "statutory obligation attached to current ownership of land survives bankruptcy."[34] Just as other current owners or operators of property may have CERCLA liability for contamination on their property that was put there prior to their ownership, a reorganized debtor is generally liable under environmental laws as the current owner or operator of the property.[35] "Having been a debtor in bankruptcy" does not authorize anyone to operate a nuisance or "excuse it from complying with laws of general application."[36]

PROTECTIVE PROOFS OF CLAIM

Due to the uncertainty surrounding the issue of when equitable remedies are dischargeable claims, many governmental agencies will file "protective" proofs of claims in bankruptcy cases that have significant environmental compliance liabilities. Here is an example of language for a protective proof of claim:

> The [governmental agency] is not required to file a proof of claim with respect to debtor's injunctive obligation to comply with work requirements imposed by environmental statutes, regulations, court orders, administrative orders, or permits, because such

33. 966 F.2d 1143 (7th Cir. 1992).

34. *Id.* at 1147; *Torwico*, 8 F.3d at 151.

35. *CMC Heartland Partners*, 966 F.2d at 1146–47. The reorganized debtor would not be liable for past costs incurred prior to confirmation. Such costs would be dischargeable claims and most environmental laws do not make a new owner or operator of property liable for past costs incurred before it became the owner or operator (unless a lien was perfected).

36. *Id.* at 1146.

obligations are not claims under 11 U.S.C. § 101(5). The debtor and any reorganized debtor must comply with such mandatory requirements, including those found in [list any consent decrees, administrative order, or other known important obligation]. The [governmental agency] reserves the right to take future actions to enforce any such obligations of debtor. While the [governmental agency] believes that its position will be upheld by the Court, the [governmental agency] has included the aforementioned obligations and requirements in this Proof of Claim in a protective fashion, to safeguard against the possibility that debtor will contend that it does not need to comply with such obligations and requirements, and the Court finds that it is not required to do so. [Therefore, a protective contingent claim is filed in the alternative for such obligations and requirements but only in the event that the Court finds that such obligations and requirements are dischargeable claims under 11 U.S.C. § 101(5), rather than obligations and requirements that any reorganized debtor must comply with.][37] The [governmental agency] estimates that the cost of performing the remaining work under [consent decree or administrative order or other known important obligation] is approximately ______.[38] Nothing in this Proof of Claim constitutes a waiver of

---

37. The bracketed language should not be included where the government agency wishes only to put parties on notice of its right to seek compliance and does not want to assert a monetary claim in the alternative if the bankruptcy court rules against its position. In making this determination, state agencies may consider whether they would be waiving sovereign immunity under the 11th Amendment. *See* 11 U.S.C. § 106(b) (filing of proof of claim waives sovereign immunity but only as to claims arising from the same transaction or occurrence); *Shieldalloy Metallurgical Corp. v. New Jersey Dep't of Env't Prot.*, 743 F. Supp. 2d 429, 437–38 (D.N.J. 2010); Chapter 5 (Key Provisions (sovereign immunity)) *supra*. Filing a protective reservation of rights (which may include a reservation of sovereign immunity) would entail less risk of a waiver of sovereign immunity than asserting an affirmative claim in the alternative. Moreover, waiver of sovereign immunity for purposes of bankruptcy cases is subject to applicable nonbankruptcy law including prohibitions against pre-enforcement review. 11 U.S.C. § 106(a)(4). Therefore, protective proofs of claim designed to preserve governmental rights should not be construed to waive bars against pre-enforcement review. References to a reorganized debtor in the preceding language should not be included in liquidation cases.

38. Sometimes the sentence providing an estimate of the cost of performing the work in question is omitted as unnecessary. In particular, if the governmental agency is uncertain as to the cost, it may decide not to include the sentence. A reason for including an estimate would be to provide the bankruptcy court and other parties of interest an idea of the magnitude of the liability which may foster resolution of issues. If an estimate is included, it would be most consistent with the theory of the protective proof of claim to use the estimated cost to the debtor

any rights of the [government agency] or an election of remedies with respect to such rights and obligations.

Additional language may be added to the protective proof of claim for sites owned by the debtor, based on the reasoning of *CMC Heartland* such as:

> Debtors have, or may in the future have, environmental liabilities for properties that are part of their bankruptcy estate and/or for the mitigation of the discharge of pollutants at property of their bankruptcy estate. Pursuant to 28 U.S.C. § 959(b), debtors are required to manage and operate estate property in accordance with non-bankruptcy law, including all applicable environmental statutes and regulations. Further, any reorganized debtor will be subject to liability under environmental law with respect to any property it owns or operates. The [governmental agency] is generally not required to file a proof of claim relating to property of the estate and reserves all rights. The [governmental agency] reserves the right to file an application for administrative expenses and to take other appropriate action in the future with respect to property of the estate.

To date, debtors have not challenged the ability of governments to file protective proofs of claim without waiving their rights to pursue an equitable remedy for compliance or injunctive relief. While there are no court decisions analyzing protective proofs of claim, they appear to be consistent with the practice of liberal pleading under federal practice.[39]

As discussed in Chapter 10 (Police or Regulatory Exception) of this Practice Guide, if the government is prepared to go forward with an action for injunctive relief, the police or regulatory exception permits it to move forward either in bankruptcy court with an adversary proceeding relating to property of the estate or in

---

of performing the remedy. If the bankruptcy court were to rule against the governmental agency and find that the liability was a claim and try to estimate it, the government might update the estimate to reflect the cost to the government (which usually is higher than the cost to a private party) given the court's ruling against the government.

39. *See, e.g.*, Fed. R. Bankr. P. 8; Fed. R. Civ. P. 8(d)(2), (3) (permitting even inconsistent pleading); *In re Sevko, Inc.*, 143 B.R. 167, 174 (Bankr. N.D. Ill. 1992).

another forum[40] having jurisdiction.[41] As discussed in Chapter 20 (Jurisdiction), if the action is filed in bankruptcy court, consideration should be given to whether or not to seek to have the reference from the district court to the bankruptcy court withdrawn so that an Article III judge will hear any action for injunctive relief.[42] If not, in exercising its "related to" jurisdiction, the bankruptcy court could only submit proposed findings of fact and conclusions of law to a district judge who would then enter judgment thereon unless all of the parties to the adversary proceeding consented to the bankruptcy court entering judgment.[43] That process may potentially result in significant delay.

Given the increase in bankruptcy cases culminating with sales of assets and liquidation,[44] consideration should be given to whether timely requests for injunctive relief should be made before the party most responsible for the contamination runs out of assets and ceases to exist. Even though an action for compliance or injunctive relief may be nondischargeable, governments will not be able to obtain relief from an entity that no longer exists. Therefore, a governmental agency may decide to pursue an action for injunctive relief prior to liquidation.[45]

---

40. The debtor will not be able to remove a police or regulatory action from another forum to the bankruptcy court. 28 U.S.C. § 1452(a); *City & Cnty. of San Francisco v. PG&E Corp.*, 433 F.3d 1115 (9th Cir. 2006).

41. If the case is in Chapter 7 (where a trustee is always appointed) or a Chapter 11 trustee has been appointed, consideration should be given as to whether or not the so-called *Barton* doctrine requires permission from the bankruptcy court overseeing the trustee before an action is brought against the trustee outside of the bankruptcy court. *See, e.g.*, *Barton v. Barbour*, 104 U.S. 126 (1881); *Chua v. Ekonomou*, 1 F.4th 948 (11th Cir. 2021); *Carroll v. Abide*, 788 F.3d 502 (5th Cir. 2015); *In re VistaCare Grp., LLC*, 678 F.3d 218 (3d Cir. 2012); *Alexander v. Hedback*, 718 F.3d 762 (8th Cir. 2013); *Satterfield v. Malloy*, 700 F.3d 1231 (10th Cir. 2012); *McDaniel v. Blust*, 668 F.3d 153 (4th Cir. 2012); *In re Triple S Restaurants, Inc.*, 519 F.3d 575 (6th Cir. 2008); *In re Crown Vantage, Inc.*, 421 F.3d 963 (9th Cir. 2005); *In re Linton*, 136 F.3d 544 (7th Cir. 1998). The *Barton* doctrine does not apply to suits for acts in carrying on a business. 28 U.S.C. § 959(a); *Muratore v. Darr*, 375 F.3d 140, 143–44 (1st Cir. 2004).

42. 28 U.S.C. § 157(d).

43. *Id.* § 157(c)(1), (2). *See also* Chapter 20 (Jurisdiction) *infra*.

44. *See* Chapter 15 (Section 363 Sales) *infra*.

45. Actions for injunctive relief require considerable resources for both the government and debtors. Before investing such resources, consideration should be given to the litigation risks presented. In *In re Venoco LLC*, 572 B.R. 105, 114–15 (Bankr. D. Del. 2017), the court denied a request for injunctive relief against a liquidating debtor because it believed that public health was not at risk, the site was

If there is a purchaser of the liquidating debtor's assets, the purchaser would be liable to address contamination on the property it is purchasing to the extent nonbankruptcy law makes purchasers of contaminated property liable for contamination on the property they acquire.[46] Many debtors will insist on an express assumption of liability in order to minimize any risk of the government seeking compliance from the estate. Questions to consider in deciding whether to focus on obtaining compliance from a purchaser include: (1) is it certain that the property has been or will be included in a sale;[47] (2) does the liability relate to property purchased;[48] (3) does the purchaser expressly assume the environmental liability in question under its asset purchase agreement;[49] (4) is the purchaser likely viable; (5) does the purchaser have any alleged defense to liability under nonbankruptcy law that the debtor would not have;[50] and (6) does the debtor have the financial ability to comply?[51]

---

not property of the estate, and the liability was a claim because money had been sought to be held as a reserve.

46. See discussion of *CMC Heartland Partners supra*. Under most environmental laws, the debtor will remain liable even after a sale. Provisions in sale orders providing otherwise may be objected to as contrary to nonbankruptcy law. *See* Chapter 15 (Section 363 Sales) *infra*.

47. Close attention should be paid to the terms of sales and lists of excluded properties. These should be requested if not part of the court docket and public record. Some debtors and purchasers have gone so far as to allow the purchaser to exclude property after the sale has been approved. Such provisions should be objected to as contrary to the Bankruptcy Code and principles of due process unless they provide for a future fair opportunity for objection.

48. The purchase will be free and clear of successor liability unrelated to what is purchased. *See* Chapter 15 (Section 363 Sales) *infra*.

49. Even in the absence of clear express assumption, the government's fixing language for sale approval order discussed in Chapter 15 (Section 363 Sales) *infra* will preserve the government's rights but an express assumption is even more reliable and entails a lower risk of litigation.

50. Some nonbankruptcy laws limit the liability of an owner of contaminated property that did not cause the contamination if it can meet specified requirements such as appropriate inquiry. For example, some statutes limit the liability of bona fide prospective purchasers, but often the prospective purchasers still must comply with specified requirements such as exercising appropriate or due care with respect to any contamination at the site. *See, e.g.*, 42 U.S.C. § 9601(40).

51. In considering this factor, one should take into account the extent to which the debtor or other interested parties such as secured creditors may contest the estate's ability to comply. *See* Chapter 12 (Priorities) *infra* (discussing the difficult issue of priority between compliance obligations and secured debt). Debtors or other creditors may well oppose requests for injunctive relief whether brought in bankruptcy court or another forum with jurisdiction.

CHAPTER 12

Bankruptcy Priorities and Environmental Law

In most bankruptcies, debtors do not have sufficient assets to satisfy their debts. Therefore, one of the main functions of the Bankruptcy Code is to set forth the priority and order of distribution of available assets to creditors.[1] Creditors are typically divided into classes of similarly situated claims. Under the absolute priority rule, an objecting class of creditors must be paid in full before more junior classes of creditors are paid anything.[2] All creditors within a class/priority level must be treated similarly, such as by pro rata distribution.[3] The highest priority for claims in bankruptcy

1. *See, e.g.*, 11 U.S.C. §§ 507, 726; *see* Chapter 2 (History and Purposes) *supra*; David A. Skeel, *The Empty Idea of "Equality of Creditors,"* 166 U. Pa. L. Rev. 699 (2018); Richard M. Hynes & Steven D. Walt, *Inequality and Equity in Bankruptcy Reorganization*, 66 U. Kan. L. Rev. 875 (2018); Pamela Elkow & Thomas Sansone, *Treatment of Environmental Liabilities in Bankruptcy*, American Bar Association, Environmental Aspects of Real Estate Transactions, ch. 7, at 192–93 (2020).

2. *See* 11 U.S.C. § 1129(b)(2); *Czyzewski v. Jevic Holding Corp.*, 137 S. Ct. 973, 983–84 (2017); *Norwest Bank Worthington v. Ahlers*, 485 U.S. 197 (1988); *Zachary v. Cal. Bank & Trust*, 811 F.3d 1191, 1194 (9th Cir. 2016); *In re Pacific Lumber Co.*, 584 F.3d 229, 244 (5th Cir. 2009). In *Jevic*, the Supreme Court held that the Bankruptcy Code does not allow a structured dismissal of a bankruptcy case that provided for final distributions that bypassed classes of creditors by way of "gifts" from a superior class. 137 S. Ct. at 985–86. The Supreme Court left open the possibility of limited departures from the absolute priority rule early in the case (such as payment of critical trade vendors or wages) where there is a clear reorganization purpose that would even make disfavored creditors better off. *Id.*

3. *See, e.g.*, 11 U.S.C. §§ 1122(a), 1123(a)(4).

goes to secured claims (which have the strongest protections outside of bankruptcy),[4] but a claim is "secured" only to the extent that collateral exists to back up (i.e., "secure") the claim.[5] The second highest priority claims are administrative expense claims, that is, the "actual, necessary costs and expenses of preserving the [bankruptcy] estate."[6] Next in line under the Bankruptcy Code are a series of priority claims for certain wages, benefits, and taxes, which rarely include any environmentally-related claims.[7] General unsecured claims come next and constitute the bulk of remaining

4. The rights of secured creditors are generally governed under state laws patterned after the Uniform Commercial Code. American Law Institute, Model Codes and Studies, Uniform Commercial Code.

5. The remainder of such a claim is a deficiency claim which is then treated as a general unsecured claim. *See* 11 U.S.C. §§ 506(a); 725, 1111(b)(1)(A), 1129(b)(2)(A); *Bank of Am. Nat'l Trust & Sav. Ass'n v. LaSalle St. P'ship*, 526 U.S. 434, 439 (1999). As is the case outside of bankruptcy, priority among secured creditors in the same collateral is based on the order of the time of perfection of the interest. *In re Darnell*, 834 F.2d 1263 (6th Cir. 1987); *In re Elder-Beerman Stores Corp.*, 221 B.R. 404 (Bankr. S.D. Ohio 1998). However, superliens can have higher priority than prior perfected liens (i.e., "prime" prior liens) in certain circumstances and will be recognized in bankruptcy as well. *In re 229 Main Street Ltd. P'ship*, 262 F.3d 1 (1st Cir. 2001); *In re Lionel Corp.*, 29 F.3d 88 (2d Cir. 1994); *In re Aznoe Abribuz, Inc.*, 416 B.R. 755, 764 (Bankr. D. Mt.). Several states provide for environmental superliens. *See* Sarah Schenck, *Buoying Environmental Burden in Bankruptcy Floodwaters*, 45 URBAN LAW. 449, 467 & n.152 (2013) (citing to laws in Connecticut, Louisiana, Maine, Massachusetts, Michigan, New Hampshire, New Jersey, Pennsylvania, and Wisconsin). In addition, 11 U.S.C. § 364 permits bankruptcy courts to provide lenders providing financing for the bankruptcy case with a first priority lien if they are unable to obtain financing without such a lien and the rights of existing lienholders are adequately protected. *See* Chapters 2 (History and Purposes), 3 (Code Chapters), 5 (Key Provisions (post-petition financing)) *supra*.

6. *See* 11 U.S.C. §§ 503(b), 507(a)(2), 726(a)(1), 1129(a)(9); *Hartford Underwriters Ins. Co. v. Union Planters Bank*, 530 U.S. 1, 4–5 (2000). Where a case converts from Chapter 11 to Chapter 7, administrative expense claims for each are categorized separately with Chapter 7 administrative expense claims paid before Chapter 11 administrative expense claims. *See In re Lazar*, 207 B.R. 668, 673 (Bankr. C.D. Cal. 1997). Domestic support claims in individual cases have a higher priority than administrative expense claims. *See* 11 U.S.C. § 507(a)(1).

7. *See* 11 U.S.C. §§ 507(a)(3)–(10), 726(a)(1). The only environmentally-related claims that the authors are aware of which may be priority tax claims are certain mining fees (Abandoned Mine Land (AML) Fees). *See United States v. Ringley*, 985 F.2d 185, 187–88 (4th Cir. 1993); *United States v. Tri-No Enters, Inc.*, 819 F.2d 154, 159 (7th Cir. 1987).

bankruptcy claims.[8] Last in line under the Bankruptcy Code are equity (stock) interests and equitably subordinated claims.[9]

Since the Bankruptcy Code does not have specific provisions that govern the priority of environmental liabilities, this chapter will cover where environmental liabilities fall in the overall priority structure. Consistent with the themes identified in Chapter 8 (Harmonization) on the harmonization of environmental law and bankruptcy law, and as discussed later in this chapter, a monetary claim relating to cleanup of contaminated property would be accorded higher priority in payment (i.e., an administrative expense priority) when such a claim relates to property of the estate and costs are incurred after the bankruptcy petition is filed than when a monetary claim relates to property outside the estate or costs incurred pre-petition (i.e., usually treated as general unsecured claims unless a lien was perfected). In addition, as discussed later and consistent with the themes of Chapter 8 (Harmonization), a strong case can be made that environmental compliance obligations must be dealt with before any monetary claims are paid, although the outcome is uncertain when competing with secured debt. Environmental monetary claims (in contrast to compliance or performance obligations), such as response costs, fines, and penalties, on the other hand, are treated like the monetary claims of similarly situated creditors and thus their priority is similarly determined.

8. *See, e.g.*, 11 U.S.C. § 726(a)(2). In Chapter 7 cases, claims for fines and penalties are subordinated below other general unsecured claims. 11 U.S.C. § 726(a)(4). However, claims for fines and penalties in all individual bankruptcies including those under Chapter 7 are not dischargeable. 11 U.S.C. § 523(a)(7).

9. *See In re Dornier Aviation (North Am.), Inc.*, 453 F.3d 225, 232 (4th Cir. 2006); *Lazar*, 207 B.R. at 675; 11 U.S.C. § 510(c). Equitable subordination of a claim requires a showing of inequitable conduct if the claimant is an insider creditor, and a showing of egregious conduct if the creditor is a non-insider creditor. *See In re Sentinel Mgmt. Group, Inc.*, 809 F.3d 958, 964 (7th Cir. 2016); *In re Winstar Commc'ns, Inc.*, 554 F.3d 382, 412 (3d Cir. 2009); *In re 604 Columbus Ave. Realty Tr.*, 968 F.2d 1332, 1362 (1st Cir. 1992); *In re Mobile Steel Co.*, 563 F.2d 692, 701–06 (5th Cir. 1977). Courts may not use equitable subordination to reorder categorical priorities established by Congress in the Code. *See United States v. Reorganized CF&I Fabricators of Utah, Inc.*, 518 U.S. 213 (1996); *United States v. Nolan*, 517 U.S. 535 (1996).

Environmental creditors may have secured claims if they have perfected a judgment or have a statutory lien.[10] Generally, a lien cannot be perfected once a bankruptcy petition is filed because the police or regulatory exception to the automatic stay does not apply to perfection of a lien.[11] Environmental creditors with a right of setoff against amounts owed to debtors are also treated as having secured claims up to the amount of the setoff right.[12] Governmental environmental creditors may wish to coordinate with other agencies within the same government, as setoffs may extend to tax refunds and other payments owed by such other agencies to debtors.[13] Environmental creditors may also have a secured-like interest in insurance proceeds as injured parties to which a debtor is liable under its insurance policies.[14] Liens supporting secured

---

10. *See, e.g.*, 28 U.S.C. § 9607(l), (r) (CERCLA liens); *In re Iezzi*, 504 B.R. 777 (Bankr. E.D. Pa. 2014) (lien for waste and recycling fees).

11. *See* 11 U.S.C. § 362(a)(4), 362(b)(4); *In re Microfab, Inc.*, 105 B.R. 152, 160 (Bankr. D. Mass. 1989). However, "superliens" that prime existing liens may be perfectable post-petition pursuant to 11 U.S.C. §§ 362(b)(3), 546(b). *See In re 229 Main St. Ltd. P'ship*, 262 F.3d 1 (1st Cir. 2001); *In re Perona Bros., Inc.*, 186 B.R. 833 (Bankr. D.N.J. 1995); *Microfab*, 105 B.R. at 155–59. Debtors may attempt to avoid the perfection of certain liens as preference if they were perfected within 90 before the filing of the bankruptcy. *See, e.g.*, *Fidelity Fin. Services, Inc. v. Fink*, 522 U.S. 211 (1998). However, debtors may not attempt to avoid as preferences statutory liens that were perfected prior to the commencement of the bankruptcy case. *See* 11 U.S.C. §§ 547(c)(6), 545; *In re Motion Mktg. Solutions, Inc.*, 403 B.R. 403 (Bankr. N.D. Tex. 2009).

12. *See* 11 U.S.C. § 506(a); *In re Buckner*, 66 F.3d 263, 265 n.3 (10th Cir. 1995). Section 553 of the Bankruptcy Code preserves creditors right of setoff under non-bankruptcy law so long as the offsetting debts are mutual. *See* Chapter 5 (Key Provisions (setoff)) *supra*; *In re Doctors Hosp. of Hyde Park, Inc.*, 337 F.3d 951, 955 (7th Cir. 2003); *Braniff Airways, Inc. v. Exxon Co., USA*, 814 F.2d 1030 (5th Cir. 1987).

13. Release of a payment to a debtor, however, may defeat the right of setoff unless it has been carefully preserved by agreement approved by the bankruptcy court. *See Citizens Bank of Maryland v. Strumpf*, 516 U.S. 16, 20 (1995); *In re Lifestyle Furnishings, LLC*, 418 B.R. 382, 387 (Bankr. D. Idaho 2009); *In re Gehrke*, 158 B.R. 465, 468 (Bankr. N.D. Iowa 1993). The United States is considered unitary for purposes of setoff. *See United States v. Maxwell*, 157 F.3d 1099, 1102–03 (7th Cir. 1998); *In re Hal, Inc.*, 122 F.3d 851 (9th Cir. 1997); *In re Chateaugay*, 94 F.3d 772 (2d Cir. 1996); *In re Turner*, 84 F.3d 1294 (10th Cir. 1996) (en banc).

14. *In re OGA Charters LLC*, 901 F.3d 599, 604 (5th Cir. 2018); *In re Allied Prods. Corp.*, 288 B.R. 533 (Bankr. N.D. Ill. 2003); *In re Sunland, Inc.*, 2014 WL 7011747 (Bankr. D.N.M. Dec. 11, 2014); *Landry v. Exxon Pipeline Co.*, 260 B.R. 769 (Bankr. M.D. La. 2001).

claims ride through a bankruptcy unaffected unless the secured creditor participates in the bankruptcy case.[15]

RESPONSE COSTS AS ADMINISTRATIVE EXPENSES

A number of courts have held that the government is entitled to an administrative expense priority for cleanup/response costs incurred post-petition with respect to property of the bankruptcy estate. The courts reason that such costs are "actual" and "necessary" costs of "preserving the estate,"[16] since the trustee or debtor-in-possession has an obligation to clean up or take care of the property. The government may obtain an allowed administrative expense claim because it fulfills that obligation and reduces the risk of further damage and liability to the estate.[17]

---

15. *See Johnson v. Home State Bank*, 501 U.S. 78, 82–83 (1991) (while personal liability is discharged, in rem liability passes through the bankruptcy); *Farrey v. Sanderfoot*, 500 U.S. 291, 297 (1991); *Long v. Bullard*, 117 U.S. 617, 620–21 (1886). 11 U.S.C. § 1141(c) permits the extinguishment of liens where the lien is dealt with in the plan and not preserved. The lien can be extinguished, however, only when the secured creditor participates in the bankruptcy case. *See In re N. New England Tel. Operations LLC*, 795 F.3d 343, 348–49 (2d Cir. 2015); *In re Ahearn Enters., Inc.*, 507 F.3d 817, 822–23 (5th Cir. 2007); *In re Penrod*, 50 F.3d 459, 463 (7th Cir. 1995). The degree of participation required is subject to debate. Therefore, a secured creditor that wishes for its lien to pass through the bankruptcy unaffected may wish to insist on a clear statement in the plan that so provides, or should object to the plan as not meeting the requirements of Section 1141(c). Secured creditors may also potentially be impacted by sales of assets under Section 363 of the Code. As explained in Chapter 15 (Section 363 Sales) *infra*, if approved, such sales may be free and clear of liens which then attach to the proceeds of sale.

16. 11 U.S.C. § 503(b)(1)(A).

17. *See, e.g.*, 28 U.S.C. § 959(b); *In re H.L.S. Energy Co.*, 151 F.3d 434, 437 (5th Cir. 1998); *Pennsylvania v. Conroy*, 24 F.3d 568, 569–70 (3d Cir. 1994); *In re Chateaugay Corp.*, 944 F.2d 997, 1009–10 (2d Cir. 1991); *In re Smith-Douglass, Inc.*, 856 F.2d 12, 17 (4th Cir. 1988); *In re Wall Tube & Metal Prods. Co.*, 831 F.2d 118, 124 (6th Cir. 1987); *In re Stevens*, 68 B.R. 774, 780–81 (D. Me. 1987); *In re Appalachian Fuels, LLC*, 521 B.R. 779, 792–99 (Bankr. E.D. Ky. 2014); *In re Am. Coastal Energy Inc.*, 399 B.R. 805 (Bankr. S.D. Tex. 2009); *In re Coal Stripping, Inc.*, 222 B.R. 78 (Bankr. W.D. Pa. 1998); *In re Peerless Plating Co.*, 70 B.R. 943 (Bankr. W.D. Mich. 1987); *In re Mowbray Eng'g Co.*, 67 B.R. 34 (Bankr. M.D. Ala. 1986); *In re Distrigas Corp.*, 66 B.R. 382 (Bankr. D. Mass. 1986); *In re T.P. Long Chemical, Inc.*, 45 B.R. 278 (Bankr. N.D. Ohio 1985); *In re Laurinburg Oil Co.*, 49 B.R. 652 (Bankr. M.D.N.C. 1984); *In re Vermont Real Estate Inv. Tr.* 25 B.R. 804 (Bankr. D. Vt. 1982). *See generally* Sarah Schenck, *Buoying Environmental Burden in Bankruptcy Floodwaters*, 45 URBAN LAW. 449, 454 (2013).

Debtors sometimes contend that environmental expenditures do not provide a benefit to the estate and therefore should not be given administrative expense priority. This argument is based on case law holding that an administrative expense must "benefit" the estate.[18] In the environmental context, though, courts have found that this "benefit" requirement should be understood as a means of testing whether an expense was "necessary" to preserve the estate as the Bankruptcy Code requires.[19] Environmental expenditures incurred with respect to property of the estate are "necessary" to comply with the law and, as such, may provide debtors with important indirect benefits, including the ability to stay in business, an orderly liquidation, or increased value of the contaminated property.[20] Indeed, as discussed in Chapter 9 (Operating Estate Property), 28 U.S.C. § 959(b) requires that debtors-in-possession manage and operate their property in accordance with nonbankruptcy law; therefore, governments contend that the costs of doing so are part of the cost of doing business.

H.L.S. Energy[21] out of the Fifth Circuit provides an instructive example. The debtor sold its valuable producing wells in Chapter 11 and a trustee was appointed when the case was converted to Chapter 7. Texas law requires that unproductive wells be properly plugged within one year of cessation of production. When the debtor did not comply with an administrative action requiring such plugging, Texas incurred the cost of doing so and sought administrative expense priority. The Fifth Circuit found that Texas's expenditures

---

18. *See, e.g., In re Whistler Energy II, L.L.C.*, 931 F.3d 432, 443 (5th Cir. 2019); *Sanchez v. Northwest Airlines, Inc.*, 659 F.3d 671, 677 (8th Cir. 2011); *In re Eagle-Picher Indus., Inc.*, 447 F.3d 461, 464 (6th Cir. 2006); *H.L.S. Energy*, 151 F.3d at 438; *In re MTE Holdings LLC*, 2021 WL 2258270 (Bankr. D. Del. June 2, 2021).

19. 11 U.S.C. § 503(b)(1)(A); *see Whistler Energy* at 443; *In re MTE Holdings LLC*, 2021 WL 2258270, at *5 (Bankr. D. Del. June 2, 2021).

20. *See In re Energy Future Holdings Corp.*, 990 F.3d. 728, 742 (3d Cir. 2021); *In re Whistler Energy II, L.L.C.*, 931 F.3d 432, 443 (5th Cir. 2019); *In re Northstar Offshore Grp. LLC*, 628 B.R. 286, 298–99 (Bankr. S.D. Tex. 2020); *Appalachian Fuels*, 521 B.R. at 799. If property is abandoned under Section 554 of the Bankruptcy Code during a bankruptcy case, this rationale for administrative expense priority would disappear on a going forward basis. (However, the estate may still be liable even for post-abandonment costs under the *Reading* theory of administrative expense priority discussed later in this chapter for costs incurred on account of post-petition, pre-abandonment releases or operation of the property.)

21. 151 F.3d 434, 437 (5th Cir. 1998).

were actual and necessary costs of preserving the estate because the bankruptcy trustee was required to comply with state law and could not abandon the wells "in contravention of a state law reasonably designed to protect public health or safety. . . . Thus, a combination of Texas and federal law placed on the trustee an inescapable obligation to plug the unproductive wells, an obligation that arose during the chapter 11 proceedings."[22] Fulfilling the estate's obligation to plug the wells benefited the estate by reducing the estate's liability related to the unplugged wells. It did not matter that oil was never produced from the wells during the bankruptcy case, because the estate had the sole operating interest during the case and thus the legal obligation to plug the well.[23]

In *H.L.S. Energy*, all of the plugging obligations accrued during the bankruptcy case (one year after the cessation of production). The Fifth Circuit therefore did not consider the situation where the obligation initially accrued pre-petition.[24] In *In re American Coastal Energy Inc.*, however, the bankruptcy court found administrative expense priority in the pre-petition accrual situation as well because there was a "continuing state-law-health-and-safety duty" that made the plugging obligation "a post-petition obligation that has pre-petition antecedents."[25]

Wall Tube[26] out of the Sixth Circuit is also an important case on administrative expenses for environmental costs. The debtor

22. *Id.* at 438. Several of the cases allowing administrative expenses for post-petition response costs have referred to limitations on a debtor's ability to abandon contaminated property. Limitations on a debtor's ability to abandon are discussed in Chapter 18 (Abandonment) *infra.* Debtors may attempt to incorporate their arguments about whether abandonment should be allowed into objections to administrative expense applications. Governments may contend that even if abandonment were permissible, any costs incurred prior to abandonment are actual and necessary costs of complying with legal requirements with respect to property that is still in the estate and therefore entitled to administrative expense priority. In addition, governments may contend that the *Reading* theory of administrative expense priority, which is discussed later in this chapter, is applicable.

23. *Id.* at 438–39.

24. *Id.* at 439. *In re National Gypsum*, 139 B.R. 397, 412–13 (N.D. Tex. 1992), held that the government was entitled to administrative expense priority only where conditions pose an imminent and identifiable threat to public health and safety. However, governments may contend that this ruling is inconsistent with the Fifth Circuit's later ruling in *H.L.S. Energy* which did not require such a showing.

25. 399 B.R. 805, 811 (Bankr. S.D. Tex. 2009).

26. 831 F.2d 118, 124 (6th Cir. 1987).

had filed for Chapter 7, and the estate included numerous leaking drums, tanks, and vats containing sludges and hazardous substances. The State of Tennessee sought administrative expense priority for response costs it incurred addressing hazards presented by this property of the estate. The Sixth Circuit first found that 28 U.S.C. § 959(b) applied because the trustee was continuing the debtor's violation of Tennessee environmental laws by exposing the public to an ongoing environmental health hazard from the estate's property.[27] The Sixth Circuit concluded that the state's costs were actual and necessary expenses to preserve the estate "in required compliance with state law and to protect the health and safety of a potentially endangered public."[28]

Similar reasoning to the aforementioned cases may support administrative expense claims of private parties fulfilling a debtor's compliance obligations.[29] Liabilities for post-petition contract services and goods associated with environmental activities are also entitled to administrative expense priority if debtors believed they would enhance the value of the business and without regard to whether they resulted in a profit.[30]

However, several courts have denied private parties (often lessors) administrative expense priority where the estate either did not own or no longer owned the property in question.[31] *In re Hanna*[32] involved an interesting situation where petroleum had leaked from debtor-owned property onto a neighboring property.

---

27. *Id.* at 122.

28. *Id.* at 124.

29. *See, e.g., In re Hemingway Transp., Inc.*, 993 F.2d 915, 935–36 (1st Cir. 1993);: *In re ATP Oil & Gas Corp.*, 2014 WL 1047818 (Bankr. S.D. Tex. Mar. 18, 2014);: *In re Virginia Builders, Inc.*, 153 B.R. 729 (Bankr. E.D. Va. 1993); *In re Great North Forest Prods., Inc.*, 135 B.R. 46, 61 (Bankr. W.D. Mich. 1991); *In re Kent Holland Die Casting & Plating, Inc.*, 125 B.R. 493, 501 (Bankr. W.D. Mich. 1991).

30. *In re MTE Holdings LLC*, 2021 WL 2258270 (Bankr. D. Del. June 2, 2021).

31. *See, e.g., In re Dant & Russell, Inc.*, 853 F.2d 700, 709 (9th Cir. 1988); *Southern Ry. Co. v. Johnson Bronze Co.*, 758 F.3d 137 (3d Cir. 1985) (clarified by later decision in *Conroy*); *Route 21 Assocs. of Belleville, Inc. v. MHC, Inc.*, 486 B.R. 75, 92 (S.D.N.Y. 2012); *In re Insilco Techs., Inc.*, 309 B.R. 111 (Bankr. D. Del. 2004); *In re G-I Holdings, Inc.*, 308 B.R. 196 (Bankr. D.N.J. 2004); *In re Mahoney-Troast Constr. Co.*, 189 B.R. 57 (Bankr. D.N.J. 1995); *In re McCrory Corp.*, 188 B.R. 763 (Bankr. S.D.N.Y. 1995). Several of these cases involved rejected leases or executory contracts which raised issues under Section 365 of the Bankruptcy Code, 11 U.S.C. § 365. *See* Chapter 5 (Key Provisions (executory contracts)) *supra*.

32. 168 B.R. 386 (9th Cir. B.A.P. 1994).

The leaks were from the debtor's pre-petition operations and the debtor did not add any significant new contamination post-petition, but the existing contamination continued to leach and migrate post-petition.[33] In a split decision, the majority of the Bankruptcy Appellate Panel denied administrative expense priority and found that the claim was a pre-petition claim because the debtor did not cause significant post-petition contamination to the neighbor's property and any migration was passive.[34] The dissent would have found administrative expense priority based on the trustee's knowing failure to stop releases from estate property.[35]

Courts have relied on *Reading Co. v. Brown*[36] as another basis for granting administrative expense priority for environmental damages or costs resulting from post-petition operations.[37] In *Reading*, the Supreme Court held that "costs ordinarily incident to operation of a business," such as damages and repair costs to another's property resulting from a fire on the debtor's premises, as in that case, are actual and necessary expenses of the estate entitled to administrative expense priority even though the estate would not "benefit," in the narrow sense of the term, from the costs paid to the third party.[38] The courts relying on *Reading* have reasoned that the estate's creditors, even if innocent themselves, should not be able to benefit from the debtor's avoidance of paying costs incurred by other innocent parties harmed through the debtor's violation of the law.[39] Courts have applied *Reading* to violations

33. *See id.* at 388.
34. *See id.* at 389.
35. *See id.* at 395.
36. 391 U.S. 471 (1968).
37. *See, e.g., H.L.S. Energy*, 151 F.3d at 437; *Hemingway*, 993 F.2d at 935; *In re N.P. Mining Co.*, 963 F.2d 1449, 1457–59 (11th Cir. 1992); *In re Wall Tube & Metal Prods. Co.*, 831 F.2d 118, 123 (6th Cir. 1987); *In re Duplan Corp.*, 212 F.3d 144, 155 (2d Cir. 2000); *In re ATP Oil & Gas Corp.*, 2014 WL 1047818 (Bankr. S.D. Tex. Mar. 18, 2014); *Kent Holland*, 125 B.R. at 503–04.
38. *Reading* can thus be viewed as either a kind of exception to the general requirement of benefit to the estate discussed earlier, or another recognition that the benefit to the estate was the underlying operation of the business. *See In re Philadelphia Newspapers, LLC*, 690 F.3d 161, 173 (3d Cir. 2012), *as corrected* (Oct. 25, 2012). *See also Ellis v. Westinghouse Elec. Co., LLC*, 11 F.4th 221, 230–31 (3d Cir. 2021); cases cited in note 20 *supra*.
39. *See, e.g., Wall Tube*, 831 F.2d at 123; *Leavell v. Karnes*, 143 B.R. 212, 219 (S.D. Ill. 1990).

that continue post-petition even where the original conduct or violation commenced pre-petition.[40]

Courts have disagreed, however, over whether the rationale of *Reading* applies to estates that are liquidating and not operating a business.[41] This disagreement is largely analogous to the disagreement among courts as to the applicability to liquidating estates of 28 U.S.C. § 959(b)'s requirement that trustees and estates manage and operate their property in accordance with nonbankruptcy law.[42]

Some courts have declined to allow administrative expenses where the claimant has not yet incurred an actual expense.[43] Other courts have allowed contingent and unliquidated administrative expense claims subject to demonstration of the future expended amounts. For example, in *In re Appalachian Fuels, LLC*,[44] the bankruptcy court held that the duty to reclaim mining properties was ongoing and therefore gave rise to an actual and necessary expense of the estate during the bankruptcy case. The bankruptcy court approved an allowed contingent administrative expense claim based on an "outside" estimate of cost and required that the trustee set aside such funds to be paid after completion of the reclamation and subject to judicial review.[45] Similarly, in *In re Hemingway Transport, Inc.*,[46] the First Circuit found that a private claimant may in the future have an allowable administrative expense claim upon the future incurrence of response costs.[47]

If the bankruptcy court allows response costs as administrative expenses, those costs would normally be subordinate to the

---

40. *See, e.g.*, *In re Mallinckrodt PLC*, 2021 WL 4876908 (Bankr. D. Del. Oct. 19, 2021).

41. *Compare, e.g.*, *Wall Tube*, 831 F.2d 118, *with NP Mining*, 963 F.2d 1449. *See also In re Res. Tech. Corp.*, 662 F.3d 472 (7th Cir. 2011); *Hemingway*, 993 F.2d at 5–6 & n.5.

42. *See* Chapter 9 (Operating Estate Property) *supra*.

43. *See, e.g.*, *In re Oldco M Corp.*, 438 B.R. 775 (Bankr. S.D.N.Y. 2010); *In re H.F. Radandt, Inc.*, 160 B.R. 323 (Bankr. W.D. Wis. 1993).

44. 521 B.R. 779, 795–96 (Bankr. E.D. Ky. 2014).

45. *See id.* at 804–05.

46. 993 F.2d 915, 935–36 (1st Cir. 1993).

47. A claim for future costs would be potentially disallowable under 11 U.S.C. § 502(e) if found to be a claim for contribution. *Id.* at 936. *See* Chapter 13 (Discharge) (claims for contribution) *infra*.

interests of secured creditors in their collateral.[48] Accordingly, if all or most of the estate's assets are subject to security interests, even administrative expenses may not be paid in full. However, under Section 506(c) of the Bankruptcy Code,[49] where response action is taken with respect to property in which a secured creditor has a security interest, the trustee or debtor-in-possession may be allowed to recover from, or surcharge against, the secured property the costs of the response action necessary to preserve the secured property.[50] The response action benefits the secured creditor's property and gives it value by bringing it into compliance with the law so that it can be sold. If the secured creditor was not required to bear those costs when obtaining the value of its collateral, it would be unjustly enriched.[51] But Section 506(c) cannot be used to surcharge property subject to the secured creditor's lien that is not itself benefited by the response action.[52]

Environmental creditors (like other creditors) had in the past been able to directly file a Section 506(c) claim to surcharge a secured creditor's collateral where the secured creditor benefited through performance of a response action that was an obligation of the estate.[53] However, in *Hartford Underwriters Insurance Company v. Union Planters Bank, N.A.*,[54] the Supreme Court held

48. *See In re Visual Indus., Inc.*, 57 F.3d 321, 324 (3d Cir. 1995); *In re Guterl Special Steel Corp.*, 316 B.R. 843, 853 (Bankr. W.D. Pa. 2004).

49. *See* 11 U.S.C. § 506(c) ("The trustee may recover from property securing an allowed secured claim the reasonable, necessary costs and expenses of preserving, or disposing of, such property to the extent of any benefit to the holder of such claim.").

50. *Guterl Steel*, 316 B.R. at 854–55; *In re Tollenaar Holsteins*, 538 B.R. 830 (Bankr. E.D. Cal. 2015); *In re Guterl Special Steel Corp.*, 198 B.R. 128, 136 (Bankr. W.D. Pa. 1996); *In re Better Bright Plating, Inc.*, 105 B.R. 912 (Bankr. E.D. Wis. 1989); *In re Mowbray Eng'g Co.*, 67 B.R. 34 (Bankr. M.D. Ala. 1986); *In re T.P. Long Chem., Inc.*, 45 B.R. 278 (Bankr. N.D. Ohio 1985). A surcharge is similar to a priority credit against the value of the secured property or collateral, which is paid first from proceeds of the sale of the property or collateral.

51. *Guterl Steel*, 316 B.R. at 853–54.

52. *See Great N. Forest Prods.*, 135 B.R. at 71; *In re Corona Plastics, Inc.*, 99 B.R. 231 (Bankr. D.N.J. 1989); *T.P. Long*, 45 B.R. at 288. Some courts require that the benefit to the property be "direct and quantifiable," but such a requirement can be met by testimony that each dollar of expense preserved the potential for at least a dollar of value. *See In re Domistyle, Inc.*, 811 F.3d 691, 701 (5th Cir. 2015).

53. *See, e.g., In re Cuyahoga Equip. Corp.*, 980 F.2d 110, 112–13 (2d Cir. 1992).

54. 530 U.S. 1 (2000).

that creditors do not have an independent right to assert Section 506(c) claims because the language of the statute refers only to trustees (and therefore debtors-in-possession who have the rights and powers of trustees).[55] The Supreme Court noted that it was not addressing the situation where an interested party acts in a trustee's stead, with permission from the bankruptcy court, because the trustee has refused to act.[56] Therefore, if an environmental creditor wishes to utilize Section 506(c) to recover its costs of protecting the value of secured creditors' collateral through performance of cleanup activities, it should in the first instance request that the trustee or debtor-in-possession undertake the cleanup and pursue a Section 506(c) claim or a settlement with the secured creditor. If the trustee or debtor-in-possession declines, the environmental creditor may then seek approval of the bankruptcy court to act derivatively on behalf of the trustee and estate.[57] Creditors hoping to utilize Section 506(c) also should be aware that larger Chapter 11 debtors nowadays often waive causes of action under Section 506(c) at the beginning of the bankruptcy case against both prepetition and post-petition lenders in connection with obtaining debtor-in-possession financing and authority to use cash collateral. Such a waiver may preclude environmental creditors from utilizing Section 506(c). Thus, environmental creditors interested in preserving the potential benefits of Section 506(c) need to pay close attention to a debtor's motions for financing or use of cash collateral.[58]

55. *See id.* at 7 n.3.

56. *See id.* at 13 n.5.

57. Providing such authority would be similar to other situations, where courts have given a creditors' committee or individual creditor's derivative standing to pursue trustee tasks when the trustee was unwilling or unable to do so. *See, e.g., In re Trailer Source, Inc.*, 555 F.3d 231, 239–44 (6th Cir. 2009); *In re Racing Servs., Inc.*, 540 F.3d 892, 898 (8th Cir. 2008); *In re Smart World Techs., LLC*, 423 F.3d 166, 176 (2d Cir. 2005); *Official Comm. of Unsecured Creditors of Cybergenics Corp. v. Chinery*, 330 F.3d 548, 579 (3d Cir. 2003) (en banc); *Fogel v. Zell*, 221 F.3d 955, 965–66 (7th Cir. 2000); *Louisiana World Exposition v. Fed. Ins. Co.*, 858 F.2d 233, 247 (5th Cir. 1988).

58. *See* Chapters 4 (Timeline (first-day hearing)), 5 (Key Provisions (post-petition financing)) *supra*. Objections could be filed against the waivers but bankruptcy courts have often overruled such objections on the ground that the debtor's agreement to the waiver was an appropriate exercise of its business judgment in connection with obtaining financing. Where an existing secured creditor's collateral is contaminated, it may be possible to contend that such a waiver of the ability to

PENALTY CLAIMS AS ADMINISTRATIVE EXPENSES

Courts have also relied on *Reading* to find that a debtor's liability for penalties for post-petition violations of environmental law are entitled to administrative expense priority as a cost ordinarily incident to the operation of a business.[59] These courts have found that it would be fundamentally unfair to allow regulated companies operating in Chapter 11 to avoid the costs associated with that regulation, including penalties for violating the law.[60] Otherwise the deterrent effect of environmental statutes would be lost, public health and safety would be placed at risk, and competitors would be placed at a disadvantage.[61] For example, in *Munce's Superior Petroleum Products*, the debtor was operating leaking fuel tanks without secondary containment systems required by a state court order. The First Circuit held that the penalties imposed on the debtor were administrative expenses.[62] This decision and others like it are consistent with the well-accepted proposition that bankruptcy courts are not a safe haven from regulatory compliance.[63] They are also consistent with Section 959(b)'s requirement

---

surcharge collateral is not good business judgment and might result in a windfall to such secured creditor.

59. *In re Munce's Superior Petroleum Prods., Inc.*, 736 F.3d 567 (1st Cir. 2013); *Cumberland Farms, Inc. v Florida Dep't of Env't Prot.*, 116 F.3d 16 (1st Cir. 1997); *In re N.P. Mining Co.*, 963 F.2d 1449, 1453 (11th Cir. 1992); *United States Dep't of Interior v. Elliott*, 761 F.2d 168 (4th Cir. 1985); *In re Charlesbank Laundry, Inc.*, 755 F.2d 200 (1st Cir. 1985); *In re Bill's Coal Co.*, 124 B.R. 827 (D. Kan. 1991); *Leavell v. Karnes*, 143 B.R. 212, 219 (S.D. Ill. 1990); *In re Coal Stripping, Inc.*, 222 B.R. 78 (Bankr. W.D. Pa. 1998); *In re Double B Distributions, Inc.*, 176 B.R. 271 (Bankr. M.D. Fla. 1994); *In re Motel Invs., Inc.*, 172 B.R. 105 (Bankr. M.D. Fla. 1994). *See also In re Steenes*, 942 F.3d 834, 838 (7th Cir. 2019) (Chapter 13 debtor's traffic fines during bankruptcy case entitled to administrative expense priority).

60. *Munce's*, 736 F.3d at 573.

61. *N.P. Mining*, 963 F.2d at 1458, 1461; *Elliott*, 761 F.2d at 172. *See also In re Res. Tech. Corp.*, 662 F.3d 472, 476 (7th Cir. 2011) (business operating in bankruptcy "would have an inefficient competitive advantage over their solvent competitors—and deficient incentive to use due care in the operation of the business").

62. *Munce's*, 736 F.3d at 569.

63. *Steenes*, 918 F.3d at 558; *In re Nortel Networks, Inc.*, 669 F.3d 128, 137 (3d Cir. 2011); *S.E.C. v. Brennan*, 230 F.3d 65, 71 (2d Cir. 2000); *In re Commonwealth Cos., Inc.*, 913 F.2d 518, 527 (8th Cir. 1990); *United States v. Nicolet, Inc.*, 857 F.2d 202, 207–08 (3d Cir. 1988); *City of New York v. Exxon Corp.*, 932 F.2d 1020, 1024 (2d Cir. 1991); *In re Commerce Oil Co.*, 847 F.2d 291, 297 (6th Cir. 1988); *Commodity Futures Trading Comm'n v. Co Petro Mktg. Grp., Inc.*, 700 F.2d 1279, 1283 (9th Cir. 1983); *Bickford v.*

that debtors-in-possession operate in accordance with applicable nonbankruptcy law.[64] However, as noted in Chapter 9 (Operating Estate Property), the courts disagree about the applicability of Section 959(b) to liquidations. In *Pennsylvania Department of Environmental Resources v. Tri-State Clinical Laboratories, Inc.*,[65] the Third Circuit held that the rationale of *Reading* did not extend to payment of noncompensatory[66] criminal penalties in a Chapter 7 case where employees of the debtor illegally disposed of infectious waste after a trustee had been appointed. The court reasoned that: (1) criminal activity could not be within the scope of ordinary and necessary operations of a business, (2) it would be unfair to Chapter 7 creditors given that there was no operation of a business as in *Reading*, and (3) noncompensatory penalties are subordinated in Chapter 7 cases.[67]

OTHER CLAIMS

As noted at the outset of this chapter, general unsecured claims for pre-petition liabilities are next in line for recovery after secured and administrative expenses and other priority claims. Examples

---

Lodestar Energy, Inc., 310 B.R. 70, 76 (E.D. Ky. 2004); *United States v. ILCO, Inc.*, 48 B.R. 1016, 1023 (N.D. Ala. 1985).

64. *See* Chapter 9 (Operating Estate Property) *supra.*

65. 178 F.3d 685 (3d Cir. 1999).

66. Noncompensatory fines or penalties are fines or penalties that are not compensation for actual pecuniary loss, as further discussed in Chapter 13 (Discharge) *infra.*

67. *Id.* at 690–98. The Third Circuit distinguished the case from a civil fine on a business in a heavily regulated industry. *Id.* at 698. *See also Resource Technology*, 662 F.3d at 477; *N.P. Mining*, 963 F.2d at 1458–61. *In re Exide Techs.*, 601 B.R. 271, 284–89 (Bankr. D. Del. 2019), *aff'd*, 613 B.R. 79 (Bankr. D. Del. 2020), extended the rationale of *Tri-State* to a Chapter 11 claim for civil penalties that it found had been conceded to be quasi-criminal. *Exide* involved an unusual situation where the debtor had closed its California hazardous waste facility during the bankruptcy case but reorganized with operations at other facilities. The bankruptcy court also found that having to enter into a criminal non-prosecution agreement and spend over $100 million in cleanup costs created a sufficient deterrent. *Exide,* 601 B.R. at 288. Although dicta in *Exide* seems to call into question whether noncompensatory civil penalties for post-petition violations of law are entitled to administrative expense priority, *see* 613 B.R. at 89–90, *Exide* fails to distinguish or even refer to the contrary decisions of three courts of appeal (*see* note 59 *supra*) and does not discuss whether *Tri-State* is distinguishable because it relied heavily on Chapter 7 provisions and legislative history relating to the subordination of penalties.

of environmental claims that may fit within the category of general unsecured claims include claims for response costs that are not related to property of the debtor or a debtor's post-petition operations, pre-petition response costs for property of the estate where a lien has not been perfected, and fines or penalties for pre-petition days of environmental violations.[68]

While the low priority for unsecured claims often results in a reduced or zero recovery for such claimants, debtors are sometimes able to pay certain unsecured pre-petition claims in full at the outset of the case pursuant to critical vendor or similar motions. Courts have allowed this preferential treatment on the ground that the ability to continue to do business with critical vendors (who might otherwise cease doing business with the debtor) or to make certain other payments may be essential to the success of the case and the potential for reorganization and is therefore of benefit to all creditors. Such payments have been approved after a hearing under Section 363(b) of the Bankruptcy Code as acceptable uses of a debtor's property.[69] Some debtors have even included certain governmental payments for pre-petition permit or license fees or royalties as critical payments needed to continue the business. However, extensive use of critical vendor and other payments at the beginning of a case portends the risk that the bulk of unsecured claims remaining in the bankruptcy case will be claims of tort victims and sometimes governmental agencies.

Claims for fines or penalties in Chapter 7 cases are subordinated below that of other unsecured claims.[70] However, while

---

68. *See, e.g., In re Dant & Russell, Inc.*, 853 F.2d 700, 709 (9th Cir. 1988); *Route 21 Assocs. of Belleville, Inc. v. MHC, Inc.*, 486 B.R. 75, 92–93 (S.D.N.Y. 2012); *In re G-I Holdings, Inc.*, 308 B.R. 196, 204 (Bankr. D.N.J. 2004); *In re Lazar*, 207 B.R. 668, 675 (Bankr. C.D. Cal. 1997); *In re Hanna*, 168 B.R. 386, 389 (9th Cir. B.A.P. 1994); *In re Wisconsin Barge Lines, Inc.*, 91 B.R. 65, 68 (Bankr. E.D. Mo. 1988). In the case of continuing violations, penalties for post-petition days of violation may be entitled to administrative expense priority as a necessary cost of post-petition operations. But debtors and not all courts agree. *See Lazar*, 207 B.R. at 684.

69. *See, e.g., Czyezewski v. Jevic Holding Corp.*, 137 S. Ct. 973, 985 (2017) (noting practice); *In re Kmart Corp.*, 359 F.3d 866, 873–74 (7th Cir. 2007); *Pacific Lumber*, 584 F.3d at 238 n.7; *Stephens Indus. v. McClung*, 789 F.2d 386, 390 (6th Cir. 1986); *In re GVM, Inc.*, 606 B.R. 220, 227 (Bankr. M.D. Pa. 2019).

70. *See* 11 U.S.C. § 726(a)(4). Section 726 does not apply in Chapter 11 cases. *See* 11 U.S.C. § 103(b). However, depending on the facts of the case, the issue of penalty subordination could come up in Chapter 11 plan confirmation in connection with

claims for fines and penalties are subordinated and dischargeable in corporate Chapter 7 bankruptcies, they are subordinated but not dischargeable in individual bankruptcies including those under Chapter 7.[71]

COMPLIANCE OBLIGATIONS

As reflected in the preceding discussion, the Bankruptcy Code only specifies priorities for liabilities that fall within the Code's definition of "claim."[72] Chapter 11 (Compliance Obligations) of this Practice Guide analyzes at length the contours of that definition. How then is a bankruptcy estate required to deal with compliance obligations (including injunctive cleanup obligations) that are not claims?

Governmental agencies may contend that compliance obligations are facts of life that the estate must comply with as they arise during the bankruptcy and thereafter.[73] If a debtor and its lenders wish for the debtor to avail itself of the protections under the Bankruptcy Code, they should understand that a corollary to that is compliance with the law while in bankruptcy and that the cost of doing so will be "actual and necessary" administrative expenses of the estate.[74] Under this view, compliance obligations take precedence over pecuniary claims and have an effective superpriority over all else.[75] In that sense, they are like other items on an estate's agenda and in its budget and follow automatically from its existence as an operating or liquidating legal entity. Compliance

---

the issue of whether creditors are recovering under a plan as much as they would in Chapter 7. *See* 11 U.S.C. § 1129(a)(7). Nonetheless, an attempt to treat penalty claims differently than other unsecured claims in Chapter 11 may also raise issues of unfair discrimination under 11 U.S.C. § 1129(a)(1). *See* Chapter 16 (Plan Objections) *infra*.

71. 11 U.S.C. § 523(a)(7).

72. *Id.* § 101(5).

73. *See* 28 U.S.C. § 959(b); Chapter 9 (Operating Estate Property) *supra*.

74. *See, e.g., In re Allegheny Int'l, Inc.*, 158 B.R. 343 (Bankr. W.D. Pa. 1992) (debtor's costs in complying with NRC consent decree and license requirements). They would, however, not per se be an administrative expense claim of the government since the government is not expending funds or seeking money. Rather, the government is simply seeking to require the debtor to comply with legal requirements.

75. *See* Joshua Macey & Jackson Salovaara, *Bankruptcy as Bailout: Coal Company Insolvency and the Erosion of Federal Law*, 71 Stan. L. Rev. 879, 956 (2019).

obligations cannot be avoided and often pass through the bankruptcy unimpaired to a reorganized debtor or liquidating plan administrator.[76]

Debtors and their secured creditors, however, may take a different view. They would point to the strong protections and primacy given to secured creditors under the law of secured transactions as well as under the Bankruptcy Code and contend that secured creditors' rights in their collateral, including cash collateral, are paramount, even ahead of compliance obligations.[77] Debtors and secured creditors are sensitive to risks that potentially diminish the value of their collateral and the availability or cost of the loans provided by lenders.

Governments might contend that as strong as the protections afforded to lenders might be, and as wide as the use and scope of security interests by lenders has become, limits are required if otherwise generally applicable legal requirements are to retain their meaning and efficacy. Police and regulatory laws and compliance do not become optional just because all of a company's assets are encumbered by liens. This is particularly so if lenders knew when making their loans that they were dealing with a regulated entity; they should have understood what the law required and that their liens and rights were subject to generally applicable legal requirements for the business in question.

If a business is operating under an ongoing loan agreement, a secured creditor should not be able to prevent a debtor from using its collateral to comply with laws applicable to the operating business.[78] The laws governing secured transactions including loan

76. However, if an estate has an inability to comply, then the government may have limited recourse. But that would be true even outside of bankruptcy. And after a company fully liquidates, it will no longer be able to comply in any event. Thus, if a government wishes to obtain compliance and cannot reach an interim settlement agreement taking into account the debtor's limited present ability to comply, it may consider bringing an action for compliance in bankruptcy court through the filing of an adversary proceeding. *See* Chapters 10 (Police or Regulatory Exception), 11 (Compliance Obligations) *supra*.

77. *See, e.g.*, 11 U.S.C. §§ 361, 362(d)(2), 364, 506, 1129(b)(2)(A); Uniform Commercial Code art. 9; Christopher G. Bradley, *Disrupting Secured Transactions*, 56 Hous. L. Rev. 965 (2019).

78. In fact, most loan agreements expressly require compliance with applicable laws including environmental laws. However, debtor-in-possession loan agreements

agreements (usually state laws based on the Uniform Commercial Code) were not intended to be a safe haven from compliance with the law any more than the bankruptcy laws were meant to be. The Uniform Commercial Code and its applications are not a license to violate applicable law. Section 959(b) confirms this principle. When the debtor files for bankruptcy, Section 959(b) expressly requires compliance with nonbankruptcy law in the debtor's ongoing operations.[79] In addition, with the help of valuation experts, sophisticated arguments can be made that secured creditors' rights do not extend to the enhanced going concern value that arises from the successful reorganization of companies and that therefore secured claims should not be a reason to allow noncompliance.[80] Finally, if a lender prohibits an operating debtor from acting to comply with the law, it risks being found liable under environmental law for acting as an operator of the business making environmental decisions.[81]

The resolution of the conflict between compliance obligations and secured interests is more uncertain in liquidating cases where a business is no longer operating. However, if a secured creditor is allowing its collateral to be used for its advantage in managing property of the estate, a case can be made that it should not be permitted to selectively choose what laws should be complied with in managing the liquidating business for its benefit. Nonetheless, there is significant litigation risk and uncertainty as to the outcome, especially in circuits that do not recognize the applicability of Section 959(b) to liquidating debtors.[82] Governmental agencies

---

also are subject to a budget approval process by lenders. *See* Chapter 5 (Key Provisions (post-petition financing)) *supra*.

79. *See* Chapter 9 (Operating Estate Property) *supra*.

80. *See* Melissa B. Jacoby & Edward Janger, *Tracing Equity: Realizing and Allocating Value in Chapter 11*, 96 Tex. L. Rev. 673 (2018).

81. *See* Chapter 5 (Key Provisions (post-petition financing)) *supra*. *See also* B. Swett, D. Foley & S. Bentley, *Aggressive, Extra-Contractual Conduct Leads to "Lender Liability" Judgment*, 41 Am. Bankr. Inst. J. 26 (2022) (noting lender liability judgment where lender injected itself into corporate governance and managed payments that would be made) (citing *Bailey Tool & Mfg. Co. v. Republic Bus. Credit*, No. 16-03025 (Bankr. N.D. Tex. Dec. 23, 2021), ECF No. 369)).

82. *See* Chapter 9 (Operating Estate Property) *supra* (discussing Circuit split on this issue); Chapter 18 (Abandonment) *infra* (noting that lack of unencumbered assets in liquidation may be relevant to motions to abandon property with environmental contamination).

will maximize their chances of success by bringing actions for compliance as early as possible and not waiting until a debtor is in full-scale liquidation mode.

The conflict between compliance obligations and secured creditors in bankruptcy (particularly in liquidating cases) is a gray area of the law that may require further clarification in environmental bankruptcy cases. Appropriate resolution will require harmonization of environmental law, bankruptcy law, and the law of secured transactions.[83] If the courts cannot reach the appropriate balance in harmonizing these conflicting areas of the law, Congress or state legislatures may step in and provide guidance to address the competing interests.[84]

83. *See* Chapter 8 (Harmonization) *supra*. Failure to harmonize these important bodies of law in a balanced and appropriate manner would threaten to effectively nullify wide areas of the law in many situations and undermine the rule of law. For an interesting debate about the impact of secured transaction laws on tort victims, *compare* Lynn M. Lopucki, *The Unsecured Creditor's Bargain*, 80 Va. L. Rev. 1887 (1994), *with* Susan Block-Lieb, *The Unsecured Creditor's Bargain: A Reply*, 80 Va. L. Rev. 1989 (1994).

84. *See* Luke Sperduto, *Three and a Half Rules for Tort Claims in (and Out of) Chapter 11*, 95 Am. Bankr. L.J. 127 (2021) (discussing similar issues from the perspective of tort claimants).

CHAPTER 13

When Environmental Claims Arise and Other Dischargeability Issues

Chapter 13 examines when environmental "claims" under Section 101(5) of the Bankruptcy Code, such as for cleanup costs, arise. The timing of when a claim arises is critical to evaluating dischargeability under the Bankruptcy Code. This chapter addresses other dischargeability issues as well.[1] Section 1141(d)(1) of the Bankruptcy Code provides that "the confirmation of a plan . . . discharges the debtor from any debt that *arose* before the date of such confirmation."[2] The term "debt" is defined as "liability on a claim."[3] Section 524(a)(2) of the Code provides for an injunction against acts to collect discharged debts.[4]

1. Whether an environmental liability such as a cleanup requirement or other equitable remedy constitutes a dischargeable "claim" under the Bankruptcy Code is covered in Chapter 11 (Compliance Obligations) of this Practice Guide.

2. 11 U.S.C. § 1141(d)(1) (emphasis added). Corporate debtors liquidating under Chapter 7 of the Code or liquidating all or substantially all of the debtor's assets under Chapter 11 of the Code are not entitled to a discharge. 11 U.S.C. §§ 727(a), 1141(d)(3).

3. 11 U.S.C. § 101(12).

4. *Id.* § 524(a)(2); U.S. Courts, Chapter 12—*Bankruptcy Basics*, https://www.uscourts.gov/services-forms/bankruptcy/bankruptcy-basics/chapter-12-bankruptcy-basics. The importance of discharge to the fresh start goals of bankruptcy is discussed in Chapter 2 (History and Purposes) *supra*.

The critical question, then, is when do environmental claims for cleanup costs arise.[5] Resolution of this issue poses a conflict between the bankruptcy goal of fresh start through discharge and the policies underlying environmental law.[6] The conflict is particularly acute in situations where the potential claimant lacks information about the existence of a claim that would enable it to fairly participate in the bankruptcy process. If a claim is not discharged, then the reorganized debtor will have to pay the claim in full even though other creditors in the bankruptcy case may have only been paid pennies on the dollar and a large claim may impact the debtor's fresh start.[7] On the other hand, if the potential claimant could not fairly participate in the bankruptcy process by filing a proof of claim because the claimant did not yet even know it had a claim, then the claimant would not have the opportunity to recover anything on the claim. This result would be unfair to the potential claimant and would undercut environmental law policies and procedural due process fairness concerns. Provision for a fresh start under bankruptcy law and the long-term liability of polluters for the harm they have caused under environmental law are thus in great tension and need to be harmonized.[8] Providing for either

5. An environmental claim for penalties arises on the day of the violation for which penalties are being sought. *See Riverkeeper, Inc. v. MirantLovett LLC*, 675 F. Supp. 2d 337 (S.D.N.Y. 2009) (confirmation discharged penalty claims for violations before plan's effective date but not thereafter). Most environmental statutes provide for penalties based on days of violation. *See, e.g.*, 33 U.S.C. § 1319(d) (Clean Water Act); 42 U.S.C. § 7413(e)(2) (Clean Air Act). The issue of when a claim arises therefore generally does not often come up in the context of claims for penalties under environmental laws. The date of violation giving rise to a penalty may also determine whether the penalty claim has administrative expense priority. *See* Chapter 12 (Priorities) *supra.* In cases of individual (as opposed to corporate) bankruptcies, noncompensatory penalties (i.e., penalties that are not compensation for actual pecuniary loss) are not dischargeable. *See* 11 U.S.C. §§ 523(a)(7), 1141(d)(2); *Kentucky Natural Res. & Env't Prot. Cabinet v. Seals*, 161 B.R. 615 (W.D. Va. 1993); *In re Thebes*, 2011 WL 1239847 (Bankr. M.D. Pa. Mar. 30, 2011); *United States v. Davis*, 2008 WL 4976271 (Bankr. S.D. Ind. Oct. 1, 2008); *In re Jones*, 311 B.R. 647 (Bankr. M.D. Ga. 2004).

6. *See In re Grossman's Inc.*, 607 F.3d 114, 125–26 n.11 (3d Cir. 2010); *In re Jensen*, 995 F.2d 925, 930 (9th Cir. 1993); *Signature Combs, Inc. v. United States*, 253 F. Supp. 2d 1028, 1038 (W.D. Tenn. 2003); *In re Nat'l Gypsum Co.*, 139 B.R. 397, 409 (N.D. Tex. 1992).

7. *See Grogan v. Garner*, 498 U.S. 279, 287 (1991) (creditors of non-discharged debts could recover "full payment").

8. *See* Chapters 1 (Introduction), 8 (Harmonization) *supra.*

(1) a discharge of environmental claims when there was not a fair opportunity to participate in a bankruptcy case or, conversely, (2) an exemption from fresh start when a claimant *could* fairly have participated in the bankruptcy case may fail to harmonize the statutes properly in both instances.

While cases dealing with the issue of when environmental claims arise tend to be fact specific, the initial question involves the determination of the proper legal test to apply.[9] This question is not unique to environmental claims; it can also emerge in the context of other kinds of latent future claims, such as tort claims, where at the time of the bankruptcy proceeding claimants may lack information regarding whether they have been exposed to a toxic chemical or are developing an injury from a harmful product. Generally speaking, courts have adopted either: (1) a conduct test or (2) variations of a fair contemplation/legal relationship test.[10] Under the conduct test, a claim arises at the time of the debtor's conduct that gives rise to the liability, regardless of whether the creditor was aware of the conduct or its consequences at that time.[11] Under the fair contemplation/legal relationship test, a claim arises when there is enough of a pre-petition legal relationship between the debtor and claimant such that the matter could be fairly contemplated and dealt with in the bankruptcy case.[12]

9. *See* Alison J. Brehn, David N. Copas & Collen K. Vossler, *To Be, or Not to Be: The Undiscovered Country of Claims Estimation in Bankruptcy*, 8 J. Bankr. L. & Prac. 197, 203–26 (1999).

10. *See* Pamela Elkow & Thomas Sansone, *Treatment of Environmental Liabilities in Bankruptcy*, American Bar Association, *Environmental Aspects of Real Estate Transactions*, ch. 7, at 206–08 (2020); David Houston, Kelly Waits & Addie Wyatt, *Bankruptcy Treatment of Environmental Liabilities,* 40-7 A.B.I. J. 18 (July 2021).

11. *See, e.g., In re Grossman's Inc.*, 607 F.3d 114 (3d Cir. 2010); *Grady v. A.H. Robins Co.*, 839 F.2d 198 (4th Cir. 1988); *68th St. Site Work Grp. v. Airgas, Inc.*, 2021 WL 4750180 (D. Md. Oct. 12, 2021). However, in *Grossman's*, the court held that even if a claim had arisen, the claim would not be discharged if due process requirements were not met. *See Grossman's*, 607 F.3d at 125–26.

12. *See, e.g., In re Motors Liquidation Co.*, 829 F.3d 135 (2d Cir. 2016) (defects in cars purchased after confirmation); *In re Lemelle v. Universal Mfg. Corp.*, 18 F.3d 1268 (5th Cir. 1994) (fire from defect in mobile home two years after plan confirmation); *In re Piper Aircraft Corp.*, 58 F.3d 1573 (11th Cir. 1995) (future claims for defects in aircraft that had not crashed by time of confirmation had not arisen and were not discharged); *In re Fairchild Aircraft Corp.*, 184 B.R. 910 (Bankr. W.D. Tex. 1995) (defective airplanes); *In re Chance Indus., Inc.*, 367 B.R. 689 (Bankr. D. Kan. 2006) (defective amusement park rides).

An older test based on when a "right to payment" accrues under nonbankruptcy law has now been largely discredited and found to be inconsistent with the Bankruptcy Code's broad definition of "claim."[13]

The majority view on when an environmental claim arises attempts to harmonize the statutory frameworks through versions of the fair contemplation/legal relationship test. Application of the fair contemplation/legal relationship test to environmental claims means that an environmental cleanup cost recovery claim arises when the claimant can tie the debtor to a release that the claimant knows will lead to response costs.[14] This test requires that the environmental claimant and the debtor have a relationship such that the claimant could fairly be expected to participate in the bankruptcy case and have its claim discharged.[15] On a related

---

13. *See, e.g.*, *In re M. Frenville Co.*, 744 F.2d 332 (3d Cir. 1982), *overruled by Grossman's*, 607 F.3d 114 (3d Cir. 2010); *In re Agway, Inc.*, 313 B.R. 31, 42 (Bankr. N.D.N.Y. 2004). However, there may be situations where a claim has not arisen because it is not within Section 101(5)'s definition of claim and the liability has not arisen under applicable nonbankruptcy law.

14. *See, e.g.*, *In re Crystal Oil Co.*, 158 F.3d 291 (5th Cir. 1998); *In re Jensen*, 995 F.2d 925 (9th Cir. 1993); *In re Chi., Milwaukee, St. Paul & Pacific R.R.*, 3 F.3d 200 (7th Cir. 1993); *Chi., Milwaukee, St. Paul & Pacific R.R.*, 974 F.2d 775 (7th Cir. 1992); *AM Int'l, Inc. v. Datacard Corp.*, 106 F.3d 1342 (7th Cir. 1997); *In re United States Pipe & Foundry Co.*, 577 B.R. 916 (Bankr. M.D. Fla. 2017); *Signature Combs, Inc. v. United States*, 253 F. Supp. 2d 1028 (W.D. Tenn. 2003); *In re Hexcel Corp.*, 239 B.R. 564 (N.D. Cal. 1999); *NCL Corp. v. Lone Star Bldg. Crs. (Eastern) Inc.*, 144 B.R. 170 (S.D. Fl. 1992); *In re Nat'l Gypsum Co.*, 139 B.R. 397 (N.D. Tex. 1992); *Reynolds Bros., Inc. v. Texaco, Inc.*, 647 N.E.2d 1205 (Mass. 1995).

15. The Second Circuit has its own version of the legal relationship test. *See In re Chateaugay Corp.*, 944 F.2d 997, 1005 (2d Cir. 1991) (focusing on the release or threatened release of a hazardous substance where there was a sufficient legal relationship with debtor); *see also In re Motors Liquidation*, 829 F.3d at 156 (requiring "pre-petition conduct fairly giving rise to the claim" and "contact or relationship between the debtor and the claimant such that the claimant is identifiable"); *In re Duplan Corp.*, 212 F.3d 144, 151 (2d Cir. 2000); *In re Manville Forest Prods. Corp.*, 209 F.3d 125, 129 (2d Cir. 2000) (environmental indemnification claim was contemplated based on legal relationship). While the Third Circuit has adopted a conduct test generally, it has reserved decision on when an environmental claim arises. *See Grossman's*, 607 F.3d at 125–26 n.11. The Third Circuit had previously held in *In re Reading Co.*, 115 F.3d 1111, 1126 (3d Cir. 1997), that environmental claims arise if: (1) all elements have accrued, or (2) a contingent claimant had sufficient knowledge of a possible claim to establish a relationship sufficient for discharge. *Grossman's* did not cite to *Reading*. Finally, an early decision adopting a right to payment/accrual test for when environmental claims arise has not been followed. *See United States v. Union Scrap Iron & Metal*, 123 B.R. 831 (D. Minn. 1990).

matter, courts have held that environmental claims under a statute cannot arise before the statute in question was enacted and became law.[16] Therefore, environmental claims under statutes that were not enacted until after confirmation of a plan would not be discharged.

Whether an environmental claimant can fairly tie a debtor to a release that will lead to response costs is a fact-intensive question. In general, a bar date notice places a duty of reasonable investigation on the environmental claimant to look for claims. If environmental authorities have discovered contamination at a site, a claim for cleanup costs at the site is likely to be found to be discharged under a duty of reasonable investigation, whether or not a claim was actually made. On the other hand, claims for contamination that would not have been revealed by a reasonable investigation at the time of the bar date may be distinct and severable and therefore found not to have arisen and are accordingly not discharged. In *Crystal Oil*, the Fifth Circuit found that a claim had arisen where a government employee saw a sign that, with the exercise of reasonable diligence, could have tied the debtor to a site with environmental contamination, provided that the debtor had not made misrepresentations to the government.[17] In *Boston & Maine*, a claim for cleanup costs of a site was not discharged because the contamination was not known and information about a nearby landfill was distinct and not known to have impacted the site.[18] In *Jensen*, a claim was discharged because an agency's inspection indicated that a tank might pose a hazard.[19] In *Exide Technologies*, a contribution claim for lead contamination in buildings was found to have arisen because the claimant knew of lead soil contamination.[20] In *Grace*, a contribution claim was discharged because the claimant

16. *See In re Duplan Corp.*, 212 F.3d at 151–52; *In re Reading Co.*, 115 F.3d 1111 (3d Cir. 1997); *In re Penn Central Transp. Co.*, 944 F.2d 164 (3d Cir. 1991); *United States v. Am. Premier Underwriters*, 2007 WL 1030487 (E.D. Pa. Apr. 4, 2007).

17. *Crystal Oil*, 158 F.3d at 296–97.

18. *In re Boston & Maine Corp.*, 2013 WL 5508248 (D. Mass. Sept. 27, 2013), *aff'd*, 2013 WL 6119313 (D. Mass. Nov. 19, 2013).

19. *In re Jensen*, 995 F.2d at 931. The Ninth Circuit imputed the knowledge of the California Water Board to the California Department of Health Services without discussing the relationship between the agencies under California law or with respect to the site. *Id.*

20. *In re Exide Techs.*, 600 B.R. 753 (Bankr. D. Del. 2019).

had been told by EPA of the possibility of asbestos damage to trees even though the claimant did not have confirmation or knowledge of the extent of damage. In *United States Pipe & Foundry*, a private nuisance claim was not discharged because releases were not known and EPA had not done any testing.[21] In *Solitron Devices*, a claim was discharged because a prior citation by authorities provided evidence of pollution.[22]

Although a debtor's duty to notify a creditor of the bankruptcy and bar date is usually analyzed separately under a different legal framework discussed later in this chapter, a claimant's notification or awareness of the bankruptcy case and the bar date (or lack thereof) may be important to a determination of "fair contemplation." On close facts, a bankruptcy court is more likely to find that contamination was "fairly" contemplated when the creditor was notified of the bankruptcy proceeding and, as a result, should have conducted a reasonable investigation to determine if it had claims as opposed to a situation in which the creditor was not even aware of the bankruptcy case and bar date.

The application of the fair contemplation test and notification of bar date requirements (as discussed later) indicate efforts by courts to harmonize bankruptcy law and environmental law and also take into account important "due process" considerations.[23] Discharging environmental claims without providing potential claimants a fair opportunity to assert their claims undermines fundamental precepts of environmental law and is at odds with due process and fairness.

---

21. *United States Pipe & Foundry Co.*, 577 B.R. at 925.

22. *In re Solitron Devices, Inc.*, 510 B.R. 890 (Bankr. S.D. Fla. 2014).

23. *See* Chapter 8 (Harmonization) *supra*; *In re Energy Future Holdings Corp.*, 949 F.3d 806, 822 (3d Cir. 2020); *Wright v. Owens Corning*, 679 F.3d 101, 108 n.7 (3d Cir. 2012).

OTHER DISCHARGEABILITY ISSUES

Notice of Bankruptcy Bar Date and Confirmation Hearing

Many cases involving the issue of when an environmental claim arises and becomes dischargeable also raise the related issue of whether the debtor had a duty to notify the creditor of the bankruptcy bar date for proofs of claim or the deadlines for objections to confirmation or a sale. Where a debtor has information that reasonably suggests a potential claim and the entity to whom the debtor would be liable is reasonably ascertainable, it is a "known" claim for which the debtor must provide notice of the bar date. In such cases, if notice is not provided, the claim is not discharged and may be pursued in full against the reorganized debtor.[24] Whether the identity of a claimant is reasonably ascertainable requires an analysis of the debtor's review of its books and records and the debtor's diligence in looking for specific information related to an actual injury for which the debtor may have liability.[25] Even if a creditor is unknown, publication notice is required and issues may arise as to the adequacy of publication notice such as whether national newspapers or newspapers where

---

24. *See, e.g., City of New York v. New York, N.H & H.R. Co.*, 344 U.S. 293, 297 (1953); *In re Arch Wireless, Inc.*, 534 F.3d 76, 83–85 (1st Cir. 2008); *Fogel v. Zell*, 221 F.3d 955, 964 (7th Cir. 2000); *Crystal Oil*, 158 F.3d at 297; *In re Maya Constr, Co.*, 78 F.3d 1395 (9th Cir. 1996); *In re Unioil*, 948 F.2d 678, 684 (10th Cir. 1991); *In re Spring Valley Farms, Inc.*, 863 F.2d 832 (11th Cir. 1989); *In re Weiand Auto. Indus.*, 612 B.R. 824, 848 (Bankr. D. Del. 2020). *Cf. Archer-Daniels-Midland Co. v. Country Visions Coop.*, 29 F.4th 956 (7th Cir. 2022) (free and clear sale not binding if notice not provided); *In re HNRC Dissolution Co.*, 3 F.4th 912 (6th Cir. 2021) (same); Chapter 15 (Section 363 Sales) *infra*. In individual cases, there is no discharge if a debt is not listed on the debtor's schedules in order to permit the creditor to file a proof of claim unless the creditor had notice or actual knowledge of the case. *See* 11 U.S.C. § 523(a)(3).

25. *See, e.g., Motors Liquidation*, 829 F.3d at 159; *Dahlin v. Lyondell Chem. Co.*, 881 F.3d 599 (8th Cir. 2018); *In re Placid Oil Co.*, 753 F.3d 151, 156 (5th Cir. 2014); *In re J.A. Jones, Inc.*, 492 F.3d 242, 251–52 (4th Cir. 2007); *In re Arch Wireless, Inc.*, 534 F.3d at 82–85; *Crystal Oil*, 158 F.3d at 297–98; *Chemetron Corp. v. Jones*, 72 F.3d 341, 346 (3d Cir. 1995); *Weiand Auto.*, 612 B.R. at 849. The issue is not whether a claim is foreseeable but whether there is specific information related to an actual injury. *Placid Oil*, 753 F.3d at 156–57. *See generally* Elkow & Sansone, *supra* note 10, ch. 7, at 201–03.

debtors operated were included.[26] As a precaution, some debtors with significant environmental liabilities also provide notice to all federal, state, and local environmental agencies (and associated attorney general offices) where they have done business. Finally, inadequate notice or faultless failure to file a claim may be a factor in a bankruptcy court's determination to permit the filing of a late proof of claim for excusable neglect in a Chapter 11 case.[27]

Post-Bankruptcy Ownership of Contaminated Property

If a creditor has a claim for response costs relating to property that is owned by a debtor, the debtor will be discharged for response costs incurred through confirmation.[28] But post-bankruptcy ownership gives rise to a liability springing anew based on the reorganized debtor's status as a post-bankruptcy owner or operator of the property, notwithstanding any discharge in bankruptcy.[29]

---

26. *See Tulsa Prof'l Collection Servs. v. Pope*, 485 U.S. 478 490 (1988); *Mullane v. Central Hanover Bank & Tr. Co.*, 339 U.S. 306, 317 (1950); *In re Waterford Energy*, 294 Fed. Appx. 900 (5th Cir. 2008) (unpublished); *Weiand Auto.*, 612 B.R. at 850; *Grand Pier Ctr. LLC v. ATC Group Sers., Inc.*, 2007 WL 2973829 (N.D. Ill. Oct. 9, 2007); *In re Buttes Gas & Oil Co.*, 182 B.R. 493 (Bankr. S.D. Tex. 1994).

27. *DPWN Holdings (USA), Inc. v. United Air Lines, Inc.*, 246 F. Supp. 3d 680, 692 (S.D.N.Y. 2017); *In re Pettibone Corp.*, 162 B.R. 791, 814 (Bankr. N.D. Ill. 1994). Other relevant factors may include prejudice to the debtor and whether a creditor was diligent upon learning of a bankruptcy bar date. *See Pioneer Inv. Servs. Co. v. Brunswick Assocs. Ltd. P'ship*, 507 U.S. 380 (1993); *In re CJ Holding Co.*, 27 F.4th 1105 (5th Cir. 2022); *In re Zilog, Inc.*, 450 F.3d 996, 1007 (9th Cir. 2006); *Jones v. Chemetron Corp.*, 212 F.3d 199 (3d Cir. 2000); *Chemetron Corp. v. Jones*, 72 F.3d at 349; *In re W.R. Grace & Co.*, 563 B.R. 160 (Bankr. D. Del. 2016).

28. Pre-petition response costs will constitute a general unsecured claim; post-petition response costs will have administrative expense priority. *See* Chapter 12 (Priorities) *supra*.

29. *See In re CMC Heartland Partners*, 966 F.2d 1143 (7th Cir. 1992) (reorganized debtor liable under CERCLA as post-bankruptcy owner for post-bankruptcy response costs even though contamination originated pre-bankruptcy); *In re Motors Liquidation Co.*, 585 B.R. 708, 726 (Bankr. S.D.N.Y. 2018) (New GM may be liable for post-sale migration of salt into groundwater from its property even though salt was dumped onto its property before it became the owner); *In re Klosterman Dev., Inc.*, 2013 WL 4605451 (Bankr. N.D. Ohio Aug. 29, 2013) at 16–17 (plan may not shield reorganized debtor from obligations to abate a post-confirmation nuisance); *In re Weiand Auto. Indus.*, 612 B.R. at 845 (reorganized debtor potentially liable for post-effective date migration of hazardous waste from its property); *In re General Motors Corp.*, 407 B.R. 463, 508 (Bankr. S.D.N.Y. 2009) (purchaser must comply with environmental responsibilities for contamination on its property starting on the

Under most environmental statutes, a current owner or operator of property is responsible even for contamination that originated before it became the owner or operator and is liable for response costs associated with such contamination.[30] The same is true for a reorganized debtor based on the well-accepted principle that no one can maintain a nuisance.[31] Another way to view this is that a claim based on a reorganized debtor's status as a post-bankruptcy owner or operator arises anew after confirmation and therefore is not discharged as a debt that arose before confirmation under Section 1141(d)(1).

Insurance Coverage

Another limitation on discharge that may be considered by environmental creditors relates to the pursuit of insurance coverage for an environmental claim. Under Section 524(e), a discharge does not affect the liability of another entity for the debt, including an insurer. Therefore, courts have held that a creditor may obtain a judgment against a discharged debtor if that is done solely for purposes of pursuing insurance coverage for a claim.[32]

Claims for Contribution

The issues of when environmental claims arise and become dischargeable and exceptions to discharge for failure to notify creditors of the bar date also arise in connection with private party environmental claims for contribution against debtors.[33] As a related matter,

---

day it obtains the property); *In re Flood*, 234 B.R. 286, 292–93 (Bankr. W.D.N.Y. 1999) (Chapter 7 bankruptcy does not permit a debtor to avoid liability for demolition of unsafe structure it owned after abandonment by estate).

30. *See, e.g.*, 42 U.S.C. § 9607(a)(1) (CERCLA).

31. *See Ohio v. Kovacs*, 469 U.S. 274, 285 (1985); *In re CMC Heartland Partners*, 966 F.2d at 1146.

32. *See* Chapter 19 (Insurance) *infra*; *In re Federal-Mogul Global Inc.*, 684 F.3d 355, 380 (3d Cir. 2012); *First Fidelity Bank v. McAteer*, 985 F.2d 114, 118 (3d Cir. 1993); *Green v. Welsh*, 956 F.2d 30, 33 (2d Cir. 1992); *In re Jet Florida Systems, Inc.*, 883 F.2d 970, 973–76 (11th Cir. 1989); *In re Hendrix*, 986 F.2d 195, 197 (7th Cir. 1993); *Weiand Auto.*, 612 B.R. at 859–60.

33. *See, e.g.*, *Boston & Maine Corp. v. Mass. Bay Transp. Auth.*, 587 F.3d 89 (1st Cir. 2009); *AM Int'l, Inc. v. Datacard Corp., DBS, Inc.*, 106 F.3d 1342, 1347–48 (7th Cir. 1997); *Reading*, 115 F.3d at 1123; *In re Revere Copper & Brass Inc.*, 172 B.R. 192

a couple of courts have held that if the government's direct claim is discharged, then there is no surviving claim for contribution by private parties because contribution claims require joint liability to the government.[34]

Claims of potentially responsible parties (PRPs) for contribution from a debtor may raise an additional issue based on Section 502(e) of the Bankruptcy Code's provision for disallowance of contingent claims for reimbursement or contribution. This provision does not affect private party claims for reimbursement of past costs that have been incurred by the private party but can result in the disallowance of claims for contribution toward expected future costs.[35] The purpose of Section 502(e) is to avoid double liability of the debtor to both a direct and contribution claimant. However, Section 502(e) can result in unfairness to a contribution claimant such as where the direct claimant is not seeking a recovery of future costs from the debtor.[36] To address this unfairness, some courts have allowed mechanisms such as a trust or a surrogate proof of claim on behalf of the direct claimant in order to protect the contribution claimant while avoiding the risk of double liability of the debtor.[37] Filing of a proof of claim by a contribution

---

(S.D.N.Y. 1994); *In re Solitron Devices, Inc.*, 510 B.R. 890 (Bankr. S.D. Fla. 2014); *In re Texaco Inc.*, 182 B.R. 937 (Bankr. S.D.N.Y. 1995).

34. *Reading*, 115 F.3d at 1124–25; *New Jersey Dep't of Env't Prot. v. Am. Thermoplatics Corp.*, 2018 WL 3536090 (D.N.J. July 23, 2018).

35. *See In re Eagle-Picher Indus., Inc.*, 131 F.3d 1185 (6th Cir. 1997); *In re Charter Co.*, 862 F.2d 1500 (11th Cir. 1989); *In re Kaiser Gypsum Co.*, 2020 Lexis 3208 ¶ 44 (Bankr. W.D.N.C. Nov. 13, 2020); *In re Chemtura Corp.*, 443 B.R. 601 (Bankr. S.D.N.Y. 2011); *In re Lyondell Chemical Co.*, 442 B.R. 236 (Bankr. S.D.N.Y. 2011); *In re Apco Liquidating Trust*, 370 B.R. 625 (Bankr. D. Del. 2007); *In re G-I Holdings, Inc.*, 308 B.R. 196, 212 (Bankr. D.N.J. 2004); *In re Kaiser Group Int'l Inc.*, 289 B.R. 597 (Bankr. D. Del. 2003); *In re Harvard Indus., Inc.*, 153 B.R. 668 (Bankr. D. Del. 1993); *In re Harvard Indus., Inc.*, 138 B.R. 10 (Bankr. D. Del. 1992); *In re Cottonwood Canyon Land Co.*, 146 B.R. 992 (Bankr. D. Colo. 1992); *In re Bicoastal Corp.*, 141 B.R. 231 (Bankr. M.D. Fla. 1992). *See generally* Elkow & Sansone, *supra* note 10, ch. 7, at 211–12.

36. *See* Henry S. Rauschenberger, *The Disallowance of Claims for Future Remediation Costs*, 40-7 A.B.I. J. 20 (July 2021). If EPA is the direct creditor and it enters into a settlement of its direct claim under CERCLA, CERCLA provides for protection against contribution claims for matters addressed. *See* 42 U.S.C. § 9613(f)(2). In the event of such a settlement, Section 502(e) would not have additional meaning since the contribution claim would already be barred by contribution protection.

37. *See In re Hemingway Transp., Inc.*, 993 F.2d 915, 927 (1st Cir. 1993); *In re Dant & Russell, Inc.*, 951 F.2d 246 (9th Cir. 1991); *Glidden Co. v FV Steel & Wire Co.*, 350 B.R. 96 (E.D. Wis. 2006); *In re Allegheny Int'l Inc.*, 126 B.R. 919 (W.D. Pa. 1991), *aff'd*,

claimant on behalf of the direct claimant can also help secure a contribution of the debtor toward future costs.[38]

Special Exceptions to Discharge of Individual Debtors

Section 523 of the Bankruptcy Code provides for several exceptions to discharge in the case of *individual* debtors (i.e., not corporate or partnership debtors and the like).[39] The exceptions to discharge in Section 523 most relevant to environmental claims are: (1) failure to provide notice, 11 U.S.C. § 523(a)(3), which was discussed earlier; (2) fines or penalties to governmental units that are not compensation for actual pecuniary loss (i.e., noncompensatory fines or penalties), 11 U.S.C. § 523(a)(7); and (3) debts for willful and malicious injury, 11 U.S.C. § 523(a)(6).[40]

Section 523(a)(7) excepts an individual debtor's liability to governmental units for fines or penalties that are not compensation for actual pecuniary loss. Nondischargeable penalties serve a "punitive or rehabilitative governmental aim, rather than a purely compensatory purpose."[41] Courts have found that penalties under most environmental laws, including clean water, mining, waste disposal, and lead paint disclosure laws, are punitive or penal rather than compensatory in nature and thus nondischargeable in individual debtor bankruptcies.[42] Key factors are whether the

---

950 F.2d 721 (3d Cir. 1991); *see AL Tech Specialty Steel Corp. v. Allegheny Int'l Credit Corp.*, 104 F.3d 601, 605 (3d Cir. 1997).

38. Section 501(b) of the Bankruptcy Code, 11 U.S.C. § 501(b), and Bankruptcy Rule 3005(a) provide that co-liable parties can file surrogate proofs of claim on behalf of the creditor within 30 days after the expiration of the bar date for that creditor.

39. Section 1141(d)(2) incorporates the exceptions to discharge set forth in Section 523 in individual Chapter 11 cases. Section 523 may also apply to corporate debtors filing under subchapter V of Chapter 11 (small businesses) or Chapter 12 (farmers). *See In re Cleary Packaging, LLC*, 36 F.4th 509 (4th Cir. 2022); *In re JRB Consol., Inc.*, 188 B.R. 373 (Bankr. W.D. Tex. 1995); 11 U.S.C. §§ 1192(2), 1228(a)(2), 1228(c).

40. *See* Chapter 2 (History and Purposes) *supra* for a more general discussion of the exceptions to discharge contained in Section 523(a).

41. *Whitehouse v. LaRoche*, 277 F.3d 568, 573 (1st Cir. 2002).

42. *In re Jones*, 311 B.R. 647 (Bankr. N.D. Ga. 2004); *Commonwealth of Ky. Natural Res. & Env't Prot. Cabinet v. Seals*, 161 B.R. 615 (W.D. Va. 1993); *In re Thebes*, 2011 WL 1239847 (Bankr. M.D. Pa. Mar. 30, 2011); *In re Davis*, 2008 WL 4976271 (Bankr.

amount of fine or penalty is calculated based on or correlated to an amount of damage or injury and whether the penalty is used to mitigate damages.[43] Note that the three-year limitation on nondischargeability found in Section 523(a)(7)(B) applies only to tax penalties and not to environmental penalties.[44] Bankruptcy and nonbankruptcy courts have concurrent jurisdiction to determine the applicability of this exception to discharge since creditors are not required to seek a ruling from the bankruptcy court that the debt is not dischargeable.[45] Nonetheless, if a plan of reorganization or other bankruptcy court document purports to determine this issue or limit a creditor's future rights, the creditor should be given notice and opportunity to object or the provision may not be binding.[46]

Section 523(a)(6) excepts an individual debtor's liability from discharge for willful and malicious injury to another entity or the property of another entity. In *Kawaauhau v. Geiger*,[47] the Supreme Court interpreted this exception narrowly and held that it applies only when the debtor intended injury. Intentional acts that cause unintended injury are not covered.[48] In an unpublished decision, although prior to *Kawaauhau*, the Sixth Circuit held that liability for

---

S.D. Ind. Oct. 1, 2008); *In re Damm*, 2001 WL 34065016 (Bankr. C.D. Ill. May 10, 2001); *In re Jimmo*, 204 B.R. 655, 658 (Bankr. D. Conn. 1997).

43. *Jones*, 311 B.R. at 656; *Seals*, 161 B.R. at 621; *Thebes*, 2011 WL 1239847, at 3–4; *Damm*, 2001 WL 34065016, at 3.

44. *Jimmo*, 204 B.R. at 658–59; *Ricketson,* 190 B.R. 684, 687 (Bankr. M.D. Fla. 1995); *Seals*, 161 B.R. at 618 n.8.

45. *See Kelly v. Robinson*, 479 U.S. 36, 43 n.4 (1986). The defense of dischargeability can therefore be considered in an enforcement proceeding without any involvement of a bankruptcy court. *See Whitehouse v. LaRoche*, 277 F.3d at 576.

46. *See* Chapter 16 (Plan Objections) *infra*. Bankruptcy Rule 7001(6) requires that requests for findings of dischargeability be filed by adversary proceeding. Fed. R. Bankr. P. 7001(6). Therefore, listing of a nondischargeable debt on the debtor's schedules does not place a burden on the creditor to object to being listed on the schedules. *See In re Galbreath*, 83 B.R. 549, 551 (Bankr. S.D. Ill. 1988). As noted in Chapter 16 (Plan Objections), however, failure to object to otherwise invalid plan provisions may result in them becoming binding on noticed creditors under *United Student Aid Funds, Inc. v. Espinosa*, 559 U.S. 260, 271 (2010).

47. 523 U.S. 57, 63 (1998).

48. *See id.* at 61–62; *In re Hansen*, 473 B.R. 240 (Bankr. E.D. Tenn. 2012) (no evidence that landlord intended environmental damage from tenant's drug lab); *In re Kirby*, 2007 WL 2492682 (Bankr. N.D. Ohio Aug. 28, 2007) (no evidence that debtor intended to cause a fire at a tire center or that the debtor intended the fire to cause environmental damage).

failure to perform reclamation on mined areas was not dischargeable where the individual debtor knowingly continued to engage in illegal mining causing injury even after being ordered to cease and desist.[49] Creditors seeking to apply this exception to discharge (as well as separate exceptions for fraud) must file a complaint in bankruptcy court seeking a determination that the debt is not subject to discharge within 60 days of the first date set for the meeting of creditors under Section 341.[50]

Section 1141(d)(6) extends only one of Section 523's exceptions to discharge to corporate debtors—the exception for debts for money or property obtained by fraud and the like in Section 523(a)(2) and then only as to the government.[51]

EXCEPTIONS TO DISCHARGE FOR CRIMINAL LIABILITIES[52]

The federal Criminal Code renders federal criminal fines and restitution obligations not dischargeable in both individual and corporate cases under Section 3613(e) and (f) of Title 18.[53] In addition, criminal fines, penalties, and restitution imposed as part of a criminal sentence are nondischargeable in an individual's Chapter 7 or 11 bankruptcy case under Section 523(a)(7)'s exception

49. *Phipps v. Commonwealth of Ky. Natural Res. & Env't Prot. Cabinet*, 980 F.2d 730 (6th Cir. 1992).

50. *See* 11 U.S.C. § 523(c); Fed. R. Bankr. P. 4007; *Whitehouse v. LaRoche*, 277 F.3d at 576.

51. In *In re Exide Techs.*, 601 B.R. 271 (Bankr. D. Del. 2019), *aff'd,* 613 B.R. 79 (D. Del. 2020), the bankruptcy court rejected a contention by a local governmental agency that a debt for a penalty based on allegedly false certifications, concealed test results, and manipulation of testing conditions relating to lead and arsenic emissions, fell within this exception. The bankruptcy court held that even if there was fraud, the exception did not apply because the debt was not for loss or damages to the agency.

52. Special thanks to Margarita Padilla, former Supervising Deputy Attorney General, Environment Section, California Department of Justice, for her contributions to this section.

53. *See In re Partida*, 862 F.3d 909 (9th Cir. 2019); *In re Robinson*, 764 F.3d 554 (6th Cir. 2014); *United States v. Hyde*, 497 F.3d 103 (1st Cir. 2007); *In re Thompson*, 418 F.3d 362 (3d Cir. 2005). Federal criminal fines were found to be dischargeable in *In re Wisconsin Barge Lines, Inc.*, 91 B.R. 65 (Bankr. E.D. Mo. 1988), but this case does not discuss Section 3613 of Title 18, which may not have yet been effective.

to discharge and the Supreme Court's ruling in *Kelly v. Robinson*.[54] Criminal fines and restitution are also nondischargeable in Chapter 13 under Section 1328(a)(3) of the Bankruptcy Code. Governments and debtors may disagree as to whether criminal fines under state law in corporate reorganization cases are dischargeable.[55]

Most restitution obligations under federal or state criminal sentences are not dischargeable in individual or corporate cases with two possible exceptions regarding state criminal sentences where courts are in disagreement.[56] First, courts have disagreed as to whether state court restitution obligations are dischargeable when payments are to be made directly to a nongovernmental party.[57] Second, the dischargeability of criminal restitution obligations under state law in corporate reorganization cases may be contested.[58] Governments may contend that state law restitution obligations in such cases are not dischargeable because they result from enforcement of criminal sentences that were exempt

54. 479 U.S. 36 (1986).

55. Governments may contend that they are not dischargeable because they are enforcement of criminal sentences that were exempt from the automatic stay under 11 U.S.C. § 362(b)(1) and that it would make little sense to exempt them only to then discharge them. Corporate debtors may contend that they are dischargeable debts under the Code's broad definition of "claim." 11 U.S.C. § 101(5). However, if the corporate debtor is liquidating under Chapter 11, the Code provides that debts are not discharged. 11 U.S.C. § 1141(d)(3). Debtors' proposed plans should be carefully reviewed for consistency with the Code and applicable case law. *See* Chapter 16 (Plan Objections) *infra*.

56. In *Kelly v. Robinson*, 479 U.S. 36 (1986), the Supreme Court held that restitution obligations were not dischargeable in individual cases under Section 523(a)(7) because they were penal in nature. The Court also noted that Congress did not intend for the Bankruptcy Code to invalidate "the results of state criminal proceedings." *Id.* at 47. However, *Kelly* was clarified and limited by *Pennsylvania Public Welfare Dep't v. Davenport*, 495 U.S. 552 (1990), which held that restitution obligations were dischargeable debts under Chapter 13 of the Code given that Section 523(a)(7) did not apply to Chapter 13 cases, *see* 11 U.S.C. § 1328(a)(2). Congress thereafter legislatively overruled *Davenport*. *See* 11 U.S.C. § 1328 (a)(3) (excepting fines or restitution in criminal sentences from discharge in Chapter 13 cases). *See also* 11 U.S.C. § 523(a)(13) (exception for payment of restitution under Title 18); 11 U.S.C. § 1141(d)(2) (making Section 523 applicable in an individual's Chapter 11 proceedings). 18 U.S.C. § 3613(f) further provides that restitution obligations arising from federal criminal sentences are not dischargeable in any bankruptcy cases.

57. *Compare, e.g., In re Dargon*, 2022 Lexis 671 (Bankr. D. Mass. Mar. 11, 2022); *In re Wilson*, 299 B.R. 380 (Bankr. E.D. Va. 2003), *with In re Troff*, 329 B.R. 85 D. Utah 2005); *In re Mills*, 290 B.R. 822 (Bankr. D. Colo. 2003).

58. There is no discharge at all in corporate liquidation cases. 11 U.S.C. § 1141(d)(3).

from the automatic stay under 11 U.S.C. § 362(b)(1), and it would make little sense to exempt them only to then discharge them.[59] Corporate debtors may contend that they are nonetheless dischargeable debts.[60] It is important to review proposed bankruptcy plans for consistency with applicable law on the discharge of criminal liabilities.[61]

WHEN IN DOUBT, SEEK A DISCHARGEABILITY RULING

If a creditor is in doubt about the dischargeability of a claim, it may consider seeking a declaratory ruling from the bankruptcy court as to whether the claim is or was dischargeable in order to minimize the risk of a discharge violation.[62] However, a creditor is not required to do so except in the few situations, as noted earlier, where the Code sets a 60–day deadline for such determinations.[63] Alternatively, if it has reasonable arguments in favor

59. For a discussion of the criminal exception to the automatic stay, *see* Chapter 10 (Police or Regulatory Exception) *supra*.

60. Debtors' argument would likely be based on reasoning similar to that set forth in *Davenport*. While *Davenport*, a Chapter 13 case, was legislatively overruled, debtors may contend that Congress' changes did not extend to state law restitution obligations in corporate reorganization bankruptcy cases.

61. As noted in Chapter 16 (Plan Objections), failure to object to otherwise invalid plan provisions may result in them becoming binding on noticed creditors under *United Student Aid Funds, Inc. v. Espinosa*, 559 U.S. 260, 271 (2010). Note also that while a liquidating corporate debtor does not receive a discharge, the debtor may no longer exist following liquidation. In such situations, governments may want to consider whether proposed liquidation plans that fail to deal with criminal liabilities are consistent with criminal laws. Likewise, governments may want to consider whether restructuring changes to corporate forms in reorganization plans are consistent with criminal laws if they would dissolve an entity that has potential criminal liability or deplete its assets.

62. *See In re Moser*, 613 B.R. 721, 727–29 (B.A.P. 9th Cir. 2020); *Whitehouse v. LaRoche*, 277 F.3d at 576.

63. Determinations of dischargeability under 11 U.S.C. § 523(a)(2) (obtaining property by false pretenses or fraud), (4) (fraud or defalcation while acting in a fiduciary capacity, embezzlement, or larceny), and (6) (willful and malicious injury) must be brought within 60 days of the first date set for the meeting of creditors under 11 U.S.C. § 341. *See* Fed. R. Bankr. P. 4004(c); 11 U.S.C. § 523(c); *Whitehouse v. LaRoche*, 277 F.3d at 576. Although many debtors/courts will provide notice of this deadline to known creditors along with the notice of a bar date for filing proofs of claim, the deadline can be found only by careful parsing of the Bankruptcy Code and Bankruptcy Rules and is therefore a potential trap to the unwary.

of nondischargeability, the creditor may elect to proceed in the nonbankruptcy tribunal with jurisdiction because jurisdiction is concurrent and not exclusive to the bankruptcy court. In that situation, the creditor may bring the action in the tribunal with jurisdiction and ask that tribunal to make a ruling as to whether the debt was discharged.[64] Creditors should keep in mind that in *Taggart v. Lorenzen*,[65] the Supreme Court held that the standard for holding a creditor in contempt for violating the discharge injunction is an objective standard of whether there was "a fair ground of doubt" about dischargeability. Subjective good faith belief of nondischargeability could be relevant but would not be dispositive.[66]

DISCRIMINATORY TREATMENT ON ACCOUNT OF FAILURE TO PAY DISCHARGED CLAIMS

Section 525 of the Bankruptcy Code provides that governmental units may not "deny, revoke, suspend, or refuse to renew" licenses, permits and similar grants or deny employment *solely* because of a debtor's bankruptcy or insolvency or because the debtor has not paid a dischargeable debt.[67] Section 525 codified the Supreme Court's decision in *Perez v. Campbell*,[68] striking down state laws denying driving privileges to debtors who did not pay tort judgments even though discharged under bankruptcy law.[69] In *Federal*

Postponement of the meeting of creditors does not automatically extend this deadline. In *In re Hawker Beechcraft, Inc.*, 515 B.R. 416 (S.D.N.Y. 2014), the court held that the exceptions to discharge under Section 1141(d)(6) were self-executing and did not incorporate the requirement for seeking a determination of dischargeability under Section 523(c).

64. *See Whitehouse v. LaRoche*, 277 F.3d at 578; 28 U.S.C. § 1334(b) (providing for nonexclusive jurisdiction over matters related to or arising in or under the Bankruptcy Code).

65. 139 S. Ct. 1795, 1802 (2019).

66. *Id.* at 1802–03.

67. 11 U.S.C. § 525(a). Government loans are not subject to Section 525(a). *Springfield Hosp., Inc.*, 28 F.4th 403 (2d Cir. 2022).

68. 402 U.S. 637 (1971).

69. *See generally In re Stoltz*, 315 F.3d 80, 87–88 (2d Cir. 2002); Karen Cordry, *Section 525: Policy Thoughts about Discriminating against Debtors*, Norton Annual Survey of Bankruptcy Law 4 (2010).

Communications Commission v. NextWave Personal Communications Inc., the Supreme Court held that Section 525 prevented the FCC from cancelling or revoking the debtor's broadband licenses for failure to make payments for the purchase of the licenses.[70] The Supreme Court interpreted the "solely because" statutory language to mean a proximate causation standard and found that it did not matter if the government had other motivations to cancel or revoke.[71] The Supreme Court also noted that, unlike the automatic stay, there is no police or regulatory exception in Section 525.[72] The Supreme Court found that failure to make the payments was a "debt" within the meaning of Section 525 even if it were also a regulatory condition, because it was still a right to payment under the Bankruptcy Code's broad definition of "claim."[73] Finally, the Court found that there was not a conflict requiring harmonization of Section 525 with the Communications Act because that statute did not preclude payments over time or security interests for the licensing fee liability.[74]

The pertinent lesson from *NextWave* for environmental matters is that governments may not deny/revoke licenses and permits on account of the reasons specified in the statute:[75] bankruptcy, prior insolvency, and failure to pay a dischargeable debt.[76] Governments

70. 537 U.S. 293 (2003).

71. *Id.* at 301–02.

72. *Id.* at 302.

73. *Id.* at 303.

74. *Id.* at 304. In contrast to the situation found by the Supreme Court in *Next Wave*, when a federal statute is found to conflict with Section 525, a much more difficult situation is presented. *See* Chapter 8 (Harmonization) *supra*. For example, Section 1259(c) in the Surface Mining Control and Reclamation Act, 30 U.S.C. § 1259(c), requires the government to consider an applicant's "history of financial solvency" in order to "self-bond," which is in direct conflict with Section 525's prohibition on considering insolvency for covered matters. In *In re Stoltz*, 315 F.3d at 93–94, the court considered a direct conflict between Sections 525 and 365 of the Bankruptcy Code and concluded that Section 525 prevailed as the more specific statutory section.

75. In *In re Stoltz*, 315 F.3d at 87–88, the court held that Section 525 applied to public housing leases as grants similar to licenses, permits, charters, or franchises.

76. *See, e.g., In re Walker*, 927 F.2d 1138 (10th Cir. 1991) (real estate license denial for failure to make payments); *In re Env't Source Corp.*, 431 B.R. 315 (Bankr. D. Mass. 2010) (failure to pay penalties for not having worker's compensation insurance); *In re Psychotherapy & Counseling Ctr., Inc.*, 195 B.R. 522 (Bankr. D.D.C. 1996); *In re Elsinore Shore Assocs.*, 66 B.R. 723 (Bankr. D.N.J. 1986); *In re Lambillotte*, 25

may, however, deny/revoke licenses and permits for other valid reasons that apply to debtors and nondebtors alike. For example, nothing in Section 525 prohibits governments from refusing to grant a permit or license or similar grant because the applicant cannot meet financial assurance, financial fitness, or other requirements applicable to all applicants.[77] Likewise, governments may refuse to grant a permit or license to violators or bad actors just as they would for other applicants as long as the justification is appropriately supported and not based simply on the failure to pay a dischargeable debt (as opposed to being based on the underlying misconduct).[78] Care should be exercised by the government in stating its reasons for its action to ensure that the government is not violating Section 525.[79]

B.R. 392, 394 (Bankr. M.D. Fla. 1982); *In re Anderson*, 15 B.R. 399, 400–01 (Bankr. S.D. Miss. 1981).

77. *See, e.g., Parkview Adventist Med. Ctr. v United States*, 842 F.3d 757, 768 (1st Cir. 2020); *Duffey v. Dollison*, 734 F.2d 265, 273–74 (6th Cir. 1984) (proof of financial responsibility for motorists); *In re Geiger*, 143 B.R. 30 (E.D. Pa. 1992) (proof of financial responsibility), *aff'd*, 993 F.2d 224 (3d Cir. 1993); *In re Will Rogers Jockey & Polo Club, Inc.*, 111 B.R. 948, 953–54 (Bankr. N.D. Okla. 1990); *In re Wengert Transp. Inc.*, 59 B.R. 226, 231 & n.1 (Bankr. N.D. Iowa 1986) (noting importance that financial fitness be determined based on post-petition assets and liabilities and track record and not based on pre-bankruptcy finances); *In re Prof'l Sales Corp.*, 56 B.R. 753, 760 n.4 (N.D. Ill. 1985).

78. *See, e.g., In re Ellis*, 493 B.R. 818 (Bankr. D. Colo. 2013) (failure to respond to documentation request); *In re Kimsey*, 263 B.R. 244 (Bankr. E.D. Ark. 2001) (violation of traffic laws). Section 525 has a broader impact in Chapter 11 corporate reorganizations than in individual bankruptcy cases given the broader exception to discharge in individual cases under Section 523. *See* Cordry, *supra* note 69.

79. For example, in *In re Alessi*, 12 B.R. 96, 97 (Bankr. N.D. Ill. 1981), the bankruptcy court, pre-*Next Wave*, found that a governmental agency could deny a license to race horses to a financially irresponsible applicant. Under *Next Wave*, it would be important that the decision not be based on a failure to pay a dischargeable debt. However, a denial based on bad conduct of issuing checks with insufficient funds (before any bankruptcy) may pass muster especially in an industry where financial honesty is important.

CHAPTER 14

Addressing Debtor-Owned Contaminated Property

Chapter 14 covers the options debtors have utilized to address environmental issues at real property they own. Commonly used options include the sale or other disposition of such properties, creation of a trust entity to hold such properties, assumption of liability by a third party, and retention by the reorganized debtor of such properties. In many instances, bankruptcy affords opportunities for creatively addressing environmental liabilities in a manner that is beneficial to debtors and governments alike and that would otherwise be difficult to achieve in a nonbankruptcy context.

At the outset, and as noted elsewhere in this Practice Guide,[1] liabilities relating to contamination remaining on a debtor's property are usually not dischargeable in bankruptcy. The reason for this is that most environmental laws make a current owner or operator of property liable for contamination on the property, regardless of when it was contaminated.[2] Accordingly, the liability of a reorganized debtor or a third-party purchaser of contaminated property "springs anew" based on its post-bankruptcy or post-sale

---

1. *See* Chapters 11 (Compliance Obligations), 13 (Discharge) *supra*, Chapter 15 (Section 363 Sales) *infra*.

2. CERCLA provides for a partial defense to liability of purchasers meeting the requirements to be bona fide prospective purchasers. *See* 42 U.S.C. § 9601(40). However, bona fide prospective purchasers must exercise appropriate care with respect to hazardous substances at the site. 42 U.S.C. § 9601(40)(B)(iv).

ownership or operation of the property.[3] This result is consistent with the harmonization theme identified in Chapter 8 (Harmonization), whereby bankruptcy law tends to give way to environmental law when property of the estate is involved. Since environmental liabilities for contamination remaining on a debtor's property are not dischargeable, debtors often rely upon the options discussed in this chapter to address environmental liabilities for owned property.

The options debtors have utilized for addressing property with environmental liabilities include:

(1) Selling debtor-owned properties that debtors do not want to retain, through a sale under Section 363 of the Bankruptcy Code, either in advance of a plan or as part of a plan, and having the purchaser assume environmental liabilities;
(2) Creating an environmental response trust where the trust takes on the responsibility for addressing environmental liabilities and ownership of the property;
(3) Utilizing a liability "transfer" or assumption arrangement whereby a third party assumes the debtor's liability for environmental contamination (and debtor often conveys fee title to the third party as well); and
(4) Retaining the property as a debtor and then as a reorganized debtor and carrying through with any environmental obligations (considered a "pass through" of environmental obligations).[4]

Some of these options can be paired with the simultaneous sale of valuable properties, which could bring in needed funding to the

3. *See* Chapter 11 (Compliance Obligations) *supra*. There are two potential exceptions to environmental liability springing anew: (1) response costs spent by the government prior to confirmation/sale when environmental law does not provide for the liability of an owner for costs spent before it became the owner, and (2) penalties for days of violation incurred by the debtor prior to confirmation/sale. If a lien was perfected or a judgment lien obtained, there may still be in rem or secured liability.

4. As noted, post-bankruptcy ownership gives rise to a springing anew of liability based on the reorganized debtor's status as a post-bankruptcy owner or operator of the property.

debtor's estate while at the same time addressing debtor's liability for the unwanted properties.

If none of these options is chosen, as a last resort, some debtors may consider attempting to abandon their contaminated property under Section 554 of the Bankruptcy Code.[5] As explained in greater detail in Chapter 18 (Abandonment) of this Practice Guide, abandonment in a Chapter 11 case is fraught with litigation risks, is likely to be strenuously contested by governmental authorities, and is of limited value to a debtor since abandonment of property ownership generally does not avoid environmental liability. The inevitable expense, delay, and unpredictability of the outcome of litigation typically result in a consensual resolution between the debtor and governmental authorities based on one of the preceding four options.

A debtor's preparation for bankruptcy in a case involving environmental issues will include a broad look at environmental liabilities for both owned and non-owned properties. Such a detailed review will provide important information for the debtor to evaluate its options for owned contaminated properties (which is the subject of this chapter) as well as addressing its other environmental liabilities. The debtor will categorize and gather information on the properties for which it may have liability to understand the scope of environmental responsibility. The key categories are:

Owned properties. These are properties currently owned by the debtor. The debtor is the fee owner of the property. (It is also useful to identify off-site migration of contamination onto adjacent properties owned by third parties.)

Operated properties. These are properties currently operated by the debtor but not owned. Typically, these are leased sites.

Formerly owned properties. These are properties that were once owned by the debtor but transferred to another party before the debtor's filing of the petition. The key point here is that the debtor is not a current owner of the property.

5. 11 U.S.C. § 554.

Formerly operated properties. These are properties that the debtor operated in the past but no longer operates. Typically, these are properties that were formerly leased by the debtor.

Never owned/never operated properties. These are generally referred to as "third-party" sites or "off-site" disposal properties and would include many federal or state Superfund sites.

After the debtor has organized the properties into these categories, the debtor should compile additional relevant information, including the status of all environmental regulatory actions or other liabilities. For example, are there any consent decrees, notices of violation, or monitoring requirements associated with a specific property? What is the current status of compliance with any such requirements? Is there a cost estimate associated with compliance? Are decisions to be made about whether and when to decommission a facility?

Once information is collected for each property for which the debtor has environmental liabilities, then, as relevant to this chapter,[6] the debtor should evaluate how to address each parcel of owned property. The importance of organizing this information is that it provides a snapshot of the debtor's environmental liabilities in connection with each owned property. For example, a debtor may own a parcel that includes a loading dock abutting a highly trafficked river. This could be valuable property for certain industries and there may be potential purchasers interested in acquiring such property. However, if the scope of addressing environmental liabilities is unduly burdensome, due to excessive cost or time and effort to address contamination, then there may be little interest in acquiring such property.

6. The debtor will benefit from undertaking a similar categorization and analysis of its environmental liabilities relating to non-owned property, but addressing debtor's environmental liabilities associated with non-owned properties is beyond the scope of this chapter.

SALE OF DEBTOR-OWNED PROPERTIES

A debtor's ability to sell contaminated properties through a Section 363 sale either as part of a plan or independent of a plan will depend on how attractive the properties are to potential purchasers and whether there is a likelihood of receiving a fair market price for the properties. Section 363 sales are discussed in more detail in Chapter 15 (Section 363 Sales) of this Practice Guide. As noted in Chapter 15, a Section 363 sale can be free and clear of many liabilities of a debtor; however, liability as a post-sale owner of property will spring anew or arise after consummation of the purchase because under most environmental laws, an owner of property is responsible for addressing contamination on its property even if the contamination originated before the purchase or transaction date. Nonetheless, while a "free and clear" order from the bankruptcy court will not protect a purchaser from environmental liability as an owner of the property, it may be beneficial to a purchaser with respect to other environmental liabilities. For example, a Section 363 order will generally state that the purchaser will not have "successor liability" for other environmental liabilities, such as past off-site waste disposal activities, torts of the debtor, or penalties for days of violation prior to the purchase. Such a "free and clear" order, combined with the auction process under bankruptcy law, may provide an advantageous price for the estate.

Many debtors have been careful to include language in purchase and sale agreements that makes it clear that purchasers are assuming environmental liability for contamination on the property they are purchasing. Clarity in such language minimizes the potential for future disputes between the debtors and purchasers as to who has primary responsibility for an environmental liability. Debtors may also wish to consider the viability of the purchaser to close the transaction and comply with the assumed liabilities to avoid the risk of secondary liability in the bankruptcy case if the purchaser is unable to perform. If debtors are parties to any consent decree or orders for cleanup of a site that has outstanding obligations or future contingent work, debtors may seek to obtain the agreement of the purchaser and the applicable governmental agency to substitute the purchaser for the debtor on the consent decree or order. It should also be noted that it is uncertain whether the option for a Section 363 sale in bankruptcy is available if a debtor previously gave a third party a right of first refusal or option to purchase.[7]

ENVIRONMENTAL RESPONSE TRUSTS

Another valuable vehicle for addressing environmentally contaminated debtor-owned property that benefits both the debtor and the government is an environmental response trust. The federal government and states can be beneficiaries of such trusts. An environmental response trust funds the costs of remediating contaminated property and facilitates beneficial reuse.

With an environmental response trust, the debtor benefits from a settlement that resolves its liability to the government for cleanup and furthers its fresh start. An environmental response trust typically offers broader protections to a debtor than a liability assumption arrangement. It usually involves a settlement agreement that requires conveyance by the debtor of contaminated real properties to a trust together with funding for cleanup. The debtor receives a covenant not to sue and has no further connection with the trust, property, or cleanup.[8] Thus, the environmental response

7. A debtor could seek to reject such a right of first refusal or purchase option as an executory contract, but there would be a litigation risk as to whether the contract would be found to be an executory contract with obligations on both sides and whether rejection of such contract would be subject to a remedy of specific performance for breach if damages are not an adequate remedy. *See* Chapter 5 (Key Provisions (executory contracts)) *supra*.

8. Environmental response trust settlements generally do not have reopeners for future cost overruns or unanticipated conditions. Due to the uncertainties and litigation risks posed by bankruptcy and the benefits of cleanup, governments may be more willing to enter into such settlements in bankruptcy than when they are dealing with responsible parties outside of bankruptcy. In contrast, cashout settlements with solvent companies that do not include reopeners for new information are not common outside of bankruptcy given the preference to hold responsible parties liable for unanticipated conditions and cost overruns. *See* Chapter 21 (Settlement Agreements) *infra* (discussing environmental bankruptcy settlements and reopeners).

trust provides the debtor with finality with respect to the properties that are transferred to the trust.

Regulators benefit from establishment of an environmental response trust in a number of ways. Through the trust vehicle, dedicated funding is specifically set aside for cleanup and the trustee who manages the trust is generally cooperative in achieving the government's remedial objectives. This is in contrast to the more confrontational approach used by some private parties in the non-trust context, which can frustrate cleanup implementation due to an overly aggressive effort to reduce costs. Additionally, the environmental response trust, as a private entity, may also be able to achieve cleanup objectives for a lower cost than a governmental agency and relieve the government of the potential burden of a future government-funded cleanup (which in all likelihood would be more expensive). The environmental response trust serves as the successor to the debtor for the limited purposes of cleanup, subject to the funding of the trust, and thus can fulfill the government preference under environmental law for responsible parties to conduct cleanup actions rather than governments undertaking publicly funded cleanups.[9] Establishment of the trust and its funding also helps to avoid the risk of abandonment of property[10] or liquidation of the debtor in the bankruptcy case without addressing environmental issues. It also avoids the risk of festering unattended environmental contamination by a reorganized debtor. Furthermore, it helps to mitigate the risk of a second bankruptcy down the road when the reorganized debtor may have even more limited resources to address environmental issues.

A threshold issue is whether the governments involved will agree to an environmental response trust. The governments will need to balance the various benefits of an environmental response trust against the downside of no longer having the responsible party (i.e., the reorganized debtor) liable to address future cost overruns or latent environmental conditions that an environmental response trust may not have funding to address (since the

9. *See, e.g., Consolidated Edison Co. v. UGI Utilities, Inc.*, 423 F.3d 90, 94 (2d Cir. 2005).

10. *See* Chapter 18 (Abandonment) *infra*.

environmental response trust only has the funding provided in the settlement to address environmental conditions). This underscores the importance to the government that the amount of funding provided to the environmental response trust be sufficient. Environmental response trusts can be particularly beneficial for the government in liquidation cases and in those cases where a debtor's financial condition is so poor that the settlement can be justified as an ability to pay settlement.[11] Environmental response trusts can also be attractive in reorganization cases if the trust is likely to facilitate a complete cleanup.

The settlement agreement providing for the creation of the environmental response trust typically identifies the proposed trustee, who is usually a signatory to both the settlement agreement and a separate trust agreement.[12] Generally speaking, the governmental parties (typically represented by the Department of Justice on behalf of EPA and sometimes other federal agencies and state attorney general offices or state regulators) will seek trustee candidates, and then engage in a collaborative interview process of the most qualified candidates.[13] The results will be discussed with the debtors and a recommendation of a trustee appointment is jointly proposed to the bankruptcy court by the debtor and the governmental beneficiaries through the settlement agreement. The trustee is usually an entity or person experienced in environmental remediation matters as well as trustee services and financial management. Experience in interacting with regulatory agencies and the public is also valuable. The trustee may be an entity headed by a professional or career environmental trustee, environmental consulting firm, an individual with a financial or environmental background, or a former judge. The environmental response trustee is

11. In significant cases, governments may hire expert consultants to help understand a debtor's financial situation.

12. Where time constraints have not permitted early selection of the trustee, a draft trust agreement can be attached to the settlement agreement. Once the trustee is identified, the trustee and final trust agreement can be submitted for bankruptcy court approval. Trustees obtain important protections against future litigation if they are appointed by the bankruptcy court. *See, e.g., Barton v. Barbour*, 104 U.S. 126 (1881) and cases cited in note 21 *infra*.

13. In a few instances, the debtor has taken the lead in the trustee selection process in consultation with the governmental entities.

usually a corporate entity with an experienced individual serving as its president.

Depending on the size of the bankruptcy and the number of debtor properties, multiple trusts may be established. The decision whether to establish multiple trusts or to use one multi-site trust depends on several factors, including the number of properties, the complexity of the various sites, the nature of the environmental work involved, and the relationships between the various governmental agencies providing oversight. Once a single trust is established, or multiple trusts as the case may be, the debtor transfers its unwanted property into the trust(s), usually by quitclaim deed. The transfer of property into the trust(s) would customarily occur on the effective date of the plan.[14] Each trust would then become the owner of the property transferred into it.

Environmental response trusts typically have a dedicated segregated trust account for each contaminated property as well as a separate account for the administrative costs of the trust. That way, each participating state can count on a known amount of cleanup funding for a property in its state and the governments can determine that the settlement is fair for all properties included. Administrative costs are limited and separate so as not to deplete funds for the cleanups. The settlement agreements often have provisions that provide for the transfer of excess funding for one property to other properties in need of additional funding, but only with approval of the relevant governmental beneficiaries. If administrative funding runs out but property cleanup funding remains, as has happened for a few of these trusts after many years, the beneficiaries will need to determine whether they wish to agree to let certain amounts of cleanup funding be used for trust administration or whether the trust should be closed and the remaining funding provided to dedicated governmental accounts for cleanup.

---

14. It is important for the agreed-upon funding to be transferred to the trust no later than when the properties are transferred into the trust. Otherwise, the trustee would lack funding to start up and protect public health and safety at the properties from the outset. In addition, bankruptcies generally are volatile situations and there can be risks of changed circumstances or unforeseen events that put funding at risk and could result in unintended abandonment of properties if funding is not simultaneously provided with transfer of the properties.

BENEFICIARIES OF THE TRUST

Typically, the United States, on behalf of EPA and other federal agencies, and the applicable state environmental agencies are the beneficiaries of environmental response trusts. The beneficiaries resolve their protective proofs of claim and causes of action against debtors for cleanup in return for the benefits provided by the settlement, including the cleanup to be undertaken by the trust.[15] The beneficiaries are designated in either the environmental response settlement agreement or trust agreement. The settlement agreement also designates the lead agency for each property. The lead agency approves the annual cleanup budget for the property. Depending on the trust, the United States and/or a state must approve annual administrative budgets. The lead agency also retains its regulatory oversight role as it would have with any other responsible party performing a cleanup. Trust agreements also often provide a nonlead state or federal agency with a right of consultation by the lead agency, if desired. Environmental response trusts are not agents of the government and act independently with fiduciary duties to their governmental beneficiaries. Separation between the entity performing the work (the trustee) and the entity overseeing the work (the regulatory agency) is important so that there is some check that the trustee is handling the work properly.

RESPONSIBILITIES OF THE TRUSTEE

The trustee's[16] responsibilities are detailed in the settlement agreement and the separate environmental response trust agreement by and among the debtor, as settling party; the trustee entity; and the beneficiaries. These agreements contain provisions governing

15. If the governments have outstanding monetary claims for response costs, the settlements can provide them with allowed claims to be paid in accordance with the plan of reorganization. Trust funding should not be used to pay for past costs incurred prior to the creation of the trust because such cost recovery claims are dischargeable claims in bankruptcy that should be treated and paid as provided in the Bankruptcy Code.

16. References in this chapter to the trustee are to the environmental response trust trustee and not to any bankruptcy trustee appointed under Sections 701, 702, or 1104 of the Code.

budgeting, cleanup, obligations and funding of the trust, acceptable investments, the activities in which the trustee can engage,[17] protections afforded the trustee against potential legal exposure such as against creditors of the debtors, and provisions relating to the future disposition of the property by the trust.

The trustee is principally responsible for managing the cleanup of the owned properties subject to budget approvals and regulatory oversight of the governmental beneficiaries. The trustee completes the required cleanup or, for a government-funded cleanup, reimburses the government. In either case, the trustee will then generally return the property to beneficial use. The trustee is also responsible for trust administration and addressing general property management concerns. The trustee is a fiduciary and must exercise its duties consistent with the purposes of the trust.

FUNDING OF TRUST

Governments are likely to require that the trust have adequate funding to address its cleanup obligations.[18] As noted in Chapter 16 (Plan Objections) of this Practice Guide, where a plan proposes an environmental response trust, the debtor must show that the plan is feasible and complies with other Bankruptcy Code Section 1129 requirements. Section 1129(a)(3) requires that a plan be confirmed only if the plan "has been proposed . . . not by any means forbidden by law." In the context of environmental response trusts, Section 1129(a)(3) and feasibility requirements require adequate funding for the trust's cleanup purposes.[19] If the governments conclude that full funding is impossible to obtain given the debtor's financial circumstances, but that it is in the governments' interest

17. Usually the trust is not permitted to operate a business. One exception was the Tronox/Savannah trust discussed in this chapter. Generally trust funding is first used for cleanup of the property owned by the trust and then for any offsite cleanup efforts provided there is remaining funding.

18. As discussed earlier, in a liquidation the government may potentially agree to less than full funding for a trust based on an ability to pay analysis.

19. *In re Eagle-Picher Holdings, Inc.*, 345 B.R. 860, 864 (Bankr. S.D. Ohio 2006)) (holding that the custodial trust must be sufficiently funded to comply with environmental law in order to meet the requirement that the plan not be forbidden by law).

for a trust to be created with less than full funding, they may decide to agree to an ability to pay settlement.[20] The settlement would include covenants not to sue and would thereby make the trust, even though underfunded, consistent with bankruptcy law requirements such as feasibility.

The trust can be funded in any number of ways. The major source of funding is usually direct payments from the debtor. Other sources may include letters of credit on some properties, surety bond proceeds, proceeds from the sale of trust assets, and insurance coverage. Furthermore, once a property is remediated, it can then be sold for redevelopment. The proceeds from that sale can be used by the trust to address other properties owned by the trust or to complete the remediation of the property sold.

To evaluate how much funding is necessary, depending on the property and status of the property's investigation, the government or debtor may have cleanup and administrative cost estimates, and either or both may retain an environmental consultant or work with in-house technical experts to develop such an estimate of the cost of cleanup and administrative costs. It can often take several weeks or a few months to develop such an estimate. The estimate is key because this estimate is the basis on which the trust is funded and approved.

TRUSTEE PROTECTIONS

In connection with the administration of the trust, the trustee has no obligation to perform any activities for which the trust has insufficient funds. Since the trustee only has the funds that are provided in the trust, its activities are limited by that financial constraint. In addition, the trustee has no personal liability in connection with its administration of the trust, except in cases of fraud or willful misconduct. This protection against personal exposure makes prospective trustees more willing to take on the work.

Furthermore, the trustee will usually receive a covenant not to sue under environmental laws from the relevant regulatory

---

20. *See, e.g.*, *In re Fruit of the Loom, Inc.*, No. 99-4497 (Bankr. D. Del. Apr. 17, 2002) discussed *infra*.

authorities, conditioned on complying with the settlement and trust agreements and the trustee's fiduciary duties. In addition, the agreements preclude other creditors from asserting claims against the trust. The environmental response trust agreement specifies that the bankruptcy court has continuing jurisdiction over trust issues and disputes, which is important because the bankruptcy court has a greater understanding of the purposes of the trust in the bankruptcy proceeding and the trust's rights, obligations, and protections from liability as compared with a district or state court. Under the *Barton* doctrine,[21] trustees appointed by the bankruptcy court may not be sued outside of the bankruptcy court for acts in their official capacity without leave of the bankruptcy court.

EXAMPLES OF ENVIRONMENTAL RESPONSE TRUSTS

Environmental response trusts have been used in a number of bankruptcy cases. Several examples are described as follows:

Tronox Inc. and 14 of Its Affiliates

Tronox, the world's third largest producer and marketer of titanium dioxide pigment, and affiliates filed petitions for relief under Chapter 11 of the Bankruptcy Code in January 2009.[22] The United States and several federal agencies, the Navajo Nation, 22 states, and several municipalities filed protective proofs of claim against Tronox for past and future response costs and cleanup under the

---

21. *Barton v. Barbour*, 104 U.S. 126 (1881); *Chua v. Ekonomou*, 1 F.4th 948 (11th Cir. 2021); *Carroll v. Abide*, 788 F.3d 502, 505 & n.12 (5th Cir. 2015); *Alexander v. Hedback*, 718 F.3d 762 (8th Cir. 2013); *Satterfield v. Malloy*, 700 F.3d 1231 (10th Cir. 2012); *Villegas v. Schmidt*, 788 F.3d 156, 158 (5th Cir. 2015); *In re VistaCare Group*, 678 F.3d 218 (3d Cir. 2012); *McDaniel v. Blust*, 668 F.3d 153, 156–57 (4th Cir. 2012); *In re Triple S Restaurants, Inc.*, 519 F.3d 575 (6th Cir. 2008); *In re Crown Vantage, Inc.*, 421 F.3d 963, 970–73 (9th Cir. 2005); *Muratore v. Darr*, 375 F.3d 140, 143–47 (1st Cir. 2004); *In re Linton*, 136 F.3d 544, 545–46 (7th Cir. 1998). 28 U.S.C. § 959(a) provides an exception to the *Barton* doctrine for acts or transactions in carrying on a business. *Muratore v. Darr*, 375 F.3d at 143–44.

22. The cases were filed in the bankruptcy court for the Southern District of New York and jointly administered. *See In re Tronox Inc.*, No. 09-10156 (Bankr. S.D.N.Y. Jan. 12, 2009).

Comprehensive Environmental Response, Compensation, and Liability Act (CERCLA),[23] and for penalties, damages, and environmental liability under various other federal and state environmental laws. Tronox's potential environmental liability was in the billions of dollars and involved more than 2,800 potentially contaminated parcels.

Debtors' plan of reorganization created five separate environmental response trusts. Each trust was allocated a portion of $270 million in cash funding, as well as a share in any future proceeds from a fraudulent conveyance proceeding, as described later. The trustees included environmental consulting firms and professional trustees skilled in administering environmental response trusts.

The largest trust, the multistate environmental response trust, held the greatest number of properties. That trust received funding to remediate approximately 30 owned properties, approximately 260 owned service stations, and approximately 1,200 non-owned service stations.[24] The West Chicago trust was responsible for remediation at and near the former Rare Earths Facility in Chicago, Illinois. The Cimarron trust was responsible for remediating property near the Cimarron facility located in Oklahoma. The Savannah trust was unique because the trust became the operator of a sulfuric acid plant at Tronox's former Savannah, Georgia, facility that it acquired as part of the settlement of the bankruptcy case. The fifth trust, the Nevada trust, held only the property in Henderson, Nevada. It was also unique because, post-bankruptcy, Tronox leased the Henderson facility from the Nevada trust and continued to operate the facility for a number of years.[25]

With respect to funding, the parties were able to agree on an allocation of the initial cash funding and future proceeds from the fraudulent transfer action. The bankruptcy court held a fraudulent

---

23. 42 U.S.C. §§ 9601–9675.

24. Environmental response trusts do not typically address non-owned properties but, due to the unusual funding structure in the Tronox settlement, certain non-owned properties were included in the scope of properties covered by the settlement.

25. U.S. Env't Prot. Agency, *Case Summary: Tronox Incorporated Bankruptcy Settlement*, https://www.epa.gov/enforcement/case-summary-tronox-incorporated-bankruptcy-settlement (last updated Sept. 9, 2021).

conveyance trial after confirmation of the plan and the creation and initial funding of the environmental response trusts. In 2013, after this four-month trial, the bankruptcy court held that Kerr-McGee Corporation had fraudulently conveyed its valuable oil and gas assets to subsidiaries of Anadarko Petroleum to avoid environmental and tort liabilities, leaving behind a chemical company (Tronox) that was saddled with legacy liabilities it could not afford.[26] The court did not determine the amount of liability; the parties thereafter reached a settlement for $5.15 billion, of which over $2 billion was paid to the five environmental response trusts.[27]

Asarco LLC

Asarco was a large copper mine, smelter, and refiner, and operated at numerous locations across the country. It filed for bankruptcy in August 2005. At the time of the filing of its bankruptcy petition,[28] Asarco had environmental liabilities at more than 80 sites, including many federal Superfund sites.[29] The bankruptcy court upheld various settlements for owned and non-owned sites after public comment and over objections by Asarco's parent company and others.[30] The Asarco settlements were the product of mediation. Three custodial trusts (as they were then referred to before the term environmental response trust was employed) were established and received a cumulative total of approximately $261 million for 24 owned contaminated properties in 13 states and the

26. *In re Tronox, Inc.*, 503 B.R. 239 (Bankr. S.D.N.Y. 2013).

27. *See In re Tronox Inc.*, 855 F.3d 84 (2d Cir. 2017); U.S. Dep't of Justice, Office of Public Affairs, *United States Announces $5.15 Billion Settlement of Litigation against Subsidiaries of Anadarko Petroleum Corp. to Remedy Fraudulent Conveyance Designed to Evade Environmental Liabilities* (Apr. 3, 2014), https://www.justice.gov/opa/pr/united-states-announces-515-billion-settlement-litigation-against-subsidiaries-anadarko.

28. *See In re Asarco LLC*, No. 05-21207 (Bankr. S.D. Tex. Aug. 9, 2005).

29. U.S. Dep't of Justice, Office of Public Affairs, *Largest Environmental Bankruptcy in U.S. History Will Result in Payment of $1.79 Billion Towards Environmental Cleanup and Restoration* (Dec. 10, 2009), https://www.justice.gov/opa/pr/largest-environmental-bankruptcy-us-history-will-result-payment-179-billion-towards.

30. *In re Asarco LLC*, 2009 WL 8176641 (Bankr. S.D. Tex. June 5, 2009).

costs of administration of the trust.[31] The settlement allowed this amount as an administrative expense of the estate.[32]

One trust was a multistate environmental custodial trust, which was established to own, remediate, and sell, if possible, approximately 18 properties previously owned by Asarco.[33] Another trust was created to own and remediate two properties in Texas. A third trust was created to own and remediate four properties in Montana.[34]

Fruit of the Loom

The *Fruit of the Loom* case was one of the earliest examples of a bankruptcy custodial trust; the trust was established in 2002.[35] The purposes of this trust were to own seven contaminated properties, carry out administrative functions related to the properties, pursue insurance coverage, manage or fund response actions or natural resource damage assessments and restoration actions selected and approved by the relevant governmental parties, and ultimately sell the seven properties, if possible. The United States and the states of Illinois, Michigan, New Jersey, and Tennessee were the government beneficiaries of the trust. The trust had limited initial funding from allowed administrative expense claims, which was supplemented by insurance and other sources. Over time, the trust received approximately $64 million for cleanup and administration. One unique feature of this trust was that the insurance policies not only provided much of the funding for the trust, but they also provided coverage to the Fruit of the Loom debtors and to a nondebtor affiliate, Velsicol Corporation. The bankruptcy settlement with Fruit of the Loom included an ability to pay settlement

31. *See* note 29 *supra*.

32. *Asarco LLC*, 2009 WL at *9, ¶ 43.

33. U.S. Env't Prot. Agency, Case Summary: ASARCO 2009 Bankruptcy Settlement (last updated Mar. 18, 2019), https://www.epa.gov/enforcement/case-summary-asarco-2009-bankruptcy-settlement.

34. *Id.*

35. *In re Fruit of the Loom, Inc.*, No. 99-4497 (Bankr. D. Del. Apr. 17, 2002). *Fruit of the Loom* actually involved two trusts, a custodial trust to hold the contaminated real property and a successor trust to hold funding. Settlement Agreement, *In re Fruit of the Loom*, No. 99-4497 (Bankr. D. Del., Apr. 17, 2002), ¶ 2, https://semspub.epa.gov/work/05/174040.pdf.

with Velsicol Corporation that enabled it to avoid filing for bankruptcy. Obtaining the insurance settlements required cooperation between the custodial trust trustee and Velsicol Corporation pursuant to the settlement.

General Motors

The General Motors bankruptcy created one of the largest environmental response trusts, known as the RACER Trust. The debtor paid over $641 million plus additional assets to the trust, which included approximately 89 properties. This trust had a unique feature of a $68 million "cushion fund" for unanticipated costs of cleanup.[36] The RACER Trust has led to many redevelopment success stories at several properties in Michigan, other Midwestern states, and New York.[37]

Eagle-Picher

Eagle-Picher involved a custodial trust for 12 properties funded with over $17 million. In contrast to most other environmental response/custodial trusts, which were consensual in nature, here, the proposal for a trust was initially not consensual. The debtors originally proposed inadequate funding for the trust as part of their plan of reorganization. The governments objected to the plan as inadequately funding the trust and, therefore, forbidden by law in contravention of the Bankruptcy Code. After extensive negotiations, partial settlements, briefing and an evidentiary hearing, the bankruptcy court approved the custodial trust.[38] This approach was unfortunate given the scarcity of available funds. It could be contended that the large amounts spent on litigation could have been better used for cleanup of the properties.

---

36. U.S. Env't Prot. Agency, *Case Summary: 2010 MLC (General Motors) Bankruptcy Settlement* (last updated Nov. 23, 2021), https://www.epa.gov/enforcement/case-summary-2010-mlc-general-motors-bankruptcy-settlement.

37. *See, e.g.*, U.S. Env't Prot. Agency Region 5, *EPA Redevelopment Success Stories*, https://storymaps.arcgis.com (July 20, 2020).

38. *In re Eagle-Picher Holdings, Inc.*, 345 B.R. 860 (Bankr. S.D. Ohio 2006); *see* Chapter 18 (Abandonment) *infra*; 11 U.S.C. § 1129(a)(3).

Exide

Exide involved creation of two environmental response trusts covering 17 properties in 11 states. The debtor, a lead recycling company, sought to abandon the 17 properties and liquidate. With help of a team of five mediators, the debtor and governmental agencies negotiated a settlement whereby abandonment was avoided by the creation of the two environmental response trusts with at least $60 million from surety bond proceeds and other funding.[39]

LIABILITY "TRANSFER" OR ASSUMPTION TRANSACTIONS

Liability "transfer" or assumption transactions typically involve the transfer of property to a company that will contractually assume the environmental liabilities associated with the property. Generally, the debtor will pay a certain sum of money in exchange for assumption of environmental liabilities, although sometimes in the case of particularly valuable property the company taking on the liability may instead make a payment to the debtor.[40] Companies in this field often refer to such transactions as environmental liability "transfer" transactions. Technically speaking, a liable party cannot avoid its liability to the government by entering into an agreement whereby a third party agrees to assume its liability.[41] However, in limited circumstances, a liable party can, as part of a bankruptcy settlement with the government, enter into a liability assumption transaction with an unrelated third party and seek a covenant not to sue from the government(s). In such a settlement, the assumption company or third party can be substituted for the responsible party in an agreement for the performance of work including

39. The *Exide* settlement is further discussed in Chapter 18 (Abandonment) *infra*.

40. In some instances the transaction can involve the contractual assumption of liabilities without transfer of ownership of the property.

41. *See, e.g.*, 42 U.S.C. § 9607(e). Indemnification agreements among private parties, however, have been recognized. *See generally* J. Sevack, Note, *Passing the Big Bucks: Contractual Transfers of Liability between Potentially Responsible Parties under CERCLA*, 75 Minn. L. Rev. 1571 (1991).

posting of financial assurance. Such a settlement is functionally similar to a transfer of liability from a practical perspective.

It is critical that there be adequate provision of funding for cleanup with a liability "transfer" or assumption transaction in order to both avoid objections by the government and facilitate resolution of a debtor's liability to the government. This means that there needs to be an estimate of the cost of cleanup that is as accurate as possible. In addition, regulatory authorities typically will seek financial assurance, which may include some buffer to protect against the potential for cost overruns or unanticipated costs. The most common forms of financial assurance are insurance, bonding, a letter of credit, or a trust fund.

A key component of the liability "transfer" or assumption transaction is that the liability assumption company becomes a signatory to the government settlement agreement and assumes all liability for environmental liabilities in accordance with the settlement agreement. As noted earlier, the regulatory authority may covenant not to sue or release the debtor from liability at the time of the transfer. However, in many instances, the government will require that the debtor retain liability until completion of all environmental work required by the agreement. The liability assumption company usually will provide indemnification to the debtor.

The typical steps for a debtor in a liability "transfer" or assumption transaction are:

(1) Identify appropriate third-party liability assumption companies that may be interested in the properties. These would usually include brownfield developers, real estate professionals, and perhaps companies interested in certain desirable features of the property (e.g., attractive location, etc.). In the case where ownership of the property is not being transferred, potential interested parties may include environmental consultants or other experts in cleanups.

(2) Prepare marketing materials that describe the properties and their significant features and related environmental liabilities, among other information.

(3) Conduct initial outreach with potential interested parties to determine interest in the transaction.

(4) Distribute marketing materials in an RFP (Request for Proposal)-type process and participate in due diligence. The prospective liability assumption company would evaluate the properties from the perspective of redevelopment potential, risk transfer analysis, scope of environmental issues, and other factors.
(5) Review proposals submitted by prospective bidders in response to the RFP.
(6) Select the liability assumption company in consultation with interested parties, including applicable regulatory authorities and other interested stakeholders. Criteria for selection include proposed funding for the transaction, plan for remediation, experience of the company, and goals for redevelopment or other future use of the property. Generally speaking, the most important criteria for the debtor in evaluating competing bids is the amount to be paid and the scope of liabilities to be assumed.
(7) Negotiate and execute the purchase and sale agreement, if applicable, or the liability "transfer" or assumption agreement, with the liability assumption company.

In the context of a bankruptcy case, the liability "transfer" or assumption transaction can occur during the bankruptcy proceeding or upon emergence. The timing will often depend upon the complexity of the transaction. The more complex the transaction, the greater the likelihood that the transaction will be completed only upon emergence from bankruptcy pursuant to a plan of reorganization. If the contaminated property raises issues of plan feasibility, it will be necessary for the issue to be addressed in the plan in order to satisfy feasibility requirements for confirmation of a plan of reorganization.[42] In the event the transaction occurs outside of a plan,[43] it is important that the agreement specify that the liability "transfer" or assumption transaction will survive and be fully effective through and after the plan process or even a conversion to Chapter 7.

---

42. *See* Chapter 16 (Plan Objections) *infra*.

43. The debtor will seek approval of the bankruptcy court for the transaction through a motion under Section 363 and/or Bankruptcy Rule 9019.

EXAMPLES OF LIABILITY "TRANSFER" OR ASSUMPTION TRANSACTIONS

A number of successful liability "transfer" or assumption transactions have been completed in the bankruptcy context. Four are described as follows:

Sparrows Point

Sparrows Point, Baltimore County, Maryland, was home to the world's largest steel mill, Bethlehem Steel, with 32,000 workers at its peak. Steel operations began there in 1889. Due to a variety of factors, the then-current operator, RG Steel, ceased operations in 2012 and filed for bankruptcy in May 2012.[44] At first, the debtor sought a buyer who would continue steel production. When it became apparent that was not an option, the property was sold to a liability assumption company for a payment of $72.5 million. As a condition of the sale, the liability assumption company agreed to assume specific legacy environmental liabilities associated with the property, which required entry into a consent order with EPA and the Maryland Department of the Environment.[45] The liability assumption company became the new responsible party (the debtor was liquidating) and placed $48 million into a remedial trust and letter of credit as financial assurance. Remedial activities have been undertaken at the property and the property is being converted into an international trade hub.[46]

---

44. *See* Peg Brickley, *RG Steel Files for Chapter 11*, Wall St. J. (Business) (May 31, 2012, 8:36 p.m.), https://www.wsj.com/articles/SB10001424052702303552104577438183180860276.

45. *See* Colleen Kokas, *ELT White Paper: How Interagency Cooperation Played a Critical Role during the Historic Environmental Transformation of Sparrows Point* (2018), https://eltransfer.com/wp-content/uploads/2018/05/ELT-White-Paper-How-Interagency-Cooperation-Played-a-Critical-Role-during-the-Historic-Environmental-Transformation-of-Sparrows-Point.pdf.

46. *See* Randall Jostes, *An In-Depth Look into the Role of Environmental Liability Transfers during Bankruptcies*, Bloomberg Law (Oct. 16, 2015, 12:00 am), https://news.bloomberglaw.com/environment-and-energy/an-in-depth-look-into-the-role-of-environmental-liability-transfers-during-bankruptcies; U.S. Env't Prot. Agency, *Hazardous Waste Cleanup: Sparrows Point Terminal LLC (TradePoint Atlantic) in Sparrows Point, Maryland*, https://www.epa.gov/hwcorrectiveactionsites/hazardous-waste-cleanup-sparrows-point-terminal-llc-tradepoint-atlantic; Natalie Sherman, *Court Approves Sparrows Point Settlement, Dismisses Bankruptcy*, Baltimore Sun (Business) (Oct. 15,

Asarco

Asarco, which was discussed earlier in this chapter in connection with environmental response trusts, also used two environmental liability "transfer" or assumption transactions as a key component of its bankruptcy reorganization. Asarco sold assets in Houston and Perth Amboy to a liability assumption company. Paying $28.9 million for the Houston property and $5.1 million for the Perth Amboy property, the liability assumption company became the responsible party, took over cleanup activities at the two properties,[47] and entered into consent orders with the New Jersey Department of Environmental Protection and the Texas Commission of Environmental Quality to remediate the properties.[48] The two state agencies, in turn, settled with Asarco, releasing it from environmental liabilities at these two properties.[49] Proceeds from the sale went to the benefit of Asarco's creditors.[50] The New Jersey Department of Environmental Protection required the liability assumption company to obtain a cost cap insurance policy[51] with a limit up to $12.8 million.[52] The Texas Commission on Environmental Quality required the liability assumption company to remove hazardous substances and restore the soil and groundwater to standards specified by Texas state regulations.[53] The liability assumption company agreed to stipulated penalties if it failed to meet cleanup or reporting deadlines.[54] The liability assumption company also agreed to indemnify and hold the agencies harmless for claims arising from its performance of cleanup activities.

2015, 11:13 p.m.), https://www.baltimoresun.com/business/bs-bz-rg-steel-settlement-20151015-story.html.

47. Jostes, *supra* note 46; *In re Asarco LLC*, No. 05-21207, Docket No. 9252 (Sept. 22, 2008).

48. *See* Texas Comm'n of Env't Quality, *Federated Metals*, https://www.tceq.texas.gov/remediation/superfund/state/fedmetal.html.

49. Jostes, *supra* note 46.

50. *Id.*

51. Cost cap insurance, also sometimes referred to as cost overrun insurance, is intended to cover actual remediation costs up to a set amount that are in excess of costs based on a cleanup cost estimate.

52. *Id.*

53. Agreed Order Regarding the Federated Metals State Superfund Site, *In re ASARCO* (No. 05-21207, T.X.S.B. Sept. 22, 2018) ¶ 11.

54. *Id.* ¶ 25.

The transfer of these two properties to the liability assumption company became an integral component of Asarco's plan of reorganization. It enabled Asarco to simultaneously dispose of these properties and address residual environmental liabilities. The governments obtained cleanup more quickly than they might otherwise have in the absence of the bankruptcy case.

Kaiser Aluminum

Kaiser Aluminum was a producer of aluminum and fabricated aluminum products. It filed for bankruptcy in 2002. The bankruptcy court confirmed Kaiser's plan in February 2006. One of the elements in Kaiser's environmental settlement included a liability assumption agreement that helped resolve Kaiser's environmental liabilities at three properties in exchange for approximately $15 million paid by Kaiser. As part of the transaction, the liability assumption company took title to the properties, assumed responsibility for environmental cleanup at the properties, and provided an indemnification to Kaiser for cleanup costs.[55] The liability assumption company signed an administrative order on consent with EPA to perform cleanup at one of the properties, securing its obligations with environmental insurance.[56]

W.R. Grace

W.R. Grace was a leading supplier of catalysts, engineered and packaging materials, specialty construction chemicals, and building materials, and had operations in more than 40 countries. It, along with 61 affiliated companies, filed for bankruptcy in 2001. A number of settlements associated with Grace's bankruptcy proceedings were consummated. One, in particular, involved the assumption of essentially all historical environmental liability relating to Grace's Hatco property in New Jersey. This environmental liability was settled through a liability assumption arrangement

55. *See* Kaiser Aluminum Corporation, Current Report (Form 8-K), 54 (Aug. 22, 2005).

56. Final Administrative Order on Consent, *In re TRC Companies; Inc. TRC Environmental Corporation; and Ravenswood Holdings Company, LLC 2/20 County Road Ravenswood, West Virginia 26164* (EPA No. RCRA-III-03-2012-0116TH) (Aug. 2012).

by which Grace provided up-front funding to a third-party environmental contractor, who in exchange for the payment assumed in perpetuity all of Grace's environmental liabilities in connection with the property. The transaction was also secured by a multimillion dollar insurance policy for cleanup costs.[57]

USE OF STATE LAND BANKS

Land banks are government entities that acquire and maintain abandoned properties, including properties that have associated environmental liabilities.[58] Land banks allow communities to more quickly redevelop and reuse buildings that would otherwise contribute to blight.[59]

CERCLA Section 101(20) exempts from liability any "unit of State or local government" that acquired property through law enforcement activity, tax delinquency, bankruptcy, abandonment, or other instances in which the government is acting as a sovereign.[60] Prior to the 2018 Better Utilization of Investments Leading to Development (BUILD) amendments to CERCLA, Section 101(20), only exempted properties that state and local governments acquired involuntarily.[61] This 2018 amendment to CERCLA allows for more expansive use of land banks with respect to contaminated properties. Land banks can be used to help facilitate environmental response trust settlements, liability assumption transactions, or potentially direct transfers to a land bank under a Section 363 sale.

One example is the *Fruit of the Loom* bankruptcy settlement and custodial trust described earlier. After nearly two decades, the trust had cleaned up many of its properties to the extent of

---

57. *See* State of New Jersey Dep't of Env't Prot., *DEP Approves $13.2 Million Hatco Site Cleanup and Land Acquisition Settlement for Wetland and Ground Water Contamination* (Apr. 21, 2005), https://www.nj.gov/dep/newsrel/2005/05_0047.htm.

58. *See* U.S. Env't Prot. Agency, *Land Revitalization Fact Sheet: Land Banking* 1 (2011), https://www.epa.gov/sites/default/files/2015-08/documents/fs_land_banking.pdf.

59. *Id.*

60. 42 U.S.C. § 9601(20)(D).

61. U.S. Env't Prot. Agency, *State and Local Government Activities and Liability Protections*, https://www.epa.gov/enforcement/state-and-local-government-activities-and-liability-protections.

available funding and many properties had been sold. However, one property in Michigan was not saleable because the cleanup was still ongoing. Meanwhile, the trust was running out of funding and preparing to wind down. Michigan's land bank agency was an attractive interim solution to own the facility while the cleanup continued. The comfort provided by the 2018 amendment to CERCLA for voluntary acquisitions out of bankruptcy by local governments facilitated the Michigan land bank agency's acquisition of the property, thereby permitting the trust to continue to wind down. Many other states also have land bank statutes.[62] Such statutes might be used in conjunction with dedicated accounts for cleanup (assuming they are available) to structure a land bank-based settlement for cleanup. Although the authors are not aware of any examples of this to date, these statutes are relatively new. In some situations, the regulators may prefer to have a response trust overseeing the cleanup and the property, but in others they may prefer to save on the administrative costs of environmental response trusts.

RETENTION BY REORGANIZED DEBTOR OF DEBTOR'S CONTAMINATED OWNED PROPERTY

A debtor may decide that the reorganized debtor will retain contaminated owned properties in those instances where the debtor is planning to emerge from bankruptcy as a reorganized debtor and will have the funding to address its environmental liabilities. As noted earlier and elsewhere in this Practice Guide,[63] liabilities for contamination on the reorganized debtor's property are not dischargeable in bankruptcy. Therefore, the reorganized debtor will have to carry through with its existing environmental obligations. This is considered a "pass through" of environmental obligations

---

62. *See, e.g.*, 68 Pa. Stat. and Cons. Stat. Ann. §§ 2103, 2104 (2021) (authorizing the creation of local land banks); Mich. Comp. Laws Ann. §§ 124.765, 124.773 (2021) (establishing a state-wide authority to create land banks); N.Y. Not-for-Profit Corp. Law § 1603 (2021) (allowing foreclosing government units to create land banks).

63. *See* Chapters 11 (Compliance Obligations), 13 (Discharge) *supra*, Chapter 15 (Section 363 Sales) *infra*.

because the reorganized debtor will continue to comply with its obligations instead of having the liabilities assumed by some other entity such as a trust, a new purchaser, or a liability assumption company. In many situations, the additional certainty provided by the other options, such as a trust or liability assumption company, if they are available, will be preferable to a debtor retaining the property and will enhance the debtor's long-term prospects. However, such options will not always be available. For example, the debtor and governments or third parties may be unable to reach agreement on the amount of funding needed for cleanup with an environmental response trust or on the amount of an appropriate ability to pay settlement. If a debtor is going to retain contaminated property, it may be tempted to, so to speak, let sleeping dogs lie. However, that may turn out to be shortsighted if the contamination festers and is aggravated by a lack of attention. That could result in significant additional liability, negative publicity, or another bankruptcy filing. In a serious case, criminal violations could even result. Therefore, it will often be in the debtor's best interest not to bury its head in the sand and to timely attend to environmental contamination on property it is retaining.

CHAPTER 15

Section 363 Sales and Environmental Issues

Once a bankruptcy proceeding has commenced, a debtor or trustee can sell assets utilizing Section 363 of the Bankruptcy Code (generally referred to as a "Section 363 sale"). Section 363(b) provides that "the trustee, after notice and a hearing, may use, sell or lease, other than in the ordinary course of business, property of the estate."[1] Section 363 provides certain protections to a purchaser against liabilities relating to the assets purchased, making a Section 363 sale attractive.[2]

A fundamental objective of a debtor in a Section 363 sale is to achieve the greatest value for a debtor's creditors while preserving the ongoing concern value of a debtor's operating businesses.[3]

---

1. 11 U.S.C. § 363(b)(1); *see also* 3 Collier on Bankruptcy ¶ 363.02[3] (16th ed. 2019).

2. 3 Collier on Bankruptcy ¶ 363.02[3] (16th ed. 2019); Am. Bankr. Inst., Commission to Study the Reform of Chapter 11, *Final Report and Recommendations, Commencing the Case*, § IV.C.2, at 83–84 (2012–2014); *id., Administering the Case,* § V.B.1, .3, at 136, 141–43; *id., Exiting the Case*, § VI.B, at 201–04 [hereinafter *ABI Report*].

3. *See* H.R. Rep. No. 95-595, 95th Cong., at 220 (1st Sess. 1977), *reprinted in* 1977 U.S.C.C.A.N. 5963, 6179 ("The purpose of a business reorganization case, unlike a liquidation case, is to restructure a business's finances so that it may continue to operate, provide its employees with jobs, pay its creditors, and produce a return for its stockholders."). *See also* National Bankruptcy Review Commission Final Report—The Next Twenty Years, ch. 3 (1997), *reprinted in* Collier on Bankruptcy (16th ed. 2019), Appendix G ("Chapter 11 of the Bankruptcy Code favors the reorganization of debtors in an effort to preserve going-concern value, retain jobs, and

Section 363 sales are relatively expedient and are generally completed within 40 to 90 days from the date the motion for approval is filed.[4] Debtors often pursue a Section 363 sale in lieu of a traditional reorganization pursuant to a Chapter 11 plan. This can avoid the delay in monetizing the estate's value through a Chapter 11 plan and attract strategic investors that are interested in a quick sale rather than a long-term restructuring.[5] Secured creditors such as lenders or hedge funds often favor Section 363 sales as the most efficient way to obtain value for a debtor's assets.[6]

Typically, a Section 363 sale process involves four main events: (1) a marketing phase where the seller enters into an asset purchase agreement with a proposed purchaser called the "stalking horse" bidder; (2) court approval of the bidding procedures and auction process; (3) the auction itself, where multiple bidders often participate (to determine if higher bidders are interested); and finally, (4) a hearing to approve the final sale.[7] In some instances, debtors do not

---

promote the efficient use of capital."); *Bankruptcy Code Section 363 Sales: Trends and Opportunities*, No. 9 NORTON BANKR. L. ADVISER 2 (2007) (noting that while "[t]raditionally, [the] goals [of reorganization] were achieved through a Chapter 11 plan . . . [i]ncreasingly debtors are turning to preplan § 363 sales to accomplish a quicker and cheaper exit from bankruptcy"). Of course, this objective can only be pursued consistent with the requirements of applicable law. *See, e.g., Zerand-Bernal, Inc. v. Cox*, 23 F.3d 159, 163 (7th Cir. 1994) ("[N]o one believes . . . a bankruptcy court enjoys a blanket power to enjoin all future lawsuits against a buyer at a bankruptcy sale [or] . . . immunizes such buyers from all state and federal laws that might reduce the value of the assets bought from the bankrupt."

4. *In re Gulf Coast Oil Corp.*, 404 B.R. 407, 415 (Bankr. S.D. Tex. 2009); *ABI Report*, *supra* note 2, § IV.C.2, at 84–85. The timing for such sales has become controversial. On the one hand, businesses, whose diminishing value while in bankruptcy is often analogized to melting ice cubes, may need quick sales. On the other hand, a rushed fire sale may reduce competition and ultimately the sales price. *Id. See also* Karen Cordry, *Section 363 Sales: Cherry-Picking the Code: Successor Liability and Lessons from Wile E. Coyote*, 28 NORTON J. BANKR. L. & PRAC. 6 (Dec. 2019). The bankruptcy court has discretion to evaluate these factors in deciding whether to approve the proposed bidding process and timeline. *Gulf Coast Oil*, 404 B.R. at 423–25.

5. 3 COLLIER ON BANKRUPTCY ¶ 363.02[3] (16th ed. 2019); *ABI Report, supra* note 2, *Exiting the Case*, § VI.B, at 201–04.

6. *Id.* (citing *In re Chrysler LLC*, 405 B.R. 84, 96 (Bankr. S.D.N.Y. 2009), *appeal dismissed*, 592 F.3d 370 (2d Cir. 2010)).

7. In large cases, debtors may file a motion to authorize de minimis sales of assets for properties with low value without an auction, further court approval, or opportunity to object at the time of such future sales. Parties in interest should carefully review such de minimis asset sale motions and may want to preserve their right to object to future sales and/or request fixing language relating to the scope of a free and clear sale as discussed in this chapter.

secure a stalking horse bidder or agreement, in which case the auction would proceed without an initial bidder in place.

This chapter examines the Section 363 sale and discusses some of the legal issues raised by such sales relating to environmental liability, including Section 363(f)'s provision for sales "free and clear" of "any interest in such property," "stalking horse" purchase agreements, the approval standard for Section 363 sales, and assumption and assignment of contracts and leases in a Section 363 sale.

"FREE AND CLEAR" LANGUAGE

An important selling point for a debtor marketing its assets to potential purchasers in a Section 363 sale is the ability to sell its assets "free and clear of any interest in such property" pursuant to Section 363(f).[8] Section 363(f) provides that "the trustee may sell property . . . free and clear of any interest in such property" if one of five listed conditions (discussed later) is met. The term "interest" is not defined in the Bankruptcy Code. Consequently, there has been a considerable amount of debate concerning the meaning and scope of the term.[9]

In the absence of a precise definition of the term "interest," courts have provided conflicting rulings regarding the meaning and scope of Section 363(f). The trend in the case law has favored a broad and expansive reading of the term "interest" which would include liens and successor liability claims.[10] For example, in

---

8. *See* 11 U.S.C. § 363(f).

9. 3 Collier on Bankruptcy ¶ 363.06[1] (16th ed. 2019) (noting that "[c]ourts have struggled to define the scope of 'interest' for purposes of section 363(f)"); *ABI Report, Administering the Case*, at 141–43; Cordry, *supra* note 4. As noted by Ms. Cordry, Section 1141(c) provides that confirmation of a plan is free and clear of all "claims and interests" and Section 106(c) allows setoff against a claim or an interest, while Section 363 only refers to an "interest."

10. *See, e.g., In re Spanish Peaks Holdings II, LLC*, 872 F.3d 892 (9th Cir. 2017) (free and clear of lease interest); *In re Motors Liquidation Co.*, 829 F.3d 135, 155 (2d Cir. 2016) (free and clear of certain successor liability); *Precision Indus., Inc. v. Qualitech Steel SBQ, LLC*, 327 F.3d 537, 545 (7th Cir. 2003) (free and clear of lease interest and noting that the "term 'interest' is a broad term no doubt selected by Congress to avoid 'rigid and technical definitions drawn from other areas of the law'"); *In re Trans World Airlines, Inc.*, 322 F.3d 283, 288–90 (3d Cir. 2003) (free and clear language protected the asset purchaser from gender discrimination claims

In re Motors Liquidation Company, the Second Circuit held that a bankruptcy court may approve a Section 363 sale free and clear of successor liability claims if such claims "flow from the debtor's ownership of the sold assets" and the claim arises from a right to payment that would have been dischargeable in the bankruptcy case because of a sufficient pre-petition relationship between the debtor and an identifiable claimant.[11]

A minority of courts, however, have interpreted "interest" under Section 363(f) narrowly to cover only in rem interests in the property being sold, such as liens and security interests, but not successor liability claims.[12] These courts note that Section 363(f) not only does not refer to claims, it does not even refer to the sale of "any interest"; rather, it refers only to the sale of "any interest in such property."[13] As such, the scope of the term "interest" should be limited to in rem interests that can only attach to property and should not include in personam liability such as successor liability.[14] Similarly, in *In re Wolverine Radio Co.*, the Sixth Circuit held that the term "interest" should be interpreted narrowly because Section 363(f) leaves out the term "claim," which, unlike "interest,"

---

against the debtor); *In re Leckie Smokeless Coal Co.*, 99 F.3d 573, 582 (4th Cir. 1996) (free and clear of coal mining health care premiums); *Folger Adam Sec., Inc.*, 209 F.3d 252, 258–60 (3d Cir. 2000); *see also In re PBBPC Inc*, 484 B.R. 860 (B.A.P. 1st Cir. 2013) (enforcing the sale of the debtor's assets free and clear of successor liability under unemployment insurance statute); *In re Sea Oaks Country Club, LLC*, 2020 WL 6588412 (Bankr. D.N.J. Nov. 10, 2020) (free and clear of lifetime memberships in a golf course); *In re K & D Indus. Servs. Holding Co., Inc.*, 602 B.R. 16 (Bankr. E.D. Mich. 2019) (assets could be sold free and clear of successor liability claims); *In re Old Carco LLC*, 538 B.R. 674, 684–85 (Bankr. S.D.N.Y. 2015) (free and clear of utilizing experience rating); *United Mine Workers of Am. Combined Benefit Fund v. Walter Energy, Inc.*, 551 B.R. 631 (N.D. Ala. 2016) (free and clear of coal mining health care premiums); *In re Mundy Ranch, Inc.*, 484 B.R. 416, 421–23 (Bankr. D.N.M. 2012) (free and clear of partition interest). *See also* George W. Kuney, *Misinterpreting Bankruptcy Code Section 363(f) and Undermining the Chapter 11 Process*, 76 AM. BANKR. L.J. 235 (2002).

11. *In re Motors Liquidation Co.*, 829 F.3d at 156.

12. *See, e.g., In re Wolverine Radio Inc.*, 930 F.2d 1132 (6th Cir. 1991); *see also In re Fairchild Aircraft Corp.*, 184 B.R. 910 (Bankr. W.D. Tex. 1995), *vacated as equitably moot*, 220 B.R. 909 (Bankr. W.D. Tex. 1998); *In re White Motor Credit Corp.*, 75 B.R. 944 (Bankr. N.D. Ohio 1987).

13. *In re Fairchild Aircraft Corp.*, 184 B.R. at 918.

14. *Id.*

is defined broadly under the Bankruptcy Code.[15] In applying this reasoning, the Sixth Circuit found that an unemployment benefits experience rating was not an "interest" that could attach to assets purchased in a Section 363 sale.[16] As a result, the successor employer was required to accept application of the debtor-seller's adverse experience rating to its own (unchanged) work force.[17]

Even under the majority view of a broad interpretation of "interest" from which purchasers will be free and clear pursuant to Section 363, the courts recognize some important limitations. In *Motors Liquidation*, the Second Circuit held that the bankruptcy court's power to bar claims against a purchaser through a Section 363 sale "is plainly no broader than its power in a traditional Chapter 11 reorganization."[18] The court held that accident claims asserted against the purchaser of assets in a Section 363 sale that had not yet arisen and become dischargeable, on the ground of an insufficient relationship between the debtor and the claimant, could be pursued against the purchaser since the debtor itself could not have discharged them in the Chapter 11 reorganization.[19] Other courts have also held that the term "interest" does

15. *See* 11 U.S.C. § 101(5). *See also* H.R. Rep. No. 595, 95th Cong, at 309 (1st Sess. 1977).

16. *Wolverine Radio*, 930 F.2d at 1132, 1145–49; *see also In re Eveleth Mines, LLC*, 312 B.R. 634, 654 (Bankr. D. Minn. 2004).

17. *See also In re Eveleth Mines*, 312 B.R. 634 (purchaser could be liable for post-sale tax even if it was calculated based on past production).

18. *Motors Liquidation*, 829 F.3d at 155.

19. *Id.* at 156–58. This rationale of *Motors Liquidation* would on its surface appear to have applicability to whether Section 363 sales can be free and clear of injunctive obligations under environmental law since most environmental injunctive or compliance obligations cannot be discharged in bankruptcy. *See* Chapter 11 (Compliance Obligations) *supra*. However, in order to find a purchaser liable, it would also have to have successor liability under the legal rules governing when an asset sale results in successor liability. Most courts have held that an unrelated third-party purchaser of assets has successor liability only where there is an express assumption of liability, a de facto merger, the mere continuation of a predecessor, or the transaction is fraudulent. *See, e.g., United States v. Gen. Battery Corp.*, 423 F.3d 294, 309 (3d Cir. 2005); *New York v. Nat'l Servs. Indus., Inc.*, 352 F.3d 682, 687 (2d Cir. 2003); *United States v. Davis*, 261 F.3d 1, 54 (1st Cir. 2001); *Atchinson, Topeka & Santa Fe Ry. Co. v. Brown & Bryant, Inc.*, 159 F.3d 358 (9th Cir. 1997); *City Mgmt. Corp. v. U.S. Chem. Co.*, 43 F.3d 244 (6th Cir. 1994); *United States v. Mexico Feed & Seed, Co.*, 980 F.2d 478, 489–90 (8th Cir. 1992).

not encompass successor liability for future or unknown claims.[20] Likewise, a Section 363 sale will not be free and clear of an interest or claim where notice is not provided to a known holder of an interest or claim.[21] And, as noted later in this chapter, many courts have found that a Section 363 sale cannot be free and clear of nonmonetary restrictions that run with the land, as these are not dischargeable in bankruptcy and cannot be satisfied through the payment of money.[22]

Another important limitation on the scope of free and clear liability arises with respect to environmental liability or other liabilities that are based on *current* owner/operator status. This kind of liability springs anew under nonbankruptcy law, which makes current owners or operators of property liable even if contamination or a condition originated prior to the purchase. In other words, environmental liability generally attaches the moment the purchaser acquires the property.[23] This means that a purchaser of a debtor's real property is liable under environmental law by virtue of the purchaser's status as an "owner" or "operator" of the property, and a Section 363 sale should not be permitted to alter

20. *See e.g., In re Mooney Aircraft, Inc.*, 730 F.2d 367 (5th Cir. 1984) (bankruptcy court did not have authority to enjoin a claim that arose several years after the sale of the debtor's assets); *In re Grumman Olson Indus., Inc.*, 445 B.R. 243 (Bankr. S.D. N.Y. 2011), *aff'd*, 467 B.R. 694 (S.D. N.Y. 2012) (sale approval order did not affect future claimants injured after the sale); *White v. Chance Indus., Inc. (In re Chance Indus., Inc.)*, 367 B.R. 689 (Bankr. D. Kan. 2006); *In re Kewanee Boiler Corp.*, 198 B.R. 519 (Bankr. N.D. Ill. 1996); *In re Ninth Ave. Remedial Grp.*, 195 B.R. 716, 732 (Bankr. N.D. Ind. 1996). *See also Pension Benefit Guar. Corp. v. Oneida Ltd.*, 562 F.3d 154, 157 (2d Cir. 2009) (pension termination premiums not discharged in bankruptcy); *Zerand-Bernal Group, Inc. v. Cox*, 23 F.3d 159, 163 (7th Cir. 1994) (bankruptcy court could not enjoin all future suits against a buyer); *CMC Heartland Partners*, 966 F.2d at 1147 ("a statutory obligation attached to current ownership of the land survives bankruptcy").

21. *See Archer-Daniels-Midland Co. v. Country Visions Coop.*, 29 F.4th 956 (7th Cir. 2022); *In re HNRC Dissolution Co.*, 3 F.4th 912 (6th Cir. 2021); *In re Savage Indus., Inc.*, 43 F.3d 714 (1st Cir. 1994); *In re Sugarloaf Holdings, LLC*, 640 B.R. 270 (Bankr. D. Utah 2022) (sale motion must provide adequate notice of how a sale will affect the rights of an impacted party).

22. *See, e.g., Sugarloaf Holdings*, 640 B.R. 270 (sale of water right could not be free and clear of forfeiture action); cases cited in note 44 *infra*.

23. *In re Gen. Motors Corp.*, 407 B.R. 463, 508 (S.D.N.Y. 2009). However, environmental laws can limit a purchaser's liability under some situations. *See, e.g.*, 42 U.S.C. § 9601(40) (CERCLA) (providing for bona fide prospective purchaser exception to liability of unaffiliated purchaser making appropriate inquiry, although such a purchaser must still exercise appropriate care).

this.[24] As emphasized by the Supreme Court, no one is entitled to maintain a nuisance,[25] and that includes a purchaser of contaminated property from a debtor.[26] Broad language in many proposed sale approval orders (also sometimes referred to as sale orders)[27] arguably violates this established rule of law with language to the effect that the purchaser shall not be liable for any act or omission related to the debtor/seller's business and shall not have any "successor" liability for acts of the debtor/seller.[28] Such attempts were criticized by the late Bankruptcy Judge John Lifland as an example

24. Since a debtor could not discharge such future liability in bankruptcy, *see In re CMC Heartland Partners*, 966 F.2d 1143 (7th Cir. 1992) (a reorganized debtor that owns property that was contaminated prior to confirmation is liable to EPA as the present owner of the property because the liability springs anew), the rationale of *Motors Liquidation* discussed earlier would apply and a Section 363 purchase should not be free and clear of a future liability that a debtor could not discharge.

25. No one is entitled to ignore hazards or disregard laws that protect the public and the environment. *See, e.g., Ohio v. Kovacs*, 469 U.S. 274, 285 (1985) ("[A]nyone in possession of [a] site . . . must comply with . . . environmental laws . . . Plainly, that person . . . may not maintain a nuisance, pollute the waters . . . [,] or refuse to remove the source of such conditions.").

26. *Gen. Motors*, 407 B.R. at 508 (a free and clear purchaser "would have to comply with its environmental responsibilities starting with the day it got the property, and if the property required remediation as of that time, any such remediation would be the buyer's responsibility").

27. For example, language such as: "Except as expressly provided by the Purchase Agreement or this Order, all persons and entities, including, but not limited to, all governmental . . . and regulatory authorities . . . , holding interests of any kind or nature whatsoever against or in the Debtors or the Assets . . . arising under or out of, in connection with, or in any way relating to, the Debtors, the Assets, the operation of the business prior to Closing . . . , hereby are forever barred, estopped, and permanently enjoined from asserting against the Purchaser, its successors or assigns, its property, or its assets (including the Assets), such persons' or entities' interests."

28. As to successor liability, technically, the liability based on status as a post-sale owner or operator is not the same liability as the debtor's presale liability because such liability is based on the purchaser's status as a post-purchase owner/operator and such liability did not exist prior to the sale. It is also different from traditional successor liability under state or federal common law. *See* note 19 *supra; United States v. Gen. Battery Corp.*, 423 F.3d 294, 309 (3d Cir. 2005); *New York v. Nat'l Servs. Indus., Inc.*, 352 F.3d 682, 687 (2d Cir. 2003). Nonetheless, the "no successor liability" language in typical sale approval orders could be read literally, or found to be ambiguous, and therefore poses risks to public health and safety if not fixed. While such language could be interpreted to refer to traditional successor liability, an argument could be made that it in fact refers to the purchaser "succeeding" to a cleanup liability similar to the liability the debtor/seller had as a past owner or operator. The latter interpretation would improperly eliminate the purchaser's liability as a current owner or operator under most environmental laws.

of "overzealousness and aggression"[29] by the debtor. Governmental agencies will generally seek to correct this defect in proposed sale approval orders by including clarifying language (also referred to as "fixing language") such as:

> Nothing in this Order or the Asset Purchase Agreement releases, nullifies, precludes, or enjoins the enforcement of any police or regulatory liability to a governmental unit that any entity would be subject to as the post-sale owner or operator of property after the date of entry of this Order. Nothing in this Order or the Asset Purchase Agreement authorizes the transfer or assignment of any governmental (a) license, (b) permit, (c) registration, (d) authorization or (e) approval, or the discontinuation of any obligation thereunder, without compliance with all applicable legal requirements and approvals under police or regulatory law. Nothing in this Order divests any tribunal of any jurisdiction it may have under police or regulatory law to interpret this Order or to adjudicate any defense asserted under this Order.

This clarifying language serves to limit overbroad free and clear liability language and was recognized in *In re Old Carco LLC (f/k/a Chrysler LLC)* as "a phrase of art commonly used and well understood by experienced bankruptcy professionals involved in sales transactions."[30] The court noted that the "self-evident" purpose of the language is that "a buyer of property under a 'free and clear' sale order cannot escape the responsibility to remediate a condition that violates safety or similar laws even if the condition pre-existed the sale."[31] This clarifying or fixing language has been obtained by the government in hundreds of sale approval orders.[32]

It is critical for governmental agencies to be on the lookout for overbroad language in proposed sale approval orders. Under the reasoning of the Supreme Court's ruling in *United Student Aid Funds, Inc. v. Espinosa*,[33] failure to object to improper language

29. *In re Blockbuster, Inc.*, No. 10-14997 (Bankr. S.D.N.Y. Mar. 10, 2011), Transcript at 12:14–13:6.

30. 551 B.R. 124, 129–30 (Bankr. S.D.N.Y. 2016).

31. *Id.* at 130.

32. Some debtors include such language in their proposed sale approval orders without request and thereby avoid governmental objections and incidental costs.

33. 559 U.S. 260 (2010).

in sale approval orders can be prejudicial and result in the order becoming binding even though it contains improper language.[34] However, when governmental agencies bring the issue of improper language to the attention of the bankruptcy court, most courts will remedy the problem. Courts are unlikely to want to keep language in a sale order that might contribute to a situation resulting in an environmental disaster. For the same reason, bankruptcy attorneys and professionals would be well advised not to seek such overbroad or ambiguous language, as it takes only one environmental disaster related to a party's erroneous presumption that it can escape liability on account of such language to cast broad disrepute on the bankruptcy system (as well as cause harm to public health and safety).[35]

As long as the previously described fixing language is obtained to cure the owner/operator liability issue, governments have generally not objected to language confirming that the purchaser does not have traditional successor environmental liability (i.e., liability not based on current owner/operator status), such as for presale

---

34. Chapter 16 (Plan Objections) of this Practice Guide discusses *Espinosa*. As noted in Chapter 16, there are limited exceptions to *Espinosa* for: (1) lack of notice (*Archer-Daniels-Midland Co. v. Country Visions Coop.*, 29 F.4th 956 (7th Cir. 2022); *In re HNRC Dissolution Co.*, 3 F.4th 912 (6th Cir. 2021); *In re Savage Indus., Inc.*, 43 F.3d 714 (1st Cir. 1994); *In re Sugarloaf Holdings, LLC*, 640 B.R. 270 (Bankr. D. Utah 2022) (sale motion must provide adequate notice of how a sale will affect the rights of an impacted party)); or (2) lack of an arguable basis for jurisdiction of the bankruptcy court (*Espinosa*, 559 U.S. at 271 (2010) (citing *United States v. Boch Oldsmobile, Inc.*, 909 F.2d 657, 661 (1st Cir. 1990); *Nemaizer v. Baker*, 793 F.2d 58, 65 (2d Cir. 1986)). In addition, bankruptcy courts have an independent duty to be on the lookout for illegal provisions and can sanction attorneys for proposing language that is illegal and has no basis in law. *Espinosa*, 559 U.S. at 277–79. A debtor's failure to disclose to the court (and the party) a known significant interest that the sale seeks to be sold free and clear of might also be contended to be fraud on the court. *See Archer-Daniels*, 29 F.4th 956.

35. For similar reasons, governmental agencies have found it unacceptable merely to qualify overbroad language in sale approval orders with language like "to the extent permitted by law." Such language is too vague and general and only adds to ambiguity and uncertainty. Environmental laws depend on the concept of deterrence whereby owners and operators know and take into account the risks of environmental liabilities. *See, e.g., Safety-Kleen, Inc. v. Wyche*, 274 F.3d 846, 865–66 (4th Cir. 2001); *Kelly v. United States Env't Prot. Agency*, 203 F.3d 519, 523 (7th Cir. 2000); *City of New York v. Exxon*, 932 F.2d 1020, 1024 (2d Cir. 1991); *United States v. Nicolet*, 857 F.2d 202, 210 (3d Cir. 1988). If a purchaser believes it may have a bankruptcy-related defense to liability, the deterrent effect of environmental law is undermined, and the risk to public health and safety increased.

disposal of waste at third-party off-site locations by the debtor/seller or penalties for days of violation prior to the sale, and have not found it necessary to request broader fixing language stating that all environmental liabilities be exempt from the free and clear language.[36] In the first place, under the majority view and trend broadly interpreting Section 363, most bankruptcy courts are likely to overrule objections seeking broader language. Second, most environmental laws do not make unrelated purchasers of assets liable for pre-purchase off-site third-party disposal liabilities of a seller or penalties for days of violation prior to the purchase (although the purchaser would be liable for days of violation that continue after the purchase) because most courts have held that environmental laws only provide for successor liability where there is an express assumption of liability, a de facto merger, the mere continuation of a predecessor, or the transaction is fraudulent.[37] Drawing the free and clear line in this manner most effectively and fairly harmonizes bankruptcy law and environmental law.[38]

An exception to be considered would be if the buyer is related to the debtor/seller such that the substantial continuity prong for successor environmental liability is met.[39] In such an instance, there might be a valid case for successor liability

36. If there are presale response costs relating to debtor-owned property being purchased or off-site presale migration of waste from debtor-owned property being purchased, the legal status of such liabilities in a Section 363 sale is uncertain. *See Pennsylvania DEP v. Trainer Custom Chemical, LLC*, 906 F.3d 85 (3d Cir. 2018); *In re Hanna*, 168 B.R. 386 (9th Cir. B.A.P. 1994). The fixing language discussed in this chapter leaves such issues for future resolution based on whether a current owner or operator of property has such liabilities under the environmental statute that is applicable.

37. *See* cases cited in note 19 *supra. But see Ninth Ave. Remedial Grp. v. Allis-Chalmers Corp.*, 195 B.R. 716 (N.D. Ind. 1996).

38. *See* Chapter 8 (Harmonization) *supra.* In most circumstances, refraining from objecting to language in the Section 363 sale approval order that the sale is free and clear of environmental liabilities (other than those liabilities the purchaser would be subject to as an owner or operator) is not depriving the government of a right that it would have under nonbankruptcy law. The purchaser is provided with clarity that the purchase will be free and clear of such liabilities and that the purchaser will not have to risk the cost of having to litigate such issues. Moreover, as long as the free and clear language is appropriately limited, it is often in the governments' interests for the sale to proceed and to have ownership of the contaminated property transferred to a third-party purchaser rather than risk abandonment, which might happen if the sale were to fail.

39. *See Ninth Ave.*, 195 B.R. at 724–25.

under environmental law, and it would be appropriate to ensure that the free and clear order does not protect against such nondischargeable environmental liability. As indicated in the preceding discussion of *Motors Liquidation*, a free and clear order should not be broader than a debtor could obtain through a discharge in bankruptcy. Governments would contend that a free and clear sale should not be permitted to allow a related buyer of assets to circumvent nondischargeable environmental causes of action.[40]

Some courts have focused less on whether a liability is an interest under Section 363(f) and more generally on whether one of the five conditions set forth in Section 363(f) for a sale free and clear has been met:[41]

(1) Applicable nonbankruptcy law permits sale of such property free and clear of such interest;
(2) Such entity [holding the interest] consents;
(3) Such interest is a lien and the price at which such property is to be sold is greater than the aggregate value of all liens on such property;
(4) Such interest is in bona fide dispute; or
(5) Such entity could be compelled, in a legal or equitable proceeding, to accept a money satisfaction of such interest.[42]

None of these conditions is satisfied with respect to environmental compliance obligations of an owner or operator. "Applicable nonbankruptcy law" (condition 1) does not permit a sale free and clear of an owner's compliance obligations under environmental law. The government does not consent to a transfer free and clear of such obligations (condition 2), the obligations are not a lien (condition 3), and the obligations of owners under environmental law are not in dispute (condition 4). Finally, the government cannot be "compelled . . . to accept a money satisfaction" (condition 5) in lieu of the purchaser's compliance with environmental law. No provision of environmental law allows an owner to force the government to

40. *See* Chapter 11 (Compliance Obligations) *supra*.

41. *See In re Energytec, Inc.*, 739 F3d 215, 225–26 (5th Cir. 2013); *In re Southland Royalty Co. LLC*, 623 B.R. 64, 97 (Bankr. D. Del. 2020).

42. 11 U.S.C. § 363(f)(1)–(5). For a detailed discussion of the application of each of these factors, *see* Cordry, *supra* note 4.

accept money instead of requiring action to protect the public. Likewise, bankruptcy law does not require the government to elect a monetary remedy over compliance.[43] For similar reasons, a bankruptcy sale of assets cannot be free and clear of covenants, deed restrictions, or equitable servitudes that run with the land if non-bankruptcy law does not permit them to be extinguished through the payment of money.[44] Some sales agreements themselves confirm that the property is being sold as is and is subject to covenants, restrictions, or easements of record that run with the land.[45]

Finally, if a sale qualifies to be free and clear of an "interest," Section 363(e) permits parties holding those interests to seek "at any time" that the sale be prohibited or conditioned as is necessary to provide "adequate protection" of their interest.[46] The concept of adequate protection is well established with respect to security interests,[47] but much less so with respect to other kinds of interests (such as claims, liabilities, or similar obligations) that

43. *See In re Mark IV Indus., Inc.*, 438 B.R. 460, 470 (Bankr. S.D.N.Y. 2010), *aff'd*, 459 B.R. 173, 186 (S.D.N.Y. 2011) (the Bankruptcy Code does not require a governmental agency entitled to an equitable remedy to select a suboptimal remedy of money damages, citing *In re Davis*, 3 F.3d 113, 116 (5th Cir. 1993)); *see also Gouveia v. Tazbir*, 37 F.3d 295, 299 (7th Cir. 1994) (a debtor could not force neighboring landowners to accept money in lieu of equitable relief). In sum, bankruptcy law cannot be used to place a buyer in a position above the law, leaving the public at risk without the protection of health and safety requirements. *See, e.g., Zerand-Bernal, Inc. v. Cox*, 23 F.3d 159, 163 (7th Cir. 1994) ("[N]o one believes . . . a bankruptcy court enjoys a blanket power to enjoin all future lawsuits against a buyer at a bankruptcy sale [or] . . . immunizes such buyers from all state and federal laws that might reduce the value of the assets bought from the bankrupt.").

44. *See, e.g., Energytec*, 739 F.3d 215; *Gouveia*, 37 F.3d 295; *In re Hassen Imps. P'ship*, 502 B.R. 851 (C.D. Cal. 2013); *Baylake Bank v. TCGC, LLC*, 2008 WL 452009 (E.D. Wis. 2008); *In re Restaurant Assoc., L.L.C.*, 2007 WL 951849 (N.D. W. Va. 2007); *In re Sugarloaf Holdings, LLC*, 640 B.R. 270 (Bankr. D. Utah 2022) (sale of water right could not be free and clear of forfeiture action); *In re Southland Royalty Co.*, 623 B.R. 64, 97–99 (Bankr. D. Del. 2020); *In re Badlands Energy, Inc.*, 608 B.R. 854, 874 (Bankr. D. Colo. 2019); *In re Banning Lewis Ranch Co.*, 532 B.R. 335 (Bankr. D. Colo. 2015); *Skyline Woods Homeowners Assoc., Inc. v. Broekemeier*, 758 N.W.2d 376, 392–93 (Neb. 2008); *see In re Skyline Woods Country Club*, 636 F.3d 467 (8th Cir. 2011); *In re WBQ P'ship*, 189 B.R. 97, 106 (Bankr. E.D. Va. 1995); *In re 523 East Fifth St. Hous. Pres. Dev. Fund Corp.*, 79 B.R. 568, 570–71 (Bankr. S.D.N.Y. 1987).

45. *See, e.g., In re Oyster Bay Cove, Ltd.*, 161 B.R. 338, 343 (Bankr. E.D.N.Y. 1993).

46. 11 U.S.C. §§ 363(e), 361 (describing permissible form of adequate protection); 3 Collier on Bankruptcy ¶ 363.05 (16th ed. 2019).

47. *See, e.g.*, 11 U.S.C. § 364(d)(1)(B); 3 Collier on Bankruptcy ¶ 363.05 (16th ed. 2019).

might be included in an expansive interpretation of "interest" under Section 363(f).[48] Parties making an objection to a Section 363 sale in connection with environmental liabilities may want to consider including, as a backup, an alternative argument that if the sale is to be allowed, it should be conditioned on ensuring adequate protection of their interest.

"STALKING HORSE" PURCHASE AGREEMENT

Typically, a debtor markets its assets broadly in order to find a purchaser willing to serve as the "stalking horse" bidder.[49] A stalking horse bidder is the initial proposed purchaser who provides a baseline, binding bid for the debtor's assets,[50] subject to court approval and other higher, better offers at a later court-approved auction.[51] A debtor selects the stalking horse bidder either pre-petition[52] or at a "mini-auction" held for receiving such offers.[53] If a debtor receives multiple offers for a stalking horse bidder, the debtor must decide

---

48. *See, e.g.*, *Illinois Dep't of Revenue v. Hanmi Bank*, 895 F.3d 465 (7th Cir. 2018); Sarah Curley, *Sellers and Buyers Beware, Recent Developments in the Sale of Assets, Part II*, 39 Am. Bankr. Inst. J. 44 (Jan. 2020). The law is undeveloped as to how adequate protection applies to liabilities connected to, or that arise from, the property being sold.

49. *See In re Grubb & Ellis Co.*, 2012 WL 1036071, at *1 (Bankr. S.D.N.Y. Mar. 27, 2012), *aff'd*, 523 B.R. 423 (S.D.N.Y. 2014) (debtor engaged in a robust marketing process to assist in negotiations with a potential stalking horse bidder).

50. *In re Westpoint Stevens, Inc.*, 600 F.3d 231, 239 n.3 (2d Cir. 2010); *In re SpecialtyChem Prod. Corp.*, 372 B.R. 434, 436 (E.D. Wis. 2007) (explaining that a stalking horse bidder is a bidder that "reaches an agreement with the debtor-in-possession to purchase assets").

51. *See* Nadia Khattak, PLC US, *Section 363 Sales: New Stalking Horse Strategies*, Practical Law (2009) (available on Westlaw) (noting that while the stalking horse bidder negotiates the threshold price for the assets, the contractual terms of the purchase agreement, and the bidding procedures, all of these negotiated items must be approved by the bankruptcy court and entered into an order).

52. *See, e.g.*, *Grubb & Ellis*, 2012 WL 1036071, at *1 (after the debtors' "prepetition secured lenders refused to provide debtor-in-possession financing to finance [the] [d]ebtors' businesses until a section 363 sale could be arranged, [the debtors' investment bankers] facilitated a purchase of the [d]ebtors' Senior Secured Debt by BGC Partners, Inc. ("BGC") . . . [and] helped negotiate a stalking horse bid by BGC, subject to higher and better offers").

53. *See, e.g.*, *In re Residential Capital, LLC*, 501 B.R. 549, 574 (Bankr. S.D.N.Y. 2013) (debtor selected its stalking horse bidder from a pre-auction auction called a "Mini Auction" that took place in advance of the sale procedures hearing).

which bid represents the most favorable economic proposal.[54] However, if the debtor receives no other offers, then the stalking horse bidder automatically becomes the purchaser.[55]

Because there is no guarantee that the stalking horse bidder will prevail over a competing bidder, the main drawback facing a stalking horse bidder is the time and effort required to conduct due diligence and negotiate the purchase agreement, including determining the initial bid price.[56] Having a seat at the table in the initial negotiations, on the other hand, can also serve as a great advantage because it is at these preliminary negotiations that the stalking horse bidder negotiates bidding protections.[57] A bid protection is a payment made to the stalking horse bidder in consideration for its time and expense in the event that the sale transaction with the bidder ultimately does not take place, which often will happen if the stalking horse bidder is not the high bidder at the auction. Absent bidding protections, many stalking horse bidders would be reluctant to invest time and effort in developing an initial bid out of the concern that the transaction would be shopped around and beaten by a competing bidder hoping to take advantage of the stalking horse bidder's initial due diligence.[58]

Those stalking horse bidding protections are generally in the form of a break-up fee, topping fee, or expense reimbursement.[59] A break-up fee is a fee paid by the debtor to the stalking horse bidder when the purchase agreement fails, when a later

---

54. *See, e.g., In re Innkeepers USA Tr.*, 448 B.R. 131, 135 (Bankr. S.D.N.Y. 2011) (debtors chose a stalking horse bid over another because it "represented the most favorable economic proposal received by the [d]ebtors and provided an opportunity to forge consensus among the [d]ebtors' constituents").

55. *In re Walter Energy, Inc.*, 542 B.R. 859, 869 (Bankr. N.D. Ala. 2015), *aff'd sub nom. United Mine Workers of Am. Combined Benefit Fund v. Walter Energy, Inc.*, 551 B.R. 631 (N.D. Ala. 2016), and *aff'd sub nom. United Mine Workers of Am. 1974 Pension Plan & Tr. v. Walter Energy, Inc.*, 579 B.R. 603 (N.D. Ala. 2016), *aff'd sub nom. In re Walter Energy, Inc.*, 911 F.3d 1121 (11th Cir. 2018).

56. 1 Collier on Bankruptcy ¶ 15.04[d] (16th ed. 2019).

57. *See id.*; Khattak, *supra* note 51.

58. *In re Integrated Res., Inc.*, 135 B.R. 746, 750 (Bankr. S.D.N.Y.), *aff'd*, 147 B.R. 650 (S.D.N.Y. 1992).

59. *In re Integrated Res., Inc.*, 135 B.R. at 750 ("In order to encourage the making of bids, debtors entice potential purchasers by utilizing various incentives, such as break-up fees, topping fees and expense reimbursement agreements."); *see also* Khattak, *supra* note 51.

bid prevails, or certain other criteria in the purchase agreement occur.[60] Break-up fees can come in the form of several types of payment arrangements, including payment of out-of-pocket expenses incurred in developing the bid or a wholly independent fee equal to the bidder's lost opportunity costs during negotiations.[61] A topping fee is a percentage, rather than a fixed amount, of the difference between the winning bid and the stalking horse's bid, or some other agreed-upon amount.[62] As an alternative to or in tandem with fees, the stalking horse bidder may seek reimbursement for expenses incurred during negotiations.[63] Importantly, however, if bidding protections are too high and competing bids are therefore too expensive because they need to account for the debtor having to pay a break-up fee, that may discourage subsequent bidders from participating in the auction.[64]

Once all aspects of the purchase agreement and bidding and sale procedures are negotiated, a debtor then seeks court approval of any stalking horse bidder and break-up fee, the bidding procedures, and the sale process. If approved, an auction will then be held to ensure that the highest and best price is obtained for the sale of the debtor's assets.[65] Typically, environmental agencies and creditors do not weigh in at the procedures phase of the sale process and instead leave that to the creditors' committee, other major creditors, and the U.S. Trustee's office to raise any issues. However, where a governmental agency or other environmental creditor has a very large interest, such party should monitor the process and keep close track of the language of the proposed bidding procedures and take appropriate steps to protect their interests. This may be important because designation of stalking horse bidders can be controversial (especially if the bidders are existing

60. *In re Twenver, Inc.*, 149 B.R. 954, 956 (Bankr. D. Colo. 1992); *Integrated Res.*, 135 B.R. at 750 .

61. *Integrated Res.*, 135 B.R. at 750

62. *In re Twenver, Inc.*, 149 B.R. at 956.

63. *In re Integrated Res., Inc.*, 135 B.R. at 750.

64. *Id.; In re Twenver, Inc.*, 149 B.R. 954, 956 (Bankr. D. Colo. 1992).

65. *In re Metaldyne Corp.*, 409 B.R. 661, 667 (Bankr. S.D.N.Y. 2009) (noting that the debtor has a duty to obtain the highest and best price, which typically requires that an auction be held).

lenders) and may warrant close scrutiny.[66] For example, language that would pre-approve credit bidding by lenders may, if not clarified, be contended to waive rights to later object to a credit bid "for cause" under Section 363(k).[67]

In addition, if the assets for sale are subject to significant environmental liabilities, consent decrees, or administrative orders, governments may want to ensure that there is a level playing field by requiring that all bids include an agreement to comply with the consent decree, administrative order, or similar liability. In cases with very significant environmental issues, governmental agencies sometimes file a notice that sets forth the fixing language they will request to be included in any sale approval order in order to avoid a potential objection by the government. That places bidders on early notice of the issues and can smooth the pathway for prompt agreement on the fixing language. For that reason, some debtors' counsel support such filings but request that they be presented as a clarification or correction so that they do not negatively impact bidding (which is usually also in the governments' interests).

---

66. *See generally* Adam Levitin, *Purdue's Poison Pill: The Breakdown of Chapter 11's Checks and Balances*, 100 Tex. L. Rev. 100, 117–20 (2022); Steven Fruchter, *Section 363 Sales After the Covid-19 Pandemic*, 95 Am. Bankr. L.J. 367, 378–80 (Spring 2021).

67. *See, e.g., In re Philadelphia Newspapers, LLC*, 599 F.3d 298, 315–16 (3d Cir. 2010); *In re Murray Metallurgical Coal Holdings, LLC*, 614 B.R. 819, 835 (Bankr. S.D. Ohio 2020); *In re Aeropostale, Inc.*, 555 B.R. 369, 414–15 (Bankr. S.D.N.Y. 2016); *In re The Free Lance-Star Publ'g Co.*, 512 B.R. 798, 805 (Bankr. E.D. Va. 2014); *In re Fisker Auto. Holdings, Inc.*, 510 B.R. 55, 59–60 (Bankr. D. Del. 2014); *In re Antaeus Technical Servs., Inc.*, 345 B.R. 556, 564 (Bankr. W.D. Va. 2005). The Supreme Court has upheld secured creditors right to credit bid in *RadLax Gateway Hotel, LLC v. Amalgamated Bank*, 566 U.S. 639 (2012). But that case did not involve an issue of an objection to a credit bid for cause under Section 363(k). As noted in Chapter 5 (Key Provisions (post-petition financing)), lenders sometimes include language providing for advance court approval of their right to credit bid in connection with providing post-petition financing. While the Bankruptcy Code does not define what constitutes "cause," such language in post-petition financing orders might preclude objections for cause under Section 363(k) if not objected to. Grounds for objection to credit bidding for cause might include that: (1) the bidder was not viable and would not have the capacity to comply with environmental law, (2) the bidder had a poor record of environmental violations, (3) the bidder would not agree to terms of sale consistent with its having to comply with police or regulatory law as discussed earlier in this chapter, or (4) the proposed bid would result in an impermissible abandonment of excluded property in contravention of abandonment requirements, *see* Chapter 18 (Abandonment) *infra*.

In important cases, governmental agencies may want to look closely at the proposed schedule for the sale process. Is there sufficient time to permit bidders to conduct due diligence to make an informed bid? Does the schedule make clear when an objection to sale approval order language is due? Is there sufficient time after the auction and filing of a proposed sale approval order and before the deadline for objections to permit evaluation and discussion of the sale and sale order language? If there are concerns with the proposed schedule, they should be timely raised to the bankruptcy court.

COURT APPROVAL OF SECTION 363 SALE OF A DEBTOR'S ASSETS

After the close of the auction, the final stage in a Section 363 sale is court approval of the sale.[68] Whether the proposed transaction involves a sale of all of the debtor's assets, substantially all of the assets, or a sale involving only the crown jewel assets, all sales are subject to careful scrutiny by the bankruptcy court.[69] To determine whether to authorize a Section 363 sale, most courts have adopted the "business judgment" standard established by the Second Circuit in *In re Lionel Corp.*[70] Notably, the "business judgment" standard in the Section 363 context is not as deferential as the "business judgment" standard in corporate law.[71] *Lionel* provides that, in evaluating a debtor's business judgment, a bankruptcy

68. Douglas Deutsch & Michael Distefano, *The Mechanics of a § 363 Sale*, 30 Am. Bankr. Inst. J. 48, 49 (Feb. 2011).

69. *See In re Gen. Motors Corp.*, 407 B.R. 463, 489 (Bankr. S.D.N.Y. 2009) (explaining that "even the entirety of a debtor's business may be sold without waiting for confirmation when there is a good business reason for doing so"); *In re Gulf Coast Oil Corp.*, 404 B.R. 407 (Bankr. S.D. Tex. 2009) (sale outside ordinary course of business is not per se prohibited simply because it involves all or virtually all property of the estate; however, such sales, or sales involving "crown jewel" assets, are subject to special scrutiny).

70. *See generally In re Lionel Corp.*, 722 F.2d 1063 (2d Cir. 1983); *see also* 17 *Collier on Bankruptcy* § 28.31 (16th ed. 2019) (citing *In re Titusville Country Club*, 25 C.B.C.2d 192, 128 B.R. 396 (Bankr. W.D. Pa. 1991); *In re Plabell Rubber Prods., Inc.*, 149 B.R. 475, 479 (Bankr. N.D. Ohio 1992); *In re Weatherly Frozen Food Grp., Inc.*, 149 B.R. 480, 483 (Bankr. N.D. Ohio 1992)). *See In re Gen. Motors Corp.*, 407 B.R. at 489.

71. *See Lionel*, 722 F.2d at 1071.

court "should consider all salient factors pertaining to the proceeding," including, but not limited, to the proportionate value of the assets to the estate as a whole and the likelihood that a plan would be confirmed.[72]

Courts have applied this standard in various ways, primarily focusing on whether: (1) the sale price was fair, (2) the assets were aggressively marketed, (3) notice was provided to all parties in interest, and (4) seller and purchaser proceeded in good faith.[73] Collusion or connections between bidders may preclude a good faith finding.[74] One case, *In re Gulf Coast Oil*, went even further to require not just a showing of a business justification for the sale but also a showing of a "valid business justification for the process occurring separate from the plan confirmation process."[75] In all cases, however, courts agree that Section 363 does not authorize a debtor to "short circuit" plan requirements by establishing a sub rosa plan.[76] A sub rosa plan refers to a sale that seeks to allocate or dictate the distribution of sale proceeds outside of the ordinary plan process, which would subvert Bankruptcy Code requirements, including the filing of a disclosure statement and satisfaction of requirements for confirmation of a plan.[77]

---

72. *Id.*

73. *See, e.g.*, 11 U.S.C. § 363(m); *In re Alaska Fishing Adventure, LLC*, 594 B.R. 883 (Bankr. D. Alaska 2018); *In re Daily Gazette Co.*, 584 B.R. 540 (Bankr. S.D. W. Va. 2018); *In re 9 Houston LLC*, 578 B.R. 600 (Bankr. S.D. Tex. 2017); *In re Sasso*, 572 B.R. 331 (Bankr. D.N.M. 2017); *In re Childers*, 526 B.R. 608 (Bankr. D.S.C. 2015); *In re Scimeca Found., Inc.*, 497 B.R. 753 (Bankr. E.D. Pa. 2013); *In re Crawford Furniture Mfg. Corp.*, 460 B.R. 586, 55 Bankr. Ct. Dec. (CRR) 238 (Bankr. W.D.N.Y. 2011). A sale is not in good faith if notice is not provided to a party with a known interest in the property. *Archer-Daniels-Midland Co. v. Country Visions Coop.*, 29 F.4th 956 (7th Cir. 2022).

74. *See In re Cold LLC*, 558 B.R. 500 (1st Cir. B.A.P. 2016), *aff'd*, 879 F.3d 376 (1st Cir. 2018); Richard Carmondy, Lisa Hedrick & Timothy Anzenberger, *Auction Sales: Disclosing Bidder Connections Prevents Surprises*, 40-3 Am. Bankr. Inst. J. 20 (Mar. 2021).

75. *Gulf Coast Oil*, 404 B.R. at 422.

76. *See, e.g.*, *In re Iridium Operating, LLC*, 478 F.3d 452, 466 (2d Cir. 2007); *In re Braniff Airways, Inc.*, 700 F.2d 935 (5th Cir. 1983); *In re Daily Gazette Co.*, 584 B.R. at 548; *In re 9 Houston LLC*, 578 B.R. at 620; *In re GSC, Inc.*, 453 B.R. 132 (Bankr. S.D. N.Y. 2011).

77. *In re GSC, Inc.*, 453 B.R. 132. *See* Chapter 16 (Plan Objections) *infra*.

ASSUMPTION AND ASSIGNMENT

Typical Section 363 sales also involve the assignment of a debtor's executory contracts and unexpired leases.[78] Such assets sometimes comprise a significant portion of a debtor's valuable property. A Section 363 sale, however, cannot be used to circumvent the requirements of assumption and assignment of executory contracts and unexpired leases under Section 365 of the Bankruptcy Code, which governs the assumption and assignment of such contracts and leases.[79] Accordingly, before an assignment of a contract or lease can take place, a debtor must satisfy the requirements of Section 365.[80]

Subject to the court's approval, Section 365(a) permits a debtor to assume or reject an executory contract or unexpired lease. Once a debtor assumes a contract or lease, Section 365(f) authorizes the assignment of such contracts if adequate protection of future performance is provided.[81] However, the Bankruptcy Code does not permit assignment without consent where applicable law excuses a counterparty from accepting performance from a party other than the debtor.[82] Therefore, when a debtor sells its assets pursuant to a Section 363 sale, it is important to identify the executory contracts and unexpired leases of the debtor associated with those assets.

---

78. For a discussion of executory contracts and the Bankruptcy Code, *see* Chapter 5 (Key Provisions (executory contracts)) *supra.*

79. *See In re Provider Meds, L.L.C.*, 907 F.3d 845 (5th Cir. 2018).

80. *See generally* 11 U.S.C. § 365; Chapter 5 (Key Provisions (executory contracts)) *supra. See also Cinicola v. Scharffenberger*, 248 F.3d 110, 124 (3d Cir. 2001).

81. 11 U.S.C. § 365(f)(2). *See also* 11 U.S.C. § 365(b)(1)(C) (requiring adequate assurance of future performance in order for debtor to assume a lease).

82. 11 U.S.C. §§ 365(c)(1)(A) (precluding assignment where applicable law excuses counterparty from accepting performance from another entity), 365(f)(2) (permitting assignment except as provided in subsections (b) and (c)). The circuit courts have adopted various interpretations of the interplay between the various provisions of Section 365, which should be consulted in any case presenting such issues. *See, e.g., In re Mirant Corp.*, 440 F.3d 238 (5th Cir. 2006); *In re Sunterra Corp.*, 361 F.3d 257 (4th Cir. 2004); *In re Catapult Ent., Inc.*, 165 F.3d 747 (9th Cir. 1999); *In re W. Elecs., Inc.*, 852 F.2d 79 (3d Cir. 1988); *Institut Pasteur v. Cambridge Biotech Corp.*, 104 F.3d 489 (1st Cir. 1997). Section 365(f) has been relied upon to override anti-assignment clauses in insurance policies and authorize the assignment of a debtor's insurance policies to a buyer. *See Pogo Res., LLC v. St. Paul Fire & Marine Ins. Co.*, 2022 WL 286206, at *13–15 (Bankr. N.D. Tex. Jan. 24, 2022).

Like a debtor's decision to pursue a sale, a debtor's decision to assume or reject a contract is subject to the business judgment rule.[83] If a debtor assumes or assigns an executory contract or unexpired lease, it must cure any default pursuant to Section 365(b).[84] Ultimately, Sections 363 and 365 work together as a way for a debtor pursuing a Section 363 sale to seek to assign its contract and lease assets. If a governmental agency or environmental creditor has a lease or contract with a debtor, it is important to view the asset purchase agreement, any supplement, and schedules to determine if the lease or contract is being assigned and what cure amount debtors are proposing. The governmental agency or creditor should determine whether it wishes to object to the assignment or the proposed cure amount. Deadlines for objections to assignments or cure amounts can be separate from other objection deadlines.

Many government leases, such as for coal or oil and gas, are issued under statutes or regulations, or have provisions, that require governmental approval of any assignment of such leases.[85] Governmental agencies' sale approval order fixing language often also contains provisions that address assignment approval requirements or cure amount issues.

OTHER ISSUES TO BE ON THE LOOKOUT FOR

Permits and Licenses

Parties should carefully review language in the proposed sale and approval order, asset purchase agreement, any supplements, and schedules relating to regulatory governmental permits and licenses. Nothing in the Bankruptcy Code permits a bankruptcy court to authorize a debtor to transfer its permits or licenses

83. *See, e.g.*, *Phar-Mor, Inc. v. Strouss Bldg. Assoc.*, 204 B.R. 948, 951–52 (N.D. Ohio 1997) ("Whether an executory contract is 'favorable' or 'unfavorable' is left to the sound business judgment of the debtor.").

84. 11 U.S.C. § 365(b).

85. *See, e.g.*, 41 U.S.C. § 6305; 43 U.S.C. § 1337(e); 30 U.S.C. § 187; 30 C.F.R. §§ 556.62, 556.72; 43 C.F.R. §§ 3453.3-1, 3453.3-2.

where nonbankruptcy law prohibits or requires prior governmental approval of such transfers.[86] Nonetheless, boilerplate language in many sale approval orders purports to authorize such transfers. The government fixing language, described earlier, corrects such improper language in a proposed sale approval order. Bankruptcy courts are not equipped to evaluate the qualifications and public health and safety requirements antecedent to regulatory permits and licenses, and few bankruptcy judges would want such a responsibility on their shoulders. Objections should be filed to such boilerplate language as bankruptcy courts may not be aware that such provisions are contrary to requirements of nonbankruptcy health and safety laws and of the risks posed by not complying with such requirements.

Some sale approval orders contain provisions authorizing a purchaser to operate temporarily under a debtor's permits and licenses pending approval of transfer. Whether such operation is legal is governed by nonbankruptcy law. Some statutes, including some mining statutes, allow such temporary operation as an agent of a permittee but may require governmental approval. Language seeking to exonerate the debtor/permittee from liability during such periods of operation would likely be contrary to nonbankruptcy law. Bankruptcy courts do not have authority to override nonbankruptcy law governing regulatory permits and licenses and certainly do not have authority to authorize anyone to operate without any required regulatory permit or license.[87]

Consent Decrees and Administrative Orders

If the property being purchased is subject to a consent decree or administrative order, interested parties, including the governmental entities or other parties that have rights under such decrees or orders, should carefully review language in the proposed sale approval order, asset purchase agreement, and any supplements

86. Sometimes debtors will include regulatory permits or licenses on lists of assumed or rejected executory contracts. Regulatory permits and licenses are not contracts because they have the force of law separate and apart from any contractual aspects. *See* note 88 *infra.*

87. *See* 28 U.S.C. § 959(b); Chapter 9 (Operating Estate Property) *supra.*

and schedules. Consent decrees and administrative orders are not mere executory contracts under the Code that the debtor can reject under Section 365, as they have the independent force of law.[88] Some decrees and orders have provisions that require government approvals or agreements prior to a sale of the property. Governments may contend that the bankruptcy court must respect these provisions because they have the force of law (under the orders of the other courts or agencies) and there is nothing in the Bankruptcy Code that overrides them.[89] In some instances, if the purchaser and government agree that the purchaser should take the place of the debtor under the decree or order, provisions should be made for the purchaser to be substituted for the debtor as appropriate.[90]

Deed Restrictions or Other In Rem Interests That Run with the Land

Parties in interest should be careful in reviewing and keeping a close eye on a Section 363 sale if there are any applicable in rem interests that might include deed restrictions or mineral or mining interests relating to the property being sold that are at risk of being potentially nullified by the sale. Debtors and purchasers have sometimes sought to override such interests without clear notification, which can lead to difficult litigation.[91] As discussed earlier

88. *See United States v. ITT Cont'l Banking Co.*, 420 U.S. 223, 236 (1975); *Saline River Props., LLC v. Johnson Controls, Inc.*, 2011 WL 4916681 (E.D. Mich. 2011); *United States v. Am. Nat'l Can Co.*, 126 F. Supp. 2d 521, 531 (N.D. Ill. 2000); *FDIC v. Frates,* 44 F. Supp. 2d 1176, 1201 (N.D. Okla. 1999); Chapter 5 (Key Provisions (executory contracts)) *supra.*

89. A bankruptcy court's authority in a Section 363 sale to impact nonbankruptcy proceedings and rights is also limited by *Stern v. Marshall*, 564 U.S. 462, 503 (2011), and the Rooker-Feldman doctrine. *See* Chapter 20 (Jurisdiction) *infra*; *In re Sugarloaf Holdings, LLC*, 640 B.R. 270 (Bankr. D. Utah 2022) (bankruptcy court did not have authority to terminate forfeiture action relating to sale of water right).

90. *See* Chapter 14 (Debtor-Owned Contaminated Property) *supra* for examples of liability transfer or assumption transactions.

91. *See, e.g., In re HNRC Dissolution Co.*, 3 F.4th 912 (6th Cir. 2021) (property sold free and clear without notice to holder of methane mining interest recorded on deed); *In re Sherwin Alumina Co., L.L.C.*, 952 F.3d 229 (5th Cir. 2020) (last minute plan changes in the middle of the night allegedly changed permitted encumbrances that would survive free and clear sale). *See also Archer-Daniels-Midland Co. v. Country Visions Coop.*, 29 F.4th 956 (7th Cir. 2022) (failure to disclose to the

in this chapter, such provisions are objectionable as not meeting the requirements of Section 363(f))(1)–(5), primarily because the interest cannot be satisfied through a money payment. If a party in interest has a lien under an environmental statute or for an environmental judgment, it should closely review the transaction and proposed sale order for the impact on its lien and whether to seek adequate protection as discussed earlier in this chapter.

Pre-enforcement Review

A purchaser (or the debtor) may not use a Section 363 sale motion to seek a ruling from the bankruptcy court as to the scope of obligations under environmental or other nonbankruptcy law. Section 106(a) of the Bankruptcy Code, which governs waiver of sovereign immunity by governmental units, provides that any order, process, or judgment of the bankruptcy court must be consistent with nonbankruptcy law applicable to the governmental unit.[92] Therefore, a purchaser or debtor may not seek a pre-enforcement determination of liability where not permitted under nonbankruptcy law.[93]

Exclusive Jurisdiction

Many proposed sale approval orders drafted by debtors include a provision stating that the bankruptcy court will have exclusive jurisdiction over all disputes relating to the sale approval order. Such language is inconsistent with the concurrent and nonexclusive jurisdiction of the bankruptcy court under 28 U.S.C. § 1334(b) over matters arising in, arising under, or related to the bankruptcy case.[94] Thus, in *Skyline Woods*, where the Nebraska Supreme Court

court and provide notice to party with known interest in property not in good faith and may be contended to be fraud on the court); *Sugarloaf Holdings,* 640 B.R. 270 (sale motion must provide adequate notice of how a sale will affect the rights of an impacted party).

92. 11 U.S.C. § 106(a)(4).

93. *See, e.g.,* 42 U.S.C. § 9613(h); *Reardon v. United* States, 947 F.2d 1509 (1st Cir. 1991) (CERCLA); *Voluntary Purchasing Grps., Inc. v. Reilly,* 889 F.2d 1380 (5th Cir. 1989) (CERCLA); *Amoco Oil Co. v. United States Env't Prot. Agency,* 959 F. Supp. 1318 (D. Colo. 1997) (RCRA). States may also object to such a request under the 11th Amendment. *See* Chapter 5 (Key Provisions (sovereign immunity)) *supra.*

94. *See* Chapter 20 (Jurisdiction) *infra.*

had ruled that a Section 363 sale could not be free and clear of a restrictive covenant on a golf course running with the land, the Eighth Circuit found that the ruling was within the concurrent jurisdiction of the state court and was entitled to res judicata.[95] The governmental fixing language, described earlier, resolves the issue by providing that the order does not divest other courts with jurisdiction to determine the meaning of provisions in the sale approval order when such provisions are asserted as defenses in actions before those courts that fall within their jurisdiction.

Distribution of Proceeds

Most sale approval orders do not have provisions governing distributions of proceeds from the sale because such provisions could raise potential objections to the sale on grounds that they are dictating the terms of a plan without going through the applicable plan approval procedures.[96] Rather, such distributions would be addressed in a plan or other resolution of the case.

When a sale is conducted done through a plan rather than just by motion under Section 363, the provisions of Section 1129 apply. Section 1129 may provide additional grounds for objection by governmental agencies and/or environmental creditors.[97] Interestingly, at least one bankruptcy court has held that certain provisions of Section 363 may not apply in a sale under a plan in accordance with Sections 1123(a)(5)(D) and 1123(b)(4) of the Bankruptcy Code.[98]

---

95. *In re Skyline Woods Country Club*, 636 F.3d 467 (8th Cir. 2011). *See also In re Mystic Tank Lines Corp.*, 544 F.3d 524 (3d Cir. 2008) ("No provision of the Bankruptcy Code requires the Bankruptcy Court to hear all 'related to' claims . . . [T]he only aspect of the bankruptcy proceeding over which the district courts and their bankruptcy units have exclusive jurisdiction is 'the bankruptcy petition itself.'") (citing *In re Wood,* 825 F.2d 90, 92 (5th Cir. 1987)).

96. *See* note 76 *supra.*

97. *See* Chapter 16 (Plan Objections) *infra.*

98. *See In re Ditech Holding Corp.*, 606 B.R. 544, 579–92 (Bankr. S.D.N.Y. 2019) (Section 363(o)'s prohibition of sales of consumer loans free and clear of creditor claims did not apply to sale under a plan.).

Excluded Property

Many asset purchase agreements allow the purchaser to exclude unwanted property from what it is purchasing. If the sale of assets would render the debtor unable to comply with the law in administering the property remaining with the estate, the motion to sell and exclude may be a de facto abandonment. Governmental agencies may object if the result would be contrary to the Supreme Court's ruling limiting debtors' ability to abandon contaminated property under Section 554(a) of the Bankruptcy Code in contravention of nonbankruptcy law.[99] If this issue is important in a particular case, close attention should be paid to the schedule that contains the final listing of excluded property and any objection deadline.

Sale of Crown Jewel Assets

If a debtor seeks to sell only its most valuable crown jewel assets, that may give rise to an impermissible de facto abandonment of the balance of the estate similar to the case of excluded property. Depending on the facts, such a sale may also be subject to an objection that the sale is improperly dictating the terms of a plan of reorganization.[100] The good faith of the transaction may be questioned if it can be shown to be an attempt to evade compliance with environmental laws or threaten public health and safety.[101] However, it may be difficult to persuade a bankruptcy judge not to allow a good faith sale of an asset for appropriate value and it may even be in the government's interest to proceed with the sale if it would further remedial activities.

---

99. *See Midlantic Nat'l Bank v. New Jersey Dep't of Env't Prot.*, 474 U.S. 494 (1986); Chapter 18 (Abandonment) *infra*. The reasoning of *Midlantic* as to the Bankruptcy Code not preempting established pre-existing police or regulatory law applies to Section 363 and other Bankruptcy Code provisions as well. *See* Robert Miller, *A Comprehensive Framework for Conflict Preemption in Federal Insolvency Proceedings*, 123 W. Va. L. Rev. 423, 460 (2020).

100. *See* note 76 *supra*. It could also make confirmation impossible, which could be grounds for conversion to Chapter 7.

101. Bankruptcy sales must be in good faith. *See, e.g., In re Abbotts Dairies of Pennsylvania, Inc.*, 788 F.2d 143, 150 (3d Cir. 1986). *See also* note 104 *infra* (courts taking into account public interest under nonbankruptcy law when interpreting or applying the provisions of the Bankruptcy Code).

If the purchaser is the debtors' lender(s) through a credit bid, a sale of only the valuable crown jewel assets that brings little or no cash into the estate might be objected to "for cause" under Section 363(k).[102] However, the Bankruptcy Code does not define what constitutes "cause"[103] and there is little case law providing guidance on this situation.[104] Finally, a governmental agency may have the right to reject requested assignment of leases for the valuable asset if the effect of approval would result in violations of its rights and the public interest for the properties left behind. To avoid this risk, a purchaser might agree to purchase all, or a larger group, of the other properties if the crown jewel assets have significant value.

Sales to Insiders

Bankruptcy sales to insiders are subject to extra scrutiny.[105] Insiders may include directors, officers, general partners, affiliates, or persons in control of the debtor.[106] Issues may include whether there was any collusion or unfair advantage.[107] In some situations, a sale to an insider or insider successor in order to evade environmental obligations (which absent free and clear protections would otherwise give rise to successor liability) might not be in good faith or might be contended not to be a true sale.

---

102. *See* note 67 *supra.*

103. In this situation, an example of a cause for objection to the proposed sale of crown jewel assets could be that the sale would result in an impermissible abandonment of property excluded from the sale due to contravention of abandonment requirements. *See* Chapter 18 (Abandonment) *infra.*

104. Several courts have taken into account the public interest under nonbankruptcy law when interpreting or applying the provisions of the Bankruptcy Code, *e.g., Midlantic*, 474 U.S. at 502 (abandonment); *In re Mirant Corp.*, 378 F.3d 511, 525 (5th Cir. 2004) (executory contracts); *In re ATP Oil & Gas Corp.*, 2013 WL 3157567, *3 (Bankr. S.D. Tex., June 19, 2013) (abandonment); *In re Pilgrim's Pride Corp.*, 403 B.R. 413, 422–25 (Bankr. N.D. Tex. 2009) (executory contracts). By doing so, the courts are effectively harmonizing bankruptcy law and environmental law). *See* Chapter 8 (Harmonization) *supra.*

105. *See In re Tempnology, LLC*, 542 B.R. 50, 65 (Bankr. D.N.H. 2015); *In re Tidal Constr. Co.*, 446 B.R. 620, 624 (Bankr. S.D. Ga. 2009).

106. 11 U.S.C. § 101(31).

107. *See In re Old Cold LLC*, 879 F.3d 376, 384–85 (1st Cir. 2018).

Post-Confirmation Sales

Section 363 is no longer available after the effective date of a confirmed plan.[108] Section 363 only permits sales of "property of the estate." Confirmation of a plan vests property of the estate in the reorganized debtor and the estate no longer exists.[109]

Appeals and Mootness

Section 363(m) of the Bankruptcy Code provides that approval of a good faith purchase of property in bankruptcy cannot be reversed unless the sale is stayed pending appeal.[110] However, challenges that do not affect the validity of the sale[111] or challenges raising the good faith of the purchaser may be considered.[112] Nonbankruptcy courts have concurrent jurisdiction to interpret the scope of a free and clear sale approval order in a matter before them.[113] Obtaining a stay may be necessary to preserve the right to appeal. Rule 6004(h) provides for an automatic stay of 14 days to permit appeals,[114] but proposed sale approval orders often seek to waive this 14-day period. Parties anticipating appeals should consider objecting to a request for waiver of the 14-day period so that they can have a fair opportunity to seek a stay and protect against an argument that their appeal has become moot.

---

108. *See In re Golf L.L.C.*, 322 B.R. 874 (Bankr. D. Neb. 2004).

109. 11 U.S.C. § 1141(b).

110. *Id.* § 363(m); *In re Walker County Hosp. Corp.*, 3 F.4th 229 (5th Cir. 2021); *In re Pursuit Capital Mgmt., LLC*, 874 F.3d 124, 133–34 (3d Cir. 2017).

111. *See, e.g., In re Energy Future Holdings Corp.*, 949 F.3d 806, 821 (3d Cir. 2020); *In re ICL Holding Co.*, 802 F.3d 547, 554 (3d Cir. 2015).

112. *See, e.g., In re Stanford*, 17 F.4th 116 (11th Cir. 2021); *Archer-Daniels-Midland Co. v. Country Visions Coop.*, 29 F.4th 956 (7th Cir. 2022) (sale not in good faith on account of failure to provide notice to known creditor).

113. *See, e.g., In re Skyline Woods Country Club*, 636 F.3d 467 (8th Cir. 2011); *Skyline Woods Homeowners Assoc. v. Broekemeier*, 758 N.W.2d 376 (Neb. 2008).

114. Bankruptcy appeals must be made within 14 days after entry of the order, judgment, or decree being appealed. Fed. R. Bankr. P. 8002.

CHAPTER 16

Objections to Bankruptcy Plans Involving Environmental Issues

The defining moment and crowning achievement of Chapter 11 bankruptcy cases is the plan and confirmation hearing.[1] The plan and confirmation hearing can be at once: (1) an expansive opportunity to negotiate a mutually beneficial resolution of environmental problems that might otherwise have taken years or even decades to deal with outside of bankruptcy, or (2) a potentially dangerous infringement on the rights of environmental creditors and parties in interest which may require strong objection. Some examples of beneficial environmental bankruptcy settlements, which are usually incorporated within the overall terms of a plan, are discussed in Chapter 21 (Settlement Agreements).

This chapter focuses on environmentally based objections to plans where settlement of the environmental issues has not yet been reached. As described later, a persuasive objection is often essential to protect environmental interests. In addition, an objection may facilitate settlement as many bankruptcy settlements are reached late in the confirmation process or even during the confirmation hearing so that the debtor can consensually resolve difficult legal issues. This chapter will first discuss plan objections

1. *See* Chapter 3 (Code Chapters) *supra*.

generally, then explain why early participation in bankruptcy cases may be important to strengthen plan objections (as well as settlement opportunities), and conclude with a discussion of the most common kinds of objections made by environmental creditors or parties in interest.

PLAN OBJECTIONS GENERALLY

Objections to Chapter 11 plans can be based on many grounds. These grounds are discussed in detail in this chapter. Objections range from assertions of illegality, such as that a discharge or release is overbroad or that the plan proposes actions that are forbidden by environmental law, to objections that a plan is not "feasible," a bankruptcy term of art. Generally speaking, the requirements that govern objections to confirmation of plans and plan contents can be found respectively in Sections 1129 and 1123 of the Bankruptcy Code.[2] Objections may be brought by any interested party, including the government, the trustee, lenders, or creditors. Objections need to be brought in advance of the objection deadline, but may also be filed well in advance of the deadline once a plan has been filed. Objections to plans are "contested matters" governed by Federal Rule of Bankruptcy Procedure 9014. Objections are considered at confirmation hearings, which may be evidentiary hearings with witnesses.[3]

It can be advantageous to raise with the debtor significant concerns about a plan as soon as possible, even before a formal objection needs to be filed. Debtors often wish to avoid filed objections to their plan, especially from governmental parties. By raising concerns early, it is often possible to negotiate with interested parties and reach agreement on the issues, thereby obviating the need for the filing of a formal objection.

---

2. 11 U.S.C. §§ 1129, 1123. The plan confirmation process starts with approval of a disclosure statement and voting solicitation procedures. *See* 11 U.S.C. § 1125. The deadline for objections to the adequacy of disclosure or voting solicitation procedures occurs earlier in the process than the deadline for objections to plans. *See* Chapter 3 (Code Chapters) *supra*.

3. Local rules should be consulted regarding deadlines for identification of witnesses and exhibits or other requirements in advance of the confirmation hearing.

IMPORTANCE OF EARLY PARTICIPATION

Early participation in the bankruptcy case is key, whether for governments[4] or other interested parties, for several reasons. First, it increases the likelihood of a beneficial settlement being reached in a timely fashion. Second, it provides time for the potential objector to learn about the case so that it will better understand often highly complex facts and the positions of other interested parties, thereby allowing an objection to be presented in the most persuasive form possible. Third, it educates the other interested parties and the court of the environmental issues and the need to resolve such issues in order for there to be a fully consensual plan process. Fourth, the bankruptcy court will appreciate early involvement, as it does any good faith attempts at consensual resolution.

Many large cases involve negotiations among the debtors and other core constituencies such as lenders and creditors' committees, whether it be in a court process or the mediation context. Such negotiations can provide an early opportunity for participation and allow for a greater understanding of the case and involvement up front. If the other interested constituencies are negotiating a "restructuring support agreement," environmental creditors and other interested parties should pay close attention and determine whether their interests may be prejudiced if they are excluded. They may wish to consider requests for a status conference or whether mediation would be beneficial either separately or as part of a larger global mediation process. They may consider objecting to requests for approval of restructuring support agreements or other products of mediations from which they were excluded.[5] If attempts for consensual resolution fail, early litigation, such as the

4. State governmental entities should evaluate whether their participation in the bankruptcy case is outweighed by an alleged waiver of sovereign immunity under the 11th Amendment. States may contend that the 11th Amendment prevents certain actions by a debtor against the state. The Bankruptcy Code does have a broad waiver of sovereign immunity in Section 106(a). This broad waiver may be limited by the 11th Amendment. However, the Supreme Court has limited the application of the 11th Amendment in bankruptcy cases, which may mean this issue is not often important. *See* Chapter 5 (Key Provisions (sovereign immunity)) *supra*.

5. *See generally* Adam Levitin, *Purdue's Poison Pill: The Breakdown of Chapter 11's Checks and Balances*, 100 Tex. L. Rev. 100, 120–22 (2022).

filing of an adversary proceeding complaint,[6] may also be considered to bring appropriate attention to important environmental issues.

Failure to participate, whether during the review of major actions in a case or in negotiations in advance of a plan, creates a risk that the environmental interests will be the only parties objecting to a plan. Under that scenario, the environmental interests would be opposing an otherwise consensual plan that has momentum, which would tend to make the court view the environmental objections as spoilers to an otherwise desirable plan. The bankruptcy court may be reluctant to address environmental interests raised late in the case and other constituencies are likely to be unwilling to reopen or extend their largely concluded negotiations. If there is a failure by the other constituencies to allow the governments or other environmental interested parties to participate in mediation or other negotiations, that should be communicated to the bankruptcy court in a timely fashion. That may make the bankruptcy court sensitive to any unfairness or illegality under a plan when it conducts its review and less likely to blame environmental parties in interest for being the only parties not to have reached agreement.[7] Some bankruptcy courts will encourage or even require the other constituencies to include environmental interests in any mediation or negotiations.

On a similar note, early actions taken in a case such as approval of financing, restructuring support agreements, substantial sales of assets, or major settlements are not supposed to be sub rosa plans

6. *See* Chapters 10 (Police or Regulatory Exception), 11 (Compliance Obligations) *supra*. Governmental parties may also consider bringing an action in a nonbankruptcy forum if it falls under the police or regulatory exception to the automatic stay. However, if that question is subject to debate, bringing the action in a nonbankruptcy forum risks shifting the focus from a debtor's violation of environmental law to the government's action and the automatic stay. In addition, even though courts have concurrent jurisdiction to determine whether the police or regulatory exception applies, some courts would prefer for the bankruptcy court to decide that question and may put the matter on hold until the bankruptcy court makes a decision.

7. Failure to include the governmental agencies in negotiations in the *First Energy* bankruptcy (after repeated attempts to participate) was noted by the bankruptcy court in ruling against the debtors on the nondebtor release issue discussed later in this chapter. *See In re First Energy Solutions Corp.*, 606 B.R. 720, 728 (Bankr. N.D. Ohio 2019).

or dictate the terms of a plan of reorganization, since they do not come with the protections built into the plan process.[8] In practice though, it can be difficult to realize when a key event in a case will effectively foreclose certain alternatives for a plan. Therefore, it is as important to be vigilant in reviewing major early actions in a bankruptcy case as it is to monitor the plan process itself.

IMPORTANCE OF VIGILANCE IN REVIEWING PROPOSED PLANS

A key theme of this chapter is the importance of vigilance in reviewing plans of reorganization (or liquidation) for improper provisions relating to environmental issues. Environmental creditors and parties in interest need to closely scrutinize proposed plans to protect their rights. Bankruptcy plans in effect are somewhat analogous to a mass settlement agreement among creditors as to the treatment of their claims.[9] Confirmation orders are final court orders approving the terms of the plan and "the provisions of a confirmed plan bind the debtor . . . and any creditor."[10] Plans and confirmation orders have res judicata effect like other final court orders.[11] That way the parties to the case can rely on plans to provide finality and move on with their affairs. That means that

---

8. *See* Chapter 3 (Code Chapters) *supra*; *In re Iridium Operating, LLC*, 478 F.3d 452, 466 (2d Cir. 2007); *In re Braniff Airways, Inc.*, 700 F.2d 935 (5th Cir. 1983); *In re Daily Gazette Co.*, 584 B.R. 540, 548 (Bankr. S.D. W. Va. 2018); *In re 9 Houston LLC*, 578 B.R. 600, 620 (Bankr. S.D. Tex. 2017); *In re GSC, Inc.*, 453 B.R. 132 (Bankr. S.D. N.Y. 2011). A sub rosa plan refers to a proceeding that seeks to allocate estate assets outside of the plan process.

9. *See In re Frontier Ins. Grp., Inc.*, 585 B.R. 685, 693 (Bankr. S.D.N.Y. 2018). With some exceptions, plans commonly (at least in larger corporate cases) only address the treatment of classes of claims and do not allow specific claims in actual amounts. It is the treatment of classes of claims under the plan that is being settled. The analogy to a settlement is not perfect, however, because each individual creditor (or party in interest) does not have to voluntarily consent or agree. *Compare* Chapter 3 (Code Chapters) *supra with* cases cited in note 78 *infra*. Plans may be more analogous to proposed in rem judgments in a collective proceeding (in contrast to in personam actions), which are binding after proper notice if a party does not successfully object.

10. 11 U.S.C. § 1141(a).

11. *Travelers Indemnity Co. v. Bailey*, 557 U.S. 137, 154 (2009); *In re Lahaye*, 17 F.4th 513, 519 & n.3 (5th Cir. 2021); *In re Am. Preferred Prescription, Inc.*, 255 F.3d 87, 92 (2d Cir. 2001); *Republic Supply Co. v. Shoaf*, 815 F.2d 1046 (5th Cir. 1987).

if a plan is not objected to at confirmation, it becomes fully final and binding (res judicata),[12] which cannot thereafter be challenged except for limited reasons,[13] such as for evident lack of jurisdiction,[14] lack of notice,[15] or fraud.[16]

The risk of failed vigilance was made evident by the Supreme Court's ruling in *United Student Aid Funds, Inc. v. Espinosa*,[17] which held that even indisputably illegal plan provisions can be binding on parties that had notice and failed to object. In *Espinosa*, the Supreme Court rejected a post-confirmation challenge to a Chapter 13 plan that declared that a student loan would be discharged. The plan lacked any finding by the bankruptcy court of undue hardship, which the statute expressly requires for such a student loan to be discharged.[18] The Supreme Court found that approval of the plan provision constituted legal error but, nevertheless, did not rise to the level of having no arguable basis for jurisdiction or

---

12. *See* 11 U.S.C. § 1141(a) ("provisions of a confirmed plan" bind a creditor "whether or not [it] has accepted the plan."); *Travelers Indem.*, 557 U.S. at 153-54; *In re Linn Energy, L.L.C.*, 927 F.3d 862, 867 (5th Cir. 2019); *In re FFS Data, Inc.*, 776 F.3d 1299, 1306–08 (11th Cir. 2015); *Corbett v. MacDonald Moving Servs., Inc.*, 124 F.3d 82, 91 (2d Cir. 1997); *Eubanks v. Fed. Deposit Ins. Corp.*, 977 F.2d 166, 170–71 (5th Cir. 1992).

13. Federal Rules of Bankruptcy Procedure 9023 and 9024 incorporate most of Federal Rules of Civil Procedure 59 and 60, which do provide some very limited grounds for relief or altering judgments.

14. Where a judgment lacks even an "arguable basis" for jurisdiction—as opposed to an error in the exercise of jurisdiction—Rule 60(b)(4) may permit relief on the ground that a judgment is void. *United Student Aid Funds, Inc. v. Espinosa*, 559 U.S. 260, 271 (2010) (citing *United States v. Boch Oldsmobile, Inc.*, 909 F.2d 657, 661 (1st Cir. 1990) and *Nemaizer v. Baker*, 793 F.2d 58, 65 (2d Cir. 1986)). However, collateral attacks on jurisdiction are rarely permitted. *Travelers Indem. Co.*, 557 U.S. at 153 n.6; *In re Lodholtz*, 769 F.3d 531, 534 (7th Cir. 2014) (permitting collateral attack only in "egregious" cases); *Wendt v. Leonard*, 431 F.3d 410, 413 (4th Cir. 2005).

15. If a party does not have proper notice of the plan, it would not be bound as a matter of due process and fairness. *In re Savage Indus., Inc.*, 43 F.3d 714, 720–21 (1st Cir. 1994). *See also Valley Historic Ltd. P'ship v. Bank of New York*, 486 F.3d 831, 839 (4th Cir. 2007) (noting exception for jurisdictional determinations over future proceedings).

16. 11 U.S.C. § 1144 provides that a confirmation order can be revoked on request of a party in interest within 180 days after date of entry "if such order was procured by fraud." Failure to disclose to the court and provide notice to a party with known interest in a plan may be contended to be not in good faith or a fraud on the court. *Cf. Archer-Daniels-Midland Co. v. Country Visions Coop.*, 29 F.4th 956 (7th Cir. 2022).

17. 559 U.S. 260 (2010).

18. *Id.* at 276–77 (citing 11 U.S.C. §§ 523(a)(8), 1328(a)(2)).

a notice failure that would make the confirmation order judgment void. The illegal provision was binding because the creditor had notice of the error and failed to object and thus had a full and fair opportunity to litigate.[19] Likewise, the debtor's failure to comply with procedural rules requiring the filing of an adversary proceeding complaint could not be pursued on appeal because the creditor had not objected in bankruptcy court to the failure to follow such rules.[20] The Eleventh Circuit recently extended the reasoning of *Espinosa* to a plan provision providing a nondebtor release in *In re Le Centre on Fourth, LLC*.[21] The creditors were served with versions of the plan and disclosure statement noting the nondebtor release. The plan did not describe the release and who it covered in conspicuous language as required by bankruptcy rules.[22] The creditors likely had failed to review the plan and disclosure statement closely because the bankruptcy court had previously lifted the automatic stay to permit litigation against certain nondebtors; the creditors had therefore wrongly assumed the bankruptcy would not interfere with continued litigation against the nondebtors.[23] The Eleventh Circuit reasoned that even if procedural rules had not been fully complied with, the creditors had been provided actual notice as in *Espinosa* and therefore due process was satisfied and the nondebtor release in the plan was upheld.[24]

Therefore, it is critical for parties in interest to closely scrutinize plans and object to illegal provisions such as overbroad

---

19. *Id.* at 275–76. *See also Stoll v. Gottlieb*, 305 U.S. 165 (1938), where the Supreme Court held that even assuming arguendo that it was improper for a bankruptcy court to cancel a third-party guarantee, the creditor would be bound if it did not object and appeal.

20. *Id.* at 275; *see* Fed. R. Bankr. P. 7001 (requiring the filing of an adversary proceeding complaint for specified proceeding including to determine the dischargeability of a debt or to obtain an injunction or other equitable relief). With regard to adequacy of notice, *Espinosa* specifically relied upon the fact that the creditor had filed a proof of claim and submitted itself to the jurisdiction of the bankruptcy court. *Id.* at 276. Therefore, even though *Espinosa* rejected any significance to that debtor's failure to file an adversary proceeding complaint seeking a determination of discharge, a party that has not filed a proof of claim or been served with an adversary proceeding complaint may still try making the argument that illegal plan provisions are not binding on it even if it was notified of the plan.

21. 17 F.4th 1326 (11th Cir. 2021).

22. *Id.* at 1332, 1336 (citing Fed. R. Bankr. P. 2002(c)).

23. *Id.* at 1330.

24. *Id.* at 1334–36.

discharges or releases that go beyond what the Bankruptcy Code provides. *Espinosa* does note that bankruptcy courts have the authority and, indeed, an *obligation* to reject illegal plan provisions.[25] *Espinosa* also notes that attorneys could potentially face sanctions for improper conduct in bankruptcy proceedings in proposing illegal provisions.[26] Unfortunately parties in interest cannot presume that these fallback safeguards will be sufficient to protect their interests. They were not sufficient in *Espinosa* even though: (1) the Bankruptcy Code expressly provided for a contrary result than that in *Espinosa* where the court permitted a discharge without a finding of undue hardship, and (2) bankruptcy rules designed to provide procedural rights enhancing notice were not followed. Moreover, debtors might contend that absent an objection, the Bankruptcy Code does not forbid discharges or releases beyond those provided for by the Code.[27] Therefore, vigilance and protective action are prudent so that bankruptcy does not become a trap for the unwary. Nonetheless, if an objection deadline is missed, parties may still want to evaluate whether the limited exceptions such as no arguable basis for jurisdiction, fraud, or lack of notice apply.[28]

---

25. 559 U.S. at 277. *See* Karen Cordry, *Setoff, Plan Provisions and Espinosa*, 29 Am. Bankr. Inst. J. 12 (Dec./Jan. 2011).

26. 559 U.S. at 278–79. Some lower courts would have gone even further and precluded bankruptcy courts from rejecting illegal provisions in the absence of an objection. *Id.* at 276. The Supreme Court rejected this as "a step too far" and contrary to statutory directive. *Id.* The Supreme Court was careful not to reach the issue of when an attorney's proposed illegal plan provisions amounted to improper conduct in bankruptcy proceedings. Where the same attorney or firm repeatedly files plans with clearly illegal provisions, there is some risk that a party in interest will contend that this is improper conduct.

27. Creditors might disagree and note the unfairness to unsuspecting creditors of overbroad discharges and releases, which are sometimes buried in lengthy and complex documents. Moreover, seeking the court's imprimatur in favor of hidden and overbroad discharges and releases without fully disclosing to the court the nature and scope of the discharges or releases could damage the debtor's credibility with the court and risk adverse reaction.

28. *See* notes 13–15 *supra*.

OBJECTIONS BASED ON FAILURE TO COMPLY WITH CODE REQUIREMENTS

What then should environmental parties in interest be looking for in plans? First, parties should determine how an environmental matter is being handled under a plan. If an environmental claim is at issue, does the plan indicate what priority it will be assigned and is that designation correct?[29] Does the plan treat an environmental claim similarly to other allowed claims or does the plan improperly discriminate in violation of the Bankruptcy Code's requirements for similar treatment of similar claims?[30] Does the plan comply with the Bankruptcy Code's requirements on classification of claims?[31] Parties in interest should also consider and evaluate the fairness of the plan's procedural provisions for allowance or estimation of claims.[32] If any provisions of the plan do not conform with Bankruptcy Code requirements, the plan cannot be confirmed because failing to comply with applicable provisions of the Bankruptcy Code violates Section 1129(a)(1) of the Code.[33]

Parties should next consult the section of the plan that deals with discharges, releases, and injunctions to see if they comply with applicable Bankruptcy Code requirements and therefore

29. *See* Chapter 12 (Priorities) *supra*.

30. *See* Chapter 3 (Code Chapters) *supra*. "One of the cardinal principles underlying bankruptcy law is equality of treatment of similarly situated creditors." 7 *Collier on Bankruptcy* ¶ 1122.03, at 1122–26 (16th ed. 2019); *see* Ralph Brubaker, *Bankruptcy Injunctions and Complex Litigation: A Critical Reappraisal*, 1997 UNIV. ILL. L. REV. 959, 981–86 (1997); *Begier v. Internal Rev. Serv.*, 496 U.S. 53, 58 (1990); *In re W.R. Grace & Co.*, 729 F.3d 332, 342–46 (3d Cir. 2013); *In re W.R. Grace & Co.*, 729 F.3d 311, 327–28 (3d Cir. 2013); *In re UAL Corp.*, 468 F.3d 456, 461 (7th Cir. 2006); *In re Dow Corning Corp.*, 280 F.3d 648, 660 (6th Cir. 2002). 11 U.S.C. § 1123(a)(4) requires that plans provide the same treatment for claims in a class, which has been interpreted to mean approximate equality. *See W.R. Grace*, 729 F.3d at 327. However, 11 U.S.C. § 1122 provides some leeway for bankruptcy courts to confirm separate classes of creditors as long as there is a reasonable, nonarbitrary basis, *W.R. Grace*, 729 F.3d at 326, and the creditors in the class are substantially similar considering the legal character of claims as they relate to the assets of the debtor. *Dow Corning*, 280 F.3d at 661–62.

31. *See* Chapter 3 (Code Chapters) *supra*; *In re W.R. Grace & Co.*, 475 B.R. 34, 109-10 (D.N.J. 2012); *In re Novinda*, 585 B.R. 145 (10th Cir. B.A.P. 2018).

32. *See* Chapter 17 (Claim Objections) *infra*.

33. 11 U.S.C. § 1129(a)(1).

Section 1129(a)(1). As noted in earlier chapters of this Practice Guide, discharge under the Bankruptcy Code in a Chapter 11 reorganization is limited to "debts" arising before confirmation. "Debt" is defined to mean a "liability on a claim."[34] "Claim" in turn is broadly defined, but does not include compliance obligations if the breach of an equitable remedy (such as a compliance obligation) has not given rise to a right to payment in lieu of compliance with that remedy.[35] A plan provision seeking to discharge "liabilities" or "causes of action" that are not "claims" under the Bankruptcy Code is, accordingly, objectionable as unlawfully providing for a discharge beyond that provided by the Bankruptcy Code.[36] Similarly, a plan provision that would discharge claims arising after confirmation, such as a provision that discharges any claim based on any action or conduct of the debtor in jurisdictions utilizing a fair contemplation test for determining when claims become dischargeable, would also be objectionable as an unlawful discharge beyond the provisions of the Bankruptcy Code.[37]

If the debtor owns contaminated property, the parties should search for language that would discharge the debtors from liabilities that the reorganized debtor would be subject to as the post-confirmation owner or operator of the contaminated property (even though the original acts of contamination occurred prior to plan confirmation). Such language discharging debtors from post-confirmation liability as an owner or operator of property is inconsistent with environmental laws that prevent anyone from exposing the public to a nuisance threatening health and safety.[38] Such language is also inconsistent with bankruptcy law to the

34. 11 U.S.C. §§ 1141(d)(1), 101(12); *see* Chapters 11 (Compliance Obligations), 13 (Discharge) *supra*.

35. *See* 11 U.S.C. § 101(5); Chapter 11 (Compliance Obligations) *supra*.

36. *See* Chapter 11 (Compliance Obligations) *supra*.

37. *See* Chapter 13 (Discharge) *supra*.

38. *See id.*; Chapter 15 (Section 363 Sales) *supra* (similar analysis for purchasers of property from debtors); *In re CMC Heartland Partners*, 966 F.2d 1143 (7th Cir. 1992).

extent it seeks to discharge liabilities that are not claims that can be discharged under the Bankruptcy Code.[39]

An example of objectionable language in a proposed plan is as follows:

> All holders of claims shall be discharged and enjoined from asserting or pursuing against the Reorganized Debtor or their assets or properties any further claims, liabilities, obligations, or causes of action based on any act or omission, transaction, or other activity of any kind or nature that occurred before the Confirmation Date.

This language would potentially discharge liabilities that do not fall within the Bankruptcy Code's definition of "claim," liabilities that may arise after confirmation, and liabilities that would be contrary to a reorganized debtor's springing anew liability for its contaminated property.[40] In hundreds of cases, governments have raised objections to such language and debtors have generally agreed to "fix" such overbroad plan discharge provisions with language similar to the following in the confirmation order:

> Nothing in this Order or the Plan discharges, releases, or precludes: (i) any liability to a governmental unit that is not a "Claim" as defined in 11 U.S.C. § 101(5); (ii) any Claim of a governmental unit arising on or after the Effective Date; (iii) any liability to a Governmental Unit that any entity would be subject to as the owner or operator of property after the Effective Date; (iv) any liability to a Governmental Unit on the part of any non-debtor; and (v) any right of setoff or recoupment by any Government Unit, all of which are preserved.[41]

---

39. *See* 11 U.S.C. §§ 1141(d)(1); 101(12); Chapter 11 (Compliance Obligations) *supra*. Section 105 of the Code is not available to expand Code language on discharge because that authority is only to "carry out" Code provisions. *Law v. Siegel*, 571 U.S. 415, 21 (2014).

40. As to the latter, debtors might contend that such liabilities are based on acts, omissions, or activity occurring before confirmation because that is when the polluting events occurred. Governments would disagree and contend that such liability is based on the reorganized debtor's post-confirmation ownership or operation of property and its obligation to protect against the continuing effects of such pollution. *See CMC Heartland Partners*, 966 F.2d 1143.

41. Some plans also seek to vest "exclusive" jurisdiction in the bankruptcy courts if scope of discharge issues arise in the future. This is objectionable as the bankruptcy court's jurisdiction is concurrent and not exclusive. *See* Chapter

Commendably, some debtors will include this fixing language without being asked and thus save the time and cost of the parties having to deal with the issue and any related objections.[42] If the parties cannot agree to fixing language, overbroad discharge provisions can be objected to under Section 1129(a)(1), which permits a court to confirm a plan only if the "plan complies with the applicable provisions of this title." Plan provisions that provide a discharge beyond that provided for by the Bankruptcy Code are not in compliance with the Code.

OBJECTIONS TO NONCONSENSUAL THIRD-PARTY RELEASES OF NONDEBTORS

One of the most controversial issues in recent bankruptcy cases has emerged when a plan provides a nonconsensual release of a nondebtor's potential liability to a third party.[43] Increasingly, plans are seeking to release a wide array of nondebtors such as officers, directors, employees, parent and affiliated corporations, insurers, lenders, and even other creditors. This issue is not specifically an environmental bankruptcy issue, as such releases would apply to any kind of liability. However, the issue can be especially perverse in the context of environmental liability because environmental law casts a wide net and many different parties can have overlapping liabilities.

---

20 (Jurisdiction) *infra*. This problem can be corrected either by deleting the word "exclusive" or with the following fixing language in the confirmation order: "Nothing in this Order divests any tribunal of any jurisdiction it may have under police or regulatory law to interpret this Order or to adjudicate any defense asserted under this Order."

42. The fixing language does not resolve what particular liabilities are or are not discharged, but insures that such issues are not prematurely determined against the government. Plan confirmation can go forward and the parties can preserve their positions on discharge for resolution at a later date if a dispute emerges.

43. *See* Brubaker, *supra* note 30; David Skeel, *The Populist Backlash in Chapter 11*, https://www.brookings.edu/research/the-populist-backlash-in-chapter-11/ (Jan. 12, 2022). Reference to "third party" in discussions of third-party releases of nondebtors means the holder of a claim or cause of action against a nondebtor (often relating in some way to the debtors).

The reason that nonconsensual nondebtor third-party releases in a bankruptcy case are so controversial is that bankruptcy law is carefully calibrated and balanced to provide the debtor a fresh start and discharge in return for the debtor making significant assets available to pay creditors. The process also requires extensive disclosures, procedural requirements, and substantive limitations. A nondebtor third-party release, though, allows nondebtors to obtain the benefits of bankruptcy without having to go through the same rigorous process and requirements.[44] Moreover, in many situations the numerous liabilities sought to be released are not evident or disclosed at the time of the plan and, consequently, there is a significant risk of lack of process that threatens to undermine confidence in the fairness of the bankruptcy system. Particularly in the case of environmental liabilities of third parties, there is a high risk of inadvertent release of liabilities of culpable nondebtors without adequate consideration or analysis. In addition, the concept of a court forcing parties to settle or release their claims without an opportunity for adjudication on the merits is somewhat alien to our legal system.[45]

The counterargument in favor of permitting nondebtor releases is strongest in situations where nondebtor third parties with integrated or derivative liabilities with debtors such as insurers, recipients of fraudulent transfers, or certain other funding parties understandably need a reasonable degree of finality as to their own future additional liabilities if they are to agree to be part of a settlement.[46] A creditor's claim against a nondebtor is a derivative claim if it is a cause of action owned by the debtor's estate on behalf of all creditors (such as many fraudulent conveyance or alter ego claims). Nonderivative or independent claims may be: (1) special or unique to the creditor, or (2) claims based on a nondebtor's

44. *In re Nat'l Staffing Servs., LLC*, 338 B.R. 35, 37 (Bankr. N.D. Ohio 2005).

45. *See Aegean Marine Petroleum Network Inc.*, 599 B.R. 717, 725 (Bankr. S.D.N.Y. 2019) (citing *United States v. Ward Baking Co.*, 376 U.S. 327, 334 (1964) and *Local No. 93, Int'l Ass'n of Firefighters v. City of Cleveland*, 478 U.S. 501, 529 (1986)).

46. *See, e.g., In re Tronox, Inc.*, 855 F.3d 84 (2d Cir. 2017) (approving settlement with third-party release of recipient of fraudulent transfer); *In re Dow Corning Corp.*, 280 F.3d 648 (6th Cir. 2002) (plan settlement providing for third-party release of insurer and shareholder, which contributed to fund for claimants injured by breast implants).

own conduct separate from the debtor.[47] Significant mutually beneficial bankruptcy settlement opportunities could be lost if a nondebtor's integrated or derivative liability cannot be resolved.[48] And a debtor may have a risk of contribution or indemnification liability that may need to be addressed in the bankruptcy if the liability to such nondebtor is not released.

RECENT TREND IN THE CASE LAW ON NONCONSENSUAL THIRD-PARTY RELEASES OF NONDEBTORS

The recent majority trend in the case law on nonconsensual third-party releases of nondebtors has been to allow them where appropriate but to limit their use to extraordinary, unique, or rare circumstances.[49] These safeguards seek to address the fairness and due process risks to affected parties. However, three circuits do not allow any nonconsensual third-party releases of nondebtors, pointing to Section 524(e), which provides that "a discharge of a debt of the debtor does not affect the liability of any other entity on, or the property of any other entity for, such debt."[50] The other circuits permit them in extraordinary, unique, or rare circumstances but also require specific factual findings based on enumer-

---

47. Nonderivative or independent claims in contrast are: (1) special or unique to the creditor, or (2) claims based on a nondebtor's own conduct separate from the debtor. *See Tronox*, 855 F.3d at 100, 106; *In re Johns-Manville Corp.*, 517 F.3d 52, 63 (2d Cir. 2008); *Steinberg v. Buczynski*, 40 F.3d 890, 893 (7th Cir. 1994); *In re Greektown Holdings, LLC*, 728 F.3d 567, 577 (6th Cir. 2013); *In re Purdue Pharma, L.P.*, 635 B.R. at 90–91; *In re Dreier LLP*, 429 B.R. 112, 133 (Bankr. S.D.N.Y. 2010); *In re Madoff*, 848 F. Supp. 2d 469, 488 (S.D.N.Y. 2012).

48. *See* Douglas Baird, Anthony Casey & Randal Picker, *The Bankruptcy Partition*, 166 U. Pa. L. Rev. 1675, 1686–90 (2018).

49. *See* Richard Epling, *Third-Party Releases in Bankruptcy Cases: Should There Be Statutory Reform?*, 75 Bus. Lawyer 1747 (2020); Dorothy Coco, *Third-Party Bankruptcy Releases: An Analysis of Consent through the Lenses of Due Process and Contract Law*, 88 Fordham L. Rev. 231, 239–44 (2019). Congress has authorized certain third-party nondebtor releases in asbestos bankruptcy cases if specified requirements are met. 11 U.S.C. § 524(g).

50. *See In re Pac. Lumber Co.*, 584 F.3d 229, 252 (5th Cir. 2009) (noting possible exception for Plans incorporating global settlements of mass claims against debtors and co-liable parties); *In re Lowenschuss*, 67 F.3d 1394, 1401–02 (9th Cir. 1995); *In re Western Real Estate*, 922 F.2d 592, 600–02 (10th Cir. 1990); *see generally* Levitin, *supra* note 5, at 129–31.

ated factors.[51] These courts reason that Section 524(e) provides that a debtor's discharge does not directly apply to nondebtors but does not preclude a release of nondebtors on other grounds.[52] Key factors that may permit such a release include whether: (1) there is an identity of interests between the debtor and third party; (2) the nondebtor has contributed substantial assets to the reorganization; (3) the release is essential to the reorganization; (4) the plan provides a mechanism that will pay fair consideration to those affected by the release; and (5) the class of creditors affected by the nondebtor release has voted for the plan.[53]

Two recent cases involving environmental liabilities are good examples of courts striking down overbroad nonconsensual nondebtor releases as improper. In *In re FirstEnergy Solutions Corp.*,[54] the debtors owned and operated coal-fired and nuclear power plants with significant environmental liabilities. The plants had been previously owned or operated by a nondebtor parent entity and affiliates for many years. The nondebtors provided significant funding to support the proposed plan and sought a broad nondebtor release including for any liabilities related to the debtors' property or business.[55] This could be contended to include environmental liabilities on account of nondebtors' own operations at the plants before the debtors even existed.[56] At the Disclosure Statement hearing, the bankruptcy court held that the plan was patently unconfirmable,[57] noting that, regardless of the circuit, nonconsensual nondebtor third-party releases were "extraordinary" and "very rare." The court cited examples where they had

51. *See In re Millenium Lab Holdings II, LLC,* 945 F.3d 126, 139 (3d Cir. 2019); *In re Seaside Engineering & Surveying, Inc.*, 783 F.3d 1070, 1076–79 (11th Cir. 2015); *Nat'l Heritage v. Highbourne Found.*, 760 F.3d 344, 347–51 (4th Cir. 2014); *In re Ingersoll, Inc.*, 562 F.3d 856, 865 (7th Cir. 2009); *Metromedia Fiber Network, Inc.*, 416 F.3d 136, 141–43 (2d Cir. 2005); *United Artists Theatre Co. v. Walton*, 315 F.3d 217, 227 (3d Cir. 2003); *In re Dow Corning Corp.*, 280 F.3d 648, 657–59 (6th Cir. 2002); *In re Cont'l Airlines*, 203 F.3d 203, 214 (3d Cir. 2000).

52. *See, e.g., Seaside Eng'g*, 783 F.3d at 1078.

53. *See, e.g., Dow Corning*, 280 F.3d at 658; *Seaside Eng'g*, 783 F.3d at 1079–81. Note that a class of creditors voting in favor is not the same as every single affected party voting in favor. *See* Chapter 3 (Code Chapters) *supra*.

54. 606 B.R. 720 (Bankr. N.D. Ohio 2019).

55. *Id.* at 729.

56. *Id.* at 730, 736.

57. *Id.* at 746.

been allowed such as where debtors were the "primary obligors or tortfeasors" but "secondarily liable nondebtor parties" had funded a plan providing for payments to the released claimants.[58] The court found that in *FirstEnergy Solutions* the release sought was different because it included liabilities from the nondebtors' operations predating the debtors and the plan did not even provide a fund for the benefit of the causes of action being released without consent.[59] The court then applied the applicable factors in the Sixth Circuit under *Dow Corning* to conclude that the release was impermissible because there was not: (1) a sufficient identity of interest between the debtors and nondebtors; (2) an essential need to avoid indirect suits against debtors; (3) a vote in favor of the release by those impacted; and (4) a mechanism to provide a benefit to those impacted.[60]

In *Aegean Marine Petroleum Network Inc.*,[61] the bankruptcy court likewise found improper a broad release of nondebtors for liabilities that "relate in any way to the Debtors," which was not limited to derivative liabilities.[62] The bankruptcy court raised concerns including whether: (1) a proper proceeding among nondebtors was before the court, (2) a court can impose an unwanted "settlement,"[63] (3) due process rights to discovery and a hearing were met, (4) extinguishing a property right without benefit would be a taking, and (5) there was no evidence of a specific recovery that would be fair value for claims taken away.[64] The bankruptcy court specifically noted that the broad categories of liabilities being released were not or could not be described or evaluated and that general support of the reorganization process was an

58. *Id.* at 734.

59. *Id.* at 736, 737, 742–43. The Court rejected debtors' argument based on the plan's provision for an initially feasible reorganized debtor that assumed the environmental liabilities in question. *Id.* at 743–44.

60. *Id.* at 739–44.

61. 599 B.R. 717 (Bankr. S.D.N.Y. 2019).

62. *Id.* at 722.

63. The court noted that courts have "no power to dictate settlement terms or to force parties to release their claims," *id.* at 725 (citing *United States v. Ward Baking Co.*, 376 U.S. 327, 334 (1964); *Local No. 93, Int'l Ass'n of Firefighters v. City of Cleveland*, 478 U.S. 501, 529 (1986)).

64. 599 B.R. at 723–28.

inadequate basis or consideration to determine the fairness of an extraordinary third-party release of nondebtors.[65]

On the other hand, in *Exide Holdings*,[66] the bankruptcy court upheld confirmation of a plan with a third-party release of a California environmental agency's claims against nondebtor noteholders who made contributions to support a plan of liquidation. Under the plan and related settlement agreement, 16 properties in ten states were placed into an environmental response trust. The plan also provided a pathway for Exide's Vernon, California, real property not to be abandoned and to be placed into an environmental response trust as long as the California Department of Toxic Substances Control provided a covenant not to sue the prospective environmental response trustee. A key difference between *Exide Holdings* and the open-ended releases in *FirstEnergy* and *Aegean Marine* was that the third-party release in *Exide Holdings* involved a specific liability for the Vernon, California, property and a specific amount of consideration for that property ($29 million plus the value of the property),[67] both of which could be evaluated by the bankruptcy court given the litigation risks and probabilities of success involved.[68] It was also important that the California agency was unable to articulate a case for the liability of the nondebtors in its briefs and therefore could not show why the consideration provided by the nondebtors was unfair. The California agency's argument rested on a premise that nonconsensual third-party releases were always invalid even where it did not or could not articulate a basis for third-party liability of the parties released.

An even more recent high profile third-party release of nondebtors issue arose, in a nonenvironmental context, in the *Purdue Pharma* Chapter 11 plan confirmation involving opioid liability.[69]

---

65. *Id.* at 726.

66. *In re Exide Holdings, Inc.*, 2021 WL 3145612 (D. Del. July 26, 2021).

67. This amount included financial assurance for closure including in part from a surety bond; the surety company was a party to the related settlement agreement.

68. The bankruptcy court's evaluation of the plan also involved analysis of other issues such as the risk of abandonment and the extent to which cleanup funding would be required given the perilous financial condition of the liquidating debtors. *See* Chapter 18 (Abandonment) *infra*.

69. *In re Purdue Pharma L.P.*, 633 B.R. 53 (Bankr. S.D.N.Y. 2021), *vacated*, 635 B.R. 26 (S.D.N.Y. 2021), *appeal pending* No. 22-85 (2d Cir. Jan. 18, 2022).

In *Purdue Pharma*, the proposed plan included a $4.275 billion contribution from the company's owners (Sacklers) in return for a nondebtor release of all of their liability. The plan utilized the $4.275 billion contribution and converted the company's assets into a public benefit corporation to address opioid addiction liabilities. The bankruptcy court upheld the third-party release of nondebtors as to the opioid liability, which was being addressed with the funding under the plan, as well as the release for derivative liability, such as for potential fraudulent conveyances or corporate veil piercing liabilities. However, the bankruptcy court refused to approve overbroad releases of nonderivative, non-opioid liability or liability that was not premised on a meaningful overlap with the debtor's conduct.[70] The court found that the plan was not addressing or using the nondebtor's contribution to provide for such liabilities and the debtors had not provided a persuasive analysis of why a nonconsensual release of non-opioid liabilities was fair.[71] On appeal, the district court went further and held that while the bankruptcy court had authority under Second Circuit decisions grounded in 11 U.S.C. § 105 to approve the estate's resolution of derivative claims (which appellants did not challenge on appeal), it lacked statutory authority to release the nonderivative claims arising out of the nondebtors' own conduct (even though such conduct may relate to the debtors).[72] Further appeals are pending.[73]

---

70. 633 B.R. at 95, 104–05. The Third Circuit had performed a somewhat similar analysis based on connection to the debtor in determining whether Section 524(g)'s requirement of derivative liability was met for purposes of a channeling injunction against asbestos claims. *See In re W.R. Grace & Co.*, 13 F.4th 279, 288–89 (3d Cir. 2021). *See also In re Boy Scouts of Am. & Delaware BSA, LLC,* 642 B.R. 504, 597-606 (Bankr. D. Del. 2022), *aff'd*, 2023 WL 2662992 (D. Del. March 28, 2023).

71. 633 B.R. at 95, 104–05. The bankruptcy court noted that nonconsensual releases of derivative causes of action owned by the estate such as alter ego, piercing the corporate veil, and fraudulent conveyance causes of action are most easily justified through analysis of the fairness of the settlement of the estate's causes of action. More complicated are releases of independent claims that are factually intertwined such as claims against officers and directors for their conduct on behalf of debtors, claims against insurance policies of co-insured nondebtors, and claims against nondebtor affiliates. *Id.*

72. 635 B.R. at 89–115.

73. No. 22-85 (2d Cir. Jan. 18, 2022). Mediation during the appeals process resulted in an additional contribution from the nondebtors of $1.5 billion but some appeals remain pending.

Similarly, in *Patterson v. Mahwah Retail Group*,[74] another district court struck down what it found to be "shocking" nondebtor releases that "have no bounds" and were not individually analyzed.

The preceding cases demonstrate that where nonconsensual third-party nondebtor releases are permitted at all, such releases should be limited to truly extraordinary circumstances, narrowly tailored, and based on fair and reasonable provision for the liabilities being released.[75] Nondebtor releases are more likely to be approved where a factually-specific demonstration can be made that the funding set aside based on the amount provided for the specific liabilities being released is at least as much as would result from a fair outcome of future litigation. Releases of derivative liability for causes of action pursued by the bankruptcy estate on behalf of all creditors (such as fraudulent conveyance, alter ego, or piercing the corporate veil) are more likely to be approved. Debtors and other parties who would benefit from third-party nondebtor releases may contend that they can be approved if they meet the range of reasonableness standard for bankruptcy settlements incorporated into plans.[76] The law in this area is evolving. The Supreme Court or Congress may decide to clarify the law in this area in the future.

WHEN ARE NONDEBTOR RELEASES CONSENSUAL?

While many courts permit consensual third-party releases of nondebtors, interested parties should look carefully at how a plan defines consent. Courts have struck down plans that found "deemed consent" to third-party nondebtor releases where: (1) a creditor had an opportunity to vote and opt out of the release but did not vote or submit an opt-out form, (2) the plan provided that a party's claims or rights against the debtors are unimpaired, or (3) a creditor's class

74. *Patterson v. Mahwah Bergen Retail Grp., Inc.*, 636 B.R. 641, 655 (E.D. Va. 2022).

75. In practice, many debtors routinely include releases in plans and contend that the factors are met. *Mahwah Bergen Retail Grp., Inc.*, 636 B.R. at 654–55; *In re Aegean Marine Petroleum Network Inc.*, 599 B.R. 717, 723 (Bankr. S.D.N.Y. 2019). Such tactics have made it more likely that nondebtor releases will be severely limited in the future by the courts or Congress.

76. *See* note 122 *infra* (discussing standard for approval of settlements).

voted in favor of the plan.[77] The courts have reasoned that these situations based on inaction do not meet the requirements for finding meaningful consent under applicable law.[78] Some plans require that creditors "opt in" to the proposed nondebtor release as part of their ballot on the plan in order to establish consent. Governments will often seek language in confirmation orders that confirms that governmental units' claims, rights, and causes of action against nondebtors are not released under the plan. As a precaution, however, governments may nevertheless want to submit and/or file an opt-out form even though doing so may be considered redundant with such language and therefore may turn out to have been unnecessary.[79] Other creditors or parties in interest should evaluate whether to opt out of the release if they are given the opportunity to do so. The deadline for opting out of a third-party nondebtor release typically is the same as the deadline for voting on confirmation of the plan. The bankruptcy court's order approving the disclosure statement and voting procedures will typically set forth the process required for submission of an opt-out form before the deadline.

JURISDICTIONAL AND CONSTITUTIONAL AUTHORITY ISSUES AND NONDEBTOR RELEASES

Nondebtor releases can raise jurisdictional issues in addition to whether the releases are permissible.[80] Bankruptcy courts have

77. *See, e.g.*, *Mahwah Bergen Retail Grp.*, 636 B.R. at 684–87; *In re Emerge Energy*, 2019 WL 7634308 at *18 (Bankr. D. Del. Dec. 5, 2019); *In re SunEdison, Inc.*, 576 B.R. 453, 458–60 (Bankr. S.D.N.Y. 2017); *In re Chassix Holdings, Inc.*, 533 B.R. 64, 80–82 (Bankr. S.D.N.Y. 2015); *In re Washington Mutual, Inc.*, 442 B.R. 314, 351–53 (Bankr. D. Del. 2011); *In re Congoleum Corp.*, 362 B.R. 167, 194 (Bankr. D.N.J. 2007); *In re Arrowmill Dev. Corp.*, 211 B.R. 497, 507 (Bankr. D.N.J. 1997).

78. *See, e.g.*, *Emerge Energy*, 2019 WL, at *18; *Sun Edison*, 576 B.R. at 459–61; *Chassix*, 533 B.R. at 80–81. *See generally* Coco, *supra* note 49; Rose Sierra, *Warning: Artificial Consent To Third-Party Releases Will Not Result in Plan Confirmation*, 37 Am. Bankr. Inst. J. 28 (2018).

79. The court's order on plan solicitation of votes provides instructions for opting out, which often, but not always, is done by submittal to a claims service company rather than through a court filing.

80. *See* Levitin, *supra* note 5, at 131; *In re Boy Scouts of Am. & Delaware BSA, LLC*, 642 B.R. 504, 597-606 (Bankr. D. Del. 2022), *aff'd*, 2023 WL 2662992 (D. Del. March 28, 2023)

jurisdiction over disputes between nondebtors only if the dispute is "related to" the bankruptcy case.[81] "Related to" jurisdiction requires that the dispute could have a conceivable effect on the administration of the bankruptcy estate.[82] In determining this question, a first step is to determine whether a creditor's claim against a nondebtor is derivative of a cause of action owned by the debtor's estate on behalf of all creditors (such as many fraudulent conveyance or alter ego claims), or whether the creditor has an independent claim that is special to the creditor.[83] However, some courts have found "related to" jurisdiction of nonderivative liabilities based on the impact or conceivable effect of the liability on the debtor's estate.[84]

In some situations, there may also be a constitutional issue as to whether a district court must approve the nondebtor release.[85] If governmental environmental liabilities of nondebtors are involved,

81. 28 U.S.C. § 1334(b).

82. *See In re Johns-Manville Corp.*, 517 F.3d at 60-65; *In re Combustion Eng'g*, 391 F.3d 190, 225–33 (3d Cir. 2004); *In re Dow Corning Corp.*, 86 F.3d 482, 489 (6th Cir. 1996); *In re Zale Corp.*, 62 F.3d 746, 751–59 (5th Cir. 1995).

83. *See In re Tronox, Inc.*, 855 F.3d 84, 100, 106 (2d Cir. 2017); *Johns-Manville Corp.*, 517 F.3d at 63; *Steinberg v. Buczynski*, 40 F.3d 890, 893 (7th Cir. 1994); *In re Greektown Holdings, LLC*, 728 F.3d 567, 577 (6th Cir. 2013); *In re Dreier LLP*, 429 B.R. 112, 133 (Bankr. S.D.N.Y. 2010); *In re Madoff*, 848 F. Supp. 2d 469, 488 (S.D.N.Y. 2012); *In re TPC Group Inc.*, 2023 WL 2168045, at *4–11 (Bankr. D. Del. Feb. 22, 2023).

84. *See, e.g., In re Purdue Pharma L.P.*, 635 B.R. at 83–89. One court has found that subject matter jurisdiction is bolstered when a nondebtor release is found in a plan. *See In re Kirwan Officers S.a.r.l.*, 592 B.R. 489, 504–05 (S.D.N.Y 2018). But even this court recognized that such an analysis poses a risk of circular bootstrapping by permitting even unrelated releases merely by insertion into plans, and that therefore further analysis was required as to whether the third-party nondebtor release fell within related to jurisdiction. *Id.* at 505–06. *See also* David Skeel, https://www.brookings.edu/research/the-populist-backlash-in-chapter-11/ (Jan. 12, 2022); *Patterson*, 636 B.R. at 670–72.

85. *In Stern v. Marshall*, 564 U.S. 462 (2011), the Supreme Court held that the Constitution requires Article III judges (not bankruptcy judges) to decide common law claims that are not integral to the restructuring of the debtor-creditor relationship. *See In re Millennium Lab Holdings II, LLC*, 943 F.3d 125 (3d Cir. 2019); *In re Purdue Pharma L.P.*, 635 B.R. at 79–82; *Patterson v. Mahwah Bergen Retail Grp., Inc.*, 636 B.R. 641, 668–76, 682–84 (E.D. Va. 2022); Eamonn O'Hagan, *On a "Related" Point: Rethinking Whether Bankruptcy Court Can "Order" The Involuntary Release of Non-Debtor Third Party Claims*, 23 Am. Bankr. Inst. L. Rev. 531 (2015). Placing resolution of the claim in a plan does not, in and of itself, provide the bankruptcy court with authority to adjudicate it. *In re Purdue Pharma L.P.*, 635 B.R. at 80; *Patterson*, 636 B.R. at 670–72.

the governmental agencies may question whether there has been a waiver of sovereign immunity (or the 11th Amendment for states).[86]

NONDEBTOR RELEASES AND INSURANCE

A special situation involving a nondebtor release may arise where a debtor has insurance coverage that might cover environmental liabilities. Pursuant to Section 524(e), a discharge does not discharge the liability of another entity, such as an insurer, for a debt.[87] Nonetheless, plan provisions may attempt to vary this rule such as where insurers are funding a settlement under a plan. Such provisions can be evaluated under the previously discussed rules permitting nondebtor releases in extraordinary circumstances.[88] Even apart from such settlements, plan provisions relating to insurance should be carefully reviewed to ensure that they do not unfairly prejudice a party's rights relating to insurance. For example, in a plan a debtor may unfairly attempt to assign insurance proceeds on account of a creditor's claim to the reorganized debtor or a trust benefiting other creditors.[89] Where a creditor may seek to pursue claims against insurers based on policies issued to a debtor or related entities, it should consider requesting that a

86. *See, e.g.*, 11 U.S.C. § 106(a)(4). The Bankruptcy Code waiver of sovereign immunity is subject to applicable nonbankruptcy law. *Id.* Many environmental laws prohibit pre-enforcement judicial review. *See, e.g.*, 42 U.S.C. § 9613(h) (CERCLA); *Amoco Oil Co. v. United States Env't Prot. Agency*, 959 F. Supp. 1318 (D. Colo. 1997) (RCRA).

87. *See In re Federal-Mogal Global Inc.*, 684 F.3d 355, 380 (3d Cir. 2012); *First Fid. Bank v. McAteer*, 985 F.2d 114, 118 (3d Cir. 1993); *Green v. Welsh*, 956 F.2d 30, 33 (2d Cir. 1992); *In re Jet Florida Sys., Inc.*, 883 F.2d 970, 973–76 (11th Cir. 1989); *In re Hendrix*, 986 F.2d 195, 197 (7th Cir. 1993); *In re Weiand Automotive Indus.*, 612 B.R. 824, 860 (Bankr. D. Del. 2020).

88. *See, e.g., In re Dow Corning*, 280 F.3d 648 (6th Cir. 2002); *In re LeCentre on Fourth*, 17 F.4th 1326 (11th Cir. 2021).

89. The debtor may attempt to justify this on the ground that it has covered costs under the policy. However, injured third parties also have vested rights and can object to any resolution that fails to take them into account appropriately. *See* Chapter 19 (Insurance) *infra* (discussing *In re Allied Prod. Corp.*, 288 B.R. 533 (Bankr. N.D. Ill. 2003)).

clear statement preserving its rights be placed in the plan or confirmation order.[90]

OBJECTIONS TO EXCULPATION CLAUSES

Exculpation clauses in plans are protective provisions against liability that are similar to releases but that focus specifically on liabilities arising from administration of the bankruptcy case by professional advisors and others. These clauses are a form of nonconsensual third-party releases of liability to nondebtors and therefore should be carefully reviewed. Exculpation clauses often include debtors and their officers and directors as exculpated parties. Appropriately narrow exculpation clauses are routinely upheld and are designed to provide fiduciaries and their professionals with reassurance that they will not be held liable post-bankruptcy for their actions in formulating a plan or other court-approved actions as long as they did not engage in willful misconduct or gross negligence.[91] Courts have struck down overbroad exculpation clauses that extend beyond fiduciaries and their professionals, go beyond court-approved matters, cover conduct before the petition date or after the plan effective date, or fail to have an exception for willful misconduct or gross negligence.[92] Environmental parties in interest may have a particular interest in objecting to overbroad exculpation clauses that extend to liability for any actions taken in connection with the bankruptcy case or anything related to a debtor's property. Such vague and overbroad language may pick up significant environmental liabilities on account of operations or

90. The Eleventh Circuit has held that a creditor might sometimes be precluded from nominally proceeding against a debtor (or a released nondebtor) for purposes of insurance coverage where there would be an economic burden. *See LeCentre on Fourth*, 17 F.4th 1326; *SuVicMon Dev., Inc. v. Morrison*, 991 F.3d 1213 (11th Cir. 2021).

91. *See, e.g.*, *In re PWS Holding Corp.*, 228 F.3d 224, 246–47 (3d Cir. 2000); *Patterson v. Mahwah Bergen Retail Grp., Inc.*, 636 B.R. 641, 701–02 (E.D. Va. 2022); *In re Aegean Marine Petroleum Network Inc.*, 599 B.R. 720–21 (Bankr. S.D.N.Y. 2019).

92. *In re Highland Capital Mgmt., L.P.*, 48 F.4th 419, 435–38 (5th Cir. 2022); *In re Pac. Lumber Co.*, 584 F.3d 229, 252 (5th Cir. 2009); *In re Mallinckrodt PLC*, 639 B.R. 837, 882–83 (Bankr. D. Del. 2022); *In re Aegean Marine Petroleum Network Inc.*, 599 B.R. 717, 720–21 (Bankr. S.D.N.Y. 2019); *In re Washington Mutual, Inc.*, 442 B.R. 314, 350–51 (Bankr. D. Del. 2011).

actions during the bankruptcy and potentially any liabilities relating to a debtor's property. This kind of language goes beyond what is intended by traditional exculpation clauses for acts by fiduciaries in proposing a plan, and would cover actions resulting in liability that were not specifically approved by or considered by the bankruptcy court. Such provisions risk varying the standard under environmental law for liability, which is beyond the authority of bankruptcy courts. Providing such immunity from liability also undermines environmental law and its deterrent effect on the conduct of companies operating while in bankruptcy to comply with the law.[93]

OBJECTIONS BASED ON PLAN FEASIBILITY

Feasibility objections to plans of reorganization are based on two different Bankruptcy Code provisions. First, Section 1129(a)(11) of the Code allows a court to confirm a Chapter 11 plan providing for reorganization only if "[c]onfirmation of the plan is not likely to be followed by the liquidation, or the need for further financial reorganization, of the debtor or any successor to the debtor under the plan."[94] Second, Section 1123(a)(5) of the Bankruptcy Code requires that a plan provide adequate means for its implementation.[95] Debtors have the burden of proof of demonstrating that

93. Where debtors are included in the parties exculpated, it is also important for there to be an exception for compliance with plan requirements so that debtors (or other parties administering the plan) are not exculpated for failing to implement the plan or from paying administrative expense liabilities.

94. 11 U.S.C. § 1129(a)(11).

95. *Id.* § 1123(a)(5). Because Section 1123(a)(5) phrases this requirement as "[n]otwithstanding any otherwise applicable nonbankruptcy law," it has sometimes been interpreted to preempt otherwise applicable state law. *See, e.g., In re FCX, Inc.*, 853 F.2d 1149, 1155 (4th Cir. 1988); *In re Pub. Serv. Co. of New Hampshire*, 108 B.R. 854, 884 (Bankr. D.N.H. 1989). However, it is well established that any such preemption does not extend to nonbankruptcy laws that concern public health, safety, or welfare given the presumption against preemption of such laws. *See In re Federal-Mogul Global Inc.*, 684 F.3d 355, 381–82 (3d Cir. 2012); *In re Irving Tanning Co.*, 496 B.R. 644, 664 (1st Cir. B.A.P. 2013); *Montgomery Cnty., Maryland v. Barwood, Inc.*, 422 B.R. 40, 44–47 (D. Md. 2009); note 5 in Chapter 8 (Harmonization) *supra*. *See also Pac. Gas & Elec. Co. v. California Dep't of Toxic Substances Control*, 350 F.3d

their proposed plan is feasible.[96] The feasibility requirement does not require a guarantee of the plan's success, but the plan must have a sufficient foundation based on evidence that it has a reasonable likelihood of success.[97] It cannot be based on a speculative visionary scheme.[98]

Accordingly, an environmental creditor, just like any other creditor, can object to a plan as infeasible if the plan's provision for a payment of a claim is speculative and does not have a reasonable likelihood of success. In addition, governments may object to plans providing for reorganization where the reorganized debtor or estate will not have the ability going forward to comply with police or regulatory laws governing its operations and/or property.[99] Governments may also object to the feasibility of a liquidating plan (such as a liquidation following an asset sale), where the plan provides for an inadequate wind-down budget to obtain environmental compliance with respect to property of the estate. Such objections sometimes are resolved by the provision of additional funding or other resources for compliance.

---

932 (9th Cir. 2003) (Section 1123(a)(5) limited to laws relating to debtor's financial condition).

96. *See, e.g., In re Briscoe Enters., Ltd. II*, 994 F.2d 1160, 1163–64 (5th Cir. 1993); *In re Ambanc La Mesa Ltd. P'ship*, 115 F.3d 650, 653 (9th Cir. 1997); *In re Trenton Ridge Investors, LLC*, 461 B.R. 440, 459 (Bankr. S.D. Ohio 2011); *In re Eagle-Picher Holdings, Inc.*, 345 B.R. 860, 861 (Bankr. S.D. Ohio 2006).

97. *See, e.g., In re Am. Capital Equip., LLC*, 688 F.3d 145, 155–56 (3d Cir. 2012); *In re WR Grace & Co.*, 729 F.3d 332, 348–49 (3d Cir. 2013); *In re Harbin*, 486 F.3d 510, 517–19 (9th Cir. 2007); *In re T-H New Orleans Ltd. P'ship*, 116 F.3d 790, 801–03 (5th Cir. 1997); *Briscoe Enters.*, 994 F.2d at 1165–66; *Kane v. Johns-Manville Corp.*, 843 F.2d 636, 649–50 (2d Cir. 1988).

98. *See, e.g., In re Clarkson*, 767 F.2d 417, 420 (8th Cir. 1985); *In re Pizza of Hawaii, Inc.*, 761 F.2d 1374, 1382 (9th Cir. 1985); 7 *Collier on Bankruptcy* ¶ 1122.03[11] (16th ed. 2019).

99. *In re Baker & Drake, Inc.*, 35 F.3d 1348, 1354 (9th Cir. 1994) (taxicab regulations) (Bankruptcy Code does not "mandate that every company be reorganized at all costs"; reorganized debtor must be able to comply with applicable laws in order to reorganize). In *In re Jager*, 609 B.R. 156, 162, 173–74 (Bankr. W.D. Pa. 2019), the court found that debtor's plan was not feasible because any source of funding for cleanup of manure piles on its property was too speculative. In *In re Lewis*, 215 B.R. 880 (Bankr. D. Alaska), the court denied confirmation of a Chapter 13 plan because it failed to provide for the cost of remediation of contaminated property.

OBJECTIONS TO PLANS "FORBIDDEN BY LAW"

Governmental agencies may object to plans based on the requirement of Section 1129(a)(3) of the Code that a plan "has been proposed in good faith *and not by any means forbidden by law*."[100] Governments may contend that that this requirement precludes confirmation of plans that would result in illegality or violations of nonbankruptcy law.[101] In some situations, this ground of objection may overlap with an objection on grounds of feasibility since a plan that does not provide adequate means for future compliance with the law may be infeasible as well as forbidden by law.[102] Governments may contend that a liquidating plan that fails to provide for compliance with civil or criminal law is forbidden by law.[103]

A plan seeking expressly to authorize a reorganized debtor to violate otherwise applicable police or regulatory law (in contrast

---

100. 11 U.S.C. § 1129(a)(3) (emphasis added).

101. 7 *Collier on Bankruptcy* ¶ 1129.02[3][b][ii] (16th ed. 2019 (plan that would violate nonbankruptcy regulatory law would be "forbidden by law" and would preclude confirmation even if no provision of title 11 was violated); *In re Cajun Elec. Power Co-op, Inc.*, 150 F.3d 503, 519 (5th Cir. 1998) (plan may not propose "independent illegality"); *In re Koelbl*, 751 F.2d 137, 139 (2d Cir. 1984) (plan did not violate employee's duty of loyalty under state law); *In re Zenith Elecs. Corp.*, 241 B.R. 92, 108 (Bankr. D. Del. 1999) (plan must comply with applicable state corporate law relating to controlling shareholders); *In re Appalachian Fuels, LLC*, 521 B.R. 779, 805 (Bankr. E.D. Ky. 2014) (plan should not have been confirmed without provision for compliance with reclamation requirements of debtor's mining permits); *In re Rent-Rite Superkegs West Ltd.*, 484 B.R. 799, 809 (Bankr. D. Colo. 2012) (plan would be forbidden by law when a significant portion of income would be derived from illegal activity); *Eagle-Picher*, 345 B.R. at 861 (debtor has burden of proof to demonstrate that plan for addressing contaminated properties complies with nonbankruptcy law); *In re Jandous Elec. Constr. Corp.*, 115 B.R. 46, 51 (Bankr. S.D.N.Y. 1990).

102. Just as the requirement of feasibility does not require the guaranteed success of a plan, the requirement that the plan not be proposed by any means forbidden by law would not require a guarantee that a reorganized debtor will not violate the law. However, a plan that is patently illegal on its face, expressly supports violations of law, or is likely to violate nonbankruptcy law would raise serious issues. To date, courts have not had to grapple with the standard of review for this part of Section 1129(a)(3) because few debtors have had the temerity to propose plans that blatantly violate nonbankruptcy law.

103. Governments may contend that a plan that does not disclose to the court if a plan attempts to evade compliance obligations or has failed to notify affected regulators is not a good faith plan. *Cf. Archer-Daniels-Midland Co. v. Country Visions Coop.*, 29 F.4th 956 (7th Cir. 2022) (sale is not in good faith if effect on interested party is not disclosed to the court and known interested party is not notified).

to a plan that merely did not provide adequate finances for future compliance) falls more squarely under the "forbidden by law" prohibition. Some courts have interpreted Section 1129(a)(3) as applying only to the mechanics of how a plan has been "proposed" in the bankruptcy case (such as the solicitation process) as opposed to whether its *implementation* would be forbidden by law.[104] Governments may disagree and contend that a plan that proposes to undertake illegal action is in fact proposed by "means forbidden by law."[105] The "means" that are "forbidden by law" may reflect the future implementation of what the plan proposes. Just as the Bankruptcy Code is not a safe haven for violators of the law while in bankruptcy,[106] it was not meant to be a vehicle authorizing future violations post-bankruptcy. Thus, for example, the Ninth Circuit in *In re Baker & Drake* held that a plan could not authorize a debtor to operate taxis without complying with a state's generally applicable regulations.[107] This interpretation of "means forbidden by law" is also useful as reinforcement, through an express provision of the Bankruptcy Code, of the court's duty to look for and not approve

---

104. *See, e.g., Garvin v. Cook Invs. NW, SPMWY, LLC*, 922 F.3d 1031, 1035 (9th Cir. 2019); *In re Irving Tanning Co.*, 496 B.R. 644, 660 (1st Cir. BAP 2013); *In re Food City, Inc.*, 110 B.R. 808, 813–14 & nn.10–12 (Bankr. W.D. Tex. 1990). Several of the courts taking this position acknowledge that plans cannot provide for violation of nonbankruptcy law if it is not preempted by the Bankruptcy Code. *See Irving Tanning*, 496 B.R. at 664; *Food City*, 110 B.R. at 813–14 & nn.10–12.

105. Governments may contend that the interpretation of this provision as covering only procedural requirements for proposing plans is too narrow given the numerous other provisions of the Code that prescribe the procedure for plan approval. *See, e.g.*, 11 U.S.C. § 1129(a)(2) (proponent of the plan must comply with applicable provisions of the Code); 11 U.S.C. § 1125 (requirements for post-petition disclosure and solicitation). Given these other provisions, a limited reading of Section 1129(a)(3) would render it largely superfluous. In addition, such a narrow interpretation could result in a plan improperly preempting and authorizing violations of many nonbankruptcy laws.

106. *See* Chapters 9 (Operating Estate Property), 10 (Police or Regulatory Exception) *supra*.

107. *In re Baker & Drake, Inc.*, 35 F.3d 1348 (9th Cir. 1994). Section 1123(a)(5) of the Bankruptcy Code (providing that plans can provide adequate means for their implementation) cannot be used to justify authorization of post-confirmation violations of police and regulatory law. *See* note 101 *supra*. Likewise Section 1123(b)(6) of the Bankruptcy Code (providing that plans may include *appropriate* provisions not inconsistent with the Code) cannot be used to justify authorization of violations of nonbankruptcy law. *See United States v. Energy Res. Co.*, 495 U.S. 545, 550 (1990).

plans that are premised on violations of law.[108] This prevents the bankruptcy system from becoming an instrument of illegality.[109]

If the debtor is subject to an existing consent decree or judicial or administrative order requiring the debtor to come into compliance with nonbankruptcy law, a plan could be objected to as "forbidden by law" if it fails to provide for the continued effectiveness of the consent decree or order. The government may seek fixing language for this issue such as: "Notwithstanding anything to the contrary in the Plan or this Confirmation Order, the applicable Reorganized Debtors shall continue to be bound by the terms of the following consent decrees, orders, or agreements: [insert citations]."[110]

OBJECTIONS TO EXPEDITED PASS-THROUGH PLANS

Some debtors file for bankruptcy only on account of a need to rearrange their bond debt. Their prearranged or prepackaged proposed plans are filed with agreement from bondholders and purport to leave other creditors or parties in interest unimpaired and unaffected. Their claims and rights purportedly "pass through" the

---

108. *See United Student Aid Funds, Inc. v. Espinosa*, 559 U.S. 260, 271 (2010).

109. That is not to say that Section 1129(a)(3) should be read so broadly that it would override other Bankruptcy Code provisions that can be fairly read to preempt state law or override other federal law. However, as noted in Chapter 8 (Harmonization), the stringent requirements for preemption of state law and for harmonization of federal law require express language making congressional intent clear, and there is a presumption against preemption of police and regulatory law. Absent express language meeting the stringent test for preemption/harmonization, governments may contend that Section 1129(a)(3) confirms the default assumption that plans seeking to override nonbankruptcy law should be viewed as forbidden by law.

110. A plan that seeks a binding ruling from the bankruptcy court as to the scope of obligations under environmental or other nonbankruptcy law may be objected to as seeking impermissible pre-enforcement review. Section 106(a) of the Bankruptcy Code, which governs waiver of sovereign immunity by governmental units, provides that any order, process, or judgment of the bankruptcy court must be consistent with nonbankruptcy law applicable to the governmental unit. A debtor may therefore not seek a pre-enforcement determination of liability where not permitted under nonbankruptcy law. *See* Chapter 5 (Key Provisions (sovereign immunity)) *supra*. States may also object to such a request as in violation of the 11th Amendment. *Id.*

bankruptcy proceeding unchanged. Indeed, proceeding through bankruptcy in a super-expedited fashion without complying with the ordinary requirements set forth in the Bankruptcy Code and the Bankruptcy Rules would be impermissible absent the consent of those affected.[111]

Nonetheless, such plans still need to be carefully scrutinized by environmental creditors and parties in interest, as debtors often include boilerplate language in such plans that may be prejudicial. Such due diligence is not possible where debtors seek confirmation without adequate opportunity for interested parties to review and object; in some instances, the confirmation hearings have been as early as on the day of filing of the bankruptcy case.[112]

Sometimes such plans have discharge and release language that would impair governmental interests even though the plans are described as nonprejudicial. Some of the plans require proofs of claim or administrative expense applications to be filed in order to obtain the benefits of pass through. Governments can object to such requirements because: (1) proofs of claim are not required for compliance obligations,[113] and (2) if debtors want to discharge monetary claims of governments they should go through the regular bankruptcy process including its various safeguards for creditors. Also, some pass-through plans might not impair a claim or cause of action against debtors but nonetheless may include an improper nondebtor release.

However, there are cases where governments may decide not to object to an expedited pass-through plan. For example, the

---

111. *See generally* Levitin, *supra* note 5, at 122–26.

112. *See* Brian Shaw & David Doyle, *Expedited Bankruptcies Are Cause for Concern*, https://www.law360.com/articles/1392553/expedited-bankruptcites-are-cause-for-concern (June 9, 2021). One debtor sought to provide advance notice of the terms of its plan to governments prior to filing its bankruptcy case and treat such advance notice as placing a burden on the government to review and be prepared to take immediate action to object if necessary upon filing. *In re HighPoint Res. Corp.*, No. 21-10565 (Bankr. D. Del.) Such extrajudicial outreach efforts are inadequate because they often will not reach the correct government personnel (who would have been entitled to service of a court filing affecting their interests) in time to permit meaningful review. Notices or deadlines that have not been approved by a bankruptcy court and are not even part of a filed case are nothing more than correspondence and are not likely to trigger timely notice or review or fairly warn of prejudicial impacts or a duty for expedited review.

113. *See* Chapter 11 (Compliance Obligations) *supra*.

debtor may agree to language in the confirmation order that clarifies that the bankruptcy is not discharging or releasing any right, claim, or cause of action of governmental units, which liability shall survive the bankruptcy case and be handled in the ordinary course as if the bankruptcy petition had never been filed. Without such language, however, governments or other interested parties are likely to object to pass-through plans and the expedited consideration of such plans as contrary to the Bankruptcy Code and due process requirements.

OBJECTIONS TO ABANDONMENT PROVISIONS IN PLANS

Environmental agencies may object to provisions in plans that provide for the actual or effective abandonment of contaminated property. As set forth in more detail in Chapter 18 (Abandonment), the Supreme Court held in *Midlantic National Bank* that bankruptcy courts lack power to authorize abandonment without including conditions requiring compliance with statutes protecting public health and safety.[114] Motions to abandon contaminated property can raise difficult factual and legal issues and therefore are usually filed well before a confirmation hearing. It should be noted that property allowed to be abandoned under Section 554 of the Bankruptcy Code reverts to the debtor (as opposed to the debtor's estate) during the bankruptcy case.[115] On confirmation, the remaining property of the estate (which has not been abandoned) vests into the (reorganized) debtor (which is holding any abandoned property) under Section 1141(b) of the Bankruptcy Code unless the plan provides otherwise. The plan's vesting provision should be checked to see whether the debtor is attempting to exclude any property of the estate (or previously abandoned property) from vesting in the reorganized debtor and evaluate whether such an attempted abandonment violates *Midlantic*. In addition, if the plan is isolating contaminated property in the estate or other non-reorganizing entity without adequate financial ability to protect

114. *Midlantic Nat'l Bank v. N.J. Dep't of Env't Prot.*, 474 U.S. 494, 506–07 (1986).
115. *See* Chapter 18 (Abandonment) *infra*.

public health and safety, then governmental agencies may contend that the plan is not feasible and/or proposed by means forbidden by law as it will be creating entities that cannot comply with applicable nonbankruptcy law. Plan provisions that permit abandonment post-confirmation may be objected to if: (1) they provide for abandonment by an entity such as a reorganized debtor because Section 554 only authorizes abandonment of "property of the estate" and the estate no longer exists, or (2) the provision does not provide the opportunity for a hearing required by Section 554.

OTHER PLAN OBJECTIONS

Several other miscellaneous grounds for plan objections may be considered. Section 1129(a)(9) of the Bankruptcy Code requires that a plan pay allowed administrative expense claims in full. As discussed in Chapter 12 (Priorities) of this Practice Guide, claims for post-petition response costs for cleanup of debtors' property and claims for penalties for post-petition violations have administrative expense priority. Failure to make adequate provision for the payment of administrative expense claims makes a plan unconfirmable if objections are raised.[116] Such an objection may make any issues about the validity and estimated magnitude of such claims (i.e., whether debtors can pay them) issues that need to be addressed at the confirmation hearing. The government would need to be prepared to provide witnesses and evidentiary support for its position at the confirmation hearing.

Section 1129(a)(7) of the Bankruptcy Code, which is known as the best interest of creditors test, requires that holders of claims receive at least as much under a plan as they would in a Chapter 7 liquidation.[117] This requirement applies to each creditor regardless of whether its class of creditors votes in favor of or against the plan. If a class of creditors votes against acceptance of a plan, there

116. *In re Hechinger Inv. Co.*, 298 F.3d 219, 224 (3d Cir. 2002); *In re Farmland Indus., Inc.*, 397 F.3d 647, 652 (3d Cir. 2005). *See* Stephen Lerner, Travis McRoberts & Kyle Arendsen, *Blackjewel and Hartshore: Overcoming § 1129(a)(9) Obstacles*, 40-8 Am. Bankr. Inst. J. 14 (Aug. 2021).

117. *See, e.g., In re PWS Holding Corp.*, 228 F.3d 224, 249–50 (3d Cir. 2000); *In re Briscoe Enter.*, 994 F.2d 1160, 1167–68 (5th Cir. 1993).

is an additional "cram down" requirement. A plan can be approved by cram down only if the court finds that it does not discriminate unfairly, is fair and equitable, and complies with the absolute priority rule, which requires that senior claims be paid in full before any amount is paid to junior claims.[118]

Plans may be objected to under Section 1129(a)(1) if they do not provide similar treatment for environmental unsecured claims and other unsecured claims.[119] Governments sometimes make such objections with respect to penalty or punitive damage claims if debtors seek to treat such claims less favorably than claims filed by commercial creditors.[120] The Supreme Court has made clear that bankruptcy courts are not free to vary the priorities of claims based on equitable considerations not provided for by Congress in the Bankruptcy Code.[121]

Interested parties may object to settlements of debtors' causes of action contained in plans. For example, a plan may settle the estate's causes of action against third parties for fraudulent conveyance, alter ego, or piercing the corporate veil. Objections to such settlements are difficult because they often require extensive discovery and expert testimony and the standard for approval of settlements under Bankruptcy Rule 9019 is somewhat deferential (using a "range of reasonableness" standard) since courts tend to encourage and favor settlements as mutually beneficial by minimizing litigation and expediting case administration.[122] Parties

---

118. *See* 11 U.S.C. § 1129(b); *Bank of Am. Nat'l Trust & Sav. Ass'n v. 203 North LaSalle Street P'ship*, 526 U.S. 434, 441–42 (1999); Chapter 12 (Priorities) *supra*.

119. *See* note 30 *supra*.

120. *See, e.g., In re A.G. Fin. Serv. Ctr., Inc.*, 395 F.3d 410, 414 (7th Cir. 2005); *In re Hyatt*, 509 B.R. 707 (Bankr. D.N.M. 2014); *In re Roman Catholic Archbishop of Portland in Oregon*, 339 B.R. 215 (Bankr. D. Or. 2006) *In re Infiltrator Sys., Inc.*, 248 B.R. 707 (Bankr. D. Conn. 2000).

121. *See United States v. Reorganized CF&I Fabricators of Utah, Inc.*, 518 U.S. 213 (1996); *United States v. Nolan*, 517 U.S. 535 (1996); Thomas C. Grant, Note & Comment, *How United States v. Noland Prohibits the Disallowance of Punitive Damages Claims in Chapter 11*, 14 Bankr. Dev. J. 199, 218 (1997).

122. *See, e.g., Protective Committee v. Anderson*, 390 U.S. 414 (1968); *In re Martin*, 91 F.3d 389, 393 (3d Cir. 1996). Bankruptcy courts must consider: (1) probabilities of success in litigation, (2) difficulties in collection, (3) the complexity and expense of litigation, and (4) the paramount interest of creditors. *Id.* But settlements that fall above the lowest point of a range of reasonableness will be approved. *See, e.g., In re Am. Cartage, Inc.*, 656 F.3d 82, 91 (1st Cir. 2011); *In re W.T. Grant Co.*, 699 F.2d 599,

considering such objections need to closely monitor the case as debtors and other constituencies may, prior to plan proceedings, seek advance approval of such settlements or of restructuring support agreements that contain them. Bankruptcy courts will often protect parties' rights to object to the settlements as part of plan proceedings if the parties file an objection that the settlement is dictating the terms of the plan. Objectors also need to weigh in on the timing and scope of discovery well before the confirmation order. Sometimes the bankruptcy court's order approving the disclosure statement and setting voting procedures will also have provisions for discovery that should be scrutinized and objected to if inadequate or one-sided. Early participation in cases with significant fraudulent conveyance, alter ego, or piercing the veil issues is important as such causes of action can provide significant consideration for payouts under plans.[123]

Finally, plans and proposed confirmation orders may be objected to under Section 1129(a)(1) if they deviate from the Bankruptcy Code's provisions on modification and substantial consummation.[124] Under Section 1127(a), a plan may be modified prior to confirmation as long as it still meets the requirements of Sections 1122 and 1123. After confirmation, modifications before substantial consummation can only occur after notice and hearing in which the bankruptcy court must find that the modified plan meets the requirements for confirmation in Section 1129.[125] Disclosure and an

608 (2d Cir. 1983); *In re Capmark Fin. Grp. Inc.*, 438 B.R. 471 (Bankr. D. Del. 2010). *See* Chapter 21 (Settlement Agreements) *infra*.

123. One of the largest fraudulent conveyance recoveries was $5.5 billion in *Tronox*, *see* DOJ Press Release, Office of Public Affairs, *United States Announces $5.15 Billion Settlement of Litigation Against Subsidiaries of Anadarko Petroleum Corp. to Remedy Fraudulent Conveyance Designed to Evade Environmental Liabilities* (Apr. 3, 2014); *In re Tronox Inc.*, 503 B.R. 239 (Bankr. S.D.N.Y. 2013); *In re Tronox, Inc.*, 2014 WL 5819821 (Bankr. S.D.N.Y. July 22, 2014), *aff'd*, 549 B.R. 21 (S.D.N.Y. 2016), *aff'd*, 855 F.3d 84, 100, 106 (2d Cir. 2017). In *Asarco*, the district court ordered the return of stock and dividends exceeding $1 billion resulting in a payout to environmental creditors of $1.79 billion. *See* DOJ Press Release, Office of Public Affairs, *Largest Environmental Bankruptcy in U.S. History Will Result in Payment of $1.79 Billion Towards Environmental Cleanup & Restoration* (Dec. 10, 2009); *In re Asarco LLC*, 441 B.R. 813 (S.D. Tex. 2010); *Asarco LLC v Americas Mining Corp.*, 404 B.R. 150 (S.D. Tex. 2009); *Asarco LLC v. Americas Mining Corp.*, 396 B.R. 278 (S.D. Tex. 2008).

124. 11 U.S.C. §§ 1127, 1144, 1101(2).

125. *Id.* § 1127(b).

opportunity for creditors to change their acceptance or rejection is also required for modification of plans.[126] After confirmation and substantial consummation, a confirmation order can be revoked only for fraud.[127] Substantial consummation of a plan may render an appeal of the plan equitably moot.[128]

CONFIRMATION ORDERS AND OTHER PLAN DOCUMENTS

Plans in complex corporate Chapter 11 cases may incorporate many side agreements or related documents. These may be filed as exhibits, as separate documents, or in a plan supplement. Sometimes these documents are not filed until after the objection deadline or even during or after the confirmation hearing. Environmental creditors and parties in interest should assert the right to review these documents as a matter of due process (as well as the right to be provided adequate information to make an informed judgment about the plan under Section 1125), even if the documents are filed late in the process or after plan confirmation, and may object to such documents for any of the reasons previously discussed. They should be carefully reviewed in the event that they introduce new issues.

Confirmation proceedings culminate in a "confirmation order" from the court, which may contain resolutions of plan objections or other new language that may introduce new issues. Proposed confirmation orders, which may be filed during or after the confirmation hearing, should be carefully reviewed and objected to if necessary. Additional reasonable time for review should be requested when necessary. If a proposed confirmation order is not filed prior to the confirmation hearing, parties in interest should attend the hearing to determine when it will be filed and preserve the opportunity for review.

Confirmation orders sometimes have language overriding inconsistent prior bankruptcy court rulings in the bankruptcy case. Thus,

126. *Id.* § 1127(c), (d).
127. *Id.* § 1144.
128. *See* Appeals of Confirmation Order and Mootness *infra.*

if there has been a prior environmental settlement or ruling, the confirmation order should be carefully reviewed for its impact.

Confirmation orders typically override any contrary language in plans or related documents. Therefore, confirmation orders are usually the best place for language fixing overbroad or illegal provisions. That said, it is important to look out for unusual language providing that in the event of conflict, some other document governs over the confirmation order.

Most but not all bankruptcy judges will require that debtors walk them through the documents and answer any questions about any last-minute changes to documents. Sometimes the bankruptcy court will require filings on the docket and provide an additional limited period for counsel to review. Therefore, it is important for counsel to monitor filings pertaining to confirmation of the proposed plan and confirmation hearings closely.

APPEALS OF CONFIRMATION ORDERS AND MOOTNESS ISSUES

If a creditor or party in interest is unsuccessful in bankruptcy court on their objections and wishes to appeal, they should evaluate whether a stay may be necessary in order to avoid their appeal becoming equitably moot.[129] Bankruptcy Rule 3020(e) stays the entry of a confirmation order for 14 days so as to provide parties an opportunity to obtain a longer stay pending appeal unless the bankruptcy court orders otherwise.[130] However, many confirmation orders in larger Chapter 11 cases contain a waiver of this 14-day stay, or some debtors may make an oral request for such a waiver at the confirmation hearing. Parties considering an appeal may wish to object to such a waiver to protect their rights.

---

129. *See* Chapter 20 (Jurisdiction) (appeals). Pursuant to Bankruptcy Rule 8007(c), a court may condition a stay on payment of a bond or other security. The United States is exempt from having to provide a bond.

130. If a plan involves a sale of assets under 11 U.S.C. § 363, Section 363(m) may also limit reversal or modification on appeal if a stay is not obtained. Appeals of the sale of property are also stayed for 14 days unless the bankruptcy court orders otherwise. *See* Bankruptcy Rule 6004(h).

The doctrine of equitable mootness is a court-made doctrine that looks to protect innocent third parties who have reasonably relied on the finality of complex plans that have been substantially consummated and would be difficult and unfair to unscramble.[131] The doctrine of equitable mootness does not preclude an appellate court from fashioning limited relief that would not cause the complete collapse of a plan.[132] Failure to seek a stay pending appeal may be a factor that an appellate court would rely on to find an appeal equitably moot.[133] In recent years, equitable mootness has become increasingly controversial and may soon be revisited by courts of appeal or the Supreme Court.[134] At a minimum, courts are likely to at least consider the issues on appeal in order to make findings as to whether any relief can be equitably constructed if an error was made.

Equitable mootness is different from statutory mootness.[135] For example, Section 363(m) of the Bankruptcy Code provides that reversal on appeal of a sale or lease of property in bankruptcy does not undo the sale or lease to a good faith purchaser if a stay was not obtained. Where a plan incorporates a Section 363 sale, appeal of the sale aspect of the plan may implicate the provisions of Section 363(m).[136] However, the statute only applies to the

---

131. *In re Highland Capital Mgmt., L.P.*, 48 F.4th 419, 429–32 (5th Cir. 2022); *In re Fin. Oversight & Mgmt. Bd. for Puerto Rico*, 987 F.3d 173 (1st Cir. 2021); *In re Abengoa Bioenergy Biomass of Kansas, LLC*, 958 F.3d 949 (10th Cir. 2020); *In re Sneed Shipbuilding, Inc.*, 916 F.3d 405, 408–09 (5th Cir. 2019); *Bennett v. Jefferson County*, 899 F.3d 1240, 1247–49 (11th Cir. 2018); *In re One2one Commc'ns, LLC*, 805 F.3d 428, 433–35 (3d Cir. 2015); *In re Tribune Media Co.*, 799 F.3d 272, 277–80 (3d Cir. 2015); *In re City of Detroit*, 838 F.3d 792, 798–99 (6th Cir. 2016); *In re Charter Commc'ns, Inc.*, 691 F.3d 476, 481–82 (2d Cir. 2012). *See generally Pragmatism v. Principle: Bankruptcy Appeals and Equitable Mootness*, 15 N.Y.U. J.L. & Bus. 477 (2019).

132. For example, appeals have been allowed on issues about the validity of third-party nondebtor releases or plan indemnifications. *See Highland Capital*, 48 F.4th at 429–32; *One2one Commc'ns*, 805 F.3d at 435; *In re Pac. Lumber Co.*, 584 F.3d 229, 251 (5th Cir. 2009); *United Artists Theatre Co. v Walton*, 315 F.3d 217, 228 (3d Cir. 2003); *In re PWS Holding Corp.*, 228 F.3d 224, 236 (3d Cir. 2000).

133. *See Jefferson Cnty.*, 899 F.3d at 1251–52; *Charter Commc'ns*, 691 F.3d at 484; *In re Paige*, 584 F.3d 1327, 1341 (10th Cir. 2009).

134. *See In re Veroblue Farms USA, Inc.*, 6 F.4th 880 (8th Cir. 2021) (citing *One2one Commc'ns*, 805 F.3d at 438–54 (Krause, C.J., concurring)).

135. Constitutional mootness also could be at issue in a situation where it was impossible for the court to create effective relief. *See Mission Prod.*, 139 S. Ct. at 1660.

136. *See In re Energy Future Holdings Corp.*, 949 F.3d 806, 820–22 (3d Cir. 2020).

validity of the sale. Therefore, collateral rulings, such as determinations concerning a governmental agency's rights against the purchaser under police or regulatory laws might still be reviewable on appeal.[137]

137. *See id.* at 822; *In re ICL Holding Co.*, 802 F.3d 547, 554 (3d Cir. 2015).

CHAPTER 17

Claim Objections and Estimation Proceedings

This chapter discusses objections to proofs of claim by debtors or parties in interest and requests for estimation of environmental claims, including procedural requirements, who can file them, and how they are adjudicated.

Objections to proofs of claim, also referred to as claims objections, are contested matters governed by Federal Rules of Bankruptcy Procedure 3007 and 9014.[1] Bankruptcy Rule 3007 requires service of an objection to a proof of claim to be sent to the address indicated for service in the creditor's proof of claim, and service must take place at least 30 days before a hearing or any deadline to request a hearing.[2] Bankruptcy court local rules and court notices should also be carefully reviewed as they often contain

1. *See, e.g. In re Franchi*, 451 B.R. 604 (Bankr. S.D. Fla. 2011); *In re Hawthorne*, 326 B.R. 1 (Bankr. D.D.C. 2005).

2. Objections to claims of United States agencies must also be served in accordance with Federal Rule of Bankruptcy Procedure 7004(b)(4) or (5). In some situations where the creditor has not already participated in the bankruptcy case and a proof of claim has been filed on its behalf, *see* Fed. R. Bankr. P. 3004, 3005, service is also required in accordance with Federal Rule of Bankruptcy Procedure 7004 (as incorporated by Rule 9014) in order to establish personal jurisdiction over the creditor. *See In re 701 Mariposa Project, LLC*, 514 B.R. 10, 16–17 (9th Cir. B.A.P, 2014). Claim objections that seek ancillary relief such as extinguishment of a lien may require the service of an adversary proceeding complaint in accordance with Federal Rule of Bankruptcy Procedure 7001. *See, e.g., In re Kleibrink*, 621 F.3d 370, 371 (5th Cir. 2010).

additional requirements and deadlines such as for responses to be filed to objections to proofs of claim.[3] Bankruptcy Rule 3007 also permits the aggregation of a debtor's objections to multiple claims on certain specified similar grounds. These aggregated objections are referred to as omnibus objections. A creditor who has filed a proof of claim should carefully review attachments to any omnibus objections to determine if they include an objection to its proof of claim.[4]

In larger cases, debtors often file motions to establish case management procedures for claims objections. These procedures, if approved by the court, may be incorporated in a case management order. Such motions and orders should be carefully reviewed, as they may contain provisions that are sensible for routine commercial claims but can be problematic for complex environmental claims. Examples of objectionable provisions include requirements for early production of relevant documents by the claimant or other one-sided provisions favoring debtors that are at variance with the rules that would otherwise apply.[5] For example, debtors may seek to exempt themselves from otherwise applicable rules of res judicata, which in theory would permit them to file multiple objections or multiple requests for estimation of claims

3. *See, e.g.*, *In re Sadlier*, 262 B.R. 17 (Bankr. D.R.I. 2001).

4. In larger cases with multiple omnibus objections, this can become a time-consuming cumbersome process requiring counsel who receive all filings in the case to hunt for objections to their claims hidden in a multiplicity of long lists of objections to claims. Note that Rule 3007 does limit the number of objections in a single filing to 100 and requires that they be alphabetically listed; however, numerous filings of objections are common in large cases. Although the process is well-established in larger cases and to some extent endorsed by the Federal Rules of Bankruptcy Procedure, it arguably is in tension with due process requirements. It also imposes significant transaction costs, including requiring governmental agencies to undertake painstaking review of multiple long lists of claims that are the subject of objections. To avoid due process and undue burden concerns, a notice of an objection could be sent to each creditor whose claim is being objected to with its name at the top of the notice. Such an approach would more meaningfully put the creditor on notice that its claim is being objected to and that action is required.

5. Federal Rule of Bankruptcy Procedure 3001(c)(1) requires that proofs of claim based on writings include the writing as an attachment. Environmental proofs of claim are based on statutory obligations, not writings. Rule 3001(c)(1) therefore does not require that documents supporting environmental proofs of claim be attached to the proof of claim or to responses to objections. *See In re Shaver*, 247 B.R. 436 (Bankr. E.D. Tenn. 1999). Such requirements are also contrary to the bankruptcy rules governing discovery in contested matters. *See* Fed. R. Bankr. P. 9014.

over lengthy periods of time. Such provisions, which could impose overwhelming burdens on creditors, have become routine in larger cases but are largely untested.

Bankruptcy Rule 9014, which governs contested matters, incorporates many but not all of the Federal Rules of Civil Procedure including most of the rules governing discovery.[6] Exceptions that are not incorporated in Bankruptcy Rule 9014 include mandatory initial disclosure requirements and expert testimony disclosures (unless otherwise ordered by the court). Thus, litigation of a contested proof of claim is similar to other civil litigation and is conducted in accordance with the Federal Rules of Evidence.[7] If an initial hearing is scheduled on an objection to a proof of claim and response thereto, it is important for the parties and the bankruptcy court to have a common understanding as to whether such a hearing will be a final evidentiary hearing with witnesses, or more in the nature of a status conference during which a schedule for the contested matter, including any discovery, will be established.

Claims can be objected to at any time during the bankruptcy case, including either before or after confirmation of Chapter 11 plans. Claim objections after Chapter 11 plan confirmations are common and can extend many years after confirmation.[8]

When a proof of claim is filed, the Bankruptcy Code states that the claim is "deemed allowed" unless a party in interest files an objection.[9] The party objecting to a proof of claim thus carries

---

6. Rule 9014 makes many of the Federal Rules of Civil Procedure applicable to contested matters through application of much of the 7000 series (Part VII) of federal bankruptcy rules that govern adversary proceedings in bankruptcy court. An "adversary proceeding" is a matter that must be initiated by a complaint as set forth in Bankruptcy Rule 7001 and includes proceedings to recover money, determine liens or interest in property, determine dischargeability, and seek injunctive or declaratory relief.

7. Fed. R. Bankr. P. 9017.

8. The claims process in *In re Exide Techns., LLC*, No. 13-11482 (Bankr. D. Del.), where a plan was confirmed in 2015, was still pending when Exide filed for bankruptcy for a third time in 2020. *In re Exide Holdings, Inc.*, No. 20-11157 (Bankr. D. Del.).

9. 11 U.S.C. § 502(a). As a practical matter, being "deemed allowed" does not normally have enormous significance because the debtor will object to any claims it does not believe should be allowed or if it disagrees with the amount of the claim. Since a claim "deemed allowed" in the amount filed would be entitled to vote on a proposed plan of reorganization, the debtor may file an objection and the voting solicitation order may provide that claimants whose claims are objected to cannot

an initial burden of coming forward with specific evidence and a legal argument rebutting the presumptive validity and amount of the claim.[10] If the objector comes forward with such evidence, the ultimate burden of proof is then determined in accordance with applicable nonbankruptcy law.[11]

The validity and amount of a proof of claim is determined by nonbankruptcy law except in the very limited circumstances where the Bankruptcy Code provides otherwise.[12] Section 502(b) of the Bankruptcy Code provides for nine exceptions to this rule, most of which usually do not arise with respect to environmental proofs of claim.[13] Moreover, none of the exceptions provides a basis for disallowance of a claim for joint and several liability; therefore,

---

vote on the plan unless the bankruptcy court estimates the claim for purposes of voting. A debtor will normally try to reach a reasonable agreement with the creditor as to the amount of its claim solely for voting purposes so that both parties can avoid the cost of an estimation hearing. However, the creditor will often need to contact debtor's counsel to reach such an agreement.

10. *See* Fed. R. Bankr. P. 3001(f) ("A proof of claim executed and filed in accordance with these rules shall constitute prima facie evidence of the validity and amount of the claim."). *See In re GG-I Holdings, Inc.*, 443 B.R. 645, 664 (Bankr. D.N.J. 2010).

11. *See Raleigh v. Illinois Dep't of Revenue*, 530 U.S. 15, 20–21 (2000).

12. *See, e.g., Travelers Cas. & Sur. Co. of Am. v. Pac. Gas & Elec. Co.*, 549 U.S. 443, 449 (2007); *Raleigh*, 530 U.S. at 15; *Grogan v. Garner*, 498 U.S. 279, 284 & n. 9 (federal law); *Butner v. United States*, 440 U.S. 48, 54 (1979); *Vanston Bondholders Protective Comm. v. Green*, 329 U.S. 156, 161 (1946); *In re Wright*, 492 F.3d 829, 832 (7th Cir. 2007). The same rule applies to estimation of claims. In estimating claims, bankruptcy courts are "bound by the legal rules which may govern the ultimate value of the claim." *Bittner v. Borne Chem. Co.*, 691 F.2d 134, 135 (3d Cir. 1982).

13. 11 U.S.C. § 502(b). The exclusion of unmatured interest, 11 U.S.C. § 502(b)(2), and late proofs of claim, 11 U.S.C. § 502(b)(9), may arise occasionally. Section 502(b)(1) provides that a proof of claim may not be objected to on the ground that it is contingent or unmatured. Inapplicable provisions include, for example, limits on the amount of damages from the termination of a rental or employment contract. In Chapter 11 cases, late proofs of claim may still be allowed for excusable neglect under Fed. R. Bankr. P. 9006(b)(1) and *Pioneer Investment Services Co. v. Brunswick Assocs. Ltd. P'ship*, 507 U.S. 380 (1993). *See In re CJ Holding Co.*, 27 F.4th 1105 (5th Cir. 2022); *In re Zilog, Inc.*, 450 F.3d 996, 1007 (9th Cir. 2006); *Jones v. Chemetron Corp.*, 212 F.3d 199 (3d Cir. 2000). In addition, Section 502(e) of the Bankruptcy Code also provides for the disallowance of contingent claims for reimbursement or contribution by co-liable parties. 11 U.S.C. § 502(e)(1)(B). Governmental claims are generally direct claims, which are unaffected by this provision. However, private party environmental claims for contribution may be impacted. The provision does not affect private party claims for reimbursement of past costs actually incurred by such party but can result in the disallowance of claims for contribution towards future costs. *See* Chapter 13 (Discharge) *supra*.

governments generally contend that a valid claim for joint and several liability under environmental law must be allowed in full.[14] Debtors may contend, however, that bankruptcy courts have the equitable authority to allocate liability and allow the government's claim only for the amount of the debtor's fair share. However, this position would need to overcome decisions limiting a bankruptcy court's authority to use equity to disallow or reprioritize otherwise valid claims where the Bankruptcy Code has not so provided.[15]

The Bankruptcy Code states that "parties in interest" may file objections to proofs of claim,[16] which provides potential standing to a wide group to object to proofs of claim.[17] However, the

---

14. *See, e.g., In re Nat'l Gypsum Co.*, 139 B.R. 397, 414–15 (N.D. Tex. 1992) (CERCLA claims to be estimated on basis of joint and several liability under applicable law). For cases discussing joint and several liability under environmental law, *see, e.g., Burlington N. & Santa Fe Ry. Co. v. United States*, 556 U.S. 599 (2009); *Pakootas v. Teck Cominco. Metals, Ltd.*, 905 F.3d 565, 588–90 (9th Cir. 2018); *PCS Nitrogen Inc. v. Ashley II of Charleston LLC*, 714 F.3d 161, 181 (4th Cir. 2013); *United States v. NCR Corp.*, 688 F.3d 833 (7th Cir. 2012). The issue of joint and several liability can also arise in nonenvironmental proofs of claim such as in the case of lenders holding joint and several claims against debtors and/or nondebtors. *See, e.g., In re CF&I Fabricators of Utah, Inc.*, 179 B.R. 704, 711–12 (D. Utah. 1994) (PBGC entitled to joint and several liability); *In re Lloyd McKee Motors, Inc.*, 157 B.R. 484 (Bankr. D.N.M. 1993) (guarantor debtor jointly and several liable to lender); *In re Ford*, 125 B.R. 735, 738 (E.D. Tex. 1991) (bank entitled to joint and several liability in bankruptcy), *aff'd*, 967 F.2d 1047 (5th Cir. 1992).

15. *See, e.g., Travelers*, 549 U.S. at 449; *United States v. Noland,* 517 U.S. 535 (1996); *United States v. Reorganized CF & I Fabricators of Utah, Inc.*, 518 U.S. 213 (1996); *In re Southmark Corp.*, 49 F.3d 1111, 1116 (5th Cir. 1995). Although governments have the right to obtain joint and several liability under many environmental statutes, they also have the discretion to enter into fair share settlements with debtors that take into account their contribution to contamination at the site, orphan shares, and the circumstances of the bankruptcy. *See* Chapter 21 (Settlement Agreements) *infra.* Governments may not be willing to do so in certain circumstances, such as where a debtor is recalcitrant or uncooperative. In any event, a debtor always has the option, if it believes it is being required to pay more than its equitable share, to bring a contribution action against other liable parties. *See, e.g., Asarco LLC v. Atlantic Richfield Co.*, 866 F.3d 1108 (9th Cir. 2017); *Asarco, LLC v. Noranda Mining, Inc.*, 844 F.3d 1201 (10th Cir. 2017); *Asarco, LLC v. Union Pac. Ry. Co.*, 762 F.3d 744 (8th Cir. 2014). *See also ASARCO, LLC v. Celanese Chem. Co.*, 792 F.3d 1203 (9th Cir. 2015) (noting that contribution action may be time-barred under statute of limitations based on date of debtor's settlement with government).

16. 11 U.S.C. § 502(a).

17. The Bankruptcy Code has numerous references to parties in interest but does not define the term, although Section 1109(b) provides examples of parties in interest. Issues as to who is a party in interest generally should be determined based on the particular matter at issue rather than in the abstract. *See generally In re Pub. Serv. Co. of New Hampshire*, 88 B.R. 546 (Bankr. D.N.H. 1988). Whether

courts are divided over whether a party in interest may object to a proof of claim if the debtor in possession or trustee is or will be objecting to the claim.[18] If the debtor in possession proposes a settlement of a proof of claim, parties in interest can object to court approval of the settlement under Bankruptcy Rule 9019(b). However, plans of reorganization sometimes have provisions that override the requirement of court approval. Plans can also specify who has standing to pursue claim objections after confirmation. If a party in interest wishes to preserve any right it has to object to a settlement or a claim, it should carefully review the plan for such provisions.[19]

REQUESTS FOR ESTIMATION OF CLAIMS

Section 502(c) of the Bankruptcy Code permits the estimation of "contingent or unliquidated" claims where "the fixing or liquidation" of the claim "would unduly delay the administration of the case."[20] Estimation of claims can be for various purposes such as voting on a plan, determining plan feasibility, or for allowance of a claim. A claim is contingent if the right to payment is not effective until the occurrence of a future event.[21] A claim is unliquidated if its amount is not fixed or readily calculable.[22] Just because a claim is disputed or a judgment has not yet been obtained does not make

---

someone is a party in interest can overlap with the issue of whether the party has standing. *See* Chapter 20 (Jurisdiction) (standing) *infra*.

18. *Compare, e.g., In re Thompson*, 965 F.2d 1136, 1147 (1st Cir. 1992) (not permitted); *Pascazi v. Fiber Consultants, Inc.*, 445 B.R. 124, 129 (S.D.N.Y. 2011) (not permitted) *with In re Weinstein Co. Holdings, LLC*, 595 B.R. 455, 463 (Bankr. 2018) (permitted); *In re Mechanicsburg Fitness, Inc.*, 592 B.R. 798, 809 (Bankr. M.D. Pa. 2018) (permitted). The courts permitting objection emphasize what they view as clear Bankruptcy Code language while the courts not so permitting emphasize the importance of orderly and efficient case administration.

19. *See* Chapter 16 (Plan Objections) *supra*.

20. 11 U.S.C. § 502(c). For a discussion of what constitutes undue delay, *see* Alison J. Brehn, David N. Copas & Colleen K. Vossler, *To Be, or Not to Be: The Undiscovered Country of Claims Estimation in Bankruptcy*, 8 J. BANKR. L. & PRAC. 197, 235–40 (1999).

21. *In re Mazzeo*, 131 F.3d 295, 303 (2d Cir. 1997); *In re Knight*, 55 F.3d 231, 236 (7th Cir. 1995).

22. *Knight*, 55 F.3d at 236.

it contingent or unliquidated.[23] Environmental claims for past costs would therefore ordinarily not be subject to estimation as the events creating liability have all occurred in the past and either: (1) the claim is readily calculable from past cost documentation, or (2) a contested claim proceeding to determine the amount of costs would not delay administration of the case.[24] Environmental claims for future costs of the claimant, however, may be subject to estimation since the amount of future costs is not readily calculable and cannot generally be determined without expert witnesses.[25]

Only rights to payment or rights to payment on account of breach of performance can be estimated. If the government is seeking performance or compliance and not payment, the government is likely to contend that such obligations are not monetary claims or rights to payment and therefore not subject to estimation. Indeed, compliance obligations are not even matters before the bankruptcy court unless the government has sought injunctive relief through an adversary proceeding in bankruptcy court.[26] However, if the government objects to the feasibility of a plan or contends that a plan is forbidden by law with respect to the reorganized debtor's ability to meet its environmental compliance obligations, the bankruptcy court may need to "estimate" the cost of compliance, solely for the purpose of confirmation of the plan.[27] Likewise, some courts have expressed doubt as to whether estimation under Section 502 of the Bankruptcy Code applies to applications for administrative expenses under Section 503 of the

---

23. *Mazzeo*, 131 F.3d at 303–05. A debt is liquidated if there is an objective method, such as an agreement or operation of law, for calculating the amount of the debt if liability is found. *Id.* at 304–05; *United States v. Verdunn*, 89 F.3d 799, 802–03 (11th Cir. 1996).

24. *See In re Continental Airlines, Inc.*, 981 F.2d 1450, 1461 (5th Cir. 1993) (claim estimation is inappropriate for claims that are not contingent or unliquidated); *In re Ford*, 967 F.2d 1047, 1053 (5th Cir. 1993).

25. In *In re Chateaugay Corp.*, 944 F.2d 997, 1006 (2d Cir. 1991), the court rejected the contention that estimation of future costs would violate CERCLA's prohibition against pre-enforcement judicial review under 42 U.S.C. § 9613(h).

26. *See* Chapter 9 (Operating Estate Property) *supra.*

27. *See, e.g., In re Eagle-Picher Holdings, Inc.*, 345 B.R. 860 (Bankr. S.D. Ohio 2006) (estimating environmental liability for purposes of determining whether plan was forbidden by law); *In re MacDonald*, 128 B.R. 161, 164 (Bankr. W.D. Tex. 1991) (tort liability).

Bankruptcy Code, but something similar to estimation may be necessary in order to determine the feasibility of a plan.[28]

Requests for estimation and estimation proceedings are contested matters under Bankruptcy Rule 9014 as discussed earlier.[29] As with other contested matters such as objections to proofs of claim, at the outset, the bankruptcy court will set the parameters for the estimation proceeding, such as the schedule for discovery and the rules and time allotted for a hearing. These rules may be set forth in a case management order. Bankruptcy courts have a fair amount of discretion in managing estimation hearings. While estimation can be "rough and speedy," the rules must comport with the purposes of the Bankruptcy Code and principles of due process.[30] The more complex the claim, the more procedure and the longer the time that should be allotted in order to obtain a reasonably accurate estimation of the claim.[31] If the matter involves risks to public health and safety, additional time may be necessary to ensure that bankruptcy law and environmental law are appropriately harmonized.[32] If the purpose of the estimation is to determine the amount of a claim in connection with voting on a plan of reorganization, then less time and formality might be necessary given the more limited consequences of the estimation.

---

28. *See In re Adelphia Bus. Solutions, Inc.*, 341 B.R. 415, 423 (Bankr. S.D.N.Y. 2003); *In re HNRC Dissolution Co.*, 371 B.R. 210, 233–34 (E.D. Ky. 2007), *aff'd*, 536 F.3d 683 (6th Cir. 2008); *In re Atcall, Inc.*, 284 B.R. 791 (Bankr. E.D. Va. 2002).

29. *See A.H. Robins Co. v. Piccinin*, 788 F.2d 994, 1011 (4th Cir. 1986).

30. *Chateaugay*, 944 F.2d at 1006; *Bittner v. Borne Chem. Co.*, 691 F.2d 134, 135 (3d Cir. 1982); *In re Brints Cotton Mktg., Inc.*, 737 F.2d 1338, 1341 (5th Cir. 1984); *In re Eagle Bus Mfg., Inc.*, 158 B.R. 421, 437 (D. Tex. 1993). Due process considerations apply to bankruptcy proceedings, including with respect to governmental agencies. *See City of New York v. New York, New Haven & Hartford R.R. Co.*, 344 U.S. 293, 297 (1953); *United States v. Cardinal Mine Supply, Inc.*, 916 F.2d 1087, 1089–92 (6th Cir. 1990); *In re Farmland Indus., Inc.*, 284 B.R. 111, 116–17 (Bankr. W.D. Mo. 2002); *MacDonald*, 128 B.R. at 166. The essence of due process is the right to be heard "at a meaningful time and in a meaningful manner." *Mathews v. Eldridge*, 424 U.S. 319, 333 (1976).

31. *See Bittner*, 691 F.2d at 135; *Brints*, 737 F.2d at 1341; *In re Avaya Inc.*, 602 B.R. 445, 453 (Bankr. S.D.N.Y. 2019); *Owens Corning v. Credit Suisse First Boston*, 322 B.R. 719, 721–22 (D. Del. 2005); *In re Wallace's Bookstores, Inc.*, 317 B.R. 720, 725 (Bankr. D. Ky. 2004); *In re Dow Corning Corp.*, 211 B.R. 545, 563 (E.D. Mich. 1997); *In re The Bible Speaks*, 65 B.R. 415, 417 (D. Mass. 1986).

32. *See* Chapter 16 (Plan Objections) *supra*.

In the *Asarco* bankruptcy, which involved complex environmental liabilities for more than 50 sites across the country, the debtors initially sought a mere eight hours for an estimation hearing for purposes of allowance to determine what eventually turned out to be over $1.7 billion in environmental liabilities.[33] Outside of bankruptcy, these environmental liabilities and related costs would have been determined over years or even decades. The United States and several states objected to debtors' proposal and after argument, the bankruptcy court entered a case management order, which provided for bands of separate estimation hearings with five days provided for each of the largest sites.[34] Competent evidence is required even in summary or truncated trials.[35]

As discussed earlier with respect to claims objections, a claim must be estimated based on applicable nonbankruptcy law, except for the limited circumstances where Section 502 provides a special basis under bankruptcy law for objection to a claim.[36] Environmental estimation hearings will frequently involve the testimony of expert witnesses concerning the cost of future required work. The government will generally contend that the bankruptcy court and experts should defer to agency decisions as to the scope of cleanup that will be required.[37] As discussed earlier, the government may

33. *See In re Asarco LLC*, 2009 WL 8176641, at 3, ¶ 14 (Bankr. S.D. Tex. June 5, 2009).

34. *In re Asarco LLC*, Docket No. 4328 (3/23/2007); *Asarco*, 2009 WL 8176641, at 5, ¶ 21 (noting that 13 days of estimation hearings were held before settlement was reached). The case management order also required mediation, which resulted in settlements that avoided the need for an estimation hearing for several sites.

35. *See MacDonald*, 128 B.R. at 166.

36. *See AL Tech Specialty Steel Corp. v. Allegheny Int'l Credit Corp.*, 104 F.3d 601 (3d Cir. 1997); *Bittner*, 691 F.2d at 135; *In re Federal-Mogul Global, Inc.*, 330 B.R. 133, 155 (D. Del. 2005); note 12 *supra*.

37. Where the government has already selected the cleanup action (which may include estimates of its cost), the court is likely to defer to the government's position since nonbankruptcy law requires such deference unless the government's position is arbitrary and capricious or not in accordance with law as determined based on the administrative record. *See* 42 U.S.C. § 9613(j)(2); *United States v. Akzo Coatings of Am., Inc.*, 949 F.2d 1409, 1423 (6th Cir. 1991); *Fairchild Holding Corp. v. Revere Copper & Brass Inc.*, 291 B.R. 29 (S.D.N.Y. 2003); *In re Eagle-Picher Indus.*, 197 B.R. 260, 269 (Bankr. S.D. Ohio 1996). Where a response action has not yet been selected, the government will still argue that deference should be given to the government's own prediction as to what it will do in the future, but debtors will argue for less deference to what it may characterize as a position in litigation. *See generally* Joel M. Gross & Suzanne LaCampagne, *Bankruptcy Estimation of CERCLA Claims:*

contend that estimation must be based on applicable principles of joint and several liability that apply under many environmental laws.[38] The bankruptcy court will need to decide whether to base its estimation on: (1) the expected cost of the most likely outcome or (2) the weighted or probabilistic cost based on the percentage likelihood of different remedies that might be selected or the degree of contamination that may ultimately be discovered.[39]

As noted earlier, estimation can be employed for different purposes depending on the needs of a case.[40] Estimation is often used to determine an estimated value of a claim for purposes of voting on a plan with allowance of the claim to be determined at a later date.[41] Estimation may be needed in connection with a determination of the feasibility of a plan or whether it is forbidden by law.[42]

In addition, estimation may be employed for purposes of claim allowance and distribution if waiting for claim resolution by traditional means would unduly delay the administration of the bankruptcy case.[43] Indeed, Section 502(c) of the Bankruptcy Code

---

The Process and the Alternative, 12 VA. ENV'T. L.J. 235 (1993); David Williams, Laurence Kirsch & Elizabeth Van Horn, *A Whole New Ball Game: Judicial Review and Estimation of CERCLA Claims in Bankruptcy*, 22 ENV'T. L. REP. 10,785 (1992).

38. *See In re Nat'l Gypsum Co.*, 139 B.R. 397, 415 (N.D. Tex. 1992) (CERCLA claims must be estimated under the usual rules under CERCLA governing joint and several liability and divisibility); *In re Ford*, 125 B.R. 735, 738 (E.D. Tex. 1991) (bank entitled to joint and several liability), *aff'd*, 967 F.2d 1047 (5th Cir. 1992).

39. *See, e.g.*, *In re POC Properties, LLC*, 580 B.R. 504, 510 (Bankr. E.D. Wis. 2017) (noting two approaches); *In re Tronox Inc.*, 503 B.R. 239, 312 (Bankr. S.D.N.Y. 2013) (describing two approaches); *In re FV Steel & Wire Co.*, 372 B.R. 446 (Bankr. E.D. Wis. 2007) (considering probability of contingency); *In re Thomson McKinnon Securities, Inc.*, 191 B.R. 976, 990 (Bankr. S.D.N.Y. 1996); *In re Windsor Plumbing Supply Co.*, 170 B.R. 503, 517–18, 536–37 (Bankr. E.D.N.Y. 1994) (using probabilistic approach); *In re Farley, Inc.*, 146 B.R. 748, 753–54 (Bankr. N.D. Ill. 1992) (same). For discussions of methods for estimating claims, *see* Brehn, Copas & Vossler, *supra* note 20, at 248–56; David S. Salsbury & Jack F. Williams, *A Statistical Approach to Claims Estimation in Bankruptcy*, 32 WAKE FOREST L. REV. 1119 (1997).

40. *See In re North Am. Health Care, Inc.*, 544 B.R. 684, 689 (Bankr. C.D. Cal. 2016); *In re Roman Catholic Archbishop of Portland in Oregon*, 339 B.R. 215 (Bankr. D. Ore. 2006); Brehn, Copas & Vosler, *supra* note 20, at 244–48.

41. *See, e.g.*, *In re Chateaugay Corp.*, 944 F.2d 997, 1006 (2d Cir. 1991); *In re Trident Shipworks, Inc.*, 247 B.R. 513 (Bankr. M.D. Fla. 2000).

42. *See, e.g.*, *In re MacDonald*, 128 B.R. 161, 164 (Bankr. W.D. Tex. 1991).

43. *See In re Asarco LLC*, 2009 WL 8176641 at *4–5 (Bankr. S.D. Tex. June 5, 2009); *In re Poole Funeral Chapel, Inc.*, 63 B.R. 527, 533 (Bankr. N.D. Ala. 1986). It should be noted that bankruptcy courts' jurisdiction over personal injury tort claims (in contrast to environmental claims of the government) is limited. *See* 28 U.S.C.

expressly states that claims may be estimated for purposes of allowance.[44] Examples of estimations of environmental claims may be found in the *Eagle-Picher*, *Allegheny*, *FV Steel*, and *Kaiser* bankruptcies.[45] The bankruptcy court similarly held several extensive estimation hearings in *Asarco*; however, settlements were reached in each instance prior to any court ruling.[46]

Section 502(j) of the Bankruptcy Code provides that claims that have been allowed or disallowed after estimation under Section 502 may be "reconsidered for cause [and] allowed or disallowed according to the equities of the case."[47] Courts have interpreted this section to have similar meaning to Rule 60(b) of the Federal Rules of Civil Procedure.[48] Until distributions to creditors have been actually made, allowed or disallowed claims based on an estimation may be potentially submitted for reconsideration under Section 502(j), if, for instance, there is newly discovered evidence emerging after the estimation.[49] After distribution, the prejudice to other creditors would make reconsideration much more difficult given the need for finality in claims administration.[50]

Where additional information is likely to emerge in the not too distant future, plans can address uncertainties by providing for reserves to deal with the possibility of higher liability based

---

§ 157(b)(2)(B). Therefore, cases discussing estimation of personal injury tort claims by bankruptcy courts for purposes of allowance and distribution have unique considerations that need to be taken into account.

44. The predecessor to the Bankruptcy Code, the Bankruptcy Act of 1988, did not provide for the allowance of unprovable future claims. Section 502(c) was meant to protect creditors whose claims cannot be definitively proven until a later date. *See In re Hemingway Transp., Inc.*, 954 F.2d 1, 8 (1st Cir. 1992).

45. *U.S. Bank Nat'l Assoc. v. United States Env't Prot. Agency*, 563 F.3d 199 (6th Cir. 2009); *In re Eagle-Picher Holdings, Inc.*, 345 B.R. 860 (Bankr. S.D. Ohio 2006); *AL Tech Specialty Steel Corp. v. Allegheny Int'l Credit Corp.*, 104 F.3d 601 (3d Cir. 1997); *In re FV Steel & Wire Co.*, 372 B.R. 446 (Bankr. E.D. 2007); *In re Kaiser Group Int'l, Inc.*, 289 B.R. 597 (Bankr. D. Del. 2003).

46. *See In re Asarco LLC*, 2009 WL 8176641 (Bankr. S.D. Tex. June 5, 2009).

47. 11 U.S.C. § 502(j).

48. *See, e.g., In re Int'l Yacht & Tennis, Inc.*, 922 F.2d 659, 662 (11th Cir. 1991); *In re Colley*, 814 F.2d 1008, 1010 (5th Cir. 1987); *In re FairPoint Commc'ns, Inc.*, 462 B.R. 75, 79 (Bankr. S.D.N.Y. 2012); *In re H.K. Porter Co.*, 156 B.R. 149, 150 (Bankr. W.D. Pa. 1993). Under Bankruptcy Rule 9024, the one-year limitation of Rule 60(b) does not apply to claims that have been allowed or disallowed "without a contest."

49. *See* Fed. R. Civ. P. 60(b)(1), (2).

50. *See, e.g., Colley*, 814 F.2d at 1010; *In re Clark*, 172 B.R. 701, 705 (Bankr. S.D. Ga. 1994).

on newly-emerging facts or resolution of future litigation. Debtors have attempted to use Section 502(c) of the Bankruptcy Code to estimate a cap on recovery for purposes of establishing a reserve. In this circumstance, the government is likely to seek that the reserve be set at a high-end cap based on an amount that is likely not to be exceeded. Otherwise, the government may object to such an estimation as unfair discrimination among similar claims since undisputed claims might end up being paid on average more than its disputed claims, which is contrary to the Bankruptcy Code's requirement of similar treatment.[51] Requiring the government to run through a gauntlet of evidentiary hearings (such as a hearing to establish a cap, a hearing to determine the final allowed amount, and/or multiple hearings on separate grounds for objection) in order to get an allowed claim may also be objected to as inequitable and contrary to finality in claims administration. Furthermore, in some situations the government may want to seek estimation of its claims for purposes of allowance or reserve so that it can share in recovery at the same time as other creditors and avoid the risk of recovering less than other creditors (on account of early payouts or inadequate reserves) or the risk of a future bankruptcy.

Where estimation of an environmental claim would require substantial and material application of nonbankruptcy law (as opposed to routine application) or where bankruptcy law and environmental law are in conflict, the government may seek withdrawal of the reference.[52] Withdrawal of the reference means that the original automatic reference of the bankruptcy case from the district court to the bankruptcy court is withdrawn with respect to a particular matter and returned to the district court for resolution; withdrawal of the reference is discussed in more detail in Chapter 20 (Jurisdiction). In particular, if a debtor is seeking estimation of a compliance liability that the government contends is not a monetary claim, considerable interpretation of bankruptcy law and environmental law and the intersection thereof may require withdrawal of the reference.[53]

---

51. *In re Mcorp Fin., Inc.*, 137 B.R. 219, 225, 227 (Bankr. S.D. Tex. 1992).

52. *See* 28 U.S.C. § 157(d); *In re Dana Corp.*, 379 B.R. 449 (S.D.N.Y. 2007) (withdrawing the reference for estimation of environmental proofs of claim that raised issues of divisibility and joint and several liability).

53. *See United States v. Delfasco, Inc.*, 409 B.R. 704 (D. Del. 2009).

CHAPTER 18

Abandonment of Contaminated Property in Bankruptcy

Chapter 18 considers the use of the abandonment power in bankruptcy, especially in the context of contaminated real property.[1] It discusses the relevant Bankruptcy Code provision governing abandonment, how that provision has been interpreted by the courts, and how debtors have used the abandonment power from a practical perspective.

As discussed previously in this Practice Guide, the Bankruptcy Code is designed to provide a debtor with a fresh start.[2] One way a debtor obtains that fresh start is to free the estate of unwanted property that is draining limited resources from the estate. Thus, among the various mechanisms in the Bankruptcy Code designed to provide a fresh start is a provision, Section 554 of the Bankruptcy Code, which permits a debtor to abandon property in certain circumstances.

However, in the environmental context, the power to abandon property under bankruptcy law can be in direct conflict with

---

1. Similar issues may arise with respect to a debtor's attempt to abandon chemicals, drums of waste, or other contaminated personal property.

2. *See* Chapter 2 (History and Purposes) *supra*.

environmental laws protecting public health and safety.[3] The concept of abandoning contaminated property therefore raises difficult questions as to how to harmonize the dual goals of bankruptcy law and environmental law. Harmonization of these laws, in turn, has important ramifications as to how compliance and remediation obligations will be addressed (and by whom), and whether estate resources should be employed to remediate property that a debtor would like to abandon.[4]

ABANDONMENT UNDER THE BANKRUPTCY CODE

Under the Bankruptcy Code, a trustee or debtor-in-possession[5] is permitted, after notice and opportunity for hearing, to abandon unprofitable burdensome assets that have inconsequential value. The specific provision in the Code, Section 554(a), provides that:

> After notice and a hearing, the trustee may abandon any property of the estate that is burdensome to the estate or that is of inconsequential value and benefit to the estate.[6]

Pursuant to this provision, the requirement for notice and a hearing can be met if notice has been given (in the form of notice to the U.S. trustee, creditors and committees pursuant to Bankruptcy Rule 6007(a))[7] and a hearing has been held or the opportunity

---

3. In some circumstances, abandonment of a hazardous substance constitutes a "release," which is prohibited under environmental law. *See Commonwealth of Pennsylvania, Dep't of Env't Res. v. Conroy*, 24 F.3d 568, 569 (3d Cir. 1994) (citing Pennsylvania law stating that abandonment is a release that is prohibited).

4. *See* Chapter 8 (Harmonization) *supra*.

5. Debtors-in-possession have the same rights as trustees to abandon estate property. *See* 11 U.S.C. § 1107(a), which provides that a "debtor-in-possession shall have all the rights . . . and powers, and shall perform all the functions and duties . . . of a trustee serving in a case under this chapter." For purposes of this chapter of the Practice Guide, the debtor-in-possession is referred to as the debtor unless otherwise indicated. *See also* Chapter 3 (Code Chapters) *supra* (discussing debtor-in-possession).

6. 11 U.S.C. § 554(a).

7. *See* Fed. R. Bankr. P. 6007, Abandonment or Disposition of Property. Rule 6007(a) provides interested parties with an opportunity to object within 14 days of mailing or such other time set by the court.

for one has been provided.[8] If the motion to abandon is opposed by any interested parties, then the bankruptcy court will need to approve the motion to abandon after a hearing in order for the trustee or debtor to proceed with abandoning the property. However, if the motion is unopposed, then the abandonment may be approved by the bankruptcy court without a hearing.[9]

While a literal reading of Section 554 appears to provide the trustee or debtor with an unconditional right to seek approval of abandonment of unwanted property without value, this power to abandon property is not in fact unqualified. As discussed later, the Supreme Court determined early on in *Midlantic National Bank* that Section 554, like prior bankruptcy law on abandonment, does not provide an unqualified power to abandon in violation of nonbankruptcy law.[10] *Midlantic* and subsequent decisions are the fruition of the courts' attempt to harmonize environmental law and bankruptcy law by filling in the details of the concept of abandonment that the Code adopted from pre-Code practice but without further elaboration.[11] The parameters courts consider when evaluating a motion to abandon contaminated estate property vary from circuit to circuit; therefore, when evaluating the merits of a

---

8. The term "after notice and a hearing". . . "(A) means after such notice as is appropriate in the particular circumstances, and such opportunity for a hearing as is appropriate in the particular circumstances; but (B) authorizes an act without an actual hearing if such notice is given properly and if—(i) such a hearing is not requested timely by a party in interest; or (ii) there is insufficient time for a hearing to be commenced before such act must be done, and the court authorizes such act." 11 U.S.C. § 102(1). Some debtors file motions for special procedures for the sale or abandonment of de minimis assets when there are numerous properties or assets with little value. Such motions provide a process for debtors to abandon such properties without an individual court hearing each time. However, a corollary to this is that there may not be individual notice to interested governmental agencies. Therefore, governmental agencies should monitor such cases closely. Debtors generally agree to provide such notice if the government will otherwise object to such motions. If an agency has not entered an appearance and request for notices, it will need to monitor the court's docket regularly for such motions.

9. There may be situations where local bankruptcy court rules or notices for meetings of creditors (discussed in Chapter 4 (Timeline) of this Practice Guide) provide alternative processes for abandonment of property. Interested parties should be alert to such situations and object as necessary.

10. *Midlantic Nat'l Bank v. New Jersey Dep't of Env't Prot.*, 474 U.S. 494, 501 (1986).

11. *See Hartford Underwriters v. Union Planters*, 530 U.S. 1, 11 (2000) (*Midlantic* "used prior practice to fill in the details of a pre-Code concept that the Code had adopted without elaboration.").

motion, it is important to closely review the relevant case law in the applicable circuit. As discussed later in this chapter, parties in interest should also consider: (1) the government's position that abandonment of property does not result in abandonment of liability, and (2) the fact that abandoned property in corporate bankruptcy cases reverts from the debtor's estate to the corporate shell of the debtor, which may create an impediment to plan confirmation proceedings.

SUPREME COURT'S MIDLANTIC RULING AND ITS IMPACT ON ABANDONMENT

Midlantic is the seminal case concerning environmental considerations with respect to abandonment rights. In that case, an oil-waste processor sought to abandon its two facilities, one in New York and one in New Jersey. Both facilities contained deteriorating and leaking containers of toxic, PCB-contaminated oil as well as contaminated soil that presented risks of explosion, fire, injury, and death.[12] The trustee alleged that the property was "burdensome" and of "inconsequential value to the estate" pursuant to Section 554 of the Bankruptcy Code.[13] Both states objected to the proposed abandonment, but the bankruptcy court nevertheless approved abandonment without requiring the trustee to take even relatively minor steps to reduce imminent danger, such as fencing, drainage, diking repairs, sealing deteriorating tanks, removing explosive agents, and security measures.[14] The Supreme Court disagreed. Recognizing that Congress did not intend a bankruptcy trustee to have "carte blanche to ignore nonbankruptcy law," the Court explained that:

> The bankruptcy court does not have the power to authorize abandonment without formulating conditions that will adequately protect the public's health and safety. . . . [A] trustee may not abandon property in contravention of a state statute or regulation

12. *Midlantic*, 474 U.S. at 497–98.
13. *Id.* at 497.
14. *Id.* at 497–99 & 499 n.3.

> that is reasonably designed to protect the public health or safety from identified hazards.[15]

Thus, *Midlantic* provides that public health and safety laws and regulations must be taken into account in any proposed abandonment of contaminated property. However, the *Midlantic* decision also contained a footnote, sometimes referred to as footnote 9, which qualified the scope and impact of its ruling:

> This exception to the abandonment power vested in the trustee by 554 is a narrow one. It does not encompass a speculative or indeterminate future violation of such laws that may stem from abandonment. The abandonment power is not to be fettered by laws or regulations not reasonably calculated to protect the public health or safety from imminent and identifiable harm.[16]

This footnote was intended to clarify when abandonment is permitted, though in practice, it has led to differing interpretations of the limits on the power of abandonment, as discussed later.

The legal underpinning of the Supreme Court's ruling was that, prior to the revisions to the Bankruptcy Code in 1978, it was well established that a trustee could not abandon property in violation of federal or state law or where doing so would threaten the public interest.[17] The Court held that where such a rule was so well established, Congress would need to clearly express its intent to override it.[18] Here, the Court found that Congress had not done so and therefore Congress had not provided for "a right to abandon property in contravention of state or local laws designed to

15. *Id.* at 506–07.

16. *Id.* at 507 n.9.

17. The Court cited to *Ottenheimer v. Whitaker*, 198 F.2d 289 (4th Cir. 1952) (barges could not be abandoned when abandonment would obstruct a navigable passage in violation of federal law); *In re Chicago Rapid Transit Co.*, 129 F.2d 1 (7th Cir. 1942) (abandonment of operation of railway had to comply with state law); *In re Lewis Jones, Inc.*, 1 Bankr. Ct. Dec. 277 (Bankr. E.D. Pa. 1974) (public utilities had to seal underground steam lines before abandoning them). *Midlantic*, 474 U.S. at 500–01.

18. The Supreme Court has applied this principle of statutory interpretation on numerous occasions in other bankruptcy law contexts, which are summarized in *In re Ultra Petroleum Corp.*, 51 F.4th 138, 153–56 (5th Cir. 2022) ("the good textualist is not a literalist") (quoting Antonin Scalia, *Common-Law Courts in a Civil-Law System: The Role of United States Federal Courts in Interpreting the Constitution and Laws*, *in* A Matter of Interpretation: Federal Courts and the Law 3, 24 (new ed. 2018)).

protect public health or safety."[19] To the contrary, the Court noted that "Congress has repeatedly expressed its legislative determination that the trustee is not to have *carte blanche* to ignore nonbankruptcy law."[20] Although *Midlantic* was a 5–4 decision, the Supreme Court has cited it more than a dozen times as a guidepost for interpreting the Bankruptcy Code.[21]

INTERPRETATION IN SUBSEQUENT CASES

Two lines of cases have emerged in interpreting and applying *Midlantic*.[22] One line of cases, favored by governmental agencies, focuses primarily on the environmental statutes or regulations at issue as opposed to the conditions at a particular site. These cases rely on the Court's references to statutes "reasonably designed to protect the public health or safety" and laws or regulations "reasonably calculated to protect the public health or safety from imminent and identifiable harm." Thus, they look more generally at the laws at issue and their purposes, as opposed to the specific risks posed by a particular site, and require full compliance with such laws. Three courts of appeal (the Third, Fifth, and Sixth Circuits) have endorsed this approach.[23]

---

19. *Midlantic*, 474 U.S. at 502.

20. *Id.* Although *Midlantic* involved state environmental laws, the court's reasoning applies to federal environmental laws as well. The court cited to federal environmental laws, *id.* at 505–06 (citing RCRA and CERCLA), and said that "nonbankruptcy law" could not be ignored, *id.* at 502. At least two courts have held that *Midlantic* precludes abandonment that would contravene federal laws designed to protect public health and safety. *In re St. Lawrence Corp.*, 248 B.R. 734, 739 (D.N.J. 2000); *In re Peerless Plating Co.*, 70 B.R. 943, 948 & n.4 (Bankr. W.D. Mich. 1987). As discussed in Chapter 8 (Harmonization) *supra*, the technical analysis when federal statutes are involved is one of harmonization; preemption analysis applies when state statutes are involved.

21. Ronald J. Mann, *Balancing Bankruptcy and Environmental Law: Midlantic National Bank v. New Jersey Department of Environmental Protection,* 42 J. S. Ct. History 101, 115 (Mar. 2017).

22. *See* Brent Bolea, *Bankruptcy Abandonment Power and Environmental Liability*, 106 Com. L.J. 83, 97–102 (2001); *In re Eagle-Picher Holdings, Inc.*, 345 B.R. 860, 862 (Bankr. S.D. Ohio 2006).

23. *In re H.L.S. Energy Co.*, 151 F.3d 434, 438 (5th Cir. 1998); *Commonwealth of Pennsylvania Dep't of Env't Res. v. Conroy*, 24 F.3d 568, 569 (3d Cir. 1994); *In re Wall Tube & Metal Prods.*, 831 F.2d 118, 120 (6th Cir. 1987) (under *Midlantic* abandonment

A second line of cases, favored by debtors, focuses on the specific language of footnote 9 that the exception to permissible abandonment does not extend to "speculative or indeterminate future violations . . . that may stem from abandonment" or laws not calculated to protect against "imminent and identifiable" harm. These cases focus primarily on the conditions on the ground at a particular site and have condensed the *Midlantic* ruling into whether risks are speculative as opposed to imminent and identifiable. The decisions of two courts of appeal (the Fourth and Tenth Circuits) and numerous lower courts are more in line with this approach.[24] Two courts adopting this approach have created multifactor tests for deciding the abandonment issue.[25]

---

is not permitted where a continuing violation of state environmental laws would occur); *see also In re Am. Coastal Energy Inc.*, 399 B.R. 805, 813 (Bankr. S.D. Tex. 2009) ("The Court reads the Supreme Court's *Midlantic* opinion to require the Court to determine whether the debtor is violating a statute 'reasonably designed to protect the public health or safety from identified hazards,' not the extent to which particular conduct imposes actual and imminent threats."); *In re Witt*, 473 B.R. 284 (Bankr. N.D. Ind. 2012); *In re Insilco Techs., Inc.*, 309 B.R. 111, 114 (Bankr. D. Del. 2004); *In re Guterl Special Steel Corp.*, 198 B.R. 128, 134–35 (W.D. Pa. 1996); *Peerless Plating Co.*, 70 B.R. at 946–47; *In re Stevens*, 68 B.R. 774, 783–84 (D. Maine 1987).

24. *In re L.F. Jennings Oil Co.*, 4 F.3d 887, 890 (10th Cir. 1993) (former gas station site "did not pose an immediate threat to public health or safety" and only violation of state law was failure to file reports); *In re Smith-Douglass*, 856 F.2d 12, 17 (4th Cir. 1988) (affirming lower courts' grant of unconditional abandonment of contaminated fertilizer plant in "absence of serious public health and safety risks" and lack of unencumbered assets); *Leavell v. Karnes*, 143 B.R. 212, 218 (S.D. Ill. 1990); *In re Venoco, LLC*, 572 B.R. 105, 114–15 (Bankr. D. Del. 2017); *In re Howard*, 533 B.R. 532, 545–47 (Bankr. S.D. Miss. 2015); *In re Unidigital, Inc.*, 262 B.R. 283, 286 (Bankr. D. Del. 2001); *In re S. Int'l Co.*, 165 B.R. 815 (Bankr. E.D. Va. 1994); *In re Sheffield Oil Co.*, 162 B.R. 339 (Bankr. M.D. Ala. 1993); *In re H.F. Radandt, Inc.*, 160 B.R. 323 (Bankr. W.D. Wis. 1993); *In re MCI, Inc.*, 151 B.R. 103 (E.D. Mich. 1992); *In re Shore Co.*, 134 B.R. 572, 578, 580 (Bankr. E.D. Tex. 1991); *In re Better Brite Plating, Inc.*, 105 B.R. 912 (Bankr. E.D. Wis. 1989); *N.J. Dep't of Env't Prot. v. N. Am. Prods. Acquisition Corp.*, 137 B.R. 8, 12 (D.N.J. 1992) (looks to whether abandonment will aggravate threat of harm or create additional harm); *In re Anthony Ferrante & Sons, Inc.*, 119 B.R. 45 (D.N.J. 1990); *In re Oklahoma Ref. Co.*, 63 B.R. 562 (Bankr. W.D. Okla. 1986).

25. *See St. Lawrence Corp.*, 248 B.R. at 739 (establishing a four-factor test, whether: (1) an identified hazard existed that posed a risk of imminent and identifiable harm to the public health and safety; (2) abandonment of the property would violate a state statute or regulation; (3) the statute or regulation being violated was reasonably designed to protect the public health and safety from imminent and identifiable harm caused by identified hazards; and (4) compliance with the statute or regulation would not be so onerous as to interfere with the bankruptcy administration itself); *In re Franklin Signal Corp.*, 65 B.R. 268, 272 (Bankr. D. Minn. 1986) (establishing a five-factor test: (1) the imminence of danger to public health

Many of the courts applying this approach have cited government delays or inaction as evidence supporting a conclusion that there is no threat of imminent and identifiable harm.[26] This reasoning seems questionable given the limited resources of governmental agencies. Many reasons, including competing priorities, may explain governmental delay or inaction. For that reason, governmental agencies are not subject to laches contentions with respect to enforcing the public interest.[27] By the same reasoning, the public should not have to bear the brunt of potential harms caused by such sites merely because there is inadequate evidence of the imminence of threats of identifiable harm. The government, in fact, may have been unaware of the scope of the threats posed or may not have the resources to deal with such threats.

Midlantic and its progeny are examples of courts' attempts to harmonize bankruptcy law and environmental law. Indeed, the entire raison d'etre of *Midlantic* was the need to harmonize bankruptcy law on abandonment with applicable nonbankruptcy law.[28] As recounted in a book and article by Professor Mann, Justice Stevens' pivotal role in deciding the outcome focused on the need to harmonize the two bodies of law.[29] The key language summarized in the preceding discussion was a result of those efforts.[30] As noted in Chapter 8 (Harmonization) of this Practice Guide, the rules for harmonization of conflicting statutes try to give maximum effect to both bodies of law unless there is clear direction for one to prevail. In particular, federal law is presumed not to preempt state

---

and safety; (2) the extent of probable harm; (3) the amount and type of waste; (4) the cost to attain compliance; and (5) the amount and type of funds available for cleanup).

26. *See, e.g.*, *Smith-Douglass*, 856 F.2d at 16; *Jennings*, 4 F.3d at 890–91; *Eagle-Picher*, 345 B.R. at 862, 863; *St. Lawrence*, 248 B.R. at 742; *Ferrante & Sons, Inc.*, 119 B.R. at 50.

27. *See, e.g.*, *United States v. Summerlin*, 310 U.S. 414, 416 (1940); *Utah Power & Light Co. v. United States*, 243 U.S. 389, 409 (1917); *United States v. Johnson*, 920 F.3d 639, 644 (10th Cir. 2019); *United States v. Mandycz*, 447 F.3d 951, 964 (6th Cir. 2006); *United States v. Peoples Household Furnishings, Inc.*, 75 F.3d 252 (6th Cir. 1996); *United States v. Ruby Co.*, 588 F.2d 697, 705 n.10 (9th Cir. 1978).

28. *Midlantic*, 474 U.S. at 501.

29. Mann, *supra* note 21, at 112–15; Ronald J. Mann, Bankruptcy and the Supreme Court 125–45 (2017).

30. Mann, *supra* note 21, at 113–14.

police power laws unless Congress has clearly and manifestly so provided.[31]

The Supreme Court in *Midlantic* provided a path to achieve harmonization when it held that the bankruptcy courts simply did not have the power to authorize abandonment without formulating conditions protective of public health and safety. Accordingly, courts have sometimes permitted abandonment where certain conditions have been met. An example of such a condition is a requirement to place funds in a separate account to cover the costs of investigation and remediation. For example, in *In re FCX, Inc.*,[32] a liquidating debtor was required to set aside funds to cover the cost of cleanup of pesticides that had been buried on-site and were considered an immediate threat to the health of those living nearby even though the harm might not manifest for several years.[33] In that case, abandonment was allowed to proceed provided that the funding condition was met. Another factor courts have utilized in the harmonization process is the extent of unencumbered assets in the estate that are available for remediation or other protective measures.[34]

In other instances, conditions are set forth in stipulations or settlement agreements where the government consents to abandonment by the debtor as long as those conditions are met, such as the debtor or trustee taking specific protective actions or providing funding for such actions. For example, in the *Outboard Marine* case, abandonment was agreed to in order to limit the estate's carrying costs. In return, the trustee agreed to several conditions including, inter alia, to remove and dispose of drums and tanks, drain and flush transformers and machines, and provide

31. *See* Chapter 8 (Harmonization) *supra*.

32. *In re FCX, Inc.*, 96 B.R. 49 (Bankr. E.D. N.C. 1989).

33. *Id.* at 55 ("[T]he danger is immediate in the sense that there is a *present* and real possibility of public exposure to those deadly substances if they are not removed.").

34. *See Smith-Douglass*, 856 F.2d at 17 ("where the estate has unencumbered assets, the bankruptcy court should require stricter compliance with state environmental law before abandonment is permitted"); *MCI*, 151 B.R. at 109; *Better Brite*, 105 B.R. at 919. If the debtor's assets are encumbered, secured creditors may contend their rights as a secured creditor take precedence. *See* Chapter 12 (Priorities) *supra* (discussing uncertainty about where environmental compliance obligations fit into bankruptcy priorities).

funding for pipe cleanup or similar work.[35] Such agreements also provide the government with a right of access, which is important because after an abandonment there may not be an available person to consent to access. Such agreements sometimes also have provisions that any abandonment is without prejudice to all parties' contentions with respect to injunctive relief or administrative expense priority, which is important because, as discussed in more detail in Chapter 12 (Priorities) of this Practice Guide, the handling of injunctive relief or administrative expense priority issues can then be addressed at a later time so as to avoid delaying the actual abandonment action.[36]

Another example is the recent *Exide* case, a Chapter 11 liquidation case filed in Delaware bankruptcy court.[37] The debtor, a lead recycling company, sought to abandon 17 properties in 11 states and liquidate. With the help of a team of five mediators, the debtor and governmental agencies negotiated a settlement for most of the sites whereby abandonment was avoided by the creation of an environmental response trust that would take title to 16 of the 17 properties and receive at least $31 million in funding from surety bond proceeds and other funding.[38] Initially, governmental agencies, including an environmental agency from California, had agreed to recommend and pursue approval of a global settlement, which would have included all 17 properties including a heavily contaminated site in Vernon, California.[39] When approval was not

35. *See In re Outboard Marine Corp.*, No. 00-37405 (Bankr. N.D. Ill.).

36. Debtors or trustees may agree to such language in order to avoid carrying costs on property to be abandoned during the bankruptcy case. As discussed later, governments generally take the position that abandonment under the Bankruptcy Code means abandonment of property and not abandonment of liability. In some situations, debtors or trustees may be willing to defer that issue to later in the case. For example, the estate may have few assets or the estate's assets may be largely encumbered and the debtor or trustee may be willing to take its chances in later contending that encumbered assets must be paid to secured creditors rather than used for cleanup. *See* further discussion in Chapter 12 (Priorities) *supra*.

37. *In re Exide Holdings, Inc.*, No. 20-11157 (Bankr. D. Del.).

38. Although this funding may not have been sufficient for full cleanups, the governmental agencies faced litigation risks given the debtor's poor financial situation, lack of unencumbered assets, and the narrow interpretation of *Midlantic* by the Delaware bankruptcy court.

39. *See In re Exide Holdings, Inc.*, 2021 WL 3145612, at *2 (D. Del. July 26, 2021) ("All government agencies, including DTSC, agreed to recommend and pursue approval of the global settlement.").

obtained for the California agency,[40] the debtor provided in its plan for either a similar environmental response trust for only the California property or abandonment together with at least $29 million in financial assurance and settlement funds for cleanup of that property. The bankruptcy court overruled the California agency's objection to the plan and found that the available funding was sufficient to deal with imminent and identifiable threats. The district court thereafter held that the California agency's appeal was moot and that, in any event, the bankruptcy court's finding that *Midlantic* did not require providing for long-term cleanup actions, such as building and foundation removal and an asphalt cap, was not clearly erroneous.[41] In the end, the California agency cooperated with the creation of an environmental response trust for the property and abandonment was thus avoided.[42]

Thus, even under a narrow reading of the *Midlantic* case, debtors have found it difficult to abandon contaminated property because of the uncertainty and litigation risk posed by the legal standard and efforts by governmental agencies and third parties to require debtors to address their contaminated property in order to protect public health and safety. Interested parties may object to abandonment and file parallel actions for injunctive relief (cleanup), which may delay resolution of the bankruptcy case.

Abandonment is particularly difficult in the context of a Chapter 11 plan because of the additional Bankruptcy Code requirements for confirmation of the plan set forth in Section 1129 of the Bankruptcy Code.[43] Section 1129 of the Bankruptcy Code lists a series of requirements that a debtor must satisfy for a court to confirm a plan of reorganization. Some of the grounds for objection, which are discussed in Chapter 16 (Plan Objections) of this Practice Guide, may apply to proposed plans that provide for abandonment of contaminated property or the transfer of contaminated property to entities with inadequate resources (which may be a de

---

40. *Id.* ("On September 15, 2020, DTSC notified Exide that [California] had rejected the global settlement.").

41. *Exide* Holdings, 2021 WL 3145612, at *8–11 (D. Del. July 26, 2021). No appeal was filed in response to the district court's ruling.

42. *Id.* at *4–5, 7.

43. 11 U.S.C. § 1129(a).

facto abandonment). For example, governments may contend that such plans are proposed by means "forbidden by law" if the abandonment would violate environmental law.[44]

Section 1129 also requires that a plan of reorganization is not likely to be followed by liquidation or the need for further reorganization—referred to in bankruptcy parlance as the Bankruptcy Code's "feasibility" requirement.[45] Objectors may contend that a proposed plan of reorganization contemplating abandonment or de facto abandonment will result in an entity without adequate resources to comply with the law and therefore would likely be followed by a future liquidation or further reorganization. This issue is further complicated by the fact that property is normally abandoned by the estate to the corporate shell of the debtor as discussed later in this chapter.[46] However, upon confirmation of a Chapter 11 plan of reorganization the Bankruptcy Code provides that property of the estate vests into the debtor (about to become the reorganized debtor) unless otherwise provided.[47] Following the language of the Bankruptcy Code, that means that abandoned property in the debtor's shell will vest into the reorganized debtor upon confirmation unless the plan provides otherwise. But if the plan of reorganization seeks to provide otherwise, whatever entity will hold the property may lack funding, which may make the plan infeasible, thereby preventing confirmation of the plan. Therefore, debtors will likely weigh the benefit of abandonment against process risks, including objections and the attendant increases in litigation and administrative costs.

Consequently, practically speaking, a Chapter 11 reorganizing debtor is most often unlikely to abandon contaminated property

---

44. *Id.* § 1129(a)(3); *see In re Eagle-Picher Holdings, Inc.*, 345 B.R. 860 (Bankr. S.D. Ohio 2006). Moreover, debtors bear the burden of proof on these issues. *Id.* at 861. *See* Chapter 16 (Plan Objections) *supra*.

45. 11 U.S.C. § 1129(a)(11) provides that a plan must demonstrate by a preponderance of the evidence that confirmation of the plan is not likely to be followed by the liquidation, or the need for further financial reorganization, of the debtor or any successor to the debtor, unless such liquidation or reorganization is proposed in the plan. *See* Chapter 16 (Plan Objections) *supra*.

46. *See* discussion *infra*.

47. 11 U.S.C. § 1141(b).

through the bankruptcy process.[48] As a result, a debtor that owns contaminated property is left in the uncomfortable position of potentially possessing non-core assets that it no longer wants but cannot abandon. This may not be in the interest of the government and public either, as unattended environmental issues may fester if the debtor does not properly address environmental concerns. In such a situation, debtors have sometimes utilized an environmental response trust vehicle, briefly noted in the preceding *Exide* description and discussed in more detail in Chapter 14 (Debtor-Owned Contaminated Property) of this Practice Guide. An environmental response trust can permit a debtor to responsibly address environmental conditions at real properties where there is acceptable funding available, while simultaneously enabling a debtor to either emerge from bankruptcy without the burdensome property or to obtain confirmation of a liquidating plan.

Private parties, as well as debtors in cases with trustees, can have standing to object to abandonment on *Midlantic* grounds if they are impacted by the abandonment.[49] For example, an owner of property may object to an abandonment of a lease, or a predecessor-in-interest of an oil well now owned by the debtor may object to abandonment of the debtor's interest in the well. However, it can be difficult to convince a court that public health and safety is at risk if the government is not asserting that position.[50] In addition, in oil and gas cases, abandonment of a well may trigger liability of the predecessors-in-interest (e.g., prior owners or operators, including lessees), which may result in a court finding that the debtor's limited resources should be dedicated to addressing those wells for which there are no liable parties other than the debtor as opposed to those wells with other liable parties.[51]

48. *See* Anne Lawton & Lynda Oswald, *Scary Stories and the Limited Liability Polluter in Chapter 11*, 65 Wash. & Lee L. Rev. 451, 474–75 (2008) ("abandonment power has been a tool almost exclusively employed by Chapter 7 trustees").

49. *See In re Lyondell Chem. Co.*, 416 B.R. 108 (Bankr. S.D.N.Y. 2009); *Howard*, 533 B.R. at 543–44; Chapter 20 (Jurisdiction) *infra*.

50. *See, e.g.*, *In re ATP Oil & Gas Corp.*, 2013 WL 3157567 (Bankr. S.D. Tex. June 19, 2013).

51. *Id.* at *2 (United States did not oppose abandonment and would presumably pursue predecessors-in-interest).

BURDEN OF PROOF

Governments have a strong argument that the trustee or party moving for abandonment has the burden of proof in demonstrating a prima facie case for the required elements for the relief being sought.[52] Under *Midlantic*, the Supreme Court describes the public health and safety law condition as a mandatory requirement for abandonment:

> The bankruptcy court does not have the power to authorize an abandonment without formulating conditions that will adequately protect the public's health and safety. . . . [A] trustee may not abandon property in contravention of a state statute or regulation that is reasonably designed to protect the public health or safety from identified hazards.[53]

If no evidence is presented on the issue by the trustee or moving party, the bankruptcy court "would not have the power" to authorize the abandonment as it could not make the required finding of conditions protecting public health and safety.[54] Therefore, governments often contend that the trustee or moving party should have the burden of proof to make a prima facie case on this issue.[55]

ABANDONMENT OF PROPERTY DOES NOT MEAN ABANDONMENT OF LIABILITY

Debtors and trustees have sometimes argued that abandonment of contaminated property means that the associated environmental liability is also abandoned. However, Section 554 speaks of

52. *See, e.g., In re Hodges*, 518 B.R. 445, 451 (E.D. Tenn. 2014); *Smoker v. Hill & Assocs., Inc.*, 204 B.R. 966, 975 (N.D. Ind. 1997); *In re Buerge*, 479 B.R. 101, 107 (Bankr. D. Kan. 2012); *In re Winsted Memorial Hospital*, 249 B.R. 588, 595 (Bankr. D. Conn. 2000); *In re DiDario*, 232 B.R. 311, 313 (Bankr. D.N.J. 1999); *In re Dillon*, 219 B.R. 781, 785 (Bankr. M.D. Tenn. 1998); *In re Siegel*, 204 B.R. 6, 8 (Bankr. W.D.N.Y. 1996).

53. 474 U.S. at 506–07.

54. *See Leavell v. Karnes*, 143 B.R. 212, 218 (S.D. Ill, 1990) (remanding for finding).

55. In *St. Lawrence*, the court stated the general rule on burdens of proof and then inexplicably concluded that *Midlantic* created an exception rather than a precondition. *In re St. Lawrence Corp.* 248 B.R. 734, 741 (D.N.J. 2000). Governments may contend that the language reads otherwise.

abandonment of "property," not abandonment of liability. While debtors may no longer be responsible for the carrying costs of a property once they have abandoned it, neither the Bankruptcy Code nor other law relieves debtors of their liability for contamination at such properties. Therefore, a debtor that abandons contaminated property is nevertheless still responsible under environmental laws for liabilities associated with its past ownership or operation of the property.[56] As the court found in *T.P. Long Chemical*, liability under CERCLA's past owner/operator provision would survive any abandonment of drums of hazardous waste.[57] As one commenter has noted, "[b]y its literal terms, section 554(a) speaks only of abandonment of property of the estate, not of the abandonment of liabilities such as those imposed by CERCLA. In fact, abandonment of property will not relieve the owner of liability under CERCLA any more than sale to a third party would."[58] This is analogous to a situation where a debtor causes a car accident and is not absolved from liability simply by abandoning the car itself.[59]

ABANDONED PROPERTY VESTS IN THE DEBTOR'S CORPORATE SHELL OR IN AN INDIVIDUAL DEBTOR

Where does property go when it is abandoned by a trustee or debtor's estate? Section 554(a) and Section 554(b) do not say.

---

56. In the unusual situation of an environmental statute that only holds the current owner or operator of property liable, the analysis would be more complicated.

57. *In re T.P. Long Chemical, Inc.*, 45 B.R. 278, 285 (Bankr. N.D. Ohio 1985). The Environmental Protection Agency had conducted a cleanup and removal of buried drums and surrounding soil contaminated with hazardous substances. The EPA sought reimbursement by the debtor's estate for the costs it had incurred. The court held that the estate's liability under CERCLA was not affected by the later abandonment of the drums and that the estate remained liable for addressing the environmental contamination associated with the abandoned property.

58. Jill Thompson Losch, *Bankruptcy v. Environmental Obligation: Clash of the Titans*, 52 La. L. Rev. 137, 150 (1991); *see also* Kristy Kutz, *Who Is Going To Pay: CERCLA v. Bankruptcy*, 31 Washburn L.J. 573, 599 & n.156 (1992) ("[A]bandonment may not eliminate the estate's financial responsibility to cleanup liability theories, such as CERCLA's, that do not depend on current ownership."). CERCLA expressly provides that a party may not contract away its CERCLA liability. 42 U.S.C. § 9607(e)(1).

59. Douglas G. Baird & T. Jackson, Cases, Problems, and Materials on Bankruptcy 591 (2d ed. 1990).

Section 554(c) gives a hint by saying that at closing of the case unadministered property is "abandoned to the debtor." Abandonment to the debtor makes sense as it conforms to the general structure of bankruptcy and Section 541 whereby an "estate" of most but not necessarily all of the debtor's property is created and administered by a trustee or "debtor-in-possession."[60] In the case of an individual debtor, exempt property[61] and certain limited post-petition acquired property[62] would remain with the debtor separate from the estate. In the case of a corporate debtor, the debtor is otherwise an empty corporate shell since all of the debtor's property has become property of the estate. As the Supreme Court has noted, the legislative history of the Bankruptcy Code confirms that property is abandoned "to the person having the possessory interest in the property."[63] That would be the debtor (an empty corporate shell in the case of corporations), which is the record title holder of the property that became part of the estate prior to its abandonment.[64] Several courts and commentators agree that property is abandoned by the estate to the debtor.[65]

---

60. *See* 11 U.S.C. §§ 541(a), 1107(a); Chapters 2 (History and Purposes), 5 (Key Provisions (property of the estate)) *supra*; *Ohio v. Kovacs*, 469 U.S. 274, 710 n.12 (1985).

61. 11 U.S.C. § 522.

62. *Compare* 11 U.S.C. § 1115 *with* 11 U.S.C. § 541(a).

63. *Kovacs*, 469 U.S. at 284 n.12 (quoting S. Rep. No. 95-989, at 92 (1978)).

64. Some courts have interpreted the legislative history language as authorizing abandonment to a secured creditor or a governmental agency. *See, e.g., In re St. Lawrence Corp.*, 239 B.R. 720, 728 (Bankr. D. N.J. 1999); *In re 82 Milbar Boulevard Inc.*, 91 B.R. 213 (Bankr. E.D.N.Y. 1988). While section 363 of the Bankruptcy Code, 11 U.S.C. § 363, would permit a consensual transfer to a secured creditor or the government by agreement, there is no authority under the Bankruptcy Code for a nonconsensual transfer. *In re Service*, 155 B.R. 512, 515 (Bankr. E.D. Mo. 1993). With respect to the federal government, real property may not be conveyed to the United States without its approval. *See* 41 U.S.C. § 6301(c); 40 U.S.C. § 3111(a); 36 Comp. Gen. 616, 618 (1957). Nothing in the Bankruptcy Code overrides this prohibition.

65. *See, e.g., In re Dewsnup*, 908 F.2d 588, 590 (10th Cir. 1990) (citing *Brown v. O'Keefe*, 300 U.S. 598, 602 (1937), *aff'd*, 502 U.S. 410 (1992); *In re Wilton Armetale, Inc.*, 618 B.R. 424, 431 n.7, 436 (Bankr. E.D. Pa. 2000); *In re Guterl Special Steel Corp.*, 316 B.R. 843, 861 (Bankr. W.D. Pa. 2004); *In re Adams*, 212 B.R. 703, 710 (Bankr. D. Mass. 1997); *In re Service*, 155 B.R. 512, 515 (Bankr. E.D. Mo. 1993); 5 *Collier on Bankruptcy* ¶ 554.02 (16th ed. 2019); Pamela Elkow & Thomas Sansone, *Treatment of Environmental Liabilities in Bankruptcy*, Am. Bar Ass'n, *Environmental Aspects of Real Estate Transactions*, ch. 7, at 199 (2020); Bolea, *supra* note 22, at 88; Lawton & Oswald, *supra* note 48, at 474–75. *See also In re Terjen*, 154 B.R. 456, 459 (E.D. Va. 1993).

ALTERNATIVES TO ABANDONMENT

Several alternatives to abandonment of contaminated property are discussed in Chapter 14 (Debtor-Owned Contaminated Property) of this Practice Guide, including adequately funded environmental response trusts. However, these alternatives require a cooperative debtor. Where a debtor is not cooperative, there are only two alternatives to abandonment: (1) permit the debtor to let sleeping dogs lie, so to speak, and defer addressing the property until the future if a viable reorganized debtor will exist, or (2) seek injunctive relief during the bankruptcy case so that the environmental issues are addressed as part of the case. The first alternative has risks because pollution problems can fester or worsen and the reorganized debtor may run into problems in the future and file for bankruptcy or simply liquidate. In addition, the first alternative also requires clear language in the plan of reorganization or confirmation order that the liability of the debtor with respect to the property is not impaired in any way.[66] The second alternative should therefore be considered if the governmental agency has authority and is prepared to move forward as such action may be the last best chance to achieve cleanup and compliance.[67] Taking affirmative action also undercuts any contention by debtors that the problem is not serious.

66. *See* Chapter 16 (Plan Objections) *supra*.

67. Such actions should fall under the police or regulatory exception whether brought in bankruptcy court by adversary proceeding or in another forum with jurisdiction. *See* Chapter 10 (Police or Regulatory Exception) *supra*.

CHAPTER 19

Bankruptcy and Insurance

Insurance issues introduce a third intricate body of law to the mix of bankruptcy law and environmental law, adding a layer of complexity and challenge that will be the focus of this chapter.

Insurance policies are property of a debtor's estate because the estate has legal title to the policies. However, the equitable interest in insurance proceeds varies depending on the facts and type of policy involved.[1] Insurance proceeds that are only payable to the insured (debtor), such as proceeds under fire, life, and casualty insurance policies, are property of the estate.[2] Insurance proceeds under liability policies present a more complex situation because the impact on the estate is indirect and injured parties may have vested rights to pursue such coverage, and therefore may have an equitable interest in the proceeds that flow from

1. *See In re OGA Charters, LLC*, 901 F.3d 599, 602–03 (5th Cir. 2018); *Am. Bankers Ins. Co. v. Maness*, 101 F.3d 358 (4th Cir. 1996); *In re Dow Corning Corp.*, 86 F.3d 482, 495 (6th Cir. 1996); *Home Ins. Co. v. Cooper & Cooper, Ltd.*, 889 F.2d 746, 748 (7th Cir. 1989); *Tringali v. Hathaway Machinery Co.*, 796 F.2d 553, 560 (1st Cir. 1986) (Breyer, J.); *In re Minoco Grp. of Cos.*, 799 F.2d 517, 519 (9th Cir. 1986); *A.H. Robins Co. v Piccinin*, 788 F.2d 994, 1001 (4th Cir. 1986); *In re Boy Scouts of Am. & Delaware BSA, LLC* 642 B.R. 504, 572 (Bankr. D. Del. 2022). *See* Hagop T. Bedoyan & Christian D. Jinkerson, *When Should the Proceeds of Liability Insurance Policies Be Treated as Property of the Estate?*, 40 ABI J. 32 (Apr. 2021), *aff'd*, 2023 WL 2662992 (D. Del. March 28, 2023).

2. *See In re Louisiana World Exposition, Inc.*, 832 F.2d 1391, 1399–1400 (5th Cir. 1987); *In re Equinox Oil Co.*, 300 F.3d 614 (5th Cir. 2002); *Landry v. Exxon Pipeline Co.*, 260 B.R. 769 (Bankr. M.D. La. 2001).

liability policies.[3] However, in *OGA Charters*, the Fifth Circuit held that where tort claims exceeded policy limits, the proceeds were property of the estate because the debtor had an interest in seeing that the insurance proceeds covered as much of the claims as possible.[4]

If insurance proceeds are property of the estate, the bankruptcy automatic stay applies to a creditor's actions to recover insurance proceeds.[5] However, bankruptcy courts often are willing to lift the stay if a creditor agrees to proceed solely against available insurance proceeds that cover such a claim.[6] Lifting the stay would be less likely, however, if the creditor's claims against insurance proceeds exceed the amount of available insurance.[7] In that situation, as noted in *OGA Charters*, different covered parties might be treated differently in a race to the courthouse outside of bankruptcy court. That would be prejudicial to parties with an interest in the proceeds and in tension with the important bankruptcy principle of similar treatment of similarly situated creditors.[8]

---

3. The scope of insurance coverage for environmental liabilities is beyond the scope of this Practice Guide. Generally speaking though, comprehensive general liability (CGL) policies issued prior to 1986 may provide coverage. Thereafter, absolute pollution exclusion clauses were usually added to CGL policies, which completely excluded environmental coverage. Other policies that provide environmental coverage include pollution legal liability, cost cap, or unknown condition policies. The names and structures of policies vary among different insurers. For further information, *see* Barry R. Ostrager & Thomas R. Newman, *Handbook on Insurance Coverage Disputes* §§ 10, 23.03 (19th ed. 2019); *Louisiana Generating LLC v. Illinois Union Ins. Co.*, 813 F.3d 618 (5th Cir. 2016); *Louisiana Generating LLC v. Illinois Union Ins. Co.*, 719 F.3d 328 (5th Cir. 2016). Parties seeking information about a debtor's insurance policies should consult: (1) the debtor's schedules and statement of financial affairs to determine if policies are listed as property or executory contracts, and (2) any disclosure statement or proposed plan. If the debtor will not provide insurance information voluntarily, parties may consider seeking a Rule 2004 examination on that subject. *See* Chapter 6 (Obtaining Information) *supra*.

4. *OGA Charters*, 901 F.3d at 604. *See also In re Titan Energy, Inc.*, 837 F.2d 325, 329 (8th Cir. 1988); *Minoco*, 799 F.2d at 519.

5. 11 U.S.C. § 362(a)(3); *see* Chapters 2 (History and Purposes), 10 (Police or Regulatory Exception) *supra*.

6. *In re Hendrix*, 986 F.2d 195 (7th Cir. 1993); *In re Shondel*, 950 F.2d 1301 (7th Cir. 1991); *In re Fernstrom Storage & Van Co.*, 938 F.2d 731 (7th Cir. 1991).

7. *OGA Charters*, 901 F.3d at 602–03. *See also AC&S, Inc. v. Travelers Cas. & Sur. Co.*, 435 F.3d 252 (3d Cir. 2006); *In re Fin. Oversight & Mgmt. Bd. for Puerto Rico*, 989 F.3d 170, 182 (1st Cir. 2021).

8. *See* Chapter 16 (Plan Objections) *supra*.

Insurance proceeds that can be paid only to the insured (debtor), which has the sole equitable interest in the proceeds, are assets of the estate that are available to all creditors in accordance with the Bankruptcy Code's priorities.[9] In contrast, even if insurance proceeds under liability policies are found to be property of the estate, such as in *OGA Charters*, the debtor's equitable interest in such proceeds is limited because of the interest of creditors whose claims are covered by the insurance policies. As such, it is settled law that such proceeds are not available for distribution to all creditors, but are reserved for creditors with claims covered by the policies.[10] In *Allied Products*, for instance, the bankruptcy court rejected a bankruptcy insurance buy-back settlement with an insurer that would have used insurance proceeds to pay general creditors.[11] The buy-back settlement was proposed as part of a Section 363 sale and the insurance company would have bought back the policy free and clear of claims of injured parties. The bankruptcy court reasoned that since state law governing liability insurance policies provides injured parties a potential right to payment from the insurer, the settlement could not be approved because it failed to provide adequate protection for the injured parties' interests.[12] Other courts have agreed with this reasoning

---

9. *See* Chapter 12 (Priorities) *supra*.

10. *OGA Charters*, 901 F.3d at 604 (debtor has no "right to pocket the proceeds"); *In re Edgeworth*, 993 F.2d 51, 56 (5th Cir. 1993) (proceeds "could not be made available for distribution to the creditors other than [covered] victims."); *Titan Energy*, 837 F.2d at 329 ("proceeds do not flow directly into the coffers of the estate"); *Landry v. Exxon Pipeline Co.*, 260 B.R. 769, 800 (M.D. La. 2001) (the insured does not have "any legal or equitable interest in the proceeds or funds to be used to pay any claims covered under" a liability policy); *In re Allied Prods. Corp.*, 288 B.R. 533 (Bankr. N.D. Ill. 2003); *In re Mahoney Hawkes LLP*, 289 B.R. 285 (Bankr. D. Mass. 2002); 3 Collier on Bankruptcy ¶ 362.03 (16th ed. 2019) (policy proceeds "are not available to all creditors . . . [but] may be available to a class of creditors whose claims are covered by insurance"). To the extent that a debtor has an independent claim for reimbursement under a liability policy, it would also have an interest in the proceeds that could be taken into account in accordance with bankruptcy law. *See, e.g.*, *OGA Charters*, 901 F.3d at 604 n.4; *In re Stinnett*, 465 F.3d 309, 313 (7th Cir. 2006). For example, to the extent that a debtor spent its own funds to satisfy a covered liability pre-bankruptcy or as part of the bankruptcy case, it would have a claim for reimbursement from insurance proceeds just as injured parties would. The limitation on a debtor's interest in proceeds protects the insurer as well by making sure that insurance proceeds are used for covered liabilities.

11. *Allied Products*, 288 B.R. 533.

12. *Id.* at 538.

based on similar state laws that vest rights in injured parties under liability policies.[13]

Nonetheless, creditors who may have insurance claims need to closely monitor bankruptcy proceedings to ensure that debtors do not seek court approval of a settlement with an insurer or propose a plan of reorganization that would prejudice them by: (1) making insurance proceeds available to general creditors, (2) limiting creditors' rights to proceed against insurers post-bankruptcy, or (3) limiting creditors' rights to proceed nominally against the debtor post-bankruptcy where necessary under applicable state law in order to pursue a claim against the insurer.[14] Failure to object to such motions or plans after proper notice could be binding on such creditors even if they would have had valid grounds for objection if made.[15]

Creditors may object to any plan provisions that unfairly discriminate against those creditors that might be covered by debtors' insurance policies.[16] Such creditors are not similarly situated to general creditors because they have a superior vested interest in potential insurance proceeds. Plan provisions that limit recovery on their claims to recovery from insurance proceeds may also

---

13. *See, e.g., In re F.O. Baroff Co., Inc.*, 555 F.2d 38, 42 (2d Cir. 1977); *Baez v. Med. Liab. Mut. Ins. Co.*, 136 B.R. 65 (S.D.N.Y. 1992). The Supreme Court has rejected challenges to such state statutes under bankruptcy law. *See Merchs. Mut. Auto. Liab. Ins. Co. v. Smart*, 267 U.S. 126, 131 (1925). *See also In re Congoleum Corp.*, 627 B.R. 62 (Bankr. D.N.J. 2021) (insurance buy-back by debtor could not strip additional insured of coverage without adequate protection); *In re SportStuff, Inc.*, 430 B.R. 170 (8th Cir. BAP 2010) (same); *In re Boy Scouts of Am. & Delaware BSA, LLC*, 642 B.R. 504, 585–86 (Bankr. D. Del. 2022) (finding that plan provides adequate protection by providing for payment in full of insured claims although noting that inchoate claims to insurance might not be entitled to adequate protection), *aff'd*, 2023 WL 2662992 (D. Del. March 28, 2023).

14. *See* note 19 *infra*.

15. *See* Chapter 16 (Plan Objections) *supra* (discussing *Espinosa*). The Eleventh Circuit has held that a creditor might be precluded from nominally proceeding against a debtor (or a released nondebtor) for purposes of insurance coverage where such a proceeding would impose an economic burden on the debtor. *See In re Le Centre on Fourth, LLC*, 17 F.4th 1326 (11th Cir. 2021); *cf. SuVicMon Dev., Inc. v. Morrison*, 991 F.3d 1213 (11th Cir. 2021) (not permitting proceeding against debtor in connection with fraudulent transfer proceeding). This result may be contrary to or not apply under state laws that seek to make insurance coverage available in the event of bankruptcy.

16. See Chapter 16 (Plan Objections) *supra* (discussing discriminatory treatment of claims).

be objectionable. Such provisions are often unfair given the difficulty of predicting whether insurance coverage will be available and what the amount of coverage will be.

Once a bankruptcy case is over, creditors are generally free to proceed with claims for insurance recovery against insurers even if the claim against debtors was discharged or if the creditor did not file a proof of claim. Under Section 524(e), a discharge in bankruptcy does not extinguish the liability itself, but only releases the debtor from personal liability. The debt can still can be collected, without reduction, from other liable companies such as insurers.[17] This makes sense since the fresh start policy of bankruptcy law is not meant to provide windfalls to insurers.[18] And while in most jurisdictions, an injured party would first need a judgment against the insured party to proceed directly against an insurer, this requirement is relaxed where the liable insured party, such as a debtor, no longer exists or the liability has been discharged in bankruptcy.[19]

Given that creditors generally have the right to proceed against insurers post-bankruptcy, it is important for creditors to be vigilant with respect to any attempt by a debtor in a plan or otherwise to provide an insurer the benefit of a debtor discharge or to

---

17. *See UNR Indus., Inc. v. Cont'l Cas. Co.*, 942 F.2d 1101 (7th Cir. 1991); cases cited in notes 18–19 *infra*.

18. *See, e.g., Edgeworth*, 993 F.2d at 53–54; *Green v. Welsh*, 956 F.2d 30, 35 (2d Cir. 1992); *In re Jet Florida Sys., Inc.*, 883 F.2d 970, 976 (11th Cir. 1989); *In re Weiand Auto. Indus.*, 612 B.R. 824, 860 (Bankr. D. Del. 2020); *In re Jason Pharm., Inc.*, 224 B.R. 315, 323 (Bankr. D. Md. 1998); *In re Dorner*, 125 B.R. 198 (Bankr. N.D. Ohio 1991); *In re Fed. Press Co.*, 104 B.R. 56, 63 (Bankr. N.D. Ind. 1989); *In re Lembke*, 93 B.R. 701, 703 (Bankr. D.N.D. 1988); *In re White*, 73 B.R. 983, 985 (Bankr. D.D.C. 1987); *Wimmer v. Mann*, 58 B.R. 953, 956–57 (Bankr. W.D. Va. 1986); *Fisher v. Lewis*, 567 N.E.2d 276, 278 (Ct. App. Ohio 1988).

19. Some courts permit the discharged debtor to be named as a nominal defendant solely for purposes of proceeding against the insurer. *See Jet Florida Systems*, 883 F.2d at 976. *See also SuVicMon*, 991 F.3d 1213. Many state laws require insurance policies to provide that the bankruptcy or insolvency of the insured or of the insured's estate does not relieve the insurer of any of its obligations. Such provisions may be interpreted to permit direct actions against an insurer when a judgment cannot be obtained against a debtor. *See, e.g., Nat'l Union Fire Ins. Co. v. Porter Hayden Co.*, 408 B.R. 66 (D. Md. 2009). Likewise, such provisions may excuse the payment of deductibles although the amount of coverage would not include the deductible amount. *See, e.g., Admiral Ins. Co. v. Grace Indus., Inc.*, 409 B.R. 275, 281 (E.D.N.Y. 2009).

pocket the insurance proceeds for the benefit of general creditors. Although not necessary, creditors that seek to pursue insurance coverage post-bankruptcy may find it helpful to seek a provision in the plan providing for a judgment in the form of an allowed claim that could be satisfied through insurance.[20] Such a provision would protect a creditor whose claim was covered by insurance because it would put to rest any contention that the bankruptcy discharged or reduced the liability of the insurer.

It should be noted that in limited circumstances where the amount of insurance coverage is less than the amount of claims that may be covered, the estate has a limited interest in the proceeds as discussed previously. In that situation, the insurer and the estate may seek to enter into a settlement that includes an injunction channeling all claims against the insurer to the settlement funds provided.[21] Such channeling injunctions are provided by statute for bankruptcy cases with asbestos liabilities and that also have a future representative who can protect the interests of future claimants.[22]

Plans may also provide for an assignment of insurance policy rights to a trustee or representative of an estate.[23] Environmental response trust settlements have provided for such assignments to

---

20. *See UNR Indus.*, 942 F.2d 1101. The plan might state that creditors can recover from insurance proceeds. However, if the insurer objects to the plan, the court would need to evaluate the fairness of the amount of the allowed claim. Alternatively, the plan could provide that the allowed claim amount is without prejudice to the insurer's right to challenge the amount of the liability in subsequent proceedings.

21. *See, e.g., In re Boy Scouts of Am. & Delaware BSA, LLC* 642 B.R. 504, 585–86 (Bankr. D. Del. 2022), *aff'd*, 2023 WL 2662992 (D. Del. March 28, 2023).

22. *See* 11 U.S.C. § 524(g). The role of a future claims representative is important to due process and fairness issues relating to future arising claims and could impact the proper scope of a channeling injunction. *See In re Johns-Manville Corp.*, 802 Fed. Appx. 20 (2d Cir. 2020); *Mahoney Hawkes, LLP*, 289 B.R. at 300–01. Channeling injunctions are examples of nondebtor releases (of insurers), which are discussed in Chapter 16 (Plan Objections) *supra.*

23. *See In re Federal-Mogul Global, Inc.*, 684 F.3d 355 (3d Cir. 2012); *In re W.R. Grace & Co.*, 475 B.R. 34, 198–99 & n. 189 (D. Del. 2012), *aff'd*, 729 F.3d 311 (3d Cir. 2013); *In re Purdue Pharma L.P.*, 633 B.R. 53, 63–65 (Bankr. S.D.N.Y. 2021), *vacated on other grounds*, 635 B.R. 26 (S.D.N.Y. 2021), *appeal pending* No. 22-85 (2d Cir. Jan. 18, 2022); 11 U.S.C. § 1123(b)(3), 1123(a)(5). In some states the assignment may be less vulnerable to attack if it is an assignment of insurance proceeds rather than the policy itself.

environmental response trustees.[24] A Chapter 7 trustee may assign insurance policy rights to a beneficiary where state law allows assignments post-loss.[25] The Bankruptcy Code's provision on executory contracts may enable a debtor to assign its rights under an insurance policy to a buyer of its assets notwithstanding a nonassignment clause.[26] Plans may also incorporate an insurance settlement that resolves a creditor's claim through the payment of insurance proceeds and resolves the debtor's claim against the insurer as well.[27] Where insurance coverage is uncertain and/or the debtor also has claims against the insurance policy, a settlement may provide for the sharing of future net insurance proceeds obtained by the debtor.[28]

24. The Fruit of the Loom and Vertellus bankruptcies both involved assignment of insurance proceeds to a trust that pursued litigation or settlements with insurers. *See Am. Int'l Specialty Lines Ins. Co.* v. *NWI-I, Inc.*, 240 F.R.D. 401, 403 (N.D. Ill. 2007); *In re VSI Liquidating Inc. f/k/a/ Vertellus Specialties Inc.*, No. 16-11290 (Bankr. D. Del.); Chapter 14 (Debtor-Owned Contaminated Property) *supra*.

25. *See In re GNI Group, Inc.* 402 B.R. 195 (S.D. Tex. 2008).

26. *See Pogo Resources, LLC v. St. Paul Fire & Marine Ins. Co.*, 2022 WL 286206, at *13–15 (Bankr. N.D. Tex. Jan. 24, 2022); Chapter 15 (Section 363 Sales) *supra*.

27. The United States entered into settlements based on recoveries in parallel insurance settlements in *In re Peabody Energy Corp.*, 16-42529-399 (Bankr. E.D. Mo. 2017), *In re LTV Steel Co.*, No. 00-43866 (Bankr. N.D. Ohio 2003), and *In re Insilco Corp.*, No. SA-92-CA-0210 (Bankr. W.D. Tex. 1993).

28. The United States entered into such a settlement in *In re Eagle-Picher Industries*, No. 1-91-00100 (Bankr. S.D. Ohio 1996).

CHAPTER 20

Bankruptcy Jurisdiction, Withdrawal of Reference, Venue, Standing, and Appeals

Bankruptcy jurisdiction is set forth in 28 U.S.C. § 1334. Section 1334(a) provides the district courts with exclusive jurisdiction of all cases filed under Title 11 of the United States Code and Section 1334(e) provides for exclusive jurisdiction of all property of the debtor and the debtor's estate.[1] At its core, the filing of a bankruptcy petition creates an in rem process to determine all claims that anyone has for recovery from the bankruptcy estate's assets.[2]

While jurisdiction is granted to the district courts, the district courts have referred bankruptcy jurisdiction to the bankruptcy courts as units of the district courts.[3] By filing a petition in bankruptcy, the debtor submits all of its property as of the commencement of the case to the exclusive in rem jurisdiction of the bankruptcy court.[4] "A bankruptcy court's in rem jurisdiction allows it to determin[e] all claims that anyone, whether named in

1. Section 1334(a) refers to the bankruptcy petition itself. *In re Wood*, 825 F.2d 90, 92 (5th Cir. 1987).

2. *See Tennessee Student Assistance Corp. v. Hood*, 541 U.S. 440, 440–41 (2004); *Katchen v. Landy*, 382 U.S. 323, 327 (1966).

3. 28 U.S.C. §§ 151, 157(a).

4. *Id.* § 1334(e).

the action or not, has to the property or thing in question. The proceeding is 'one against the world.'"[5]

"ARISING UNDER," "ARISING IN," AND "RELATED TO" JURISDICTION

28 U.S.C. § 1334(b) provides the district courts with original but not exclusive jurisdiction of civil proceedings "arising under title 11, or arising in or related to cases under title 11." Proceedings "arising under title 11" are matters dealing with substantive rights created or determined by the Bankruptcy Code and thus would arise only in the context of a bankruptcy case.[6] Examples include fraudulent conveyance actions under 11 U.S.C. § 548, preference actions under 11 U.S.C. § 547, bankruptcy automatic stay violations, and assumptions of executory contracts.[7] Proceedings "arising in" cases under Title 11 are matters that are not based on any right created by the Bankruptcy Code, but matters that by their nature could only have arisen as a result of the bankruptcy of the debtor.[8] Examples include: litigation over allowance and disallowance of proofs of claim;[9] the dischargeability of debts; the turnover of property; the validity, extent, or priority of liens; and general

---

5. *Hood*, 541 U.S. at 448 (quoting 16 J. Moore, et al., Moore's Federal Practice § 108.70[1] (3d ed. 2004)).

6. *See Gupta v. Quincy Medical Ctr.*, 858 F.3d 657, 664 (1st Cir. 2017); *In re Robert Plan Corp.*, 777 F.3d 594, 596–97 (2d Cir. 2015); *In re Wishire Courtyard*, 729 F.3d 1279, 1285 (9th Cir. 2013); *In re Ray*, 624 F.3d 1124, 1131 (9th Cir. 2010); *In re Toledo*, 170 F.3d 1340, 1345 (11 Cir. 1999); *Zerand-Bernal Group, Inc.*, 23 F.3d 159, 162–63 (7th Cir. 1994); *Wood*, 825 F.2d at 96.

7. *See, e.g., In re Point Ctr. Fin., Inc.*, 957 F.3d 990, 997 (9th Cir. 2020); *In re Galaz*, 841 F.3d 316, 322 (5th Cir. 2016); *In re Pintlar Corp.*, 133 F.3d 1141, 1146 (9th Cir. 1998); *In re Lionel Corp.*, 29 F.3d 88, 92 (2d Cir. 1994).

8. *Gupta*, 858 F.3d at 662–63; *In re Motors Liquidation Co.*, 829 F.3d 135, 153 (2d Cir. 2016); *In re Farmland Indus., Inc.*, 567 F.3d 1010, 1018 (8th Cir. 2009); *Stoe v. Flaherty*, 436 F.3d 209, 218 (3d Cir. 2006); *Valley Historic Ltd. P'ship v. Bank of New York*, 486 F.3d 831, 835–36 (4th Cir. 2007); *Wood*, 825 F.2d at 96; 1 Collier on Bankruptcy ¶ 3.01[3][e][i] (16th ed. 2019). For example, *Gupta* held that a dispute about the terms of an asset purchase agreement entered into by a debtor would not fall under "arising in" jurisdiction if the issues did not require interpretation of bankruptcy law.

9. Adjudication of proofs of claim is an integral part of the bankruptcy courts' in rem process. *Hood*, 541 U.S. at 447–48; *see Granfinanciera, S.A. v. Nordberg*, 492 U.S. 33, 57–58 (1989); *Langenkamp v. Culp*, 498 U.S. 42, 44–45 (1991).

bankruptcy administrative matters.[10] 28 U.S.C. § 157(b)(2) sets forth several examples of proceedings "arising under" Title 11 or "arising in" a case under Title 11; these are referred to as "core proceedings."

Proceedings "related to" cases under Title 11 are those that could have a conceivable effect on the bankruptcy estate, but are not based on rights created by the Bankruptcy Code or matters that could only arise in a bankruptcy case.[11] Litigation over the debtor's assets or liabilities arising under nonbankruptcy law (outside of the proof of claim process) are classic examples of "related to" matters. However, just because a matter is related to a bankruptcy does not mean that it has to be heard in bankruptcy court.[12] Placing an unrelated matter in a proposed plan should not be used to bootstrap or manufacture "related to" jurisdiction.[13] In reorganization cases, "related to" jurisdiction diminishes upon confirmation of a plan; post-confirmation jurisdiction requires a close nexus to the plan or trusts created by the plan.[14] As a consequence,

---

10. *In re Ortiz*, 665 F.3d 906, 911–12 (7th Cir. 2011); *In re Repository Techs., Inc.*, 601 F.3d 710, 719 (7th Cir. 2010); *Stoe*, 436 F.3d at 218; *In re Middlesex Power Equip. & Marine, Inc.*, 292 F.3d 61, 68 (1st Cir. 2002); *Wood*, 825 F.2d at 97; 1 Collier on Bankruptcy ¶ 3.01[3][e][iv] (16th ed. 2019).

11. *Exec. Benefits Ins. Agency v. Arkison*, 573 U.S. 25, 38 (2014); *Celotex Corp. v. Edwards*, 514 U.S. 300, 307–09 & n.6 (1995); *In re Fundamental Long Term Care, Inc.*, 873 F.3d 1325, 1336–38 (11th Cir. 2017); *In re Greektown Holdings, LLC*, 728 F.3d 567, 577–79 (6th Cir. 2013); *In re W.R. Grace & Co.*, 591 F.3d 164, 172 (3d Cir. 2009); *In re Fed. Mogul, Inc.*, 300 F.3d 368 (3d Cir. 2002); *In re Dow Corning*, 86 F.3d 482, 488–95 (6th Cir. 1996); *In re Walker*, 51 F.3d 562, 569 (5th Cir. 1995); *In re Xonics, Inc.*, 813 F.2d 127, 131 (7th Cir. 1987); *Pacor, Inc. v. Higgins*, 743 F.2d 984, 994–95 (3d Cir. 1984); 1 Collier on Bankruptcy ¶ 3.01[3][e][ii] (16th ed. 2019).

12. *See In re Mystic Tank Lines Corp.*, 544 F.3d 524, 528 (3d Cir. 2008) ("[n]o provision of the Bankruptcy Code requires the Bankruptcy Court to hear all 'related to' claims"). However, if the matter is stayed by the automatic stay, the bankruptcy court would have to lift the stay for it to be heard in another forum. *See* 11 U.S.C. § 362(c).

13. *See Greektown Holdings, LLC*, 728 F.3d at 578; *In re Johns-Manville Corp.*, 517 F.3d 52, 60–65 (2d Cir. 2008); *In re Combustion Eng'g, Inc.*, 391 F.3d 190, 225 (3d Cir. 2004); *In re Midway Gold*, 575 B.R. 475, 519 (Bankr. D. Colo. 2017); *In re Dreier LLP*, 429 B.R. 112, 131 (Bankr. S.D.N.Y. 2010). *But see In re Munford, Inc.*, 97 F.3d 449, 454 (11th Cir. 1996).

14. *In re GenOn Mid-Atlantic Dev., L.L.C.*, 42 F.4th 523 (5th Cir. 2022); *Greektown Holdings, LLC*, 728 F.3d at 578; *Nuveen Municipal Trust v. Withumsmith Brown, P.C.*, 692 F.3d 283, 294 (3d Cir. 2012); *In re Pegasus Gold Corp.*, 394 F.3d 1189, 1194 (9th Cir. 2005); *In re Resorts Int'l, Inc.*, 372 F.3d 154, 164–65 (3d Cir. 2004); *In re Craig's Stores of Texas, Inc.*, 266 F.3d 388, 390–91 (5th Cir. 2001); *Pettibone Corp. v. Easley*,

post-confirmation disputes with reorganized debtors over environmental compliance are outside of "related to" jurisdiction and would therefore be heard in nonbankruptcy tribunals.[15]

As expressly provided in 28 U.S.C. § 1334(b), "arising in," "arising under," and "related to" jurisdiction provide for concurrent, nonexclusive jurisdiction.[16] Examples of matters that can be addressed by other forums exercising concurrent jurisdiction include: police or regulatory actions against debtors, including whether the police or regulatory exception applies;[17] determinations of the dischargeability of debts;[18] and disputes under bankruptcy court sale orders or plans.[19] Where state courts are involved, an unresolved issue is whether the state court's decision

---

935 F.2d 120, 122 (7th Cir. 1991); *In re Stillwater Asset Backed Offshore Fund Ltd.*, 559 B.R. 563, 573–74 (Bankr. S.D.N.Y. 2016). Related to jurisdiction may not be as diminished in the case of core proceedings, interpretation of a bankruptcy court's order, and liquidations. *In re Essar Steel Minnesota, LLC*, 47 F.4th 193 (3d Cir. 2022); *In re Boston Reg'l Med. Ctr., Inc.*, 410 F.3d 100, 106–07 (1st Cir. 2005).

15. *Shieldalloy Metallurgical Corp. v. New Jersey Dep't of Env't Prot.*, 743 F. Supp. 2d 429 (D.N.J. 2010).

16. It is less likely that matters "arising in" or "arising under" will also fall under the jurisdiction of nonbankruptcy forums since they by definition have a closer nexus to bankruptcy law. One example, however, is proofs of claim for police or regulatory liability that fall under the police or regulatory exception to the automatic stay. A nonbankruptcy forum with jurisdiction could adjudicate the same liability asserted in the proof of claim. Technically, the nonbankruptcy forum would not be allowing or disallowing a proof of claim, but its decision would be entitled to res judicata effect as to the validity and amount of the liability. *See In re Am. Metrocomm Corp.*, 303 B.R. 32 (Bankr. D. Del. 2003).

17. *Bd. of Governors of Fed. Reserve Sys. v. MCorp Fin., Inc.*, 502 U.S. 32, 41 (1991); *Mystic Tank Lines*, 544 F.3d at 528; *Lockyer v. Mirant Corp.*, 398 F.3d 1098, 1107 (9th Cir. 2005); *United States Dep't of Hous. & Urban Dev. v. Cost Control Mktg. & Sales Mgt. of Virginia, Inc.*, 64 F.3d 920, 926 n.11 (4th Cir. 1995); *Pico v. Global Marine Drilling Co.*, 900 F.2d 846, 850 (5th Cir. 1990); *Brock v. Morysville Body Works, Inc.*, 829 F.2d 383, 387 (3d Cir. 1987); *N.L.R.B. v. Edward Cooper Painting Inc.*, 804 F.2d 934, 938–39 (6th Cir. 1986); *In re Baldwin-United Corp. Litigation*, 765 F.2d 343, 347 (2d Cir. 1985). *See also In re Mahurkar Double Lumen Hemodialysis Catheter Patent Litigation*, 140 B.R. 969 (N.D. Ill. 1992) (concurrent jurisdiction over whether automatic stay applies).

18. *In re Apex Oil Co.*, 406 F.3d 538, 542 (8th Cir. 2005); *Eden v. Robert A. Chapski, Ltd.*, 405 F.3d 582, 586 (7th Cir. 2005); *Whitehouse v. LaRouche*, 277 F.3d 568, 578–79 (1st Cir. 2002); *Erspan v. Badgett*, 647 F.2d 550, 556 (5th Cir. 1981); *Signature Combs, Inc. v. United States*, 253 F. Supp. 2d 1028 (W.D. Tenn. 2003).

19. *In re Haven Eldercare, LLC*, 503 Fed. Appx. 13, 15 (2d Cir. 2012); *In re Skyline Woods Country Club*, 636 F.3d 467, 471 (8th Cir. 2011); *In re Middlesex Power Equip. & Marine, Inc.*, 292 F.3d 61, 66–67 (1st Cir. 2002).

will have res judicata effect or whether it can thereafter be challenged in federal court as incorrectly decided and void ab initio.[20]

28 U.S.C. § 1334(c)(1) permits federal courts to abstain from hearing a matter "arising under," "arising in," or "related to" jurisdiction in the interest of justice or comity with state courts or respect for state law.[21] 28 U.S.C. § 1334(c)(2) requires, upon timely motion, abstention from hearing "related to" matters for which there would be no federal jurisdiction absent a bankruptcy proceeding if the action is commenced and can be timely adjudicated in state court.[22] Bankruptcy courts have accordingly abstained from hearing environmental actions removed from state courts and returned those actions to state courts to be resolved.[23] If a state court with concurrent jurisdiction issues a ruling, the so-called Rooker-Feldman doctrine requires that the debtor file an appeal in state court rather than attempt to collaterally attack that ruling in bankruptcy court.[24]

---

20. *Compare, e.g., Skyline*, 636 F.3d at 470–71 (finding that res judicata applies in cases of concurrent jurisdiction in contrast to exclusive jurisdiction, which would make another forum's ruling void ab initio), *In re Gandy*, 327 B.R. 796, 801 (Bankr. S.D. Tex. 2005), and *In re Siskin*, 258 B.R. 554, 563 (Bankr. E.D.N.Y. 2001) *with In re Gruntz*, 202 F.3d 1074 (9th Cir. 2000) (en banc) (permitting federal court determination of whether exception to automatic stay for criminal proceedings applied after state court ruling); *In re Hamilton*, 540 F.3d 367 (6th Cir. 2008). *See also Inn World Report, Inc. v. MB Financial Bank NA*, 2022 WL 17841529 (2d Cir. Dec. 20, 2022). *Gruntz* in any event should have no applicability to district court cases in federal court given that *Gruntz* relied heavily on the role of states vis a vis federal bankruptcy jurisdiction. *See Lockyer*, 398 F.3d at 1105–06. The Ninth Circuit's decision in *Gruntz* has been strongly criticized. Karen Cordry, *The Ninth Circuit and In re Gruntz*, 2000 Norton Bankr. L. Adviser, No. 4, at 1 (2000).

21. *See In re Harris*, 966 F.3d 439, 442 (6th Cir. 2020); *Middlesex Power*, 292 F.3d at 69; *In re Chicago, Milwaukee, St. Paul & Pacific R.R. Co.*, 6 F.3d 1184, 1189 (7th Cir. 1993). It should be noted that the "interest of justice" alternative under this section is not limited to state law issues or cases. *See In re Paolo*, 619 F.3d 100 (1st Cir. 2010). The decision to abstain or not abstain under Section 1334(c)(1) is not subject to appellate review. *See* 28 U.S.C. § 1334(d).

22. *See Parmalat Cap. Fin. Ltd. v. Bank of Am. Corp.*, 671 F.3d 261 (2d Cir. 2012); *Stoe v. Flaherty*, 436 F.3d 209, 214 (3d Cir. 2006); *In re Dune Energy, Inc.*, 575 B.R. 716 (W.D. Tex. 2017).

23. *In re Mexico Farms, LLC*, 2011 WL 1131532 (Bankr. D. Md. Mar. 28, 2011); *In re Commercial Oil Serv., Inc.*, 58 B.R. 311 (Bankr. N.D. Ohio 1986), *aff'd*, 88 B.R. 126 (N.D. Ohio 1987). One court declined abstention where a complaint in bankruptcy court alleging alter ego and unjust enrichment was for the benefit of all creditors and a state proceeding was not. *In re Maxus Energy Corp.*, 597 B.R. 235 (Bankr. D. Del. 2019).

24. *See Exxon Mobil Corp. v. Saudi Basic Indus. Corp.*, 544 U.S. 280 (2005); *Inn World Report*, 2022 WL 17841529; *Behr v. Campbell*, 8 F.4th 1206 (11th Cir. 2021); *In*

Another statute, 28 U.S.C. § 1452(a), permits debtors to remove civil actions related to bankruptcy cases from other courts but this statute does not apply to actions by governmental units to enforce police or regulatory power.[25] Under the doctrine of "primary jurisdiction," courts may refer or stay a proceeding to permit the parties to obtain a ruling within the special expertise of an administrative agency.[26] Bankruptcy jurisdiction does not extend to nonfinal administrative proceedings that may proceed under the police or regulatory exception to the automatic stay.[27]

As noted earlier, Section 1334 grants the previously described bankruptcy jurisdiction to district courts. Both 28 U.S.C. §§ 151 and 157(a) designate bankruptcy courts as units of district courts and authorize the district courts to "refer" bankruptcy cases and proceedings arising under Title 11 or arising in or related to a case under Title 11 to bankruptcy judges.[28] All district courts have standing general orders of reference to bankruptcy courts that are in place with respect to all bankruptcy cases.[29] The concept of "reference" to bankruptcy courts was Congress's response to the Supreme Court's decision in *Northern Pipeline Construction Co. v. Marathon Pipe Line Co.*,[30] which held that the Constitution requires that certain matters (i.e., those that fall under "related to" jurisdiction under the current statute) be resolved by Article III lifetime judges rather than term-limited bankruptcy judges.[31] 28 U.S.C.

---

re Isaacs, 895 F.3d 904 (6th Cir. 2018); *In re Philadelphia Entm't & Dev. Partners*, 879 F.3d 492 (3d Cir. 2018); *In re Knapper*, 407 F.3d 573 (3d Cir. 2005); *Safety-Kleen, Inc. (Pinewood) v. Wyche*, 274 F.3d 846, 857–58 (4th Cir. 2001); *In re Ferren*, 203 F.3d 559, 560 (8th Cir. 2000).

25. *Mayor & City Council of Baltimore v. BP P.L.C.*, 31 F.4th 178, 224–25 (4th Cir. 2022). However, a motion to remand may be required. *See City & Cnty. of San Francisco v. PG & E Corp.*, 433 F.3d 1115 (9th Cir. 2006).

26. *Reiter v. Cooper*, 507 U.S. 258, 268–69 (1993); *Rilling v. Burlington N. R.R. Co.*, 909 F.2d 399 (9th Cir. 1990).

27. *Bd. of Governors of Fed. Reserve Sys. V. MCorp Fin., Inc.*, 502 U.S. 32, 41–42 (1991); *see* Chapter 10 (Police or Regulatory Exception) *supra*.

28. *See United States v. Gurley*, 434 F.3d 1064, 1067 (8th Cir. 2006).

29. *See, e.g.*, *In re Point Ctr. Fin., Inc.*, 957 F.3d 990, 998 (9th Cir. 2020); *In re Atherotech, Inc.*, 582 B.R. 251, 258 (Bankr. N.D. Ala. 2017).

30. 458 U.S. 50 (1982).

31. Lifetime appointments protect the integrity and independence of the judiciary. *Stern v. Marshall*, 564 U.S. 462, 483 (2011); *Wellness Int'l Network, Ltd. v. Sharif*, 575 U.S. 665, 668 (2015). Bankruptcy judges are appointed by the courts of appeal and serve 14-year terms. 28 U.S.C. § 152.

§ 157(b)(1) provides that bankruptcy judges can hear and determine cases under Title 11 and "core proceedings" arising under Title 11 or arising in a case under Title 11.[32] 28 U.S.C. § 157(b)(2) provides a nonexclusive list of the core proceedings. 28 U.S.C. § 157(c)(1) provides that bankruptcy judges can also hear "related to" cases but must submit proposed findings of fact and conclusions of law to a district judge who will review the matter de novo.

In *Stern v. Marshall*, the Supreme Court held that Section 157(b) was unconstitutional to the extent that it permitted a non-Article III judge to enter a final judgement on a state law counterclaim on a noncore matter filed by the debtor against a creditor (tortious interference in that case) where the noncore matter was not necessarily resolved by the bankruptcy court's rulings on the creditor's proof of claim.[33] In *Executive Benefits Insurance Agency v. Arkison*, the Supreme Court clarified that so-called *Stern* claims (in *Arkison*, a fraudulent transfer claim) can be handled as noncore claims under Section 157 and that bankruptcy courts may make recommendations of findings of fact and conclusions of law on such matters.[34] In *Wellness International Network, Ltd. v Sharif*, the Supreme Court held that bankruptcy courts can also hear and resolve *Stern*-type claims if there is knowing and voluntary consent by all parties, which consent can be express or implied.[35]

The main relevance of *Stern* to environmental bankruptcy cases is in those instances where critical litigation on *Stern*-type claims is occurring in the bankruptcy case, such as the fraudulent conveyance litigation in *Tronox*.[36] Such claims may be dealt with by the bankruptcy court by consent under *Wellness* or the bankruptcy court may make recommendations to the district court. Alternatively, the bankruptcy court may issue a ruling that is either: (1) a judgment with findings of facts and conclusions of law, or (2) rec-

32. An exception is made for personal injury tort and wrongful death claims. These can only be tried in district courts. 28 U.S.C. § 157(b)(5).

33. 564 U.S. 462, 503 (2011). The Court noted a "public rights" exception to the requirement of an Article III court for the adjudication of rights under federal regulatory schemes in particularized areas of the law. *Id.* at 490–94.

34. 573 U.S. 25, 38 (2014).

35. 575 U.S. 665 (2015).

36. *In re Tronox Inc.*, 503 B.R. 239 (2013). *Tronox* is discussed Chapter 21 (Settlement Agreements) *infra*.

ommendations to the district court given that the legal issues relating to the applicability of *Stern* are uncertain.

The impact of *Stern* has not yet been considered with respect to environmental litigation in bankruptcy cases. *Stern* does not apply to the claims allowance process[37] or the approval of settlements.[38] And it is somewhat rare for parties in interest to bring other environmental litigation in bankruptcy court, such as by way of the filing of an adversary complaint for injunctive relief. Governments, acting in their police or regulatory capacity, can bring such litigation in other courts pursuant to the police or regulatory exception.[39] Where it is more efficient to proceed with such litigation under bankruptcy "related to" jurisdiction, *Stern* may require the involvement of district courts unless the parties consent to proceeding in bankruptcy court.[40] In order to meet the requirements of *Stern*, it may be necessary to either withdraw the reference, as discussed later, or for the bankruptcy court to make recommendations to the district court.

WITHDRAWAL OF THE REFERENCE

As noted previously, district courts have standing general orders that refer bankruptcy cases and proceedings to bankruptcy judges in their district in accordance with 28 U.S.C. § 157(a). However, 28 U.S.C. § 157(d) provides that the district court "shall, on timely motion of a party" *withdraw* the reference of a proceeding to the bankruptcy court if the district court determines that resolution of the proceeding requires consideration of both bankruptcy law and "laws of the United States regulating organizations or activities affecting interstate commerce." In addition to this provision

37. *Stern*, 564 U.S. at 499; *In re Millenium Lab Holdings II, LLC*, 945 F.3d 126, 138 (3d Cir. 2019).

38. *In re Madoff*, 848 F. Supp. 2d 469 (S.D.N.Y. 2012), *aff'd*, 740 F.3d 81 (2d Cir. 2014); *In re Land Resource, LLC*, 505 B.R. 571 (M.D. Fla. 2014); *In re Murray Energy Holdings Co.*, 615 B.R. 461 (Bankr. S.D. Ohio 2020).

39. *See* Chapter 10 (Police or Regulatory Exception) *supra*. The fact that environmental litigation can be brought in other courts under the police or regulatory exception does not mean it has to be brought there and cannot be brought in bankruptcy court.

40. *Wellness*, 575 U.S. at 679.

for mandatory withdrawal of the reference,[41] 28 U.S.C. § 157(d) also provides for permissive withdrawal of the reference "for cause shown." Since the authority for federal environmental laws is the regulation of interstate commerce, environmental matters in bankruptcy cases are prime candidates for withdrawal of the reference.[42]

Motions for withdrawal of the reference are filed in bankruptcy court but are decided by a district judge.[43] Local rules should be consulted for the exact procedure in each district, but typically the clerk's office will gather the briefs for and against the motion and transmit them to the district court for its ruling.[44] In some districts, the bankruptcy court makes a recommendation to the district court as to whether the reference should be withdrawn.[45] The filing of a motion to withdraw the reference does not automatically stay proceedings in bankruptcy court, but the bankruptcy judge or district judge can enter a stay.[46] However, most bankruptcy judges will not proceed with the matter at issue in deference to the district court's right to determine the motion and as a matter of judicial efficiency.

District courts have granted mandatory withdrawal of the reference with respect to objections to environmental proofs of claim,[47] determinations of whether an injunctive compliance obligation is a dischargeable or stayed claim,[48] adversary proceedings

---

41. The term "shall" makes withdrawal mandatory. *In re Nat'l Gypsum Co.*, 134 B.R. 188, 191 (N.D. Tex. 1991); *In re Combustion Equip. Assocs., Inc.*, 67 B.R. 709, 711 (S.D.N.Y. 1986).

42. *See, e.g.*, *Hodel v. Virginia Surface Mining & Reclamation Assoc.*, 452 U.S. 264, 281–82 (1981); *United States v. Delfasco, Inc.*, 409 B.R. 704, 707 (D. Del. 2009).

43. Fed. R. Bankr. P. 5011(a).

44. *See, e.g.*, Del. Bankr. Ct. Local Rule 5011-1. Some local rules such as in Delaware bankruptcy court require the movant to seek a concurrent determination as to whether the bankruptcy court should enter final orders and judgments as opposed to making recommendations of findings of fact and conclusions of law. Del. Bankr. Ct. Local Rule 5011-1.

45. *See, e.g.*, S.D. Tex. Bankr. Ct. Local Rule 5011-1.

46. Fed. R. Bankr. P. 5011(c).

47. *In re Nat'l Gypsum Co.*, 134 B.R. 188 (N.D. Tex. 1991); *see United States v. Gurley*, 434 F.3d 1064 (8th Cir. 2006).

48. *Chemtura Corp. v. United States*, 2010 WL 1379752 (S.D.N.Y. Mar. 26, 2010); *In re Insilco Corp.*, No. 92-0210 (W.D. Tex. Apr. 6, 1992); *In re Combustion Equip. Assocs., Inc.*, 67 B.R. 709 (S.D.N.Y. 1986); *In re Johns-Manville Corp.*, 63 B.R. 600 (S.D.N.Y. 1986).

seeking injunctive or declaratory relief relating to environmental law by either the government or debtor,[49] and actions by a trustee for contribution from other liable parties.[50] Some courts will not withdraw the reference if the environmental issue is routine and the law is settled and does not require substantial and material consideration of environmental law.[51] Cases at the intersection of the conflict between environmental law and bankruptcy law are the strongest candidates for withdrawal of the reference.[52] Most commonly, the district court will only withdraw the reference on particular contested matters or adversary proceedings,[53] but where the issues are intertwined throughout the case it is possible to withdraw the reference of the entire bankruptcy case.[54] A district court may also withdraw the reference to decide issues of interpretation of nonbankruptcy law and then refer the matter back to the bankruptcy court to apply its ruling.[55]

If read literally, the statute providing for withdrawal of the reference requires that, for the reference to be withdrawn, the matter at issue would require consideration of both bankruptcy and non-bankruptcy law. Most environmental matters arising in bankruptcy

---

49. *United States v. Delfasco, Inc.*, 409 B.R. 704 (D. Del. 2009); *United States v. Moglia*, No. 02-6131 (N.D. Ill. Jan. 6, 2003); *In re Feinstein Family P'ship*, No. 96-232-24 (M.D. Fla. May 28, 1998 and Aug. 17, 1999); *In re Hawaiian Western Steel, Ltd.*, No. 93-00527 (D. Haw. June 30, 1993); *Hatzel & Buehler, Inc. v. Orange & Rockland Utilities, Inc.*, 107 B.R. 34 (D. Del. 1989); *In re ILCO, Inc.*, 48 B.R. 1016 (N.D. Ala. 1985).

50. *AT&T v. Chateaugay Corp.*, 88 B.R. 581 (S.D.N.Y. 1988); *In re Lajet, Inc.*, 1995 WL 72428 (E.D. La. Feb. 21, 1995).

51. Although the literal statutory language does not contain this limitation, courts have interpreted "consideration" narrowly in order to avoid creating an escape hatch for most of the work of bankruptcy courts. *In re Vicars Ins. Agency, Inc.*, 96 F.3d 949, 952 (7th Cir. 1996). *See LTV Steel Co. v. Union Carbide Corp.*, 193 B.R. 669 (S.D.N.Y. 1996); *In re C-TC 9th Ave. P'ship*, 177 B.R. 760 (N.D.N.Y. 1995); *In re Revere Copper & Brass Inc.*, 172 B.R. 192 (S.D.N.Y. 1994). The requirement of substantial and material consideration or significant interpretation of nonbankruptcy law for withdrawal of the reference applies to nonbankruptcy laws other than environmental law as well. *See, e.g., Vicars*; *City of New York v. Exxon Corp.*, 932 F.2d 1020, 1026 (2d Cir. 1991); *In re Ionosphere Clubs, Inc.*, 922 F.2d 984, 995 (2d Cir. 1990).

52. *In re Dana Corp.*, 379 B.R. at 461; *In re Nat'l Gypsum Co.*, 134 B.R. 188, 192 (N.D. Tex. 1991); *ILCO*, 48 B.R. at 1021.

53. Proceedings in bankruptcy court are most commonly either contested matters under Fed. R. Bankr. P. 9014 or adversary proceedings initiated by complaint under Part VII of Fed. R. Bankr. P.

54. *See, e.g., United States v. Merritt*, No. 94-0026 (D. Wyo. Mar. 10, 1994).

55. *Nat'l Gypsum*, 134 B.R. 188 (N.D. Tex. 1991).

court also require consideration of bankruptcy law, such as allowance or priority issues or bankruptcy defenses but that may not always be the case. However, courts have noted that it would be odd for a bankruptcy court to retain the sole right to hear a matter that only involved nonbankruptcy law on the theory that it did not involve bankruptcy law.[56] Post-*Stern*, the bankruptcy court could in any event only make recommendations to the district court on a matter that is "related to" the bankruptcy case (as opposed to "arising in" or "arising under" the bankruptcy case) given that no bankruptcy law issues are involved. Such matters may also be candidates for permissive withdrawal of the reference for cause.

Motions for mandatory withdrawal of the reference must be "timely" filed under 28 U.S.C. § 157(d) in order to discourage stalling tactics, inefficient administration of justice, and unfair burdens on the parties.[57] A motion to withdraw the reference is considered timely if it is done without "undue delay" given the circumstances of the proceeding, but the statute sets no precise time limit.[58] Even a five-month delay was found to be timely where there were no indications of tactical delays or forum shopping and the bankruptcy court had not made findings or invested significant time on the matter.[59] Nevertheless, if one intends to file such a motion, it would be prudent to do so as soon as reasonably practicable.

Withdrawal of the reference for cause (sometimes referred to as permissive withdrawal of the reference) is based on several factors including judicial economy and efficient use of judicial resources, uniform bankruptcy administration, reduction of forum shopping, expediting the bankruptcy process, and conservation of parties' resources.[60] While motions to withdraw the reference on environmental matters often seek withdrawal for cause in the alternative, district courts do not need to reach the issue if mandatory withdrawal applies. If mandatory withdrawal is found not to apply,

---

56. *See In re St. Mary Hospital*, 115 B.R. 495, 497 (E.D. Pa. 1990).
57. *In re Giorgio*, 50 B.R. 327, 328–29 (D.R.I. 1985).
58. *In re Baldwin-United Corp.*, 57 B.R. 751, 753 (S.D. Ohio 1985).
59. *In re VWE Group, Inc.*, 359 B.R. 441 (S.D.N.Y. 2007).
60. *See, e.g.*, *In re Canter*, 299 F.3d 1150, 1154 (9th Cir. 2002); *In re Orion Pictures Corp.*, 4 F.3d 1095, 1101 (2d Cir. 1993); *In re Pruitt*, 910 F.2d 1160, 1168 (3d Cir. 1990); *Holland Am. Ins. Co. v. Succession of Roy*, 777 F.2d 992, 999 (5th Cir. 1985).

district courts are often reluctant to find cause for permissive withdrawal as they often have heavy caseloads and may prefer for bankruptcy judges to handle the matter.

The decision of whether to move for withdrawal of the reference on complex environmental matters in a bankruptcy case can be delicate and difficult. On the one hand, the statutory language of mandatory withdrawal is clear and strong. In addition, as noted elsewhere in this Practice Guide, addressing environmental bankruptcy issues requires the careful harmonization of bankruptcy law and environmental law and it is the need for such harmonization that underpins the requirements for withdrawal of the reference by the district court.[61] While many bankruptcy courts have been able to fairly and neutrally undertake such harmonization in a balanced way, there often can be doubt as to whether a *bankruptcy* court will fairly consider both bodies of law given the bankruptcy court's focus on bankruptcy law and the problems faced by debtors. Furthermore, withdrawal motions may antagonize some bankruptcy judges who could view them as an affront to their capability to handle such matters. Even some district courts may view the motions warily in view of their heavy caseloads. Filing a motion to withdraw the reference therefore could have negative repercussions in some districts as to the pending matter or future matters. Moreover, motions to withdraw the reference often cause delay and expense, which may be counterproductive and not in the movant's interest given the limited resources available in bankruptcy. Accordingly, if there is a reasonable likelihood that the matter can be amicably settled in bankruptcy court, it may be more efficient to leave the matter in bankruptcy court. That said, the requirement of timeliness for withdrawal motions necessitates early decisions on whether to seek withdrawal of the reference. Finally, the fact that a matter might be subject to withdrawal of the reference, if a timely motion were filed, does not in any way deprive the bankruptcy court of its referred bankruptcy jurisdiction from the district court if the reference is not actually withdrawn.[62]

61. *See* Chapter 8 (Harmonization) *supra*.

62. *See, e.g.*, *U.S. Bank Nat'l Assoc. v. United States Env't Prot. Agency*, 563 F.3d 199 (6th Cir. 2009); *AL Tech Specialty Steel Corp. v. Allegheny Int'l Credit Corp.*, 104 F.3d 601 (3d Cir. 1997); *In re Dant & Russell, Inc.*, 951 F.2d 246 (9th Cir. 1991);

VENUE

28 U.S.C. § 1408 provides for a wide range of venue options for corporations filing for bankruptcy. A single corporation may file where it is incorporated, has had its principal business or principal assets for 180 days,[63] and also where any of its affiliates have a pending case.[64] The affiliate option for venue selection has sometimes resulted in the creation of affiliates for the sole purpose of obtaining bankruptcy venue.[65] However, 28 U.S.C. § 1412 provides that a bankruptcy case or proceeding may be transferred to another district "in the interest of justice" or "for the convenience of the parties." While a debtor's choice of forum is entitled to great weight where venue is proper, courts have considered other factors such as efficient and economic case administration, judicial economy, fairness and integrity of the bankruptcy system, proximity of creditors, proximity of the debtor, proximity of witnesses, a state's interest in having local controversies decided within its borders, and location of assets.[66] An adversary proceeding bearing

---

Fairchild Holding Corp. v. Revere Copper & Brass, Inc., 291 B.R. 29 (S.D.N.Y. 2003); *In re Kaiser Group Int'l, Inc.*, 289 B.R. 597 (Bankr. D. Del. 2003); *In re Eagle-Picher Indus.*, 197 B.R. 260, 271 (S.D. Ohio 1996*), aff'd*, 1997 U.S. Dist. LEXIS 15436, No. 1-96-821 (S.D. Ohio July 14, 1997); *In re U.E. Systems, Inc.*, 1992 WL 472113 (Bankr. N.D. Ind. Sept. 28, 1992); *In re Peerless Plating Co.*, 70 B.R. 943 (Bankr. W.D. Mich. 1987); *In re T.P. Long Chem.*, Inc., 45 B.R. 278 (Bankr. N.D. Ohio 1985).

63. Individuals may file where they have resided or are domiciled for 180 days. 28 U.S.C. § 1408.

64. *In re Peachtree Lane Assocs., Ltd.*, 150 F.3d 788, 795 (7th Cir. 1998); *In re Commonwealth Oil Refining Co.*, 596 F.2d 1239, 1241 (5th Cir. 1979); *In re Think3, Inc.*, 529 B.R. 147, 208–09 (Bankr. W.D. Tex. 2015); *In re Barrington Spring House, LLC*, 509 B.R. 587, 604 (Bankr. S.D. Ohio 2014); *In re Patriot Coal Corp.*, 482 B.R. 718, 741–46 (Bankr. S.D.N.Y. 2012). A corporation's principal place of business is where its major business decisions are made. *Peachtree Lane Assocs.*, 150 F.3d at 795; *In re Commonwealth Oil,* 596 F.2d at 1241.

65. *See, e.g., In re LTL Mgmt. LLC*, 2021 WL 5343945 (Bankr. W.D.N.C. Nov. 16, 2021) (affiliate created two days before bankruptcy filing); *In re Patriot Coal Corp.*, 482 B.R. at 741 (also citing to Winn-Dixie bankruptcy case); *see generally* Adam J. Levitin, *Purdue's Poison Pill: The Breakdown of Chapter 11's Checks and Balances*, 100 Tex. L. Rev. 100, 152–53 (2022). The venue provisions of the Bankruptcy Code have been criticized in the literature and could be changed by Congress. *Id.*; Mark Pfeiffer, *Let's Talk About Chapter 11 Venue Again*, 39 ABI J. 5, 20–21, 55 (May 2020).

66. *See In re Commonwealth Oil Ref. Co.*, 596 F.2d 1239, 1248 (5th Cir. 1979); *LTL Mgmt.*, 2021 WL at *3; *Patriot Coal*, 482 B.R. at 740 n.31; *In re Safety-Kleen Corp.*, 2001 WL 1820321 (Bankr. D. Del. Aug. 27, 2001); *In re Scotia Dev., LLC*, 2007 WL 1192137 (Bankr. S.D. Tex. Apr. 20, 2007); *In re F.S Airlease II, Inc.*, 67 B.R. 428, 432 (Bankr. W.D. Pa. 1985); *In re Thomasson*, 60 B.R. 629, 632 (Bankr. M.D. Tenn. 1986).

on environmental issues about property in a different state from where the main bankruptcy case is filed may be transferred after consideration of the preceding factors, even if the main case is not transferred.[67] The venue for proceedings arising out of post-bankruptcy operations would be the place of operations as provided by applicable nonbankruptcy venue statutes.[68]

STANDING

Standing is a doctrine that preserves the separation of powers between the judicial, legislative, and executive branches, and conserves the resources of courts and litigants so that only injured parties with live cases or controversies can take part in judicial proceedings. Standing requirements seek to avoid the courts becoming forums for persons or bystanders with agendas that are not real parties in interest to a live case or controversy. There are at least two levels of standing requirements that may apply to bankruptcy matters. First, Article III of the Constitution only permits courts to adjudicate "cases" and "controversies." The Supreme Court has explained that standing to sue is a key component of a case or controversy and requires parties to demonstrate: (1) injury in fact, (2) with a causal connection to the conduct complained of, and (3) that is likely to be redressed by a judicial decision in the matter.[69] "Injury in fact" means particularized and concrete injury that is not conjectural or hypothetical.[70] Second, courts consider statutory or prudential standing limitations that prohibit litigants that are outside the "zone of interest" protected or authorized by the particular law to bring matters to a court;

---

67. *See, e.g., In re Safety-Kleen Corp.*, 2001 WL 1820321 (Bankr. D. Del. Aug. 27, 2001) (declaratory judgment action about hazardous waste disposal facility's compliance with consent order transferred); *Safety-Kleen, Inc. (Pinewood) v. Wyche*, 274 F.3d 846 (4th Cir. 2001).

68. 28 U.S.C. § 1409(e); *In re Pan Am Corp.*, 177 B.R. 1014 (Bankr. S.D. Fla. 1995).

69. *TransUnion LLC v. Ramirez*, 141 S. Ct. 2190 (2021); *Spokeo, Inc. v. Robins*, 578 U.S. 330, 338 (2016); *DaimlerChrysler Corp. v. Cuno*, 547 U.S. 332, 342 (2006); *Lujan v. Defenders of Wildlife*, 504 U.S. 555, 561 (1992); *In re Wilton Armetale, Inc.*, 968 F.3d 273, 281 (3d Cir. 2020); *In re Capital Contracting Co.*, 924 F.3d 890, 897–98 (6th Cir. 2019).

70. *Carney v. Adams*, 141 S. Ct. 493 (2020); *Spokeo*, 578 U.S. at 339–40.

parties cannot invoke generalized grievances or the rights of other parties to give themselves standing.[71] For example, individual creditors may not have standing (or more precisely statutory authority) to bring certain derivative actions that belong to the trustee or estate on behalf of all creditors.[72] Both constitutional and statutory requirements for standing may apply to bankruptcy matters, although the status of bankruptcy courts as non-Article III courts that are adjuncts of district courts may be considered relevant to an analysis of constitutional standing as limited by Article III.[73]

Section 1109 of the Bankruptcy Code is relevant to statutory standing in bankruptcy court. It provides that a "party in interest," as well as committees and creditors, may appear and be heard on any issue.[74] Federal Rule of Bankruptcy Procedure 2018(a) provides "any interested entity" the right to intervene "generally or

---

71. *Lexmark Int'l, Inc.*, 572 U.S. 118, 127 (2014); *Warth v. Seldin*, 422 U.S. 490, 499 (1995). In *Lexmark*, the Supreme Court clarified that prudential (in the sense of exercising discretion or prudence) standing limitations should be viewed as a "zone of interest" question of statutory interpretation or authorization instead of as a prudential exercise of discretion. 572 U.S. at 127. However, the Court left open the question of whether third-party standing cases might involve a kind of prudential standing. *Id.* at 127 n.3.

72. *See, e.g.*, *Wilton Armetale*, 968 F.3d at 280–83. Derivative causes are general to the estate as opposed to personal to a specific creditor. *Id.* at 282; *In re Tronox, Inc.*, 855 F.3d 84, 103 (2d Cir. 2017). Likewise, certain Bankruptcy Code provisions provide the trustee with standing to bring certain causes of action on behalf of the estate. *See* 11 U.S.C. §§ 544–549, 506(c); *Hartford Underwriters Ins. Co. v. Union Planters Bank, N.A*, 530 U.S. 1 (2000).

73. *Capital Contracting*, 924 F.3d at 894–95; *In re Technicool Sys., Inc.*, 896 F.3d 382, 385 (5th Cir. 2018); *see Czyzewski v. Jevic Holding Corp.*, 137 S. Ct. 973, 982 (2017); *Wilton Armetale*, 968 F.3d at 280–81; *In re Sisk*, 962 F.3d 1133, 1141–42 (9th Cir. 2020); *Kane v. Johns-Manville Corp.*, 843 F.3d 636, 643–44 (2d Cir. 1988). Bankruptcy judges are not Article III judges but their authority derives from reference from district courts.

74. 11 U.S.C. § 1109. Certain other provisions of the Bankruptcy Code also provide parties in interest certain rights. *See, e.g.*, 11 U.S.C. § 502(a) (objections to proofs of claim); 11 U.S.C. § 707 (motions to convert or dismiss); 11 U.S.C. § 1104 (motions for appointment of a trustee); 11 U.S.C. § 1121 (filing of a plan after the expiration of debtor's exclusive right). However, several courts have held that efficient administration of the estate limits standing of other parties to object to proofs of claims to situations where the trustee or debtor in possession, as applicable, has declined to pursue an objection. *See, e.g., In re Thompson*, 965 F.2d 1136, 1147 (1st Cir. 1992); *In re Magnesium Corp.*, 583 B.R. 637 (Bankr. S.D.N.Y. 2018); *In re Trusted Net Media Holdings, LLC*, 324 B.R. 470 (Bankr. N.D. Ga. 2005). Others disagree based on a literal reading of Section 502(a). *See, e.g., In re Zimmer*, 2020 WL 7090170 (Bankr. W.D. Pa. Dec. 4, 2020); *In re Mechanicsburg Fitness, Inc.*, 592 B.R. 798 (Bankr. M.D. Pa. 2018). 11 U.S.C. § 704 provides that trustees have a duty to

with respect to any specified matter" in any case under the Bankruptcy Code. While the Bankruptcy Code does not define "party in interest" or "interested entity," courts have found that the terms include any party with a pecuniary or practical stake or legal interest that might be affected by the case.[75] Standing can be based on a party's rights being aggrieved or burdened and is not limited to financial or pecuniary interests.[76] Governmental agencies have been found to have public interest standing when their rights in connection with a bankruptcy case are at issue.[77] The Third Circuit has held that party in interest standing is broad and coextensive with Article III standing requirements.[78] Where a party has a legally protected interest or stake that could be affected, it has standing to be heard.[79] Governmental agencies with a statutory mandate to protect the public interest that would be impacted by a bankruptcy proceeding may also be interested parties with standing.[80] Citizen groups must meet additional requirements for associational

---

examine and object to improper proofs of claim, and 11 U.S.C. § 1107(a) assigns this duty to debtors-in-possession in cases without a trustee.

75. *In re Global Indus. Techs., Inc.*, 645 F.3d 201, 210 (3d Cir. 2011); *In re James Wilson Assoc.*, 965 F.2d 160, 169 (7th Cir. 1992).

76. *In re Cmty. Home Fin. Servs., Inc.*, 990 F.3d 422, 426–27 (5th Cir. 2021); *Global Industries*, 645 F.3d at 212–15; *In re Zarnel*, 619 F.3d 156, 162 (2d Cir. 2010); *In re Congoleum Corp.*, 426 F.3d 675, 685 (3d Cir. 2005); *In re Revco D.S., Inc.*, 898 F.2d 498, 499–500 (6th Cir. 1990); *In re Clark*, 927 F.3d 793, 796 (4th Cir. 1991).

77. *See In re Kaspar Town of Putnam Valley v. Kaspar*, 2021 WL 1226586 (S.D.N.Y. Mar. 13, 2021) (citing *Penn Terra Ltd. v. Dep't of Env't Res.*, 733 F.2d 267 (3d Cir. 1984); *In re Commerce Oil Co.*, 847 F.2d 291 (6th Cir. 1988); *In re First Alliance Mortgage Co.*, 264 B.R. 634 (C.D. Cal. 2001); *In re Allegheny Health Education & Research Found.*, 252 B.R. 309 (W.D. Pa. 1999)).

78. *Global Indus.*, 645 F.3d at 211. The Supreme Court's emphasis on statutes in standing analysis in *Lexmark*, 572 U.S. at 126, may mean that prudential standing does not apply in Chapter 11 cases and that the relevant standing questions are constitutional and within the scope of Section 1109(b).

79. *Global Indus.*, 645 F.3d at 212. While a few courts occasionally make reference to a requirement of a pecuniary interest for standing, the authors are not aware of any case that has rejected a party's standing merely because it is the party's nonpecuniary rights that are impaired or burdened. Cases mentioning the lack of pecuniary impact when rejecting the standing of parties that have neither a pecuniary or nonpecuniary right or interest that is impaired or burdened are therefore inapposite to the standing of governmental agencies that may have nonpecuniary rights or interests.

80. *In re Zarnel*, 619 F.3d 156, 162 (2d Cir. 2010) (citing *SEC v. U.S. Realty & Improvement Co.*, 310 U.S. 434, 459–60 (1940)); *In re Revco D.S., Inc.*, 898 F.2d 498, 499–500 (6th Cir. 1990).

standing in order to participate in a bankruptcy case on behalf of impacted citizen members with a legally protected interest.[81] Citizen groups have been found to have standing on issues relating to the applicability of or lifting of the automatic stay for the purpose of bringing a citizen suit during a bankruptcy case.[82]

Finally, standing analysis is applied anew when a bankruptcy decision is appealed. Some courts apply more stringent standing analysis in evaluating whether the bankruptcy court's ruling has injured or aggrieved a party sufficiently for purposes of appellate standing. These cases seek to avoid overwhelming numbers of appeals by parties that are only indirectly affected by a bankruptcy court ruling.[83]

APPEALS

Bankruptcy appeals are governed by 28 U.S.C. § 158 and Part VIII of the Federal Rules of Bankruptcy Procedure.[84] Appeals ordinarily proceed to the district court, or in some circuits, a bankruptcy appellate panel (i.e., sometimes referred to as a BAP), which consists of three bankruptcy judges designated to hear such appeals.[85] In circuits with BAPs, appeals go to the BAP unless either party timely opts to have the matter heard by the district court instead.[86]

81. *Friends of the Earth, Inc. v. Laidlaw Env't Servs. (TOC), Inc.*, 528 U.S. 167 (2000); *Lujan v. Defenders of Wildlife*, 504 U.S. 55 (1992); *see In re First Energy Sols. Corp.*, 828 Fed. Appx. 321 (6th Cir. 2020) (citing *Hollingsworth v. Perry*, 570 U.S. 693 (2013)); *In re Alpha Natural Res. Inc.*, 544 B.R. 848 (Bankr. E.D. Va. 2016).

82. *In re Taylor*, 572 B.R. 592 (Bankr. E.D.N.C 2017); *In re Peabody Energy Corp.*, No. 16-42529 (Bankr. E.D. Mo. July 20, 2016) (Docket No. 946); *In re Edison Mission Energy*, 502 B.R. 830 (Bankr. N.D. Ill. 2013); *In re Edison Mission Energy*, 2013 WL 6504710 (Bankr. N.D. Ill. Dec. 11, 2013); *In re Kish*, 41 B.R. 620 (Bankr. E.D. Mich. 1984).

83. *In re Imerys Talc Am., Inc.*, 38 F.4th 361 (3d Cir. 2022); *In re Point Ctr. Fin., Inc.*, 890 F.3d 1188 (9th Cir. 2018); *In re Wigley*, 886 F.3d 681 (8th Cir. 2018); *Opportunity Fin., LLC v. Kelley*, 822 F.3d 451 (8th Cir. 2016); *In re Ernie Haire Ford, Inc.*, 764 F.3d 1321 (11th Cir. 2014); *Kane v. Johns-Manville Corp.*, 843 F.2d 636 (2d Cir. 1988); *In re Murray Energy Holdings Co.*, 624 B.R. 606 (6th Cir. Bankr. App. P. 2021).

84. 28 U.S.C. § 158; FED. R. BANKR. P. 8001–8028. *See generally Bullard v. Blue Hills Bank*, 575 U.S. 496 (2015).

85. The First, Sixth, Eighth, Ninth, and Tenth Circuits use Bankruptcy Appellate Panels unless any party provides notice of an election to proceed in district court.

86. 28 U.S.C. § 158(c)(1); FED. R. BANKR. P. 8005.

The appeal itself is filed in the bankruptcy court which will then transmit it to the higher court.[87]

Appeals must be filed within 14 days after entry of the final order, judgment, or decree being appealed.[88] What constitutes a final decision in bankruptcy can be a very difficult question because bankruptcy involves multiple overlapping controversies. Discrete disputes may be appealed only if they have been finally resolved, but determining whether that has occurred is not always easy.[89] Congress has also made special provision where specified criteria are met for interlocutory appeals of bankruptcy court rulings to the district court, from the district court to the court of appeals, and/or directly from the bankruptcy court to the court of appeals.[90] As noted earlier, some courts apply more stringent standing analysis in evaluating whether the bankruptcy court's ruling has injured a party sufficiently for purposes of appellate standing.

When appealing a bankruptcy court ruling, it is important to consider seeking a stay so that the appeal is not found to be equitably moot.[91] Requests for stay must first be made to the bankruptcy court.[92] Bonds may be required for a stay, but not for appeals by or at the direction of the United States.[93]

87. Fed. R. Bankr. P. 8004.

88. 28 U.S.C. § 158(a); Fed. R. Bankr. P. 8002.

89. *Ritzen Grp., Inc. v. Jackson Masonry, LLC*, 140 S. Ct. 582 (2020); *Bullard*, 575 U.S. at 501. Parties must often file protective appeals in case a ruling is found to be final because failure to appeal a final ruling would be res judicata and bar any later appeal.

90. 28 U.S.C. § 158(a)(3), 158(d)(2); *Ritzen Grp.*, 140 S. Ct. at 587.

91. *See* Chapters 15 (Section 363 Sales), 16 (Plan Objections) *supra*.

92. Fed. R. Bankr. P. 8007.

93. Fed. R. Bankr. P. 8007(c), (d).

CHAPTER 21

Environmental Bankruptcy Settlement Agreements

In the bankruptcy context, an environmental settlement agreement is the document in which a debtor can settle environmental liabilities with the government. Often a settlement can be reached during a bankruptcy proceeding that might otherwise take years to obtain outside of the bankruptcy context.[1] By entering into a settlement agreement, the debtor and the government avoid the protracted costs of litigating the environmental bankruptcy issues discussed in this Practice Guide as well as any number of underlying environmental issues. In addition, a settlement agreement between the debtor and the government helps ease the path for approval of the plan of reorganization. In larger cases, typically the debtor negotiates the terms of a settlement agreement with the government at the same time as the debtor develops its plan of reorganization (or in some instances, its plan of liquidation) and then the settlement agreement is incorporated into the plan by reference. This chapter will discuss key components of environmental bankruptcy settlement agreements entered into between the debtor and the government and concludes with case examples of significant environmental settlements.[2]

1. As noted in Chapter 16 (Plan Objections) *supra*, bankruptcy is inherently a collective settlement-oriented process that incentivizes settlement.

2. This chapter does not cover issues relating to pre-bankruptcy settlements.

PARTIES TO THE SETTLEMENT AGREEMENT

The first consideration for developing an environmental settlement agreement concerns who will be party to the settlement. Depending upon a variety of factors, the settlement may involve only federal agencies, in which case the parties to the agreement would be the United States through the Department of Justice on behalf of the applicable federal agencies and the debtor.[3] This would generally occur when: (1) there is a federal agency interest in the case, but not a state agency interest, or (2) when the timeframe for settling with the federal agencies and applicable state agencies, or the nature of the respective liabilities being pursued by the governments, is so different that it is more efficient to settle separately with the federal agency. In other instances, the parties to the settlement agreement could include the United States and a state (or state agency), or a group of states (or state agencies). In such a case, the settlement would involve settling liabilities under both federal and state laws. Other parties to a settlement agreement may include Native American nations/tribes and local governmental entities. While the negotiation process can take longer if multiple parties are at the table and numerous interests need to be balanced, ultimately such a settlement can result in a simpler resolution because overlapping potential environmental liabilities are addressed in one document.[4]

As noted in Chapter 5 (Key Provisions) (executory contracts) *supra*, pre-bankruptcy settlement agreements with the government for performance of work or compliance have the force of law and are binding on debtors-in-possession and their successors. They may not be rejected as executory contracts. Likewise, where a proposed consent decree for performance of work or compliance is lodged with a district court prior to a bankruptcy filing, entry of the proposed consent decree as a judgment is permitted under the police or regulatory exception to the automatic stay. 11 U.S.C. § 362(b)(4); *New York v. Mirant N.Y., Inc.*, 300 B.R. 174 (S.D.N.Y. 2003).

3. The Department of Justice represents federal agencies in bankruptcy cases. *See* 28 U.S.C. § 516.

4. *See In re Tronox Inc.*, Case No. 09-10156 (Bankr. S.D.N.Y. Jan. 12, 2009) (Consent Decree and Environmental Settlement Agreement).

TIMING OF SETTLEMENT AND THE SETTLEMENT AGREEMENT

Bankruptcy settlements can occur at any point in a bankruptcy case. An early settlement, entered into prior to and independent of plan proceedings, can resolve an allowed claim or group of claims and may be an efficient way to proceed for relatively small claims. In such a case, the government or interested party may then be able obtain information from large creditors or a creditors' committee to help ensure the fairness of recovery under the plan as the case proceeds.

However, in larger cases or where there are significant environmental liabilities that are paramount in the case, it may be a better strategy to time any settlement to coincide with plan proceedings and then have the plan incorporate the proposed settlement. Settling before the terms of the plan are known is risky, because, for example, if the settlement provides for any allowed general unsecured claims for the government,[5] the government would not have knowledge of how such allowed claims would be treated under a plan. A future plan might propose little or no payment for such allowed general unsecured claims. In large corporate cases involving multiple debtors, there would be a risk that debtors and other parties in interest would seek confirmation of a plan that disadvantages the recovery for allowed claims against the particular debtor for which the government has its allowed claim under the settlement. Or the plan might over-reserve assets for the future operation of the reorganized debtor to the detriment of creditors. In the absence of a plan, the government will not know what its likely range of recovery from the settlement will be. While the government might be able to protect its interest through an objection to the plan, that can be a costly process and require the retention of expert witnesses. It may also be difficult for a bankruptcy court to reject a plan that is supported by multiple other constituencies.

Bankruptcy settlements can also take place after a plan has been confirmed. However, governments or interested parties

5. Allowance of proofs of claim or administrative expense claims is the mechanism for creditors to share in proceeds being provided to creditors under a plan. *See* Chapter 7 (Proofs of Claim) *supra*.

would need to carefully scrutinize the proposed plan for its impact on the still unresolved environmental liabilities as discussed in Chapter 16 (Plan Objections) of this Practice Guide.

SCOPE OF THE SETTLEMENT AGREEMENT

Some environmental bankruptcy settlements focus on specific claims and liabilities. Others are "global"[6] or "multi-site" and address multiple properties owned and/or operated by debtors and other liabilities. The advantage of one global or multi-site settlement agreement is that the issues are all addressed in one document, but the difficulty is that often many more parties need to be included. Therefore, the more properties involved in a settlement, the more cumbersome the agreement may be to negotiate.[7]

In *Tronox*, which is described in greater detail later in this chapter, there was one global settlement agreement involving 22 states, eight federal agencies, a tribe, and two local governments, which incorporated thousands of sites owned or operated by Tronox, formerly owned or operated by Tronox, or those never owned but associated with Tronox, such as third-party disposal sites.[8] One reason for utilizing a global settlement agreement in the *Tronox* case was that part of the funding behind the settlement included an allocation of litigation proceeds from Tronox's then-pending fraudulent conveyance litigation against Kerr-McGee and Anadarko, should the litigation prove successful. By having one settlement agreement, the agreement provided a roadmap for the allocation of those proceeds among the settling parties. Other cases have contained several settlement agreements. For example, in *W.R. Grace*, there were, among other settlements: (1) a multi-site

---

6. Global settlements are broader in scope than multi-site settlements because they cover a larger range of sites for which debtor may have liability. They are discussed later in this chapter.

7. However, the United States and state attorney general offices have a longstanding track record of coordination on environmental bankruptcy cases. The National Association of Attorneys General has also been heavily involved in helping resolve large, complex bankruptcy cases such as General Motors, Tronox, and Circle K (described in Chapter 4 (Timeline) *supra*).

8. *Tronox*, Settlement Agreement, Sections V–IX.

settlement with EPA and other federal agencies that resolved claims at a number of formerly owned sites, third-party sites, and sites where companies licensed by Grace operated; (2) a separate settlement covering the Curtis Bay FUSRAP[9] site in Baltimore Maryland; (3) a CERCLA settlement relating to former vermiculite mining operations in Libby, Montana, and (4) a settlement with Montana DEQ involving the Libby, Montana site.[10] In *W.R Grace*, it was more efficient to enter into several discrete settlement agreements because the environmental issues were separate and the timetable for settlement varied. Likewise, in the *General Motors* bankruptcy settlement agreements, described in more detail later in this chapter, there were several settlement agreements covering different groups of sites.[11]

Environmental bankruptcy settlements specify consideration or compliance obligations by site and also by applicable statute and agency. Historically, governments have not been willing to enter into cash out settlements covering all of a debtor's environmental liabilities in gross, without an allocation of settlement payments amongst various sites, because it is difficult for the government and the courts to evaluate the fairness and reasonableness of such settlements under environmental laws. The settlement agreement should provide a transparent allocation. Without that, there could also be a risk that other liable parties would claim credit against their liability from the settlement in amounts greater than that

9. FUSRAP refers to a "formerly utilized sites remedial action program" to address contamination caused by atomic energy programs of federal agencies. *See Sevenson Env't Servs., Inc. v. United States*, 76 Fed. Cl. 51, 61 (Ct. Cl. 2007); Cliff Carpenter, Nicki Fatherly & Rebecca Roberts, *Life-Cycle Baseline Customization for the Formerly Utilized Sites Remedial Action Program—20304* (2020WM: 46 Annual Waste Mgmt. Conference, 2020), https://www.energy.gov/sites/default/files/2020/04/f74/20304_FUSRAP%20LCB.pdf.

10. *In re W.R. Grace & Co.*, No. 01-01139 (Bankr. D. Del. June 2, 2008) (settlements with the United States provided for $250 million cash payment for the Libby Asbestos Site in Montana and an allowed general unsecured claim of $34.065 million and allowed administrative expense claim of $2.294 million for 28 other sites).

11. *In re Motors Liquidation Co.*, No. 09-50026 (Bankr. S.D.N.Y. Mar. 3, 2011, Mar. 29, 2011, and June 17, 2011). *See also In re Kaiser Aluminum Corp.*, No. 02-10429 (Bankr. D. Del. Oct. 27, 2003) (multi-site Superfund settlement with EPA, DOI, NOAA, California regulators, and Washington).

which the government believed they were entitled.[12] There could also be a risk of extensive litigation, which would undermine the benefits of settlement.

AUTHORITY TO ENTER INTO SETTLEMENT AGREEMENTS

The majority of environmental settlement agreements in bankruptcy involve settling CERCLA (or Superfund) liability. Section 122 of CERCLA provides authority for the United States to enter into certain categories of settlements such as for response actions, past costs, and de minimis settlements.[13] While debtors could enter into any of these types of settlements while in bankruptcy, they would not be filed in bankruptcy court (other than by debtors in order to obtain authority from the bankruptcy court to enter into the settlement) but would instead follow the procedures and mechanisms provided for in Section 122. For example, work settlements (e.g., settlements describing cleanup work to be performed) are normally handled either administratively or under the auspices of a district court consent decree. Past cost settlements in the non-bankruptcy context also are often handled administratively and generally do not address liability for future costs (unless an inherent authority settlement is added). De minimis settlements are limited to situations where the party has de minimis liability. However, these provisions for settlement are limited in applicability, and most settlements in bankruptcy are broader and are entered into under the inherent authority of the Attorney General to resolve disputes involving federal agencies[14] and not under one of

---

12. CERCLA provides that a settlement reduces the potential liability of other liable parties "by the amount of the settlement." 42 U.S.C. § 9613(f)(2). The amount of the settlement for a site would potentially be subject to dispute if there were no site by site breakdowns.

13. *See* 42 U.S.C. § 9622(d), (g), (h).

14. *See Swift & Co. v. United States*, 276 U.S. 311, 331–32 (1928); *see, e.g., United States v. Hercules, Inc.*, 961 F.2d 796, 798 (8th Cir. 1992); *Tosco Corp. v. Hodel*, 804 F.2d 590, 591 (10th Cir. 1986); *Applegate v. United States*, 52 Fed. Cl. 751, 757–58 (Fed. Cl. 2002); *United States v. Asarco, Inc.*, 814 F. Supp. 951, 957 (D. Colo. 1993); *Halbach v. Markham*, 106 F. Supp. 475, 479–80 (D.N.J. 1952), *aff'd*, 207 F.2d 503 (3d Cir. 1953). "Courts have upheld the United States' entry into numerous environmental bankruptcy settlements under the Attorney General's inherent authority that have

the specific provisions of Section 122. The Department of Justice, on behalf of EPA, has wide discretion under its inherent authority to enter into environmental bankruptcy settlement agreements as long as they are fair, reasonable, and consistent with environmental law.[15] Bankruptcy settlement agreements can also sometimes resolve disputes under the Clean Water Act, Resource Conservation and Recovery Act (RCRA), Clean Air Act, and other federal environmental statutes.[16]

COVENANT NOT TO SUE

To encourage settlement in the bankruptcy context, EPA or a state may provide a covenant not to sue to the debtor for civil actions with respect to specified sites under specified statutes. From the debtor's perspective, in some respects, this is the most critical protection in the settlement agreement because it allows the debtor's business to go forward without a future risk of further liability for the environmental liabilities that are the subject of the settlement. Unlike private settlements, the United States and several states do not provide "releases" in their environmental settlements—in or outside of bankruptcy—and instead provide covenants not to sue.[17]

One benefit of an environmental bankruptcy settlement agreement entered into under the Department of Justice's inherent

---

obtained important benefits for the public . . . ." *In re Asarco, LLC*, 2009 WL 8176641, at *46 (Bankr. S.D. Tex. June 5, 2009) (citing *In re Cuyahoga Equip. Corp.*, 980 F.2d 110, 112–13, 119–20 (2d Cir. 1992); *In re Eagle-Picher Indus., Inc.*, 197 B.R. 260 (Bankr. S.D. Ohio 1996), *aff'd*, 1997 U.S. Dist. LEXIS 15436, at *46 (July 14, 1997 S.D. Ohio); *In re Energy Coop., Inc.*, 173 B.R. 363, 372 (N.D. Ill. 1994).

15. Congress can limit the Attorney General's exercise of inherent authority settlements but such limitations on a discretionary function such as settlement must be clearly and unambiguously expressed and not merely inferred. *See United States v. California*, 332 U.S. 19, 27–28 (1947); *United States v. Morgan*, 222 U.S. 274, 282 (1911); *United States v. Hercules*, 961 F.2d at 798–99.

16. *See, e.g.*, *In re PES Holdings, LLC*, No. 18-10122 (Bankr. D. Del. Apr. 4, 2018) (Clean Air Act settlement with refiner relating to compliance with past renewable fuel standard program requirements for renewable identification number credits (RINs)).

17. One explanation for this may have to do with the fact that governments have related causes of action against other liable parties. The governments would not want a "release" to be interpreted as a release of nonparties by operation of law.

authority as described previously is that the covenant not to sue in such settlements comports well with the "fresh start" policy under bankruptcy law. An inherent authority settlement does not usually require the standard "reopener" for unknown information that is required in most nonbankruptcy settlements. This provides added finality to the settling parties, subject to certain limited exceptions. In nonbankruptcy settlements, reopeners for unknown information are generally required for settlements under Section 122 absent extraordinary circumstances or entry into a de minimis settlement.[18]

When negotiating a covenant not to sue, it is important to consider the breadth of the protection given by the covenant. There are several specific factors that will determine how broad the covenant not to sue will be. For one, which statutes will be covered? While CERCLA is commonly included in a covenant not to sue for Superfund sites, parties may also seek protection against liability under RCRA, the Clean Water Act, or other federal statutes and state law equivalents. The government is generally unwilling to include a statute in the covenant unless the debtor can demonstrate the statute has been invoked or is at issue for the site. Adding additional statutes typically requires a government office to consult with other offices in the government that handle such statutes. If the statute has already been considered with respect to a site, the burden on the government might be limited and it may agree to include that statute in the covenant not to sue. But if the statute has not previously been considered for a site, it may be unreasonably burdensome to expect the government to bring in other officials who have no information to evaluate a settlement under such statute. It may be a poor use of government resources to even consider expanding the covenant especially where it is very unlikely that the additional statute may ever be relevant. A special situation is presented by Section 7003 of RCRA when CERCLA has already been invoked,[19] given that a cause of action under the "imminent and substantial

18. 42 U.S.C. § 9613(f)(6). As noted earlier, Section 122 applies to certain settlements for work. Even where Section 122 applies, financial inability to pay may be part of the basis for a finding of extraordinary circumstances.

19. 42 U.S.C. § 9673.

endangerment" Section of RCRA may overlap with a CERCLA cause of action under Section 106 of CERCLA.[20]

A second consideration is the entities that should be covered. Although the debtor itself (and reorganized debtor) will receive covenant not to sue protection, the debtor may have to negotiate with the government for the inclusion of other parties, such as affiliates, subsidiaries, parents, successors and assigns, and officers, directors, shareholders, and employees. The federal government generally has been willing, in bankruptcy cases, to extend its covenants to include successors and assigns and officers, directors, and employees, but only in their capacity as such. It would not be appropriate to include any independent liability that they might have. The government generally is not willing to include generic categories like affiliates, subsidiaries, parents, and shareholders because without identifying the specific parties, the government cannot evaluate the appropriateness of including them.

Third, the covenant not to sue should conform to the scope of the agreement. As a matter of good government, the government will insist that covenants be limited to specified sites and that consideration be specifically allocated so that the fairness and reasonableness of the settlement can be properly evaluated. The settlement will have a reservation of rights paragraph that clearly sets forth what is not being settled. The government will also require a parallel covenant not to sue from the debtor.[21] In

20. *See* Kenneth K. Kilbert, *Re-Exploring Contribution Under RCRA's Imminent Hazard Provisions*, 87 Neb. L. Rev. 420, 432–33 (2008).

21. Most settlements with the United States require the debtor to covenant not to sue all agencies of the United States with respect to the site or matters being settled. On first thought, this might seem to be incongruous with the covenant of the United States, which will be limited to the settling federal agencies involved. However, there is only one United States, which is a unitary creditor in bankruptcy. *Cherry Cotton Mills, Inc. v. United States*, 327 U.S. 536, 539–40 (1946); *United States v. Maxwell*, 157 F.3d 1099, 1102 (7th Cir. 1998); *In re Chateaugay Corp.*, 94 F.3d 772, 778–79 (2d Cir. 1996); *In re Turner*, 84 F.3d 1294, 1296–97 (10th Cir. 1996). Therefore, this incongruence only reflects the different positions of the government and debtors in the settlement. From the perspective of the government, it would not be an actual settlement for the debtor to pay money only to seek its recovery from another federal agency that is part of the United States. The same situation is not present with respect to the debtor as the government is not paying the debtor money. In unusual situations where there is a known liability of another federal agency to the debtor relating to the site/settlement that is not ripe for settlement, the United States may agree that the debtor can reserve its claim for such liability.

settlements with "additional sites" provisions (discussed later), such sites will not receive a covenant not to sue in the bankruptcy settlement because litigation and settlement of them is reserved for a future date.

In more routine bankruptcy settlements, the trustee or debtor and the federal government may wish to avoid the time-consuming negotiation of covenants and reservations of rights by simply providing that the settlement resolves the settling federal agency's proof of claim and that the settling agency agrees not to file any further claim for the site/liability being settled.

CONTRIBUTION PROTECTION; CREDIT TO CO-LIABLE PARTIES

Another key benefit provided to a debtor that enters into a settlement agreement is that the debtor receives contribution protection under CERCLA, which protects a debtor from suits by co-liable parties for contribution. Section 113(f)(2) of CERCLA states that, "a person who has resolved its liability to the United States or a State in an administrative or judicially approved settlement shall not be liable for claims for contribution regarding matters addressed in the settlement."[22] It protects parties who have settled their liability with the federal government from suit by other parties.[23] This provision has been used as an incentive to settlement by providing finality with respect to liability concerning the sites at issue.

In addition, bankruptcy settlement agreements with the United States that provide for allowed claims under CERCLA also contain clarifying language providing:

> Only the amount of cash received by EPA (and net cash received upon sale of any non-cash distributions) pursuant to this Settlement Agreement for the EPA Allowed Claim, and not the total amount of the EPA Allowed Claim, shall be credited as a recovery

---

22. 42 U.S.C. § 9613(f)(2)

23. *United States v. Southeastern Pa. Transp. Auth.*, 235 F.3d 817, 822–23 (3d Cir. 2000); *Akzo Coatings, Inc. v. Aigner Corp.*, 30 F.3d 761 (7th Cir. 1994); *United States v. Pretty Prods., Inc.*, 780 F. Supp. 1488 (S.D. Ohio 1991). *See also Cannons Eng'g*, 899 F.2d at 92; *O'Neil v. Picillo*, 883 F.2d 176, 178–79 (1st Cir. 1989).

> by EPA for the Site, which credit shall reduce the liability of non-settling potentially responsible parties for that site by the amount of the credit.[24]

This language forecloses any risk to the government that a responsible party could claim a reduction to its liability in the amount of the allowed claim rather than the amount actually received. If the government risked reduction of its claim against other parties on account of pursuing a bankruptcy claim and not getting paid in full, it might be deterred from filing claims against debtors when it has the option of bringing joint and several liability claims against solvent parties.[25] The clarifying language is consistent with the language of CERCLA itself, which provides that the amount of the reduction in liability is "the amount of the settlement."[26] In a bankruptcy settlement, the terms of the settlement include a payout amount or value that is determined in accordance with a plan of reorganization. The "amount of the settlement," therefore, is the amount or value that is received under the plan. The preceding clarifying language is also consistent with Section 113(f)(3) of CERCLA, which allows the United States to pursue other liable parties when it obtains "less than complete relief" from settling parties.[27]

GLOBAL SETTLEMENTS AND "ADDITIONAL SITES"

Historically, the United States and some states and state agencies entered into global settlements that addressed different categories of liabilities and sites. Such settlements provided for: (1) allowed claims

---

24. *See, e.g.*, Amended Settlement Agreement Regarding Miscellaneous Federal and State Environmental Sites ¶ 12, *In re Asarco LLC*, No. 05-21207 (Docket No. 10540).

25. *See, e.g., In re Eagle-Picher Indus., Inc.*, 197 B.R. 260, 272 (Bankr. S.D. Ohio 1996), *aff'd*, 1997 U.S. Dist. LEXIS 15436 (July 14, 1997 S.D. Ohio).

26. 42 U.S.C. § 9613(f)(2).

27. *Id.* § 9613(f)(3). Legislative history further confirms this by stating that non-settling parties "remain potentially liable for the *amounts not received* by the government through the settlement." *See* 131 Cong. Rec. 34,646 (Dec. 5, 1985) (emphasis added) (remarks of Rep. Glickman incorporating House Judiciary Committee explanations of amendments to CERCLA); H.R. Rep. No. 253, 99th Cong., 1st Sess., pt. 3, at 19 (1985), *reprinted in* 1986 U.S. Code Cong. & Admin. News 3042.

for "Liquidated Sites," (2) the pass-through of most liabilities for currently owned or operated sites consistent with their treatment under environmental bankruptcy law,[28] (3) ongoing compliance with currently existing work consent decrees and administrative orders, and (4) compromise treatment for "Additional Sites."[29]

The so-called Additional Sites were defined as: (1) unknown sites that may arise or be identified in the future, or (2) in some cases, known sites where both the government and debtor believed that there was inadequate information to liquidate the liability at the time of the bankruptcy and that it was in the parties' interest to delay liquidation and potential litigation until investigations were further along in the ordinary course. Under the compromise treatment given to Additional Sites: (1) pre-petition liabilities under CERCLA for Additional Sites were discharged through the terms of the confirmed plan of reorganization and such liabilities were treated as general unsecured claims; and (2) any injunctive cleanup orders against the debtor for such sites could not be pursued. However, no payments would be made by the debtor with respect to the Additional Sites at the time of the bankruptcy. Instead, these liabilities would be paid later, typically post-bankruptcy, through a future settlement or judgment, in accordance with the treatment provided in the plan for general unsecured claims once the government later undertook enforcement action. The practical effect of this was that these liabilities would be paid in "bankruptcy dollars," but at a later date.[30] The federal government has not entered into a global settlement with an Additional Sites provision in several years.[31] Historically, these settlements were more in the government's interest where: (1) the global settlement confirmed that (a) significant ongoing

---

28. *See* Chapter 13 (Discharge) *supra*.

29. Categories 2 and 3 are nowadays typically addressed by confirmation fixing language as discussed in Chapter 16 (Plan Objections) *supra*.

30. *In re W.R. Grace & Co.*, No. 01-01139 (Bankr. D. Del. June 2, 2008). *See also In re Lyondell Chem. Co.*, No. 09-10023 (Bankr. S.D.N.Y. Apr. 23, 2010); *Eagle-Picher Indus.*, 197 B.R. at 264; *In re Kaiser Aluminum Corp.*, No. 02-10429 (Bankr. D. Del. Oct. 27, 2003).

31. However, governments still enter into settlements for allowed claims or cleanup work for specific known sites, as appropriate. Further, as discussed in Chapter 16 (Plan Objections) *supra*, governments seek plan fixing language relating to owned or operated sites and compliance with consent decrees and work orders.

compliance obligations under consent decrees and administrative orders remain unimpaired and (b) owned site liabilities remained unimpaired and (2) there was a high payout to unsecured creditors so that the waiver of injunctive cleanup order authority with respect to the so-called Additional Sites was a less significant compromise in the overall settlement.[32]

COMMENT PERIOD/NOTICES

Environmental bankruptcy settlement agreements with the federal government and certain states or state agencies often include an opportunity for public notice and comment.[33] In addition, settlements containing a covenant under Section 7003(d) of RCRA[34] may require an opportunity for a public meeting. It is important to be aware of any requirements to avoid procedural challenges to the settlement and to be aware of the impact they may have on the timing of approval for a settlement. Most comment periods by the United States in environmental bankruptcy settlements provide for a 30-day public comment period.[35] Some states or state agencies may require a longer public comment period, and some may run as long as 90 days.

NOTICE OF LODGING

For a settlement agreement involving the federal government as a party, the proposed consent decree and environmental settlement agreement is lodged with the bankruptcy court and public notice is published in the *Federal Register*. The Department of Justice will accept comments for the specified period (normally 30 days), on behalf of the federal agencies it represents, and at the conclusion

32. *See* Chapter 11 (Compliance Obligations) *supra* (discussing cases holding that cleanup order liability for non-owned sites may be nondischargeable).

33. Many environmental bankruptcy settlements do not fall under statutory requirements for public comment, *see, e.g.*, 42 U.S.C. § 9622(d)(2); 28 C.F.R. ¶ 50.7, but the government takes public comment as a matter of policy but at its discretion.

34. 42 U.S.C. § 9673(d).

35. The Department of Justice can sometimes shorten this period but only for good reasons.

of the federal comment period, the United States will file with the court any comments received as well as responses to those comments and, if appropriate, will then request that the court approve the proposed settlement agreement. The debtor will also file a motion seeking approval of the debtor's entry into the settlement under Bankruptcy Rule 9019. For a settlement agreement that involves only settling state parties, with no federal government involvement, the process will follow the applicable federal or state law requirements. The applicable state law or laws will be those of the state(s) where the property is located.

OTHER PROVISIONS

If the government understands the settlement agreement to provide for an allowed general unsecured or administrative expense claim, it is important for the settlement agreement to state that such claim is "allowed." Debtors' draft settlements often omit the word "allowed," which could be contended to mean that a claim is contested. Such an argument would seem totally contrary to the idea of entering into a settlement to resolve the claim. In order to avoid any contention that the settlement does not provide for an agreed upon allowed claim, it is best to avoid any future need for litigation by ensuring that the word "allowed" is included.

Likewise, the settlement agreement should clearly indicate the priority and treatment of the allowed claim under a plan. Generally, the government will also want language confirming that the allowed claim will receive similar treatment to other allowed claims such as:

> The [allowed claim] shall receive the same treatment under the Plan of Reorganization, without discrimination, as all other allowed Class __ Unsecured Claims, with all attendant rights provided by the Bankruptcy Code and other applicable law, and shall not be entitled to any priority in distribution over other allowed Class __ Unsecured Claims. In no event shall the [allowed claim] be subordinated to any other allowed Class __ Unsecured Claim pursuant to any provision of the Bankruptcy Code or other applicable law that authorizes or provides for subordination of allowed claims, including, without limitation, Sections 105, 510, and 726(a)(4) of the Bankruptcy Code.

Environmental bankruptcy settlement agreements creating environmental response trusts are discussed in greater detail in Chapter 14 (Debtor-Owned Contaminated Property) of this Practice Guide. Other provisions to consider when negotiating such settlement agreements in the bankruptcy context include document sharing provisions, both regarding electronic information and paper files; status of environmental permits; treatment of natural resource damage claims; and status of existing consent decrees or orders.

Many environmental bankruptcy settlements have a stated effective date of either the date of approval by the bankruptcy court or the effective date of the plan (which often incorporates the environmental bankruptcy settlement agreement). As discussed in Chapter 20 (Jurisdiction) of this Practice Guide, such provisions can have the effect of making appeals equitably moot. The alternative of waiting for time-consuming appeals may delay cleanup or compliance under the settlement to the detriment of public health and safety.

APPROVAL OF ENVIRONMENTAL BANKRUPTCY SETTLEMENTS: DEFERENTIAL STANDARD OF REVIEW

Environmental bankruptcy settlements usually need two kinds of approvals from the bankruptcy court. First, under Bankruptcy Rule 9019, bankruptcy court approval is needed for the debtor's entry into the agreement.[36] The standard for review of a debtor's entry into a settlement is a deferential one that requires only that it be within a range of reasonableness.[37] Second, the government will need approval of the bankruptcy court that the settlement is fair and reasonable under environmental law, and consistent with environmental law.[38] The standard for review under environmental law

36. However, some confirmed plans provide that reorganized debtors can enter into settlements without further approval of the bankruptcy court.

37. *See, e.g., In re Martin*, 91 F.3d 389, 393 (3d Cir. 1996); *In re Am. Cartage, Inc.*, 656 F.3d 82, 91 (1st Cir. 2011); *In re W.T. Grant Co.*, 699 F.2d 599, 608 (2d Cir. 1983); *In re Capmark Fin. Grp. Inc.*, 438 B.R. 471 (Bankr. D. Del. 2010).

38. *United States v. Southeastern Pa. Transp. Auth.*, 235 F.3d 817, 823 (3d Cir. 2000); *In re Cuyahoga Equip. Corp.*, 980 F.2d 110, 118–20 (2d Cir. 1992); *In re Tutu Water Wells CERCLA Litigation*, 326 F.3d 201 (3d Cir. 2003); *In re Energy Cooperative, Inc.*, 173 B.R. 363, 367 (N.D. Ill. 1994); *In re Asarco LLC*, 2009 WL 8176641, at *2

is also a deferential one so that settlement is encouraged.[39] The presumption in favor of settlement "is particularly strong where a consent decree has been negotiated by the Department of Justice on behalf of a federal administrative agency like EPA which enjoys substantial expertise in the environmental field."[40]

There is no hard and fast rule regarding the timing of the required approvals under bankruptcy law and environmental law. The timing is flexible as to the order or whether approvals proceed simultaneously as long as it is made clear that both approvals are required before the settlement is effective.

NOTABLE EXAMPLES OF BENEFICIAL ENVIRONMENTAL SETTLEMENT AGREEMENTS

Tronox

Tronox Incorporated, the world's third largest producer and marketer of titanium dioxide pigment at the time, was formed when Kerr-McGee Corporation, its former parent, issued shares via an initial public offering in November 2005. Tronox was officially separated from Kerr-McGee in March 2006. Due in part to a significant amount of environmental liabilities inherited by Tronox during its spin-off from Kerr-McGee, which was subsequently acquired by Anadarko Petroleum Corporation (Anadarko), Tronox and 14 of its affiliates filed petitions for relief under Chapter 11 of the Bankruptcy Code on January 12, 2009.

The United States and several federal agencies, the Navajo Nation, 22 states, and several municipalities filed protective proofs of claim against Tronox and its affiliates for past and future response costs under CERCLA; civil penalties under RCRA; and

(Bankr. S.D. Tex. June 5, 2009); *In re Eagle–Picher Indus., Inc.*, 197 B.R. 260 (Bankr. S.D. Ohio 1996), *aff'd*, 1997 U.S. Dist. LEXIS 15436, at *46 (July 14, 1997 S.D. Ohio).

39. *Pennwalt Corp. v. Plough, Inc.*, 676 F.2d 77, 80 (3d Cir. 1982); *Autera v. Robinson*, 419 F.2d 1197, 1199 (D.C. Cir. 1969).

40. *United States v. Akzo Coatings of Am., Inc.*, 949 F.2d 1409, 1436 (6th Cir. 1991); *United States v. Bechtel Corp.*, 648 F.2d 660, 666 (9th Cir. 1981); *United States v. Assoc. Milk Producers, Inc.*, 534 F.2d 113, 117 (8th Cir. 1976).

for penalties, damages, and environmental liability under various other federal and state environmental laws. Tronox's potential environmental liability was in the billions of dollars and involved more than 2,800 potentially contaminated parcels. Debtors and the governments entered into a global settlement agreement, which was incorporated into its proposed plan of reorganization. The settlement created five separate environmental response trusts to manage and implement environmental actions at debtor-owned sites. Each environmental response trust was allocated a portion of $270 million in cash funding, as well as a share in future proceeds from a fraudulent conveyance proceeding, which ultimately was settled for $5.15 billion.[41] $4.4 billion of this amount was allocated for environmental liabilities, including more than $2 billion for the five environmental response trusts.

Asarco

Asarco was the third largest copper producer in the United States. It had operated for more than 100 years in the mining, smelting, and refining businesses. Asarco filed for bankruptcy on August 9, 2005. At the time of the filing of its bankruptcy petition, Asarco had environmental liabilities for more than 80 sites, including 20 federal Superfund sites. The federal government and 16 states or state agencies filed protective proofs of claims.[42] Asarco originally proposed to estimate all of its environmental liabilities in a one-day hearing, but the bankruptcy court, after consideration of the governments' collective objections to Asarco's proposal, instead established an orderly schedule and conducted several estimation hearings before referring the matter to successful mediation.[43]

The bankruptcy court upheld various settlements for owned and non-owned sites after public comment and over objections by Asarco's parent company and others.[44] Originally, the settlements

41. *See Case Summary: Tronox Incorporated Bankruptcy Settlement*, EPA: Enforcement (last updated Sept. 9, 2021), https://www.epa.gov/enforcement/case-summary-tronox-incorporated-bankruptcy-settlement; *In re Tronox Inc.*, 855 F.3d 84 (2d Cir. 2017).

42. *See In re Asarco LLC*, Case No. 05-21207 (Bankr. S.D. Tex. Aug. 9, 2005).

43. *In re Asarco LLC*, 2009 WL 8176641 (Bankr. S.D. Tex. June 5, 2009).

44. *Id.*

were approved as part of a proposed plan of reorganization involving the sale of certain of Asarco's owned properties to a third party. When that sale and associated plan of reorganization fell through, some of the environmental bankruptcy settlements had to be modified. While they were no longer dependent on any particular plan, the settlements did not become effective until a plan was confirmed. The settlement resulted in the payment of approximately $1.79 billion for environmental liabilities. The United States received approximately $776 million for more than 35 sites; 14 states received in excess of $321 million for more than 36 sites; the Coeur d'Alene Work Trust received $436 million for cleanup of a site in Idaho; and three custodial trusts[45] were established and received a cumulative total of approximately $261 million for 24 contaminated sites in 13 states and administration of the trust.[46]

General Motors

General Motors Corporation, one of the United States' oldest automobile manufacturers and the second-largest automotive manufacturer in the world at the time, filed for bankruptcy on June 1, 2009. The United States entered into at least 12 environmental bankruptcy settlements with the debtor, which resulted in recoveries or allowed claim amounts of more than $904 million.[47]

The largest and most significant settlement was a 2010 agreement that settled liabilities to the United States, 14 states, and the Saint Regis Mohawk Tribe pursuant to CERCLA, RCRA, and the Clean Air Act.[48] The settlement provided for the transfer of 89 properties into an environmental response trust as part of a $773 million settlement. Funding included $68 million in pooled "cushion"

---

45. Custodial trusts are now referred to as environmental response trusts but are the same.

46. *Asarco LLC*, 2009 WL 8176641, at ¶ 3; *Largest Environmental Bankruptcy in U.S. History Will Result in Payment of $1.79 Billion towards Environmental Cleanup & Restoration*, justice.gov, press release (Dec. 19, 2009).

47. *United States Announces $5.5 Million Settlement with GM to Resolve Natural Resource Damage Claims at Onondaga Lake Superfund Site Near Syracuse*, justice.gov, United States Attorney's Office Southern District of New York, press release (Apr. 11, 2013).

48. *In re Motors Liquidation Co.*, No. 09-50026 (Bankr. S.D.N.Y.). *See* James M. Redwine & David C. McMurtry, *The GM Bankruptcy—The Environmental Story*, Corp. Counsel Bus. J., www.ccbjournal.com (Sept. 2012).

funding to deal with unforeseen conditions. The settlement paved the way for redevelopment and the return to beneficial use of many contaminated sites. The environmental response trust in the GM case was the largest environmental trust in U.S. history.[49]

COMPLIANCE PLANS

When a debtor is out of compliance with the law and needs time to make progress toward compliance, a bankruptcy court may approve a compliance plan settlement with the government to the same extent that a party outside of bankruptcy could enter into such a plan approved by a district court. Two examples of this type of settlement are settlements in the *Safety-Kleen* and *Alpha Natural Resources* bankruptcy cases. Both involved debtors that were out of compliance with financial assurance requirements for their operations. In *Alpha Natural Resources*, the debtors and state regulators entered into a compromise by which debtors increased their financial assurance to some degree and were allowed additional time to come into compliance with mining law financial assurance requirements while they reordered their affairs in bankruptcy.[50] In *Safety-Kleen*, the hazardous waste disposal company's bonding company for hundreds of its facilities lost its approval status with the government. The debtor entered into a compliance agreement that provided a framework for coming into full compliance.[51] In these types of settlements, it is important that the regulated party agree to continue its progress toward compliance as soon as it is able as the government and courts do not otherwise have authority to allow an entity to operate in violation of the law.[52]

49. *United States Announces $5.5 Million Settlement with GM to Resolve Natural Resource Damage Claims at Onondaga Lake Superfund Site Near Syracuse*, justice.gov, United States Attorney's Office Southern District of New York, press release (Apr. 11, 2013).

50. *See In re Alpha Natural Resources Inc.*, 544 B.R. 848 (Bankr. E.D. Va. 2016). In *Alpha*, the bankruptcy court found that citizen groups had not demonstrated that they met the requirements to establish standing to object to the settlement. *Id. at* 854–56; *see* Chapter 20 (Jurisdiction) *supra*. The bankruptcy court noted that anyone who had standing to do so could still object to the regulators' actions under nonbankruptcy law in a nonbankruptcy forum. *Id.* at 858–59.

51. *See In re Safety-Kleen Corp.*, EPA Docket No. MM-HQ-2000-0005. The debtor was required to pay a penalty for its noncompliance.

52. *See* Chapter 9 (Operating Estate Property) *supra*.

Table of Cases

Index